Legal Writing
Custom Edition

Aspen Custom Publishing Series

Legal Writing
Custom Edition

Curated by

Wayne Law Legal Research and Writing Department

Wayne State University Law School

Selected pages from

Just Memos, Fourth Edition
by Laurel Currie Oates and Anne Enquist

Just Briefs, Third Edition
by Laurel Currie Oates, Anne Enquist, and Connie Krontz

Wolters Kluwer

Published by Wolters Kluwer in New York.

Wolters Kluwer Legal & Regulatory US serves customers worldwide with CCH, Aspen Publishers, and Kluwer Law International products. (www.WKLegaledu.com)

To contact Customer Service, e-mail customer.service@wolterskluwer.com,
call 1-800-234-1660, fax 1-800-901-9075, or mail correspondence to:

Wolters Kluwer
Attn: Order Department
PO Box 990
Frederick,MD 21705

Printed in the United States of America.

1 2 3 4 5 6 7 8 9 0

978-1-4548-8191-9

CONTENTS

CHAPTER 1

MAKING THE TRANSITION 1

Laurel Currie Oates and Anne Enquist, *Just Memos*, 4E

CHAPTER 2

THE UNITED STATES LEGAL SYSTEM 13

Laurel Currie Oates and Anne Enquist, *Just Memos*, 4E

CHAPTER 3

UNDERSTANDING STATUTES 29

Laurel Currie Oates and Anne Enquist, *Just Memos*, 4E

CHAPTER 4

UNDERSTANDING JUDICIAL OPINIONS 45

Laurel Currie Oates and Anne Enquist, *Just Memos*, 4E

CHAPTER 9

DRAFTING LETTERS 207

Laurel Currie Oates and Anne Enquist, *Just Memos*, 4E

CHAPTER 10

WRITING A MOTION BRIEF 223

Laurel Currie Oates, Anne Enquist, and Connie Krontz, *Just Briefs*, 3E

CHAPTER 1

Making the Transition

Everyone comes to law school with some writing experience. Whether you were an undergraduate or graduate student at a university, a business person, scientist, poet, paralegal, student, or attorney from a country other than the United States, you have come to a U.S. law school with a range of writing skills and experience that shape who you are as a writer.

For example, if you are coming to law school immediately after receiving your undergraduate degree, you have undoubtedly been shaped as a writer by the expectations of your undergraduate professors, particularly those in your major. Consciously or subconsciously, you have absorbed some of the customs and conventions of academic writing and the specific conventions of your major's discipline.

Similarly, if your most recent writing experiences have been from work, whether it be as a businessperson, social worker, police officer, or other professional, you too have absorbed the writing conventions of your field. The various writing projects and reports you wrote and read for work have shaped your beliefs about what is "good writing" and how it is done.

Even if you wrote for a living—as a novelist, journalist, poet, technical writer—or perhaps we should say, especially if you wrote for a living, you have been shaped as a writer by the work you did before law school. As a writer, you are more likely to be consciously aware of the conventions of the genre in which you were writing before entering law school, and you have undoubtedly honed the writing skills necessary to write successfully in that genre. The challenge, of course, will be to adapt those writing strengths to a new genre, legal writing, and to new readers, lawyers and judges in the U.S. legal community.

Whatever you were doing before law school, you were part of a specific culture—whether it be the world of health care, the world of school children, the world of wildlife biologists—and the writing that was done in those cultures was tailored for specific purposes and specific readers. The change to legal writing will require an adjustment.

Those of you who are coming to a U.S. law school from another country may have a more obvious cultural adjustment to make when it comes to writing. In some cases it will include the challenge of learning the writing conventions of another language, but even in cases in which the language of your home country is English, there will undoubtedly be cultural differences in what your new readers will expect from your written work.

In short, everyone coming to law school is making a transition from the writing he or she did before law school to the writing of the U.S. legal community. The trick will be to figure out what are the obvious and subtle similarities and differences between the writing culture you are coming from and the writing culture you are joining. Even if you were a paralegal before law school, you will have to figure out what was specific to the firm or legal setting in which you worked and what is generally true about writing for the larger, more generic legal community. At the very least, your specific role as a writer will have changed from paralegal to attorney, and that change alone will make a difference in the expectations your readers will have for your writing.

This chapter is designed to help law students make the transition to legal writing as smoothly and painlessly as possible. Several concepts are the keys to a successful transition: (1) understand the purpose of the new type of writing you are learning; (2) know what your new readers want and need from what you write; (3) understand your role as the writer in this genre; and (4) learn the specific conventions of the new type of writing you are adding to your writing repertoire.

A. UNDERSTANDING THE PURPOSE OF A PIECE OF LEGAL WRITING

Here's an important truth that will help you make effective choices as you work as a writer: Once you understand what a piece of writing is supposed to accomplish—its purpose—you will have a sound basis for the many decisions you as the writer will make in creating a document. Put another way, you have about 90 percent of the information you need for creating a document once you know

- ☐ why you are writing something,
- ☐ what the document is supposed to do, and
- ☐ what the reader hopes to achieve by reading it.

Like other types of writing, legal writing exists to communicate. Lawyers write because they want to communicate information to their readers. But the broad term "communicate" is not specific enough to be particularly helpful as you transition to the new genre of legal writing.

Most legal writing exists for one or more of these three specific reasons:

1. to explain,
2. to persuade,
3. to memorialize.

Whether you are writing a letter to a client, an office memo for a senior partner, or a brief for a judge, you will undoubtedly have as one of your primary purposes the goal of explaining. You might be explaining to the client that the law is on her side and therefore she is likely to be successful if she sues her employer. You might be explaining to a partner how the courts have interpreted a statute and why that interpretation means the firm's biggest client should not include a particular term in a contract. You might be explaining to a judge why an application of the law to your client's facts would lead to a just result.

If clear explanation is the first goal of most legal writing, then the goal of effective persuasion is not far behind. Sometimes the persuasion is subtle. In writing an opinion letter, you may be persuading a client to see the strengths and weaknesses of his or her legal position. You may also be subtly persuading that client to see not only the limitations of his or her options but also the wisdom of adopting one particular option.

Persuasion is also part of legal memoranda. Although you will see in Chapters 11-14 that an office memorandum should be an objective assessment of the law and its application to a case, a good office memo also includes persuasion in the sense that it anticipates the arguments each side is likely to make and, in doing so, showcases which ones will be more or less persuasive.

The goal of persuasion is most obvious, and important, in brief writing. When writing to a court, you will be working to get a judge or justice to see the law, precedent, the facts, and the arguments from your side's point of view. You will want that judge or justice to view the case from your perspective so he or she will rule in your favor. When you write for a court, you will have clear-cut evidence of whether you succeeded or failed in your goal to persuade, and that will be what the court decides as a result of reading your writing.

The third goal of most legal writing—to memorialize—is especially evident in documents like contracts and wills. The document exists as a statement of what the contracting parties agreed to or how the deceased person wanted his or her assets distributed. Opinion letters, office memos, and briefs also have a goal of memorializing the work an attorney has done. Because the work is preserved in writing, the client can go back over a letter and review the advice. An office memo written for one client's case may be used by other attorneys in the office working on that case. Undoubtedly, it will be filed for future consideration, and it might be reviewed and used again, at least in part, if the client has a similar problem or even if another client has a similar problem. In litigation, a brief written in support of or opposition to a pretrial motion can become part of the record on appeal, recording what the parties did, or did not argue, to the trial court.

Before leaving the topic of purpose in legal writing, let's think again about the transition most new law students are making from writing they did before they came to law school to writing they will do as lawyers. Note how different the purposes of student writing are from the purposes of "real world" legal writing. Student writers write to prove that they have learned something. They write to demonstrate knowledge and mastery of a subject, and quite frankly, to get a good grade. As a general rule, readers of student writing (professors) do not read student essays, reports, and research papers to gain information or learn anything new. Because professors are already experts in the subject matter, their purpose in reading is to evaluate how well the writer has learned the material. This difference between student writing and real world writing is actually a rather profound one, and one that accounts for many of the other differences between writing that is done for class and writing that is done for professional reasons.

Keep in mind, then, as you work on the assignments for your legal writing and research classes that, even though the assignments are part of a law class, in almost every case, the writing tasks are intended to simulate real world practice situations. In other words, you are not supposed to be writing like you are a student with the purposes of a student writer. You are supposed to be writing as if you are a practicing lawyer with one or more of the real world goals of explaining, persuading, and memorializing. Even though you are still a student learning how to write like a lawyer (and hoping for a good grade), stay focused on key concept number 1: Know your purpose for writing.

COMMON MISTAKE 1

Some students in legal writing courses mistakenly assume that their legal writing professors will be reading and evaluating their papers as though they, the professors, are the real readers. Consequently, these students leave things out of the writing on the assumption that "my professor already knows that." While it is true that your professor undoubtedly researched the problem and knows the analysis inside out, he or she will be evaluating your writing from the point of view of a "real world" reader—someone who is depending on the writer's research and analysis and who was not in class and participating in the class discussions on the issues.

COMMON MISTAKE 2

Some new legal writers make the "undergraduate mistake" when they are writing their first office memos: They want to make sure their legal writing professor or their supervising attorney knows how much work they did and how thoroughly they researched the problem. Consequently, they include far more cases than are necessary to understand the analysis or make the arguments. This mistake often comes directly from their undergraduate experience. As undergraduates, many of us were rewarded for writing papers that showed how much work we had done. Length often translated into high grades. Law school and law firm writing is different. Legal writers should adopt the real world reader's point of view about length, which is "I'm busy. Tell me what I need to know and then stop writing."

B. WRITING FOR LEGAL READERS

Closely related to understanding your purpose in writing is understanding who your reader or readers are. In legal writing, the goal is not just to explain or persuade in the abstract. Instead, you are writing to real readers, readers who need your writing with all of its research, analysis, arguments, citations, conclusions, and insights in order to do their jobs.

Real legal readers include both lawyers and nonlawyers. When writing for a reader who is not a lawyer, keep in mind how much or how little experience that person may have with law and legal matters. For example, clients who are not lawyers and are not experienced in matters related to law may need explanations in lay terms. Other nonlawyer readers may have a sophisticated understanding of law and their legal issues and would find a watered down explanation condescending. The point, of course, is that an effective writer will adjust his or her approach accordingly.

To some extent, you may have to make similar adjustments for readers who are lawyers.[1] All lawyers do not have the same background or practice experience. In some situations, a senior partner who is the reader for a given memo about a tax issue may be the firm's tax expert. In such a situation, the writer can assume much more knowledge and start the discussion further into the law and analysis. Writing a memo for a different reader, maybe someone who hasn't looked at tax law since law school, would require an adjustment. In this second situation, the smart writer will give a quick refresher and enough background to get that kind of reader up to speed quickly so that he or she is ready to follow the analysis.

Anticipating your reader's knowledge base is only the beginning of writing for legal readers. Most legal readers, whether they are senior partners or judges, tend to have a few common characteristics, and these characteristics have shaped their notions of what is good legal writing. First, they tend to be very busy. Consequently, they appreciate writing that gets to the point quickly and lays out information clearly. They don't want writers to take them down every blind alley the writer had to explore before figuring out that information was irrelevant. They don't give extra credit for discussing additional cases or extra arguments if those cases or arguments aren't needed. They are annoyed, not impressed, if they think the writer is padding the document. Therefore, before including something in a piece of legal writing, ask yourself, "does my reader need to know this?" Notice that this question is different from "did I need to know this in order to analyze the problem?" Legal readers will expect legal writers to be selective about what they include in the document and to synthesize the relevant material. They will expect legal writers to understand that their time is valuable and to write, and edit, with that in mind.

Second, legal readers appreciate—actually demand—clear organization. They want the information they need laid out in a well-structured, easy-to-follow fashion. They appreciate roadmaps that give them an overview of the analysis and signposts that guide them through it, all the while focusing their attention on "where the fight is." They like transitions that help them see the connections between ideas and follow the writer's line of reasoning. They appreciate mini-conclusions that summarize a section and macro conclusions that summarize all the main pieces of a large document. In short, it is hard to over-emphasize how important a clear and explicit organization is to most legal readers.

The fact that experienced, sophisticated attorneys want such explicit organization and analysis may come as a surprise to some new legal writers. After all, not all cultures value explicitness in the same way the U.S. legal culture does. In fact, leaving things unsaid and for readers to figure out is a mark of sophisticated writing in some academic cultures and in some Asian and Middle Eastern cultures. Stating one's point so directly may be considered not just unsophisticated but also brash and even rude. For writers coming from these backgrounds, it may feel unnatural at first to spell out points so clearly and explicitly, but over time it

1. The generalizations in this section about legal readers refer to U.S. legal readers.

will become second nature as these writers better understand how writing works in the U.S. legal culture.

Third, because legal readers need the writing they read in order to do their jobs well, they insist on the highest levels of professionalism. This means that accuracy and precision are critical virtues in legal writing—no playing loose with the facts or the law. Legal readers depend on their writers to get the facts and law right and to be strictly accurate in how they are represented.

The emphasis on professionalism also means that mistakes such as poor citation form; the misspelling, especially of a name; and grammar, punctuation, and proofreading errors matter more than they do in other kinds of writing. Being accurate, precise, and polished in written documents are all critical parts of being professional that legal readers expect.

If accuracy, brevity, clarity, precision, and professionalism are high priorities for legal readers, then the next obvious question is what isn't such a high priority for them? Unlike a great deal of undergraduate writing, legal writing places less emphasis on creativity. While the professor reader in an undergraduate course in poetry or creative writing might reward an unusual approach to a topic or a novel twist in a plot, readers of legal writing tend to prefer writing that is far more conventional. Creativity is nice, especially if a creative argument turns out to be a winning argument, but remember that legal readers are not reading to be entertained. The writing is all about work and getting a job done, so creative introductions or unusual analytical approaches take a back seat to accuracy, brevity, and clarity for legal readers.

Similarly, legal readers resent unnecessary complexity. Consequently, when it comes to things like sentence structure and word choice, the acronym KISS for "keep it simple stupid" is useful advice. Legal readers do not want to puzzle over a sentence or word. For them, the sign of a well-written sentence is one that can be understood the first time they read it. For them, the well-chosen word is, more often than not, one they already know. If an unfamiliar word is required in a given instance, they expect the writer to define it immediately within the writing. Legal writers don't need to worry that they are "dumbing down" the writing when they present information as simply as possible. For legal readers, clear communication is the goal; they don't want to be dazzled by the writer's vocabulary or convoluted syntax.

Does this mean that legal readers are incapable of handling complexity or that they have weak vocabularies? Certainly not. The appreciation for simplicity goes back to the initial point about how busy legal readers are. The legal issues are often so inherently complex that no one wants added unnecessary complexity that will simply take up time and attention.

COMMON MISTAKE 3

Some new legal writers make the mistake of "dressing up their ideas." They fear that if they state things simply they will seem unsophisticated. Here again, the mistake may be the result of an undergraduate writing experience that rewarded students for making simple ideas seem complex. The opposite is true in legal writing: You will be rewarded and appreciated if you can make complex ideas seem simple.

C. UNDERSTANDING YOUR ROLE AS A LEGAL WRITER

When a junior associate or a legal intern is assigned to research and write a client letter, office memo, or brief, the expectation is that the associate or intern will spend many hours researching and analyzing the legal problem and then write up that work in a document that will take the client, assigning attorney, or judge approximately fifteen minutes to read and understand.

An underlying assumption of the U.S. legal culture, then, is that the reader's time is more valuable than the writer's time. Legal readers, including supervising attorneys, partners in law firms, and judges, tend to have positions of authority over the writers of legal memos. Consequently, writers are expected to expend their time and energy writing clearly so that readers do not have to spend extra time and energy understanding what they are reading.

This does not mean, then, that the writer's role is unimportant—far from it. As the writer, your role is to become the expert on a given case. Through careful study of the facts and thorough research, you will be the one who knows what law is the controlling law and which cases are the key cases. In addition, after reading the arguments set out in the cases and the courts' evaluation of those arguments, you will be the one who is in the best position to predict what each side will argue and how the court will view those arguments.

Ultimately, your role as the writer of a client letter is to be the one who advises the client about what he or she should do next and why. Your role as the writer of an office memo is to give your educated opinion about what the court is likely to do in the current case and be clear about how you reached that opinion. Your role as the writer of a brief is to figure out what approach and arguments will persuade the court to rule in your client's favor. In short, your role is to exercise expert judgment, and in fact, that is exactly what you are paid to do when you are assigned to write a client letter, office memorandum, or brief.

You need to exercise judgment

- ☐ about what are the legally significant facts,
- ☐ about what statute(s) or common law doctrine will govern,
- ☐ about which cases are the key analogous cases, and
- ☐ about which arguments the court will find persuasive.

As new attorneys or law students, many find the legal writer's role a bit intimidating. It can be hard enough to be confident that you have found the right law and key cases without trying to create brand new, never-seen-before arguments, or worse, predicting what a court will do or convincing a court what it should do. Take heart, though. Many of the arguments will be variations of ones you see in the cases (no one is expecting you to make this all up from scratch), and law school is exactly the right place to learn and practice these skills.

A key part of your role as well will be to cite authority (at least in office memos and briefs) to support each of the points you make. The citations show that you have the support of the law, other courts, and other legal minds behind your analysis. Furthermore, by including the source for the facts and correctly citing the record, statutes, cases, books, law review articles, and other secondary sources, you create a document in which everything about the case comes together. Thus, one major aspect of your role as a legal writer is to be the synthesizer—the one who brings all the relevant material together and presents it in a way that gets the job done.

One final point about your role as a legal writer: Every piece of writing you create in your role as a lawyer reflects on your professionalism. Words are the tools of your trade, so how you use words represents how seriously you take your work. In the heat of the moment or in the thick of an argument, it can be tempting to slip into a sarcastic or denigrating tone. Resist the temptation. Be particularly careful to maintain a professional tone in all the writing you do. As a lawyer, your writing, including the tone you use, is a big part of how you are representing your client and yourself.

D. LEARNING THE CONVENTIONS OF LEGAL WRITING

In the earlier discussion of the purposes of legal writing, legal readers, and the writer's role, a number of the common practices and conventions of legal writing have already been mentioned:

1. a high priority on clarity, brevity, precision, and organization
2. an appreciation for explicit roadmaps, signposts, topic sentences, and transitions
3. an expectation for easy-to-read sentences and paragraphs, but not bullet points or charts
4. a requirement for citations to authority
5. an expectation about professional tone.

In addition, new legal writers may be struck by a number of other conventions of legal writing. For example, specific formats are often expected and sometimes required in legal writing. Legal readers expect an office memo to have an issue statement, sometimes called a Question Presented, which seems to be an artifact from an earlier time. Briefs have required cover pages, tables of authorities, argumentative headings, and page and paragraph numbering systems. Therefore, when you are assigned a new type of legal writing, check to see whether there are court rules governing the format and review some samples or models of that type of writing. Knowing format requirements before starting to write is more efficient than spending a lot of time creating a format only to find it does not meet expectations.

Less surprising is the convention to set out a rule before applying it to the facts or making an argument using the rule. Also not surprising, at least for some, is the custom of setting out general rules before more specific rules. In fact, throughout legal writing the convention is to organize material from general to specific.

Writers of academic prose may be immediately comfortable with other conventions, such as the tendency not to use contractions or the use of the third person rather than the first person "I" or "we" or the second person "you." The practice of staying in the third person means that language such as "I think," "I believe," or "I feel" is not typically used in legal writing. Rather than write "I think the court is unlikely to find," most lawyers write "the court is unlikely to find."

Some firms do make an exception and use the first person "our" when referring to "our client" or "our case," but others maintain the more formal "the client" or the client's name when referring to the case.

E. ADVICE FOR SPECIFIC GROUPS

Even though it can be a bit risky to generalize about the customs and conventions of any given community of writers, knowing about some patterns in different writing cultures can ease a writer's transition into legal writing. Making that knowledge more explicit can help a writer look at his or her assumptions about "good writing" and see which assumptions apply and which do not apply to legal writing.

Below is a list of different communities of writers and some of the common assumptions those communities have about writing and how those assumptions are similar to or different from the underlying assumptions that shape legal writing. In creating this list, however, we do not mean to suggest that legal writing is somehow "right" in its assumptions about what makes good writing and these other fields or cultures are somehow "wrong." In fact, we would argue that the differences make sense given the differences in readers, purpose, and culture. Nor do we mean to suggest that writers need to erase and replace what they know about how to write for the communities they were part of before joining the legal community. Instead we would suggest that writers think of the experience of learning to do legal writing as adding a new category or genre of writing to their writing repertoire.

One final point: Although we cannot discuss every undergraduate major, previous profession, or culture, we hope that the insights about how different disciplines and cultures view writing will help you make a smooth transition into legal writing.

1. English Majors

Most English majors come to law school believing that they will do exceptionally well in their legal writing classes. In most cases, this proves to be true, but their success tends to happen more toward the end of the course rather than at the beginning. Early in the course, English majors may resist what they consider the formulaic and restrictive nature of legal writing. They complain that it "stifles their creativity," and they are frustrated because they cannot show off their vocabularies and sophisticated writing style. Once they accept the idea that they are learning a new genre, in much the way a poet would adapt when learning to write screenplays, they stop resisting, start adapting, and then gradually see how they can channel some of their earlier skills into legal writing. Their storytelling ability helps them write the facts; they apply their creativity to constructing arguments; and they bring the close reading skills they developed for literature and poetry to their reading of statutes and rules.

2. *Philosophy Majors*

Like English majors, philosophy majors are likely to feel that their creativity is stifled and their analytic ability tightly restricted by the standard modes of legal analysis. In their doctrinal courses, they may be initially surprised by the heavy emphasis on precedent and the layers of doctrine, as well as disappointed by what may appear to them to be the law's emphasis on rhetoric.

As they learn to write office memos, philosophy majors are likely to find the construction of rules paragraphs to be arbitrary; their natural instinct will be to think about the validity of the rules rather than simply lay them out for the readers. Once they get to the arguments, philosophy majors are likely to feel at home, and it is here that their background in logic can give them an edge.

3. *Journalism Majors and Journalists*

Like their "cousins" the English majors, journalism students and journalists bring an interesting combination of advantages and disadvantages to legal writing. Perhaps most important is the simple fact that they have fresh writing skills. They come to law school and the practice of law with their writing skills honed by lots of practice. In addition, journalists are already well schooled in the concept of writing for a specific audience. Many of them have learned to adjust their style to the varying demands of straight news reporting to the specific conventions of the sports page, the op-ed page, the lifestyle and feature sections, or a blog. Initially some journalists may resent having to tone down their style a bit for legal writing, particularly if they have grown accustomed to writing "zinger" sentences or writing with vivid language and extended metaphors for the sports page.

Yet another advantage that journalists bring to legal writing is their thoroughness and accuracy with the facts. They are used to answering the questions "who," "what," "when," "where," and "how," and they are also used to being required to state the source for the facts.

Organization and paragraph length are usually the two areas in which journalists will have to adjust. The typical journalism piece is written in an inverted-pyramid, front-loaded style so the editors can cut the piece from the end to fit space limitations and, if a reader loses interest and stops reading midway in a story, he or she still will have gotten the key ideas in the opening sentences. While much of legal writing also puts key points (rules, the best cases, and arguments) up front, the organizational structure is shaped by very different considerations and reader expectations. A threshold issue will almost always be treated first, even if it is relatively easy to resolve. Even though legal readers are busy, most will read a memo through to the end and not treat the last pages or lines as optional. For the most part, true paragraphs do not exist in journalism. Because of the narrow width of many newspaper columns, the convention in journalism is to write mostly one-sentence paragraphs. Journalists transitioning into writing about law have to learn to write longer paragraphs.

Finally, most journalists have learned to be extraordinarily careful with spelling, particularly the spelling of proper names, which is an asset that carries over nicely into legal writing. Punctuation, however, may be a different matter. Journalism prefers "open punctuation," which means using as little punctuation as the rules will allow; legal writing, by contrast, tends to used "closed punctuation," which means that lawyers lean in the other direction and use commas when the rules give them the option to do so. The serial comma, for example, is generally omitted in journalism (no comma before the "and" in "red, white and blue") but is included in legal writing ("red, white, and blue").

4. *Science Majors and Scientists*

Science majors and scientists bring a strong set of skills in critical thinking and formal analysis that individuals in many other professions or disciplines may lack. The ability to evaluate evidence, make logical connections, and draw plausible conclusions forms the very basis of substantive legal analysis. However, legal writing diverges from scientific writing in several ways that may prove challenging or even frustrating.

In terms of writing style, legal writing favors active voice sentences, not the passive voice sentences used as the professional standard in scientific writing. Formal organization of various legal writing projects requires a different organizational structure than scientific writing (e.g., title, hypothesis, materials, methods, observations, results, conclusion), although experience working with any formal structure will be of help in legal writing.

In terms of substantive analysis, deriving governing rules and tests from case law precedent or statutory language is similar to formulating the hypothesis and methods sections of a scientific paper. However, on a practical level jurisprudence has little in common with scientific laws and validity studies. Science majors and scientists may find their experience similar to the frustration experienced by philosophy students. "Law" is not created by systematic application of the scientific method in order to discover logically necessary, objective truths with universal application that can be repeated and verified by any scientist in a variety of conditions. Rather, "law" is created by a combination of individual circumstances, public policies, concepts of fairness, tradition, emotion, credibility, economic realities, political considerations, and persuasive argument, among other factors.

In fact, legal reasoning and persuasive argument may represent the greatest challenges to science majors and scientists engaged in legal writing. Although persuasive argument skills have a subtle use in the results and conclusion parts of a scientific paper, the rhetorical strategies and skills necessary for legal writing will likely draw on a legal writer's experience in non-scientific areas of life. Consequently, science majors and scientists transitioning into writing about law should be prepared to merge an "objective" approach with a more subjective "relational" approach.

5. *Writers from Other Cultures*

Each of us absorbs the writing preferences of our first language and our native culture. Those preferences are often so deeply embedded in the many aspects of writing that they are hard to see and even harder to articulate. Often we are unaware that different cultures (and different professions) have different ideas about what makes something "good writing."

The U.S. culture, and specifically the U.S. legal culture, is no different from any other professional culture. It has expectations and preferences that have developed over time about how something should be written. Students who come to U.S. law schools wanting to learn U.S. legal writing may find it useful to begin by examining the cultural preferences related to writing from their native cultures and languages and then compare those preferences with those of the U.S. legal culture.

CHAPTER 2

The United States Legal System

The United States system of government. For some, it is the secret to democracy, the power to elect one's leaders and the right to speak freely. For others, it is a horrendous bureaucracy, a maze through which one must struggle to obtain a benefit, to change a law, or to get a day in court. For still others, it is more abstract—a chart in an eighth-grade civics book describing the three branches of government and explaining the system of checks and balances.

For lawyers, the United States system of government is all of these things and more. It is the foundation for their knowledge of the law, the stage on which they play out their professional roles, the arena for the very serious game of law.

No matter which metaphor you prefer—foundation, stage, arena—the point is the same. To be an effective researcher, you must understand the system. You must know the framework before you can work well within it.

Like most complex systems, the United States system of government can be analyzed in a number of different ways. You can focus on its three branches—the executive branch, the legislative branch, and the judicial branch—or you can focus on the system's two parts, the federal government and the state governments.

In this chapter we do both. We look first at the three branches, examining both their individual functions and their interrelationships. We then examine the relationship between state and federal government, again with an eye toward their individual functions and powers.

A. THE THREE BRANCHES OF GOVERNMENT

Just as the medical student must understand both the various organs that make up the human body and their relationship to each other, the law student must understand both the three branches of government and the relationships among them.

1. *The Executive Branch*

The first of the three branches is the executive branch. In the federal system, the executive power is vested in the President; in the states, it is vested in the governor. (See Article II, Section 1 of the United States Constitution and the constitutions of the various states.) In general, the executive branch has the power to implement and enforce laws. It oversees public projects, administers public benefit programs, and controls law enforcement agencies.

The executive branch also has powers that directly affect our system of law. For example, the President (or a governor) can control the law-making function of the legislative branch by exercising his or her power to convene and adjourn the Congress (or state legislature) or by vetoing legislation. Similarly, the President (or a governor) can shape the decisions of the courts through his or her judicial nominations or by directing the attorney general to enforce or not to enforce certain laws.

2. The Legislative Branch

The second branch is the legislative branch. Congress's powers are enumerated in Article I, Section 8, of the United States Constitution, which gives Congress, among other things, the power to lay and collect taxes, borrow money, regulate commerce with foreign nations and among the states, establish uniform naturalization and bankruptcy laws, promote the progress of science and the useful arts by creating copyright laws, and punish counterfeiting. Powers not granted Congress are given to the states or left to the people. (See the Tenth Amendment to the United States Constitution.) The state constitutions enumerate the powers given to the state legislatures.

Like the executive branch, the legislative branch exercises power over the other two branches. It can check the actions of the executive branch by enacting or refusing to enact legislation requested by the executive, by controlling the budget and, at least at the federal level, by consenting or refusing to consent to nominations made by the executive.

The legislative branch's power over the judicial branch is less obvious. At one level, it can control the judiciary through its power to establish courts (Article I, Section 8, grants Congress the power to establish inferior federal courts) and its power to consent to or reject the executive branch's judicial nominations. However, the most obvious control it has over the judiciary is its power to enact legislation that supersedes, or replaces, a common law or court-made doctrine or rule.

The legislative branch also shares its law-making power with the executive branch. In enacting legislation, it sometimes gives the executive branch the power to promulgate the regulations needed to implement or enforce the legislation. For example, although Congress (the legislative branch) enacted the Internal Revenue Code, the Internal Revenue Service (part of the executive branch) promulgates the regulations needed to implement that code.

3. The Judicial Branch

The third branch is the judicial branch. Article III, Section 1, of the United States Constitution vests the judicial power of the United States in one supreme court and in such inferior courts as Congress may establish. The state constitutions establish and grant power to the state courts.

a. The Hierarchical Nature of the Court System

Both the federal and the state court systems are hierarchical. At the lowest level are the trial courts, whose primary function is fact-finding. The judge or jury hears the evidence and enters a judgment.

At the next level are the intermediate courts of appeals. These courts hear the majority of appeals, deciding (1) whether the trial court applied the right law and (2) whether there is sufficient evidence to support the jury's verdict or the trial judge's findings of fact and conclusions of law. Unlike the trial courts, these courts do not conduct trials. There are no witnesses, and the only exhibits are the exhibits that were admitted during trial. The decisions of the appellate courts are based solely on the written trial record and the attorneys' arguments.

At the top level are the states' highest courts and the Supreme Court of the United States. The primary function of these courts is to make law. They hear only those cases that involve issues of great public import or cases in which different divisions or circuits have adopted or applied conflicting rules of law. Like the intermediate courts of appeals, these courts do not hear evidence; they only review the trial court record. See Exhibit 2.1.

An example illustrates the role each court plays. In *State v. Strong*, a criminal case, the defendant, Mr. Strong, was charged with possession of a controlled substance. At the trial court level, both the State and the defendant presented witnesses and physical evidence. On the basis of this evidence, the trial court decided the case on its merits, with the trial judge deciding the questions of law (whether the evidence should be suppressed) and the jury deciding the questions of fact (whether the State had proved all of the elements of the crime beyond a reasonable doubt).

Both issues were decided against the defendant: The trial court judge ruled that the evidence was admissible, and the jury found that the State had met its burden of proof. Disagreeing with both determinations, the defendant filed an appeal with the intermediate court of appeals.

In deciding this appeal, the appellate court could consider only two issues: whether the trial court judge erred when he denied the defendant's motion to suppress and whether there was sufficient evidence to support the jury's verdict.

Because the first issue raised a question of law, the appellate court could review the issue de novo. The court did not need to defer to the judgment of the trial court judge. Instead, the appellate court could exercise its own independent judgment to decide the issue on its merits.

The appellate court had much less latitude with respect to the second issue. Because the second issue raised a question of fact rather than law, the appellate court could not substitute its judgment for that of the jury. It could only review the jury's findings to make sure that they were supported by the evidence. When the question is one of fact, the appellate court may decide only (1) whether there is sufficient evidence to support the jury's verdict or (2) whether the jury's verdict is clearly erroneous. It may not substitute its judgment for the judgment of the jury.

EXHIBIT 2.1 THE ROLES OF THE TRIAL, INTERMEDIATE, AND SUPREME COURTS

Trial Court

- ☐ The trial court hears witnesses and views evidence.
- ☐ The trial court judge decides issues of law; the jury decides questions of fact. (When there is no jury, the trial court judge decides both the questions of law and the questions of fact.)

Intermediate Court of Appeals

- ☐ The intermediate court of appeals reviews the written record and exhibits from the trial court.
- ☐ When an issue raises a question of law, the intermediate court of appeals may substitute its judgment for the judgment of the trial court judge; when an issue raises a question of fact, the appellate court must defer to the decision of the finder of fact (the jury or, if there was no jury, the trial judge).

Supreme, or Highest, Court

- ☐ Like the intermediate court of appeals, it reviews the written record and exhibits from the trial court.
- ☐ Like the intermediate court of appeals, it has broad powers to review questions of law: It determines whether the trial court and intermediate court of appeals applied the right law correctly. Its power to review factual issues is, however, very limited. Like the intermediate court of appeals, it can determine only whether there is sufficient evidence to support the decision of the jury or, if there was no jury, the decision of the trial court judge.

Regardless of the type of issue (fact or law), the appellate court must base its decision on the written trial court record and exhibits and the attorneys' arguments. Consequently, in *Strong*, the intermediate court of appeals did not see or hear any of the witnesses. The only people present when the appeal was argued were the appellate court judges assigned to hear the case and Strong's and the State's attorneys. Not even the defendant, Mr. Strong, was present.

If Mr. Strong lost his first appeal, he could petition the state supreme court (through a petition for discretionary review) and ask that court to review the intermediate court of appeals' decision. If the state supreme court granted the petition, its review, like that of the intermediate court of appeals, would be limited. Although the supreme court would review the issue of law de novo, it would have to defer to the jury's decision on the questions of fact.

Most of the cases that appear in law school casebooks are appellate court decisions, for example, decisions of the United States Court of Appeals or the United

States Supreme Court or decisions from state appellate courts. These cases, however, represent only a small, and perhaps not representative, percentage of the disputes that lawyers see during the course of their practice.

Accordingly, as you read the cases in the casebooks, remember that you are seeing only the proverbial tip of the iceberg. For a case to reach the United States Supreme Court, the parties must have had the financial means to pursue it, and the Court must have found that the issue raised was significant enough to grant review.

PRACTICE POINTER

As you will learn in Civil Procedure, to hear a case a court must have both subject matter jurisdiction and personal jurisdiction. Stated very simply, a court has subject matter jurisdiction when it has power to hear a particular type of case. For example, the federal courts have subject matter jurisdiction to hear cases involving the United States Constitution and United States statutes, state courts of general jurisdiction have subject matter jurisdiction to hear cases involving the state constitution and state statutes, and municipal courts have subject matter jurisdiction to hear cases involving city ordinances. It is not, though, enough that a court has subject matter jurisdiction. The court must also have personal jurisdiction or the power to hear and decide cases involving the parties to the case or controversy.

b. The Federal Courts

In the federal system, most cases are heard initially in the federal district courts, the primary trial courts in that system. These courts have original jurisdiction over most federal questions and have the power to review the decisions of some administrative agencies. Each state has at least one district court, and many have several. For example, Indiana has the District Court for Northern Indiana and the District Court for Southern Indiana. Cases that are not heard in the district court are usually heard in one of several specialized courts, for example, the United States Tax Court, the United States Court of Federal Claims, or the United States Court of International Trade.

In the federal system, the intermediate court of appeals is the United States Court of Appeals. There are currently thirteen circuits: eleven numbered circuits, the District of Columbia Circuit, and the Federal Circuit. See Exhibit 2.2. The Federal Circuit, which was created in 1982, reviews the decisions of the United States Court of Federal Claims and the United States Court of International Trade, as well as some administrative decisions.

PRACTICE POINTER

For an electronic copy of a map showing the federal circuits, see *http://www.uscourts.gov/court_locator.aspx*

EXHIBIT 2.2 THE THIRTEEN FEDERAL JUDICIAL CIRCUITS

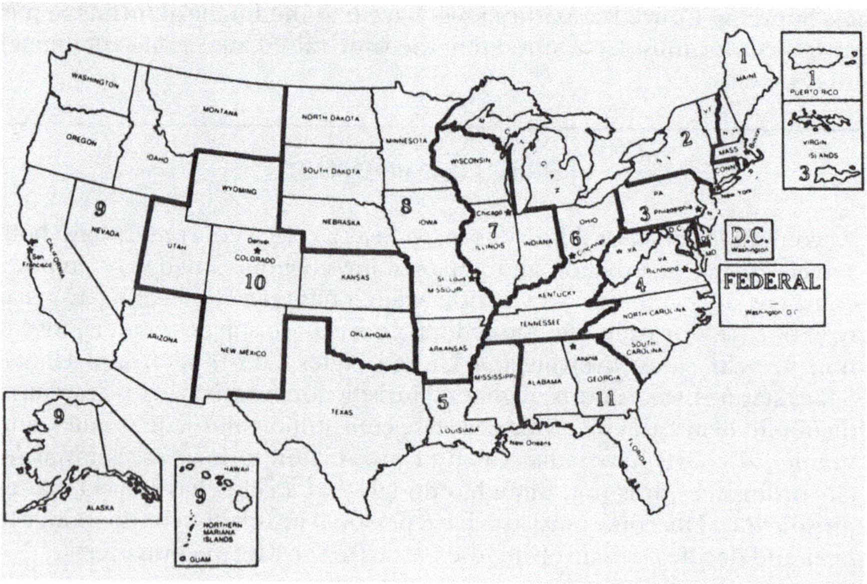

Reprinted from *Federal Reporter* (West's National Reporter System) with permission of West, a Thomson Reuters business.

The highest federal court is the United States Supreme Court. Although many people believe that the Supreme Court is all-powerful, in fact it is not. As with other courts, there are limits on the Supreme Court's powers. It can play only one of two roles.

In one role, the United States Supreme Court is similar to the state supreme courts. In the federal system, the United States Supreme Court is the highest court, the court of last resort. In contrast, in its other role, it is the final arbiter of federal constitutional law, interpreting the United States Constitution and determining whether the federal government or a state has violated rights granted under the United States Constitution.

Thus, although people often assert that they will take their case all the way to the Supreme Court, they may not be able to. As a general rule, the Supreme Court may hear a case only if it involves a question of federal constitutional law or a federal statute. The Supreme Court does not have the power to hear cases involving only questions of state law. For example, although the United States Supreme Court has the power to determine whether a state's marriage dissolution statutes are constitutional, the Court does not have the power to hear purely factual questions, such as whether it would be in the best interests of a child for custody to be granted to the father or whether child support should be set at $300 rather than $400 per month.

Each year the United States Supreme Court receives more than 7,000 requests for review (writs of certiorari). Of the approximately 100 cases that the Court actually hears, the overwhelming majority are appeals from the federal courts.

Exhibit 2.3 illustrates the relationships among the various federal courts.

Because the United States District Courts and Courts of Appeals hear so many cases, not all of their decisions are "published." When they are published, decisions from the United States District Courts are published in either the *Federal Supplement*, or *Federal Rules Decisions*, and decisions from the United States Courts of Appeals are published in the *Federal Reporter*. (Decisions from the specialized courts are published in specialized reporters.

PRACTICE POINTER

A "published" decision is a decision that is published in a set of books called a "reporter." (For more about reporters, see § 4.2.4b.) Thus, decisions that appear on Lexis Advance®, WestlawNext™, Bloomberg Law, or a free website but that are not in a reporter are not published decisions. They are unpublished, or unreported, decisions. In some jurisdictions, you cannot cite to an unpublished decision in a brief to that jurisdiction's courts. To find out whether you can cite to an unpublished decision, see your local court rules.

All United States Supreme Court decisions are published. The official reporter is *United States Reports*, and the two unofficial reporters are *Supreme Court Reporter* and *United States Supreme Court Reports, Lawyers' Edition*.

EXHIBIT 2.3 THE FEDERAL COURT SYSTEM

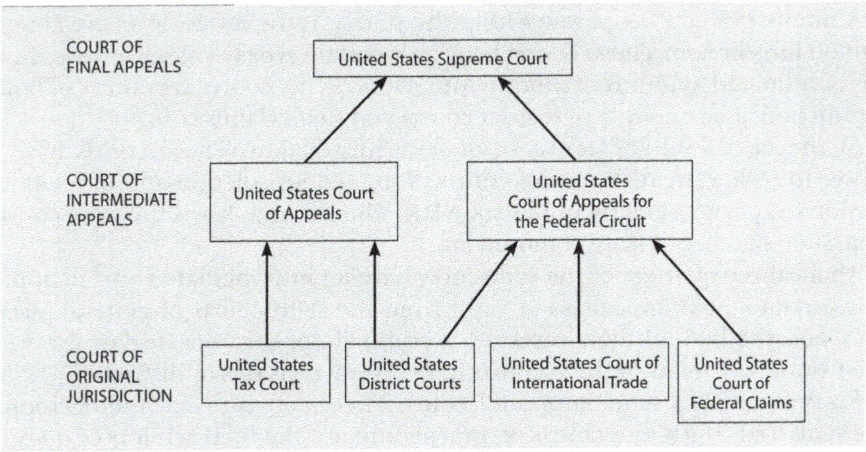

EXHIBIT 2.4 THE STATE COURT SYSTEM

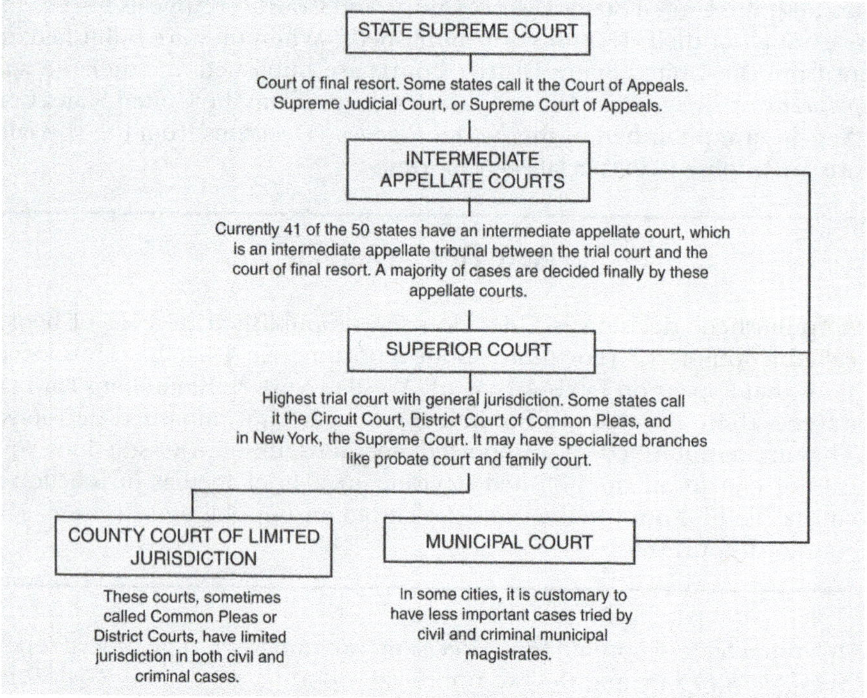

c. State Courts

A number of courts operate within the states. At the lowest level are courts of limited jurisdiction. These courts hear only certain types of cases or cases involving only limited amounts of money. Municipal or city courts are courts of limited jurisdiction, as are county or district courts and small claims courts.

At the next level are courts of general jurisdiction. These courts have the power to review the decisions of courts of limited jurisdiction and original jurisdiction over claims arising under state law, whether that law is the state constitution, state statutes, or state common law.

About three-quarters of the states now have an intermediate court of appeals. These courts hear appeals as of right from the state courts of general jurisdiction, and the bulk of their caseload is criminal appeals. Because of the size of their workload, many of these courts have several divisions or districts.

Every state has a state "supreme" court. These courts review the decisions of the state trial courts and courts of appeals and are the final arbiters of questions of state constitutional, statutory, and common law. Exhibit 2.4 illustrates the typical relationship among the various state courts.

PRACTICE POINTER

Not all states call their highest court the supreme court. For example, in New York, the highest court is called the Court of Appeals, and the trial courts are called the supreme courts.

Decisions of state trial courts are not usually published. In addition, because of the volume, not all decisions of intermediate state courts of appeals are published. Those that are, and all decisions of the state supreme court, appear in one of West Publishing Company's regional reporters and, if the state has one, the state's official reporter.

d. Other Courts

There are also several other court systems. As sovereign entities, many Native American tribes have their own judicial systems, as does the United States military.

B. THE RELATIONSHIP BETWEEN THE FEDERAL AND STATE GOVERNMENTS

It is not enough, however, to look at our system of government only from the perspective of its three branches. To understand the system, you must also understand the relationship between the federal and state governments.

1. A Short History

Like most things, our system of government is the product of our history. From the early 1600s until 1781, the "united states" were not united. Instead, the "country" was composed of independent colonies, all operating under different charters and each having its own laws and legal system. Although the colonies traded with each other, the relationship among the colonies was no closer than the relationship among the European countries prior to 1992. It was not until the Articles of Confederation were adopted in 1781 that the "states" ceded any of their rights to a federal government.

Even though the states ceded more rights when the Constitution became effective in 1789, they preserved most of their own law. Each state retained its own executive, its own legislature and laws, and its own court system.

Thus, our system of government is really two systems, a federal system and the fifty state systems, with the United States Constitution brokering the relationship between the two.

2. The Relationship Between Laws Enacted by Congress and Those Enacted by the State Legislatures

As citizens of the United States, we are subject to two sets of laws: federal law and the law of the state in which we are citizens (or in which we act). Most of the time, there is no conflict between these two sets of laws: federal law governs some conduct; state law, other conduct. For example, federal law governs bankruptcy proceedings, and state law governs divorce.

Occasionally, however, both Congress and a state legislature enact laws governing the same conduct. Sometimes these laws coexist. For example, both Congress and the states have enacted drug laws. Acting under the powers granted to it under the Commerce Clause, Congress has made it illegal to import controlled substances or to transport them across state lines. The states, acting consistently with the powers reserved to them, have made illegal the possession or sale of controlled substances within the state. In such instances, citizens are subject to both laws. A defendant may be charged under federal law with transporting a drug across state lines and under state law with possession.

There are times, however, when federal and state law do not complement each other and cannot coexist. An act can be legal under federal law but illegal under state law. In such instances, federal law preempts state law, provided that the federal law is constitutional. As provided in the Supremacy Clause, laws enacted by Congress under the powers granted to it under the Constitution are the "supreme Law of the Land; and the Judges in every State shall be bound thereby. . . ."

The issue is different when the conflicting laws are from different states. Although there are more and more uniform laws (the Uniform Child Custody Act, the Uniform Commercial Code), an activity that is legal in one state may be illegal in another state. For instance, although prostitution is legal in Nevada as a local option, it is illegal in other states.

3. The Relationship Between Federal and State Courts

The relationship between the federal and state court systems is complex. Although each system is autonomous, in certain circumstances the state courts may hear cases brought under federal law, and the federal courts may hear cases brought under state law.

For example, although the majority of cases heard in state courts are brought under state law, state courts also have jurisdiction when a case is brought under a provision of the United States Constitution, a treaty, and certain federal statutes. Similarly, although the majority of cases heard in the federal courts involve questions of federal law, the federal courts have jurisdiction over cases involving questions of state law when the parties are from different states (diversity jurisdiction).

The appellate jurisdiction of the courts is somewhat simpler. In the federal system, the United States Court of Appeals has appellate jurisdiction to review the decisions of the United States District Courts and certain administrative agencies, and the United States Supreme Court is the court of last resort, having the power to review the decisions of the lower federal courts. Similarly, if a state has an intermediate court of appeals, that court has the power to review the decisions of the lower courts within its geographic jurisdiction, and the state's highest, or supreme court, is the court of last resort.

4. *The Relationship Among Federal, State, and Local Prosecutors*

The power to prosecute cases arising under the United States Constitution and federal statutes is vested in the Department of Justice, which is headed by the Attorney General of the United States, a presidential appointee. Assisting the United States Attorney General are the United States Attorneys for each federal judicial district. The individual United States Attorneys' offices have two divisions: a civil division and a criminal division. The civil division handles civil cases arising under federal law, and the criminal division handles cases involving alleged violations of federal criminal statutes.

At the state level, the system is slightly different. In most states, the attorney for the state is the state attorney general, usually an elected official. Working for the state attorney general are a number of assistant attorneys general. However, unlike the United States attorneys, most state attorneys general do not handle criminal cases. Their clients are the various state agencies. For example, an assistant attorney general may be assigned to a state's department of social and health services, the department of licensing, the consumer protection bureau, or the department of workers' compensation, providing advice to the agency and representing the agency in civil litigation.

Criminal prosecutions are handled by county and city prosecutors. Each county has its own prosecutor's office, which has both a civil and a criminal division. Attorneys working for the civil division play much the same role as state assistant attorneys general. They represent the county and its agencies, providing both advice and representation. In contrast, the attorneys assigned to the criminal division are responsible for prosecutions under the state's criminal code. The county prosecutor's office decides whom to charge and then tries the cases.

Like the counties, cities have their own city attorney's office, which, at least in large cities, has civil and criminal divisions. Attorneys working in the civil division advise city departments and agencies and represent the city in civil litigation; attorneys in the criminal division prosecute criminal cases brought under city ordinances. State, county, and city prosecutors do not represent federal departments or agencies, nor do they handle cases brought under federal law.

C. DECIDING HOW MUCH WEIGHT TO GIVE TO A PARTICULAR AUTHORITY

Not all enacted and common law is given equal weight. In deciding which law to apply, courts distinguish between mandatory and persuasive authority.

Mandatory authority is law that is binding on the court deciding the case. The court must apply that law. In contrast, persuasive authority is law that is not binding. Although the court may look to that law for guidance, it need not apply it.

Determining whether a particular statute or case is mandatory or persuasive authority is a two-step process. You must first determine which jurisdiction's law applies (that is, whether federal or state law applies and, if state law applies, which state's law); you must then determine which of that jurisdiction's statutes and cases are binding on the court that will be deciding the case.

1. *Which Jurisdiction's Law Applies?*

Sometimes determining which jurisdiction's law applies is easy. For example, common knowledge (and common sense) tells you that federal law probably governs whether a federal PLUS loan constitutes income for federal income tax purposes. Similarly, you would probably guess that a will executed in California by a California resident would be governed by California state law. At other times, though, the determination is much more difficult. You probably would not know which jurisdiction's law governs a real estate contract between a resident of New York and a resident of Pennsylvania for a piece of property located in Florida.

Although the rules governing the determination of which jurisdiction's law applies are beyond the scope of this book (they are studied in Civil Procedure, Federal Courts, and Conflicts), keep two things in mind.

First, remember that in our legal system, federal law almost always preempts, or takes precedence over, state law. Consequently, if there is both a federal and a state statute on the same topic, the federal statute will preempt the state statute to the extent that the two are inconsistent. For example, if a federal statute makes it illegal to discriminate on the basis of familial status when renting an apartment but under a state statute such discrimination is lawful, the federal statute governs—it is illegal to discriminate on the basis of familial status. There are a few instances, however, when a state constitutional provision or a state statute will govern. If the state constitution gives a criminal defendant more rights than does the federal constitution, the state constitution applies. While states can grant an individual more protection, they cannot take away or restrict rights granted by the federal constitution or a federal statute.

Second, in the federal system there is not the same body of common law that there is in the states. Unlike the state systems, in the federal system there are no common law rules governing adverse possession or intentional torts such as assault and battery, false imprisonment, or the intentional infliction of emotional distress. As a consequence, if the cause of action is based on a common law doctrine, the case is probably governed by state and not federal law.

2. *What "Law" Will Be Binding on the Court?*

Within each jurisdiction, the authorities are ranked. The United States Constitution is the highest authority, binding both state and federal courts. Other federal and state law is under the United States Constitution.

In the federal system, the highest authority is the Constitution. Under the Constitution are the federal statutes and regulations, and under the federal statutes and regulations are the cases interpreting and applying them.

In the state system, the ranking is similar. The highest authority is the state constitution, followed by state statutes and regulations and the cases interpreting and applying those statutes and regulations and state common law.

In addition, the cases themselves are ranked. In both the federal and state systems, decisions of the United States Supreme Court carry the most weight: When deciding a case involving the same law and similar facts, both the courts of appeals and the trial courts are bound by the decisions of the supreme, or highest, state courts. Decisions of intermediate courts of appeals come next; the trial courts under the jurisdiction of the intermediate courts of appeals are bound by the courts of appeals' decisions. At the bottom are the trial courts. Trial court decisions are binding only on the parties involved in the particular case.

Statutes and cases are also ranked by date. More recent statutes supersede earlier versions, and more recent common law rules supersede early rules by the same level court. Courts are bound by the highest court's most recent decision. For example, if there is a 1967 state intermediate court of appeals decision that makes an activity legal and a 1986 state supreme court decision that makes it illegal, in the absence of a statute, the 1986 supreme court decision governs. The 1986 decision would be mandatory authority, and all the courts within that jurisdiction would be bound by that decision.

D. EXERCISE

1. In 1930, in Case A, the Supreme Court of your state set out a common law rule. In 1956, in Case B, the Supreme Court of your state changed that rule. In your state, which case would be binding on a trial court: Case A or Case B?
2. Same facts as in Question 1 except that in 1981, in Case C, the Supreme Court of your state modified the rule set out in Case B, adding a requirement. In your state, which test would a trial court use: the test set out in Case A, the test set out in Case B, or the test set out in Case C?

Case A	State Supreme Court	1930
Case B	State Supreme Court	1956
Case C	State Supreme Court	1981

3. Same facts as in Question 2 except that in 1983 your state legislature enacted a statute that completely changed the common law rule. What is now binding on the trial court: the cases or the statute?

Case A	State Supreme Court	1930
Case B	State Supreme Court	1956
Case C	State Supreme Court	1981
State Statute		1983

4. Same facts as in Question 3 except that in 1985, in Case D, a case involving the application of the 1983 statute, the Court of Appeals of your state gives one of the words in the statute a broad interpretation. (The word was not defined in the statute.) In applying the statute, which courts are bound by

the Court of Appeals' decision in Case D: a trial court within the Court of Appeals' geographic jurisdiction? A trial court outside the Court of Appeals' geographic jurisdiction? The division of the Court of Appeals that decided Case D? A division of the Court of Appeals other than the division that decided Case D? Your state's Supreme Court?

State Statute	1983
Case D	1985

5. In 1995, in Case E, a different division of the Court of Appeals applies the 1983 statute. In reaching its decision, the court declines to follow the decision in Case D. Instead of interpreting the word broadly, the court interprets it narrowly. The losing party disagrees with this decision and files an appeal with your state's Supreme Court. In deciding the appeal, is the Supreme Court bound by the Court of Appeals' decision in Case D? The Court of Appeals' decision in Case E?

State Statute		1983
Case D	Court of Appeals	1985
Case E	Court of Appeals	1995

6. Same facts as in Question 5 except that in 1999 the state legislature amends that statute, explicitly defining the word that was the subject of debate in Cases D and E. The legislature elects to give the word a very narrow meaning. In Case F, which is brought before a state trial court in 2008, what would be controlling: the 1983 version of the statute? The 1985 decision in Case D? The 1995 decision in Case E? The amended version of the statute?

   Note: In Case E, the Supreme Court reversed the Court of Appeals and interpreted the term broadly.

State Statute		1983
Case D	Court of Appeals	1985
Case E	Court of Appeals	1995
Case E	Supreme Court	1996
Amended State Statute		1999

Chapter 2 Quiz

Draft answers for each of the following questions. Make your points clearly and concisely, and write sentences that are easy to read and that are grammatical and correctly punctuated.

1. Which branch of the federal government has the power to enact statutes?
2. Which branch of the federal government is responsible for enforcing federal statutes?
3. Which branch of the federal government has the power to determine whether a federal statute is constitutional?
4. What is the difference between a statute and a regulation?
5. At trial, what is the role of the judge? The role of the jury?

6. What role do the appellate courts play?
   a. Do they hear testimony?
   b. Do they decide issues of fact?
   c. Do they determine whether there was sufficient evidence to support the trial court's judgment?
   d. Do they determine whether the trial court applied the right law and applied that law correctly?
7. In the federal system, what is the name of the trial court? The intermediate court of appeals? What courts operate in your state? (To find this information, you will need to do an Internet search.)
8. What do lawyers and judges mean when they say that a federal statute "preempts" a state statute?
9. What do lawyers and judges mean when they say that a court has "jurisdiction" to hear a particular type of case?
10. Are all of the court decisions that appear on the Internet (for example, on Lexis Advance and WestlawNext) "published" decisions? What makes a decision a "published opinion"?

CHAPTER 3

Understanding Statutes

> The last fifty to eighty years have seen a fundamental change in American law. In this time we have gone from a legal system dominated by the common law, divined by courts, to one in which statutes, enacted by legislatures, have become the primary source of law. The consequences of the "orgy of statute making," in Grant Gilmore's felicitous phrase, are just beginning to be recognized. The change itself and its effect on our whole legal-political system have not been systemically treated.
>
> Guido Calabresi,
> A Common Law for the Age of Statutes

The "orgy of statute making" Guido Calabresi described has created a legal system dominated by statutes. Although no one knows for sure how many statutes there are, one fact is certain: The ability to read and analyze statutes is a skill that every attorney needs.

A. HOW STATUTES ARE ENACTED

Because attorneys are sometimes called upon to make arguments based on a statute's legislative history, we begin this chapter by briefly describing the processes through which federal and state statutes are enacted. If you are already familiar with this process, you can skip to section 3.B. If, however, you are not familiar with the process, or if all you remember is the song from the "Schoolhouse Rock" video, I'm Just a Bill, then read the following two subsections, noting both how complex the process is and the names of the documents that are created at each stage.

1. Federal Statutes

In the United States, federal statutes are enacted by Congress, which is made up of two houses, the House of Representatives and the Senate. See section 2.1.2. All federal statutes begin as a bill, which is the name used to refer to proposed statutes. Although a bill may be drafted by anyone, only a member of Congress can introduce, or present, a bill to Congress. The member of Congress who introduces the bill becomes the bill's sponsor and usually works to get the bill passed into law.

For the purpose of this example, presume that the bill's sponsor is a member of the United States House of Representatives. To introduce the bill, the sponsor places a copy of the bill in the "hopper," which is a box located on the platform where the Speaker of the House of Representatives sits. After the bill is placed in the hopper, the Clerk of the House assigns the bill a number that begins with "H.R.," which stands for House of Representatives, and the bill is sent to one of the House of Representatives' twenty standing committees, for example, the Committee on Agriculture, the Committee on Homeland Security, or the Committee on International Relations.

The standing committee reviews the bill, debates its merits and, if it chooses, makes changes to it. If, after debating the bill, a majority of the members of the standing committee believe that the bill is unnecessary or unwise, the standing committee can vote to table the bill or can let the bill "die in committee." If, however, the standing committee decides that the bill has merit, the committee will usually refer it to a subcommittee for further study and debate. The subcommittee may conduct hearings, during which experts, supporters, and opponents may testify or speak about the need for the bill and its effect. After these hearings and debate, the members of the subcommittee can vote to table the bill, let the bill die, or vote to send the bill back to the standing committee for further action. If the subcommittee sends the bill back to the standing committee, the standing committee can vote to table the bill, let it die, or release the bill and send it, along with a committee report that explains the bill, back to the full House of Representatives.

When the House of Representatives receives a bill from a standing committee, the Clerk of the House places the bill on the House of Representatives' calendar, scheduling it for consideration by the membership of the House of Representatives. During these public debates, members of the House of Representatives can offer amendments, which will be voted on by all of the members of the House of Representatives. At the close of the debates, the bill is placed before the membership for a vote. If a majority of the House of Representatives approves the bill, the engrossed bill, which is the version of the bill passed by the House of Representatives, is sent to the Senate for its consideration.

When the Senate receives a bill, or act, from the House of Representatives, it refers it to one of the Senate's sixteen standing committees. This standing committee will consider the bill and do one or more of the following: (1) approve the bill as it was passed by the House of Representatives and send it back to the full Senate for a vote; (2) send the bill to a Senate subcommittee for further consideration, including additional hearings; (3) send the bill to a joint subcommittee made up of members of the House of Representatives and the Senate, which will attempt to draft a compromise bill that is acceptable to both the members of the House of Representatives and the Senate; or (4) let the bill die. If the Senate standing committee recommends passage of the bill as it was passed by the House of Representatives, it will release the bill and send it to the full Senate for its consideration and its vote. If, however, the Senate subcommittee sends the bill to a joint committee, any compromise bills that are drafted must be approved by the membership of both the House of Representatives and the Senate.

Once a bill has been approved by both the House of Representatives and the Senate, the enrolled bill, which is a bill that has been passed by both houses, is sent to the President. If the President signs the bill, the bill is assigned a public law number (beginning with "P.L."). If, however, the President vetoes the bill, the bill does not become law unless both the House of Representatives and the Senate override that veto by a two-thirds vote. Chart 3-1 summarizes the process and lists the documents that are created at each stage in the process.

CHART 3-1
HOW A BILL INTRODUCED IN THE UNITED STATES HOUSE OF REPRESENTATIVES BECOMES A LAW

Step	Document
1. A member of the House of Representatives introduces the bill.	• Bill
2. The bill is referred to a committee. The committee may then refer the bill to a subcommittee. (Most bills die in committee.)	• Transcripts from Committee Hearings • Committee Print
3. If the bill does not die in committee, the committee submits its report on the bill to the House.	• Committee Report
4. The bill is presented to the House for debate, amendments, and a vote.	• Engrossed Bill
5. If bill is approved, it is sent to the Senate. The Senate repeats steps 1-4.	• Engrossed Bill
6. If the Senate passes the bill, it returns the bill, with any amendments, to the House. The House then approves the amendments, determines that the amendments are unacceptable, or creates a Conference Committee to create a compromise bill	• Conference Committee Report • Enrolled Bill
7. If both House and Senate pass the same version of the bill, the bill is sent to the President for signature. If the President signs the bill, it becomes law.	• Presidential Statement • Public Law

The process is the same if a bill is introduced in the Senate. The only difference is that when a Senator introduces a bill, the bill is assigned a number that begins with an "S." and if the majority of the Senate approves the bill, it is then sent to the House of Representatives for consideration.

Once a bill has been signed into law, it is assigned a public law number, and the law is codified, or placed into the appropriate section or sections of the United States Code (U.S.C.).

PRACTICE POINTER

For a more detailed explanation of how federal statutes are enacted, see *http://beta.congress.gov/legislative-process*

2. *State Statutes*

In the forty-nine states that have a bicameral legislature—a legislature with two houses or chambers—the process is similar. A member of one of the state's two houses will introduce a bill, the bill will be read and referred to a committee, and the committee will debate the bill and either let it die or send it back to the house in which the bill originated. If that chamber approves the bill, the bill will be sent to the other chamber for its consideration. If the other chamber approves the bill, the bill will be sent to the governor, who can either sign the bill, making it law, or veto the bill. If the governor vetoes the bill, the state legislature can overturn that veto by a two-thirds vote. The exception is Nebraska: The Nebraska legislature has only one house.

B. HOW REGULATIONS ARE PROMULGATED

In enacting statutes, the legislative branch can give the executive branch the power to promulgate regulations implementing the provisions set out in the statute. If the executive branch does not exceed the powers granted to it by the legislative branch, these regulations have the force of law. For example, in enacting the Clean Air Act, a federal statute, Congress gave the Environmental Protection Agency, an agency created by the President, the power to promulgate regulations implementing the Clean Air Act.

The process of promulgating a federal regulation is relatively straightforward. The federal agency that has been given the power to promulgate regulations publishes proposed regulations in the Federal Register and invites comments from the public. After the comment period ends, the agency considers the comments and prepares the final version of the regulations. The final versions of federal regulations are published in the Federal Register and then in the Code of Federal Regulations (C.F.R.), which is republished each year.

At the state level, the process is similar. The state agency that has been given the power to promulgate regulations publishes proposed regulations in some type of state register, and invites public comment. When the comment period ends, the state agency considers the comments and then publishes the final version of the regulations in its state administrative code.

C. THE RELATIONSHIP AMONG STATUTES, REGULATIONS, AND CASES

The relationships among statutes, regulations, and cases are both simple and complex. They are simple in the sense that there is a hierarchy: Statutes, which set out the law, are at the top; regulations, which implement the law, are in the middle; and cases, which apply the statutes and regulations, are at the bottom.

Statute
↓
Regulations Implementing Statutes
↓
Cases Applying the Statute and Regulations

The relationships are, however, also complex in that they involve both the federal government and the state governments and, within each of those governments, the system of checks and balances that the drafters of our Constitution created. See section 2.2.

Federal Statutes	State Statutes
Statutes (Legislative Branch)	Statutes (Legislative Branch)
Regulations (Executive Branch)	Regulations (Executive Branch)
Cases (Judicial Branch)	Cases (Judicial Branch)

We start with two simple examples and then move to some of the more complex situations that you may encounter.

1. *Federal Statute Governs*

Presume for a moment that you have been asked to research an immigration issue. Historically, there was no common law governing immigration and, under the United States Constitution, only the federal government has the power to regulate immigration. Thus, immigration issues are governed by federal statutes, federal regulations, and federal cases that have applied those statutes and regulations.

Because the statutes are the "highest authority," you will want to start your research, and your analysis, with these statutes. You will, however, also need to look for federal regulations. While the federal statutes will set out the general principles and rules, the federal regulations will provide more specific information, for example, definitions, standards, and procedures. If the statute and/or regulations are ambiguous, you will also want to look for cases that have applied the statutes and regulations. In looking for cases, look first for mandatory authority: a United States Supreme Court decision or, if there are no United States Supreme Court decisions, for a decision from the court of appeals for the circuit that will hear the case. If there are no court of appeals decisions from the circuit that will hear the case, look for decisions from other circuits and for district court decisions. For more on mandatory and persuasive authority, see section 2.3.

Immigration Issue

Federal Statutes Governing Immigration
Title 8 of the *United States Code*
See, for example, 8 U.S.C. § 1551 (2012)

↓

Federal Regulations Governing Immigration
Title 8 of the *Code of Federal Regulations*
See, for example, 8 C.F.R. § 2.1 (2012)

↓

United States Supreme Court Cases

↓

United States Court of Appeals Cases

↓

United States District Court Cases

In reading federal statutes, regulations, and cases, keep the following "checks and balances" in mind. First, in promulgating regulations, a federal agency cannot exceed the authority granted to it by Congress. Therefore, a federal agency cannot promulgate regulations unless Congress has authorized it to do so, and the regulations that it promulgates cannot contradict the statute. Second, while the federal courts have the power to hold that a federal statute is unconstitutional, if the statute is constitutional, the courts must interpret and apply the statute in a way that is consistent with the statutory language and Congress's intent.

2. *State Statute Governs*

Now presume that you have been asked to work on a landlord-tenant case involving a house located in California. Because the United States Constitution does not give the federal government the power to regulate relationships between landlords and tenants in California, the case will be governed by California law. Although historically, most state law was common law, today much of that common law has been replaced by enacted law, that is, by statutes. Consequently, you would begin researching a California landlord-tenant issue by looking for California statutes.

While in some instances state legislatures give state agencies the power to promulgate regulations implementing a state statute, the California legislature has not authorized a state agency to promulgate regulations relating to landlord-tenant issues. Therefore, your issue will be governed by the California statutes and by the California cases that have applied those statutes. Although a California court might, in some circumstances, look to court decisions from other states, those decisions will never be more than persuasive authority. For more on mandatory and persuasive authority, see section 2.3.

Landlord-Tenant Issues in California

California Landlord-Tenant Statutes
↓
California Supreme Court Cases
↓
California Court of Appeals Cases

3. *Both Federal and State Statutes Govern*

Sometimes an issue will be governed by both federal and state law. For example, a company operating in New York will have to comply both with federal statutes governing employment and with New York laws governing employment.

In general, federal laws establish the minimum standards. For example, there is a federal statute that establishes the federal minimum wage, a federal statute that establishes minimum safety standards, and a federal statute that guarantees family leave benefits to some classes of employees. While a state cannot enact a statute that reduces these benefits, it can enact a statute that gives employees additional benefits. For example, a state can enact a statute that provides for a higher minimum wage than that provided for by the federal statute, a state can enact a statute that imposes additional safety standards, and a state can enact a statute that provides additional classes of employees with family leave benefits.

When there is both a federal and a state statute that govern, you will need to look not only for the federal statute, federal regulations implementing that federal statute, and federal cases interpreting and applying that statute but also for the state statute, any applicable state regulations, and state cases interpreting and applying the state statute and state regulations.

Federal Statute Sets Minimum	**State Statute Provides Additional Benefits**
Federal Statutes	State Statute
↓	↓
Federal Regulations	State Regulations
↓	↓
Federal Cases	State Cases

In working on cases that are governed by both federal and state law, keep the following in mind.

1. In general, federal law preempts, or takes precedence over, state law. (See United States Constitution, Article VI, Clause 2, which states that laws enacted by Congress under the powers granted to it under the Constitution are the "supreme Law of the Land; and the Judges in every State shall be bound thereby. . . . ")

   Thus, if the state statute provides fewer benefits or protections, it will not be enforced. In some instances, however, a state can provide its citizens with additional benefits.
2. Federal regulations implement federal statutes, and state regulations implement state statutes.

3. In most instances, it is the federal courts that interpret and apply federal statutes and the state courts that interpret and apply state statutes.

4. *Party Argues that a Statute Is Unconstitutional*

Occasionally, a party will argue that a statute is unconstitutional either because the legislative body that enacted the statute did not have the authority to enact the statute or because the statute is unconstitutionally vague and/or overbroad.

When the statute at issue is a federal statute, it is the federal courts that must decide whether the statute is, or is not, unconstitutional. While most of these cases are first heard in a United States District Court, a party who loses at the District Court level can file an appeal, asking the appropriate United States Court of Appeals to review the District Court's decision. In addition, the party losing at the United States Court of Appeals level can file a petition for a writ of certiorari with the United States Supreme Court, asking the United States Supreme Court to review the United States Court of Appeals' decision.

When the statute is a state statute, the issue is a bit more complicated. If the party challenging the statute alleges that the statute violates the state's constitution, then the challenge will be decided by the state's courts. While initially the issue will be decided by a state trial court, the party that loses at the trial court level can appeal to the state's intermediate court of appeals, if the state has such a court, or to the state's highest appellate court. If, however, the party challenging the statute alleges that the statute violates the federal constitution, the party can raise the issue in either a state court or a federal court. In such instances, the final arbiter is not the state's highest court but the United States Supreme Court.

5. *Party Argues that an Agency Exceeded Its Authority in Promulgating a Particular Regulation*

Some cases involving federal regulations are first heard, not in the federal courts, but by an administrative law judge who is employed by the executive branch of the federal government. For instance, an individual who believes that the Social Security Administration has incorrectly denied his or her claim for disability benefits can appeal the agency's decision, asking a federal administrative law judge to review that decision. In these cases, claims that a regulation is invalid because the agency that promulgated it exceeded the authority granted to it by Congress will be decided by the administrative law judge. The losing party can, however, appeal the administrative law judge's decision. These appeals are heard initially by a United States District Court.However, the party losing at the District Court level can ask the United States Court of Appeals to review the District Court's decision, and the party losing at the United States Court of Appeals level can ask the United States Supreme Court to review the United States Court of Appeals' decision.

In other cases, for example, cases in which an individual or a company has been charged in a United States District Court with violating a federal statute and regulation, the individual or company can, as part of its defense, argue that the regulation is invalid. In this situation, the United States District Court will make the initial decision about whether the regulation is invalid, and the losing party can appeal the decision to the United States Court of Appeals, and the party that loses at the United States Court of Appeals can file a petition for a writ of certiorari, asking the United States Supreme Court to review the United States Court of Appeals' decision.

Likewise, some cases involving state regulations are heard first by state administrative law judges who are employed by the executive branch of the state government. For example, an individual who believes that the state has improperly denied his or her claim for state worker's compensation benefits can ask a state administrative law judge to review the agency's decision. In these situations, an individual's claim that a state regulation is invalid will be decided by the state administrative law judge, subject to review by the state's courts. In contrast, in cases in which an individual has been charged in a state court with violating a state statute and regulation, the state courts will decide whether or not the regulation is invalid. The only time that a federal court will review a state regulation is when a party claims that the state regulation violates the United States Constitution.

PRACTICE POINTER

Given the relationships between federal and state statutes and regulations and the relationships among the various branches, the statements set out in the left-hand column are **incorrect.**

The state statute **preempts** federal statute	If there is a conflict between a state statute and federal statute, the federalstatute governs unless the state statute provides additional protections.
The court **overruled** the statute	Although courts can hold that a statute is unconstitutional, they cannot **overrule** a statute. If a statute is constitutional, the court must apply that statute.
The regulations **supersede** the statute	Although the regulations are promulgated after the statute is enacted, the regulations **do not supersede** the statute. In promulgating regulations, administrative agencies can only exercise the authority granted to them by the legislative branch. Regulations implement, but do not add to, subtract from, or change the statute itself.

D. READING AND ANALYZING STATUTES

Statutes can be difficult to read. Sometimes, a statute is difficult to read because the person or group that drafted the original bill did not do a good job drafting the bill; more often, though, a statute is hard to read because statutes are the product of a system that requires compromise to get a bill enacted into law. Although the initial bill may have been well written, during the legislative process the bill was amended one or more times to get the votes needed to get the bill out of committee, to get the votes needed to have the first house or chamber approve the bill, to get the votes needed to have the second house or chamber approve the bill, and/or to ensure that the President or governor will sign and not veto the bill.

Although reading and analyzing statutes is time consuming, it is time well-spent. When an issue is governed by a state statute, that statute is the "highest" authority: The regulations must be consistent with the statute and, unless the courts decide that the statute is unconstitutional, they must apply the statute as it is written and not as they wish it had been written.

The following subsections walk you through the process of finding, reading, and analyzing a statute.

1. Finding Statutes Using the Citation

If you have been given the citation to the applicable statute, finding the statute is easy. Simply locate the statute in the book version of the applicable code, on a free website, or on a fee-based service (e.g., Lexis Advance or WestlawNext).

PRACTICE POINTER

You can find federal statutes on the following free websites:

- ☐ *http://uscode.house.gov*
- ☐ *http://www.law.cornell.edu/uscode*

You can find state statutes on the following free websites:

- ☐ *http://www.law.cornell.edu/states/listing*
- ☐ *http://www.llsdc.org/state-legislation*
- ☐ Each state's official website

Although the citation formats vary from jurisdiction to jurisdiction, most citations to statutes contain three types of information: (1) an abbreviation that identifies the name of the code in which the statute can be found, (2) the title and section number, and (3) the year of the code. Look at the following citation, which is a citation to a federal statute.

42 U.S.C. § 12101 (2012)

In this citation, the letters "U.S.C." identify the code: "U.S.C." stands for United States Code, which is the official code for federal statutes. The number before "U.S.C." is the title number; the cited statute is in Title 42 of the United States Code. The number following "U.S.C" is the section number: The cited statute is section 12101 of Title 42 of the United States Code. The final number, which is in parentheses, is the year of the code. To find the cited statute, you need to look at the 2012 version of the United States Code.

42	U.S.C.	§ 12101	(2012)
Title	Name of Code	Section	Year of Code

Now look at the following citation, which is the citation to the Florida statute governing service of process.

Fla. Stat. § 48.031 (2012)

In this citation, "Fla. Stat." is the abbreviation for Florida's official code, which is called the Florida Statutes. The number that follows that abbreviation is the title and section number; the number before the period, the "48," is the title, and the number following the period, "031," is the section number. The last number, the number in parentheses, is the year of the code.

Fla. Stat.	§ 48.031	(2012)
Name of Code	Title and Section Number	Year of Code

PRACTICE POINTER

To find the name of each state's code or codes and the abbreviations that are used for the codes, see Appendix 1 in *ALWD Guide to Legal Citation, Fifth Edition, or Table 1 in The Bluebook, A Uniform System of Citation, Nineteenth Edition.*

If you have not been given the citation to the statute, finding the applicable statutory section or sections can be more difficult. If you are using books, the easiest way to find a statute is to use the index that comes with the book version of the code. (This index is usually set out in a separate volume at the end of the code.) If you are using a fee-based service, such as Lexis Advance or WestlawNext, the easiest way is to use either the table of contents option or the index option. If you are using a free source, use the table of contents or index option if the source offers that option. Otherwise, locate the applicable sections using the search text box.

For more information on finding state statutes and regulations, see Chapter 4 in Just Research, and for more information on finding federal statutes and regulations, see Chapter 5 in *Just Research.* For more information on finding county and city ordinances, see Chapter 6 in *Just Research.*

2. *Distinguishing Between the Text of the Statute and Other Material Provided by the Publisher*

What you find when you look up a statute will depend on the source that you use. If you use a free website, more likely than not, you will find only the text of the statute, credits, and historical notes. If, however, you use a fee-based service or the book form of an annotated code, you will find not only the text of the statute, credits, and historical notes but also other material provided by the publisher, for example, cross-references to other sources and notes of decisions/case notes that you can use to locate cases that have applied the statute. See the screen shot below from the Westlaw version of Fla. Stat. § 48.031 (2012).

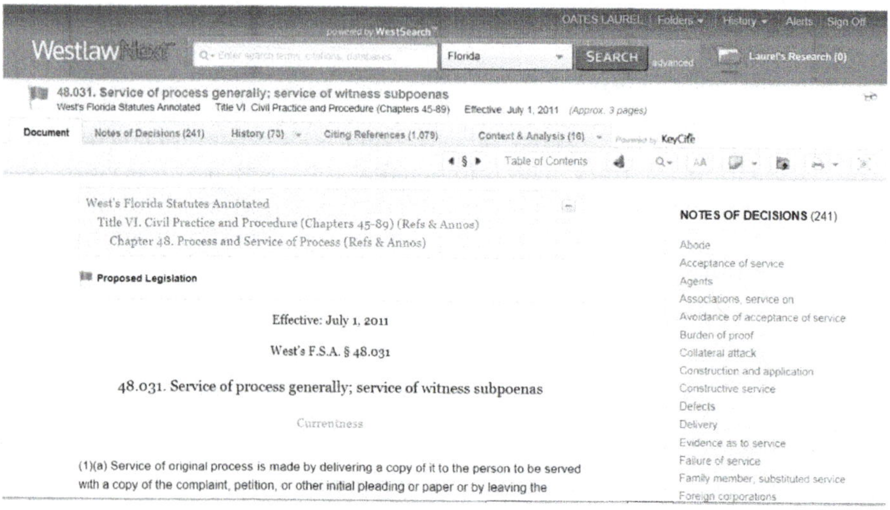

3. Making Sure You Have the Right Version of the Statute

Before spending time reading and analyzing a statute, make sure that you are reading the right version of the statute. If the issue that you have been asked to research involves an event that happened in the past, you will need to find the version of the statute that was in effect at the time that event occurred. In contrast, if the client has asked you to determine what he or she can do next month, you need to find the version of the statute that will be in effect next month.

To determine whether the version of the statute that you have found is the right version, use the credits and historical notes that are set out after the text of the statute. If the statute has been amended since your cause of action arose, use the version of the statute that was in effect on the applicable date. If you are advising a client about what it can or cannot do in the future, use an online source to see if there is pending legislation.

4. Identifying the Elements or Requirements

While some disciplines and cultures focus on the "whole," as law is practiced in the United States, the focus is on the "parts." Thus, in reading a statute, most United States attorneys are looking for the elements, that is, for the requirements set out in the statute. For example, in reading the following Florida statute dealing with substituted service of process, an attorney would try to identify the elements, or requirements, for substituted service of process.

Fla. Stat. § 48.031. Service of process generally; service of witness subpoenas

(1)(a) Service of original process is made by delivering a copy of it to the person to be served with a copy of the complaint, petition, or other initial pleading or paper or by leaving the copies at his or her usual place of abode with any person residing therein who is 15 years of age or older and informing the person of their contents . . . .

While sometimes Congress or the state legislature sets out the elements in a list, most of the time the elements are embedded in the text of the statute. In these situations, you will need to read and reread the statute, determining, as best you can, what the elements are. One of the easiest, and most reliable ways of doing this type of analysis is to do a form of sentence diagramming. Begin by identifying each clause and phrase. For example, in analyzing Fla. Stat. § 48.031(a)(1) (2012), you find the following clauses and phrases.

Fla. Stat. § 48.031(a)(1) (2012)

Service of original process is made

by delivering a copy of it
to the person to be served
with a copy of the complaint, petition, or other initial pleading or paper
or by leaving the copies at his or her usual place of abode
with any person residing therein
who is 15 years of age or older
and informing the person of their contents.

Once you have listed the clauses and phrases, look at the words that the legislature used to connect those clauses and phrases and the words in those clauses and phrases. In particular, note whether the clauses, phrases, and words are connected with "and" or with "or." In addition, try to determine what modifies what.

In our example, the statute begins with a subject, "service of original process," and a verb, "is made." This subject and verb are followed by two phrases that begin with the word "by": "by delivering" or "by leaving." Thus, it appears that service of process can be made either (1) by delivering a copy of the process to the person to be served or (2) by leaving a copy at his or her usual place of abode. A close reading of the language used to describe the second option suggests that there are four sub-elements or requirements: (a) the process must be left at the person's usual place of abode, (b) the process must be left with a person residing therein, (c) the person with whom the process is left must be fifteen years or older, and (d) the person serving the process must inform the person served about "their contents." By reformatting your first list of phrases and clauses, you can see the two options and the requirements for each option.

Service of original process is made
by delivering a copy of it to the person to be served with a copy of the complaint, petition, or other initial pleading or paper

or
by leaving the copies at

a. his or her usual place of abode
b. with any person residing therein
c. who is 15 years of age or older
and
d. informing the person of their contents.

The next step is to look for other statutory sections that are on point. Begin by looking for statutory definitions. Are the terms in the subsection that you just read defined in a different subsection of the same statute or in a different section of the same chapter or act? If there are statutory definitions, you need to use those definitions. If the statutory language is ambiguous, also look for a findings and purpose section that explains why the statute was enacted and what drafters hoped to accomplish. Finally, if your statute contains cross references to other statutes, look up and read those cross references.

Once you have done your own analysis of the statute, check your analysis against the analysis that others have done. For example, have the courts, in interpreting and applying the statute, listed the elements and does their list match yours? In cases in which a jury would decide whether the statute has or has not been violated, are there any pattern jury instructions, and how are the elements listed in those jury instructions? Is the statute discussed in a practice manual, a treatise, a law review article, or other secondary source and, if it has, how has the source listed the elements?

If your list matches the list set out in the cases, the jury instructions, and secondary sources, you can be confident that you have read the statute correctly. If your list does not match those lists, you will usually want to go with the list set out in a case that is mandatory authority or in the pattern jury instructions unless that reading of the statute does not favor your client and you can make a good faith argument that the courts or the authors of the pattern jury instructions have misread the statute.

E. EXERCISE

Read the following statute and then answer the questions.

Text of statute:

Wash. Rev. Code § 9A.46.110 (2012):

(1) A person commits the crime of stalking if, without lawful authority and under circumstances not amounting to a felony attempt of another crime:

a. He or she intentionally and repeatedly harasses or repeatedly follows another person; and
b. The person being harassed or followed is placed in fear that the stalker intends to injure the person, another person, or property of the person or of

another person. The feeling of fear must be one that a reasonable person in the same situation would experience under all the circumstances; and

c. The stalker either:
   i. Intends to frighten, intimidate, or harass the person; or
   ii. Knows or reasonably should know that the person is afraid, intimidated, or harassed even if the stalker did not intend to place the person in fear or intimidate or harass the person.

(2) (a) It is not a defense to the crime of stalking under subsection (1)(c)(i) of this section that the stalker was not given actual notice that the person did not want the stalker to contact or follow the person; and

. It is not a defense to the crime of stalking under subsection (1)(c)(ii) of this section that the stalker did not intend to frighten, intimidate, or harass the person.

(3) It shall be a defense to the crime of stalking that the defendant is a licensed private investigator acting within the capacity of his or her license as provided by chapter 18.165 RCW.
(4) Attempts to contact or follow the person after being given actual notice that the person does not want to be contacted or followed constitutes prima facie evidence that the stalker intends to intimidate or harass the person. . . .

. . .

(6) As used in this section:

a. "Follows" means deliberately maintaining visual or physical proximity to a specific person over a period of time. A finding that the alleged stalker repeatedly and deliberately appears at the person's home, school, place of employment, business, or any other location to maintain visual or physical proximity to the person is sufficient to find that the alleged stalker follows the person. It is not necessary to establish that the alleged stalker follows the person while in transit from one location to another.
b. "Harasses" means unlawful harassment as defined in RCW 10.14.020.

. . .

d. "Repeatedly" means on two or more separate occasions.

Questions:

1. How would you determine whether the statute above governs acts that occurred in April 2014? Any new between '12 & '14?
2. To convict an individual of stalking, what does the State have to prove? List the elements.
3. What is and is not a defense to the crime of stalking?
4. What other types of statutory sections would you want to look for?
5. What other statutory sections would you want to read and analyze?

CHAPTER

4

Understanding Judicial Opinions

Although sometimes a statute will answer the question that you have been asked to research, more often than not you will also need to look at judicial decisions, which are also called judicial opinions or, more simply, cases. If the issue is governed by common law, you will be looking at the cases to find the common law rule and examples of how that common law rule has been applied in analogous cases. In contrast, if the issue is governed by a statute, you will be looking at the cases to determine how the courts have applied the statute, or a particular part of the statute, in cases that are analogous, or similar to, your client's case.

A. WHICH CASES ARE BINDING ON WHICH COURTS

The image created by most casebooks, TV shows, and news articles is that all cases are created equal. Nothing could be further from the truth. Even though a criminal law casebook may set out cases from United States District Court for the Northern District of California, from the United States Court of Appeals for the Third Circuit, and from the Mississippi Supreme Court, in practice your search for cases will be more focused. While casebooks are designed to illustrate the historical development of a rule or the ways in which different jurisdictions have approached the same issue, as a practicing attorney you will look first for cases that are mandatory authority, that is, cases that are binding on the court that will be deciding your case. You will look at persuasive authority, for example cases from outside your jurisdiction, only when there is no mandatory authority or when you are asking a court to overrule, or invalidate, one of its decisions.

Three examples illustrate when cases from a particular court are mandatory authority. In the first example, the issue is governed by a state statute and the cases that have interpreted and applied that statute. In the second example, the issue is governed by federal statutes and regulations and the cases that have interpreted and applied those statutes and regulations. The third example involves an issue governed by common law.

1. *Issue Governed by State Statute and Cases that Have Interpreted and Applied that Statute*

Presume for a moment that the State of Oregon has charged Martin Obote with assault under an Oregon statute. Because Mr. Obote has been charged under an Oregon statute, the case will be heard by the Oregon courts and, in deciding whether Mr. Obote is guilty, the Oregon courts will apply the Oregon statute and Oregon cases that have interpreted and applied that statute.

Initially, the case will be heard by one of Oregon's circuit courts, which are trial courts that have jurisdiction to hear cases in which the defendant is charged under an Oregon statute with a misdemeanor, gross misdemeanor, or a felony. Mr. Obote can choose to have a bench trial or a jury trial. If Mr. Obote chooses to have a bench trial, there will not be a jury, and the trial court judge will decide both issues of fact and issues of law. If, however, Mr. Obote chooses a jury trial, the judge will decide issues of law, and the jury will decide issues of fact. Under both options, the State has the burden of proof and must prove each element of the crime beyond a reasonable doubt.

At the trial court level, the Oregon statute, Oregon Supreme Court cases, and Oregon Court of Appeals cases are mandatory authority. Thus, in deciding issues of law, the trial court must apply the Oregon statute in a manner that is consistent with the ways in which the Oregon Supreme Court and Oregon Court of Appeals have applied that statute in analogous cases. The only exception is for issues that involve a right guaranteed by the United States Constitution, for example, an individual's Fourth Amendment right to be free from unreasonable searches and seizures. When the issue involves a right guaranteed under the United States Constitution, United States Supreme Court decisions are mandatory authority.

If, after hearing the witnesses and viewing the exhibits, the judge or jury finds that Mr. Obote is guilty, Mr. Obote can file an appeal, which in most instances will be heard by the Oregon Court of Appeals, which is Oregon's intermediate court of appeals. The Oregon Court of Appeals does not conduct trials. Instead, it reviews the written record from the trial conducted before the circuit court and any exhibits that were admitted at trial. With only a few exceptions, the Oregon Court of Appeals can hear and decide only four types of issues: (1) whether a statute is constitutional, (2) whether the trial court applied the right law and properly instructed the jury, (3) whether the trial court judge abused his or her discretion in granting or denying a motion or granting or denying an objection, and (4) whether there is sufficient evidence to support the trial court judge's findings of fact or the jury's verdict.

In deciding these issues, the Oregon Court of Appeals must apply mandatory authority. Consequently, if the issue is an issue of state law, the Oregon Court of Appeals must apply the rules set out in decisions by the Oregon Supreme Court. In contrast, if the issue involves a right guaranteed under the United States Constitution, the Oregon Court of Appeals must apply the rules set out by the United States Supreme Court. While most of the time the Oregon Court of Appeals will follow its own prior decisions, it is not required to do so.

If the Oregon Court of Appeals affirms Mr. Obote's conviction, Mr. Obote can file a petition for discretionary review, asking the Oregon Supreme Court, which is Oregon's highest court, to hear his case. If the Oregon Supreme Court grants

Mr. Obote's petition, it will review his conviction; if it denies his petition, it will not review the conviction, and the Oregon Court of Appeals' decision is the final decision.

Like the Oregon Court of Appeals, the Oregon Supreme Court does not conduct trials. Instead, like the Oregon Court of Appeals, it reviews the written record from the trial court and reviews exhibits introduced at trial. In addition, like the Oregon Court of Appeals, it can decide only certain types of issues. With just a few exceptions, it can determine only (1) whether the statute is constitutional; (2) whether the trial court applied the right law and correctly instructed the jury; (3) whether the trial court judge abused his or her discretion in granting or denying a motion or granting or denying an objection; and (4) whether there is sufficient evidence to support the trial court judge's findings of fact or the jury's verdict.

Just as the Oregon Court of Appeals is not bound by its earlier decisions, the Oregon Supreme Court is not bound by its earlier decisions. Thus, in cases heard by the Oregon Supreme Court, the only mandatory authority are United States Supreme Court decisions, and those decisions are only mandatory authority insofar as they involve rights guaranteed by the United States Constitution.

Although the names of the courts will vary from state to state, for example, in New York the trial court is called the "Supreme Court," the roles that trial courts, intermediate courts of appeal, and the highest court play are the same in each state. Chart 4-1 summarizes the role that each court plays and lists the authorities that are mandatory authority.

CHART 4-1
CHART ROLE EACH STATE COURT PLAYS AND LIST OF AUTHORITIES THAT ARE MANDATORY AUTHORITY

Court	Role	Mandatory Authority
State trial courts	• Conducts trial • In a bench trial, the judge decides questions of law and questions of fact and enters findings of fact and conclusions of law. • In a jury trial, the judge decides questions of law, and the jury decides questions of fact and enters a verdict.	• If the issue is governed by a state statute, the state statute and decisions of the state's highest court and, if it has one, intermediate court of appeals are mandatory authority. • If the issue is governed by the United States Constitution, United States Supreme Court decisions are mandatory authority.
State intermediate courts of appeals	• Does not conduct trials, hear testimony, or accept new evidence.	• If the issue is governed by a state statute, the state statute and decisions of the state's

Court	Role	Mandatory Authority
Note: Some of the smaller states (e.g., Nevada) do not have an intermediate court of appeals.	• Reviews trial court record to determine whether (1) the statute is constitutional, (2) the trial court applied the right law and correctly instructed the jury, (3) the trial court judge abused his or her discretion in granting or denying a motion or granting or denying an objection, and (4) there is sufficient evidence to support the trial court judge's or the jury's findings of fact.	highest court are mandatory authority. • If the issue is governed by the United States Constitution, United States Supreme Court decisions are mandatory authority. • Although a state's intermediate court of appeals will usually follow its own prior decisions, those decisions are not mandatory authority.
State's highest court or court of last resort Note: In many states this court is called the Supreme Court.	• Does not conduct trials, hear testimony, or accept new evidence. • Reviews trial court record to determine (1) whether the statute is constitutional; (2) whether the trial court applied the right law correctly; (3) whether the trial court judge abused his or her discretion in granting or denying a motion or granting or denying an objection; and (4) whether there is sufficient evidence to support the trial court judge's findings of fact or the jury's verdict.	• If constitutional, the state statutes are mandatory authority. • For issues governed by United States Constitution, United States Supreme Court decisions are mandatory authority. • Although the state's highest court will usually follow its own prior decisions, those decisions are not mandatory authority.

2. *Issue Governed by a Federal Statute and Regulations and Cases that Have Interpreted that Federal Statute and the Federal Regulations*

In our second example, Sanjee Singh wants to sue her employer under the Family and Medical Leave Act (FMLA) on the grounds that her employer illegally fired her after she took three weeks off from work to care for her dying mother. Because the FMLA is a federal statute, the issue is governed by the FMLA, the regulations that implement the FMLA, and the federal cases that have applied the FMLA.

If Ms. Singh does sue her employer, her case would be heard by a United States District Court. As in the state system, Ms. Singh can ask for a bench trial, in which the trial court judge will decide both issues of fact and issues of law, or a jury trial, in which the judge would decide issues of law, and the jury would decide issues of fact. As the plaintiff, Ms. Singh would have the burden of proof. At the District Court, or trial court level, the FMLA, the applicable federal regulations, United States Supreme Court decisions, and United States Court of Appeals decisions from the same circuit as the circuit in which the District Court is located are mandatory authority.

If Ms. Singh loses at the district court level, she can appeal that decision to the United States Court of Appeals for the circuit in which the District Court that heard the case is located. Similarly, if Ms. Singh wins, her employer can file an appeal. Like state intermediate courts of appeals, the United States Court of Appeals does not conduct trials, hear witnesses, or admit new exhibits. Instead, it just reviews the written record from the trial court and the exhibits admitted at trial. In addition, just as the state intermediate court of appeals can decide only certain types of issues, the United States Court of Appeals can decide only certain types of issues: (1) whether the statute is constitutional, (2) whether the regulations are valid, (3) whether the district court judge applied the right law and correctly instructed the jury, (4) whether the district court judge abused his or her discretion in granting or denying a motion or granting or denying an objection, and (5) whether there is sufficient evidence to support the trial court judge's findings of fact or the jury's verdict. When a case is heard by a United States Court of Appeals, the statute, the regulations, and United States Supreme Court decisions are mandatory authority.

Although the United States Supreme Court hears relatively few cases each year, the party that loses at the Court of Appeals level has the right to file a petition for a writ of certiorari asking the United States Supreme Court to review the United States Court of Appeals' decision. If the United States Supreme Court accepts review, it would review the trial court record and determine (1) whether the statute is constitutional, (2) whether the regulations are valid, (3) whether the district court judge applied the right law correctly and correctly instructed the jury, (4) whether the trial court judge abused his or her discretion in granting or denying a motion or granting or denying an objection, and (5) whether there is sufficient evidence to support the district court judge's findings of fact or the jury's verdict. The only mandatory authority would be statutes and regulations, and those statutes and regulations are only mandatory authority if the statute is constitutional and the regulations are valid.

Chart 4-2 summarizes the role each federal court plays, and it identifies the authorities that are mandatory authority.

CHART 4-2
ROLE EACH FEDERAL COURT PLAYS AND LIST OF AUTHORITIES THAT ARE MANDATORY AUTHORITY

Court	Role	Mandatory Authority
United States District Court (trial court)	• Conducts trial. • In a bench trial, judge decides questions of law and questions of fact and enters findings of fact and conclusions of law. • In a jury trial, judge decides questions of law, and the jury hears questions of fact and enters verdict.	• Federal statutes.* • Federal regulations.** • United States Supreme Court decisions. • United States Court of Appeals decisions from same circuit in which District Court is located.
United States Court of Appeals	• Does not conduct trials, hear testimony, or accept new evidence. • Reviews trial court record to determine whether (1) the statute is constitutional, (2) the regulations are valid, (3) the district court judge applied the right law and correctly instructed the jury, (4) the district court judge abused his or her discretion in granting or denying a motion or granting or denying an objection, and (5) whether there is sufficient evidence to support the district court judge's or the jury's findings of fact.	• Federal statutes.* • Federal regulations.** • United States supreme Court decisions. • Although the United States Courts of Appeals will usually follow their own prior decisions, those decisions are not mandatory authority.

Court	Role	Mandatory Authority
United States of supreme Court	• Does not conduct trials, hear testimony, or accept new evidence. • Reviews trial court record to determine (1) whether the statute is constitutional, (2) whether regulations are valid, (3) whether the trial court applied the applicable law correctly, (4) whether the trial court judge abused his or her discretion in granting or denying a motion or granting or denying an objection, and (5) whether there is sufficient evidence to support the trial court judge's findings of fact or the jury's verdict.	• Federal statutes.* • Federal regulations.** • Although the United States Supreme Court will usually follow its own decisions, those decisions are not mandatory authority.

* If constitutional
** If valid

3. *Issue Governed by Common Law*

For this last example, presume that you represent Mr. Garcia, who is concerned that a group that runs a summer camp has obtained, through adverse possession, title to land that he owns in Washington. Because adverse possession is a common law doctrine, the only statute that is on point is a Washington statute that sets out the statutory period for adverse possession.

Because the land is located in Washington, the case would be heard by one of Washington's trial courts, the Superior Court. In hearing the case, the Superior Court would apply the common law rules set out in Washington cases and the statutory time periods set out in Washington statutes. Because Washington has an intermediate court of appeals, the decisions of that court, the decisions of the Washington Supreme Court, and Washington statutes are mandatory authority.

The party that loses at trial can file an appeal with the Washington Court of Appeals. At the Washington Court of Appeals, the only mandatory authorities are decisions by the Washington Supreme Court and the Washington statutes that set out the length of time a person must possess the property to establish title through adverse possession. Although in most situations the Washington Court of Appeals would follow its own earlier decisions, those decisions are not mandatory authority. The party that loses at the Court of Appeals level can ask the Washington Supreme Court to review the Washington Court of Appeals' decision. If the Washington Supreme Court accepts review, the only authority that is mandatory authority is the statute that sets out the time limits.

B. HOW ATTORNEYS USE CASES

Attorneys use cases in two ways: (1) as authority for a common law rule or for a rule that the courts have created in interpreting and applying a statute or regulation and (2) to illustrate how the courts have applied a common law rule or a statute or regulation in analogous cases.

> Sometimes an attorney will use one case as authority for a rule and another case to illustrate how that rule has been applied. At other times, an attorney will use the same case both as authority for a rule and as an analogous case to illustrate how that rule has been applied.

1. *Case as Authority for Rule*

When an issue is governed by a common law rule, you will cite to one or more cases as authority for that common law rule. For instance, in the adverse possession case described in section 4.A.3, you would need to cite to a case or cases for both the general rules, that is, for the test the courts apply in determining whether an individual has gained title to land through adverse possession, and for the specific rules, that is, for the tests that the courts apply in determining whether a particular element is or is not met.

Example 1 **Author Cites Cases as Authority for the Common Law Rule**

> To establish title through adverse possession, the claimant must prove that its possession was (1) exclusive, (2) actual and uninterrupted, (3) open and notorious, and (4) hostile for the statutory period. *ITT Rayonier, Inc. v. Bell*, 112 Wn.2d 754, 757, 774 P.2d 6 (1989); *Chaplin v. Sanders*, 100 Wn.2d 853, 857, 676 P.2d 431 (1984).[1]

When the issue is governed by a statute, you will cite to the statute for the rules set out in the statute but to the cases for the rules that the courts have created in applying that statute. For example, if the courts have defined a word that is used in the statute, you will set out that definition and then cite a case as authority. Likewise, if

1. Because the issue would be decided by a Washington court, the author has used the Washington Style Sheet. See Appendix 2 in the ALWD Guide to Legal Citation, 5th ed.

the courts have set out rules or tests for determining whether a particular element is met, you will set out those rules or tests and cite a case or cases as authority.

Example 2 **Author Sets Out Definition Developed by Florida Courts in Interpreting and Applying Florida's Service of Process Statute**

> The Florida courts have defined "usual place of abode"as "the fixed place of residence for the time being when the service is made." *Shurman v. A. Mortg. & Inv. Corp.*, 795 So. 2d 952, 953-54 (Fla. 2001). "If a person has more than one residence, a summons must be served at the residence at which the defendant is actually living at the time of service." *Id.* at 954.

If there are only one or two cases that have set out a common law, or court-made rule, cite those one or two cases as authority. If, however, there are a number of cases that have set out the same rules, do not cite all of the cases. Instead, select the one or two "best" cases. Begin by identifying the cases that are mandatory authority. From this group, you will usually want to select cases from higher courts over cases from lower courts and more recent cases over older cases. The exception is when all of the decisions from the higher courts are quite old. In this situation, you will usually want to cite one of the older higher court cases to show that the rule was established by the jurisdiction's highest court and then cite to one of the newer lower court decisions to show that the rule is still good law.

Selecting Cases to Cite as Authority for a Common Law or Court-Made Rule

1. Select cases that are mandatory authority over cases that are persuasive authority.
2. Of those cases that are mandatory authority, select cases that are from higher courts over cases from lower courts.
3. Of those cases that are from higher courts, select more recent cases over older cases.

Exception:

> If all of the cases from higher courts are old, also cite to a more recent lower court decision to show that the rule is still being applied by the courts.

For more on setting out the general and specific rules, see Chapters 7 and 8.

2. *Using Analogous Cases to Illustrate How the Courts have Applied a Statute or Common Law Rule*

In addition to citing cases as authority for a common law, or court-made, rule, attorneys also use cases to illustrate how the courts have applied a particular rule. For example, attorneys will use cases to illustrate the types of situations in which the courts have held that a particular element of a statute or common law rule was met or not met. In selecting these analogous cases, most attorneys try to select cases that illustrate the types of situations in which the courts have held that the element was met and cases that illustrate the types of situations in which the courts have held that the element was not met. The attorneys then place those cases and their client's case along a continuum, arguing either that their client's case is more like the cases in which the element was met or more like the cases in which the element was not met.

Element Met	Client's Case	Element Not Met

The criteria for selecting analogous cases are a bit different from the criteria for selecting cases to cite as authority for a rule. Although you want to select cases that are mandatory authority over cases that are only persuasive authority, you will not always choose cases from higher courts over cases from lower courts or more recent cases over older cases. Instead, the cases that will be the "best" cases will be those that are most factually analogous to your case. Thus, you might select an intermediate court of appeals decision over a case from the jurisdiction's highest appellate court if the facts in the intermediate court of appeals decision are more similar to the facts in your case. Similarly, you might select an older case over a more recent one if the facts in the older case are more analogous to the facts in your case.

Selecting Analogous Cases

1. Select cases that are mandatory authority over cases that are persuasive authority.
2. Select cases that are more factually analogous over cases that are less factually analogous.
3. When possible, select representative cases in which the element was met and representative cases in which the element was not met.

C. READING AND ANALYZING CASES

Just as some statutes are hard to read and analyze, so too are some cases. Sometimes, a case is difficult to read and analyze because it has a complicated set of facts and a complicated procedural history. In these cases, just figuring out who the parties are and who did what may take effort. At other times, the case is difficult to read and analyze because it involves a complicated area of law and a complicated issue or set of issues. Unless you already understand the area of law, you will have a difficult time understanding the court's opinion. At still other times, the judge simply did a bad job writing the opinion: The opinion is poorly organized, the sentences are hard to read, or the writing is wordy or imprecise.

In the end, though, it does not matter whether a case is easy or difficult to read and analyze or why that might be the case. To do your job, you need to figure out what the case says and does not say and how the case might be applied.

1. Finding Cases Using the Citation

Just as you can use the citation to a statute to find a copy of the statute (see section 3.D.1), you can use the case citation to find a copy of the case in the book form of a reporter, which is the name that is given to the sets of books that contain copies of judicial opinions. For more on state reporters, see section 4.2.4 in Just

Research; for more on federal reporters, see section 5.2.3 in Just Research. You can also use the citation to find copies of cases on fee-based services—for example, on Lexis Advance, WestlawNext, or Bloomberg Law—or on free websites.

Most case citations contain three parts: the name of the case; references to the reporter or reporters in which the case can be found; and a parenthetical that includes, at a minimum, the year in which the opinion was issued. A case citation may also include a subsequent history section that provides information about what happened after the court issued its opinion and a parenthetical that provides the reader with additional information about the case. The following citation is a typical case citation.

Thompson v. State, Dept. of Revenue, 867 So. 2d 603 (Fla. App. 1 Dist., 2004).

In this citation, the first piece of information is the name of the case: Thompson v. State, Dept. of Rcvenue. In the second slot is set out the information that you will need to find a copy of the case. The first number, "867," is the volume number; the letters "So. 2d" are the abbreviation for the reporter; and the second number, "603," is the page on which the case begins. Thus, you can find a copy of Thompson v. State, Dept. of Revenue in volume 867 of the Southern Reporter, Second Series, beginning on page 603. The parenthetical gives you the information you need to determine whether the case is mandatory or persuasive authority: the name of the court that decided the case and the year of the decision.

Thompson v. State, Dept. of Revenue, 867 So. 2d 603 (Fla. App. 1 Dist., 2004).

Case Name Vol. Reporter Page Court Year

PRACTICE POINTER

For more on case citations, see Rule 12 in *ALWD Guide to Legal Citation, Fifth Edition*; Rule 10 in *The Bluebook, Nineteenth Edition*; or your jurisdiction's citation rules.

To find a copy of a case in the book form of a reporter, locate the appropriate set of reporters in the library, locate the correct volume, and then turn to the correct page. To find a copy of a case on a fee-based or free website, type the citation in the search text box.

PRACTICE POINTER

The following websites are free websites that contain the text of court opinions.

A. Federal Cases

1. United States Supreme Court
http://www.supremecourtus.gov/opinions/opinions.html

http://www.gpoaccess.gov/judicial.html
http://supct.law.cornell.edu/supct/
2. United States Courts of Appeal, United States District Courts, and Specialized Courts
http://www.uscourts.gov/links.html
http://www.gpoaccess.gov/judicial.html
http://www.law.cornell.edu/federal/opinions.html
http://www.law.emory.edu/FEDCTS/

B. State Cases

http://www.law.cornell.edu/opinions.html
state court websites

2. *Distinguishing Between the Text of an Opinion and Material Added by the Publisher*

What you see when you locate a copy of a case depends on the source in which you have looked up that case. If you have found a copy of the case on a free website, more likely than not all that you will see is the text of the court's opinion. If, however, you have looked up the case in the book form of a reporter or on a fee-based website such as Lexis Advance, WestlawNext, or Bloomberg Law, you will find not only the text of the court's opinion but also editorial enhancements, for example, a syllabus and headnotes. Although these editorial enhancements are not part of the court's opinion and cannot, therefore, be cited as authority, they are useful tools for obtaining an overview of the opinion and for locating those parts of the opinion that are most relevant to the issue you have been asked to research.

Chart 4-3 walks you through the WestlawNext version of Thompson v. State, Dept. of Revenue.

CHART 4-3
THOMPSON V. STATE, DEPT. OF REVENUE, AS IT APPEARS ON WESTLAWNEXT

Original Image of 867 So.2d 603 (PDF)	This is a link to the PDF version of the case.
867 So.2d 603 District Court of Appeal of Florida, First District.	Caption: • Citation • Court
Calvin THOMPSON, Appellant, v. STATE of Florida, DEPARTMENT OF REVENUE, Appellee.	• Parties
No. 1D03-2975.	Case number
March 5, 2004.	Date of decision

Synopsis

This is the publisher's (West's) synopsis of the court's decision

Background: Department of Revenue filed action against father to establish and enforce child support for daughter. The Circuit Court, Duval County, E. McRae Mathis, J., denied father's motion to quash service of process. Father appealed.

Holding: The District Court of Appeal, Van Nortwick, J., held that father made prima facie showing that Department's petition was not served on him at his usual place of abode.

Reversed and remanded.

West Headnotes (5)Collapse West Headnotes

West headnotes are written by attorneys employed by Thomson Publishing Company, the company that operates Westlaw Classic and WestlawNext. The attorney who is assigned case reads the case and, for each rule of law set out by the court, prepares a one-sentence statement. These statements are then placed at the beginning of the case as headnotes, in West's digests, and if the case involves a statute, in the notes of decision following the statute in the West version of the code.

Change View

1 Child Support
Father's affidavit stating that he was separated from wife and had not resided with her for over three years was sufficient to make a prima facie showing that Department of Revenue's petition to establish and enforce child support, which was left with wife at her residence, was not served on father at his usual place of abode, for purposes of Department's attempt to establish valid substituted service. West's F.S.A. § 48.031.
0 Case that cites this headnote

76EChild Support
76EVProceedings
76EV(A)In General
76Ek180Process

To find the place in the court's opinion from which the attorney drew the statement, click on the number that is next to the headnote or scroll through the opinion until you find the number. For example, to find the place from which the attorney drew the "rule" set out in headnote 2, click on the "2."

2 Process
The requirement that substituted service of process be at a defendant's "usual place of abode" means the place where the defendant is actually living at the time of service. West's F.S.A. § 48.031.
3 Cases that cite this headnote

313Process
313IIService
313II(B)Substituted Service
313k76Mode and Sufficiency of Service
313k78Leaving copy at residence or other place

(continues)

3 Process
The burden of proof to sustain the validity of service of process is upon the person who seeks to invoke the jurisdiction of the court and, without proper service of process, the court lacks personal jurisdiction over the defendant. West's F.S.A. § 48.031.
2 Cases that cite this headnote

To find cases that have cited *Thompson* click "Cases that cite this headnote."

To find cases that have been indexed under the same key number, click on the applicable key number.

313Process
313IIService
313II(A)Personal Service in General
313k48Nature and necessity in general

313Process
313IIService
313II(E)Return and Proof of Service
313k144Evidence as to Service
313k145Presumptions and burden of proof

4 Process
A process server's return of service on a defendant which is regular on its face is presumed to be valid absent clear and convincing evidence presented to the contrary.
3 Cases that cite this headnote

313Process
313IIService
313II(E)Return and Proof of Service
313k144Evidence as to Service
313k145Presumptions and burden of proof
(Formerly 313k149)

5 Process
A simple denial of having received service is not sufficient to contradict a process server's return of service that is regular on its face.
2 Cases that cite this headnote

313Process
313IIService
313II(E)Return and Proof of Service
313k144Evidence as to Service
313k148Evidence to impeach or contradict return, certificate, or affidavit of service

Attorneys and Law Firms

These are the attorneys of record in the case

*604 Esther A. Zaretsky, West Palm Beach, for Appellant.
Charles J. Crist, Jr., Attorney General and Toni C. Bernstein and William H. Branch, Assistant Attorneys General, Tallahassee, for Appellee.

The *604 tells you that the text following the *604 is at the top of page 604 in the official reporter.

Opinion

This is where the court's opinion begins.

VAN NORTWICK, J.

In this case, Judge Van Nortwick wrote the opinion. (The "J" stands for judge or justice.)

Calvin Thompson appeals a non-final order denying his motion to quash service of process in this support-administrative paternity action filed by the Department of Revenue. We reverse and remand for an evidentiary hearing pursuant to *Venetian Salami Co. v. Parthenais*, 554 So.2d 499, 502-03 (Fla.1989).

Pursuant to section 409.2564, Florida Statutes (2002), the Department filed an action to establish and enforce child support for Thompson's four year-old daughter. The petition was served at 625 F Covenant Drive, Belle Glade, Florida 33430, and accepted by Thompson's wife. Thompson filed a motion to dismiss/quash for lack of service of process stating that he was not present at the Belle Glade address and was not personally served. In his attached affidavit, Thompson stated that he has been separated from his wife, that he has not resided at that address for over three years, and that he did not authorize anyone to accept service of process on his behalf.

The trial court entered an order ruling that any jurisdictional defect could be cured by mailing a copy of the petition and accompanying documents to Thompson's attorney, "who has made a general appearance." The Department correctly concedes that the jurisdictional defect cannot *605 be cured in the manner suggested by the trial court and that Thompson's argument that the trial court lacked personal jurisdiction was not waived because Thompson neither took affirmative action nor sought affirmative relief prior to raising the alleged defect. *See Coto-Ojeda v. Samuel*, 642 So.2d 587, 588 (Fla. 3d DCA 1994)(Cope, J., specially concurring).

The *605 tells you that this is where page 604 ends and page 605 begins.

1 2 3 Turning to the merits, "[s]ection 48.031 expressly requires that substituted service be at the person's usual place of abode." *Shurman v. Atlantic Mortgage & Investment Corp.*, 795 So.2d 952, 954 (Fla.2001). The requirement "usual place of abode" means "the place where the defendant is actually living at the time of service." *Id., citing State ex rel. Merritt v. Heffernan*, 142 Fla. 496, 195 So. 145, 147 (1940). The burden of proof to sustain the validity of service of process is upon the person who seeks to invoke the jurisdiction of the court and, without proper service of process, the court lacks personal jurisdiction over the defendant. *M.J.W. v. Department of Children and Families*, 825 So.2d 1038, 1041 (Fla. 1st DCA 2002).

The numbers 1, 2, and 3 tell you that this is the portion of the opinion from which the West attorney drew headnotes 1, 2, and 3.

4 5 "[A] process server's return of service on a defendant which is regular on its face is presumed to be valid absent clear and convincing evidence presented to the contrary." *Telf Corp. v. Gomez*, 671 So.2d 818 (Fla. 3d DCA 1996). Although simple denial of service is not sufficient, *id.* at 819, Thompson's motion and affidavit are based on the fact that the service did not comply with section 48.031 and was therefore legally deficient. *National Safety Associates, Inc. v. Allstate Insurance Co.*, 799 So.2d 316, 317 (Fla. 2d DCA 2001). Thompson's affidavit makes a prima facie showing that he was not served at his usual

The numbers 4 and 5 tell you that this is the portion of the opinion from which the West attorney drew headnotes 4 and 5.

(continues)

place of abode by valid substituted service. *See, e.g., S.H. v. Department of Children and Families*, 837 So.2d 1117, 1118 (Fla. 4th DCA 2003) (invalidating substituted service on father at mother's address, where mother's residence was not father's "usual place of abode" at the time of service); *Gonzalez v. Totalbank*, 472 So.2d 861 (Fla. 3d DCA 1985) (invalidating substituted service when wife was separated from husband and not living at address where service was attempted). Having raised the issue of personal jurisdiction, Thompson's motion and accompanying affidavit placed the burden on the Department to establish the validity of service of process. *M.J.W.*, 825 So.2d at 1041. Accordingly, the cause is reversed and remanded for an evidentiary hearing to determine whether the attempted service of Thompson pursuant to section 48.031, Florida Statutes (2003), was valid. *See Venetian Salami*, 554 So.2d at 502-03; *Mowrey Elevator of Florida, Inc. v. Automated Integration*, 745 So.2d 1046, 1047-48 (Fla. 1st DCA 1999).

REVERSED and REMANDED.

KAHN and BENTON, JJ., concur.

This is the end of the court's opinion.

Parallel Citations

29 Fla. L. Weekly D566

These are the names of the judges who concurred in the court's decision. (JJ means judges or justices.)

---

3. *Reading the Opinion*

If the opinion is relatively short, for example, only two or three pages long, you will usually want to begin by reading quickly through the entire case. If, however, the case is longer, you will want to make sure that the case is on point or relevant to the issue you have been asked to research before you invest too much time reading and analyzing it. Therefore, if the case is more than a few pages long, begin by reading any introductory material, for example, the background section or the syllabus and the headnotes. If the introductory material or headnotes indicate that the case deals with the statute, common law doctrine, or issue that you have been asked to research, use the headnote numbers to locate those portions of the opinion from which the headnotes were drawn, and read those portions of the opinion. If those portions of the opinion appear to be on point, go back and read the entire opinion.

PRACTICE POINTER

While the time saved by reading just the headnotes may seem to outweigh the cost of taking the time to read the entire case, you cannot cite headnotes. Because the headnotes are written by an attorney working for a publishing company and not by the court, they are not authority.

When you read the full opinion, look for specific types of information. First, identify the issue. If the opinion is a trial court opinion, was the issue a procedural issue, for example, whether the plaintiff was entitled to summary judgment, or did the court decide the case on its merits? In contrast, if the opinion is from an appellate court, was the issue (1) whether the statute is constitutional, (2) whether the regulations are valid, (3) whether the trial court set out the law correctly or correctly instructed the jury, (4) whether the trial court judge abused his or her discretion in granting or denying a motion or granting or denying an objection, or (5) whether there is sufficient evidence to support the trial court judge's or the jury's findings of fact?

Second, if the opinion is from an appellate court, determine what standard of review the appellate court applied. If the issue involves an issue of law, the standard of review is usually de novo. Under this standard of review, the appellate court does not defer to the trial court. Instead, it makes its own independent determination of what law applies or what the law is. In contrast, if the issue involves an issue of fact or an exercise of judgment, the standard of review is usually more deferential. For example, in reviewing most factual determinations, the standard of review is a sufficiency of the evidence standard. The appellate court looks to see only if there is sufficient evidence to support the trial court's findings of fact or the jury's verdict. Similarly, in reviewing a trial court's decision to admit evidence, the appellate courts usually defer to the trial court, reversing the trial court only when the appellate court determines that the trial court judge abused his or her discretion.

Third, determine what rule or test the court applied in deciding the issue. Begin by determining whether the parties agreed about what the rule was. If the parties agreed on the rule, the issue is not what the rule is but how that rule should be applied in a particular fact situation. If the parties did not agree about what the rule was, what rule did the plaintiff ask the court to apply? What rule did the defendant ask the court to apply? What rule did the court choose?

Fourth, evaluate the court's reasoning. If the parties agreed about what the rule was, what facts did the court consider in applying that rule to the facts of the case? If the parties disagreed about what the rule was, why did the court pick one rule over another? For example, in deciding how to interpret a statute, did the court rely on the plain language of the statute, on the canons of statutory construction, or on the statute's legislative history?

Fifth, look carefully at the court's disposition of the case. Did the court affirm the trial court? Reverse the trial court? Remand the case back to the trial court for further action?

Last, think about how you might be able to the use the case. Can you use the case as authority for a rule? To illustrate how the courts have applied a particular rule? Similarly, think about how the other side might use the case, about how a trial court might use the case, and how the appellate court might use the case.

As the preceding paragraphs indicate, in reading and analyzing a case, your role is anything but that of a passive reader. Instead, you are reading the case as a lawyer, looking not only for the rules and how those rules have been applied, but also for how you and any other parties might be able to use the case.

Chart 4-4 demonstrates how an attorney would approach the reading of an opinion on Westlaw. In this "think aloud," the attorney who is reading the case represents Ms. Olsen, a woman who wants to overturn a decision terminating her parental rights on the grounds that she was not properly served. At the time of service, Ms. Olsen was spending four nights each week at a halfway house for recovering addicts and three nights each week at her sister's house. The summons was left with her sister at her sister's house on a day on which Ms. Olsen was not at her sister's house. The text of the opinion is in the left-hand column and what the defense attorney thought as she read the opinion is in the right-hand column. Because the case is short, the attorney read the entire case.

CHART 4-4
DEFENSE ATTORNEY'S THOUGHTS WHILE READING THOMPSON V. STATE, DEPT. OF REVENUE

Original Image of 867 So.2d 603 (PDF)	**What Attorney Thought as She Read Opinion**
867 So.2d 603 District Court of Appeal of Florida, First District. Calvin THOMPSON, Appellant, v. STATE of Florida, DEPARTMENT OF REVENUE, Appellee. No. 1D03-2975. March 5, 2004.	Okay, because this is a Florida case, it is mandatory authority. I need to remember to cite check it to make sure that it is still good law.
Synopsis	I am going to read the synopsis to see if the case is on point.
Background: Department of Revenue filed action against father to establish and enforce child support for daughter. The Circuit Court, Duval County, E. McRae Mathis, J., denied father's motion to quash service of process. Father appealed.	The father wanted the same thing that I want: to quash service.
Holding: The District Court of Appeal, Van Nortwick, J., held that father made prima facie showing that Department's petition was not served on him at his usual place of abode. Reversed and remanded. West Headnotes [1] KeyCite Notes	Good. The issue in this case seems to be the same as the issue in my case. I want to establish that the sister's house was not my client's usual place of abode.

76E Child Support
76EV Proceedings
76EV(A) In General
76Ek180 k. Process. Most Cited Cases

Father's affidavit stating that he was separated from wife and had not resided with her for over three years was sufficient to make a prima facie showing that Department of Revenue's petition to establish and enforce child support, which was left with wife at her residence, was not served on father at his usual place of abode, for purposes of Department's attempt to establish valid substituted service. West's F.S.A. § 48.031.

The facts in this case seem to be pretty different from the facts in my case. My client was staying with her sister a couple of nights a week. I may not be able to use this case as an analogous case.

[2] KeyCite Notes

313 Process
313II Service
313II(B) Substituted Service
313k76 Mode and Sufficiency of Service
313k78 k. Leaving Copy at Residence or Other Place. Most Cited Cases

The requirement that substituted service of process be at a defendant's "usual place of abode" means the place where the defendant is actually living at the time of service. West's F.S.A. § 48.031.

This looks like the rule. It also looks like a rule that I can use to support our argument. I need to look at this part of the opinion.

[3] KeyCite Notes

313 Process
313II Service
313II(A) Personal Service in General
313k48 k. Nature and Necessity in General. Most Cited Cases

313 Process KeyCite Notes
313II Service
313II(E) Return and Proof of Service
313k144 Evidence as to Service
313k145 k. Presumptions and Burden of Proof. Most Cited Cases

The burden of proof to sustain the validity of service of process is upon the person who seeks to invoke the jurisdiction of the court and, without proper service of process, the court lacks personal jurisdiction over the defendant. West's F.S.A. § 48.031.

Good. Here is the rule about burden of proof. It looks like the state has the burden. I need to look at this part of the opinion.

[4] KeyCite Notes

313 Process
313II Service
313II(E) Return and Proof of Service

313k144 Evidence as to Service
313k145 k. Presumptions and Burden of Proof. Most Cited Cases

313 Process KeyCite Notes
313II Service
313II(E) Return and Proof of Service
313k144 Evidence as to Service
313k149 k. Weight and Sufficiency. Most Cited Cases

A process server's return of service on a defendant which is regular on its face is presumed to be valid absent clear and convincing evidence presented to the contrary.

[5] KeyCite Notes

313 Process
313II Service
313II(E) Return and Proof of Service
313k144 Evidence as to Service
313k148 k. Evidence to Impeach or Contradict Return, Certificate, or Affidavit of Service. Most Cited Cases

A simple denial of having received service is not sufficient to contradict a process server's return of service that is regular on its face.

This rule may hurt us. If the phrase "return of service" means what I think it does, then there will be a presumption that the service is valid, and we will have to present clear and convincing evidence. I need to read this part of the opinion, make sure that I know what return of service means, and check the file to see if in our case the return of service was regular.

*604 Esther A. Zaretsky, West Palm Beach, for Appellant. Charles J. Crist, Jr., Attorney General and Toni C. Bernstein and William H. Branch, Assistant Attorneys General, Tallahassee, for Appellee.

VAN NORTWICK, J.

Calvin Thompson appeals a non-final order denying his motion to quash service of process in this support-administrative paternity action filed by the Department of Revenue. We reverse and remand for an evidentiary hearing pursuant to *Venetian Salami Co. v. Parthenais*, 554 So.2d 499, 502-03 (Fla.1989).

This is just the procedural history. This was a paternity action. Thompson, who seems to be the father, moved to quash service.

Pursuant to section 409.2564, Florida Statutes (2002), the Department filed an action to establish and enforce child support for Thompson's four year-old daughter. The petition was served at 625 F Covenant Drive, Belle Glade, Florida 33430, and accepted by Thompson's wife. Thompson filed a motion to dismiss/quash for lack of service of process stating that he was not present at the Belle Glade address and was not personally served. In his attached affidavit, Thompson stated that he has been separated from his wife, that he has not resided at that address for over three years, and that he did not authorize anyone to accept service of process on his behalf. The trial court entered an order ruling that any jurisdictional defect could be cured by mailing a copy of the petition and accompanying documents to Thompson's attorney, "who has made a general appearance." The Department correctly concedes that the jurisdictional defect cannot

Okay, the court is setting out the facts.

The petition was served at his wife's house, and his wife accepted service.

Thompson filed an affidavit stating

*605 be cured in the manner suggested by the trial court and that Thompson's argument that the trial court lacked personal jurisdiction was not waived because Thompson neither took affirmative action nor sought affirmative relief prior to raising the alleged defect. *See Coto-Ojeda v. Samuel*, 642 So.2d 587, 588 (Fla. 3d DCA 1994)(Cope, J., specially concurring).

that he had been separated from his wife and had not resided at her house for three years.

Given our facts, most of this does not seem relevant.

[1] [2] [3] Turning to the merits, "[s]ection 48.031 expressly requires that substituted service be at the person's usual place of abode." *Shurman v. A. Mortg. & Investment Corp., 795 So.2d 952, 954 (Fla.2001).* The requirement "usual place of abode" means "the place where the defendant is actually living at the time of service." *Id., citing State ex rel. Merritt v. Heffernan*, 142 Fla. 496, 195 So. 145, 147 (1940).

Although the court does not set out the issue on appeal, the issue seems to be whether the service was at the defendant's usual place of abode.

Good. Here is a definition of usual place of abode. Court cites an old Florida Supreme Court decision as authority.

The burden of proof to sustain the validity of service of process is upon the person who seeks to invoke the jurisdiction of the court and, without proper service of process, the court lacks personal jurisdiction over the defendant. *M.J.W. v. Department of Children and Families*, 825 So.2d 1038, 1041 (Fla. 1st DCA 2002).

Here are the rules about the burden of proof.

[4] [5] "[A] process server's return of service on a defendant which is regular on its face is presumed to be valid absent clear and convincing evidence presented to the contrary." *Telf Corp. v. Gomez*, 671 So.2d 818 (Fla. 3d DCA 1996). Although simple denial of service is not sufficient, *id.* at 819, Thompson's motion and affidavit are based on the fact that the service did not comply with section 48.031 and was therefore legally deficient. *National Safety Associates, Inc. v. Allstate Insurance Co.*, 799 So.2d 316, 317 (Fla. 2d DCA 2001). Thompson's affidavit makes a *prima facie* showing that he was not served at his usual place of abode by valid substituted service. *See, e.g., S.H. v. Department of Children and Families*, 837 So.2d 1117, 1118 (Fla. 4th DCA 2003) (invalidating substituted service on father at mother's address, where mother's residence was not father's "usual place of abode" at the time of service); *Gonzalez v. Totalbank*, 472 So.2d 861 (Fla. 3d DCA 1985) (invalidating substituted service when wife was separated from husband and not living at address where service was attempted). Having raised the issue of personal jurisdiction, Thompson's motion and accompanying

Okay, we are going to have to do more than just allege that the sister's house is not our client's usual place of abode. We are going to have to submit an affidavit establishing that her residence was somewhere else.

These cases look like they are on point. I need to look at them once I finish reading this case.

affidavit placed the burden on the Department to establish the validity of service of process. *M.J.W.*, 825 So.2d at 1041. Accordingly, the cause is reversed and remanded for an evidentiary hearing to determine whether the attempted service of Thompson pursuant to section 48.031, Florida Statutes (2003), was valid. *See Venetian Salami*, 554 So.2d at 502-03; *Mowrey Elevator of Florida, Inc. v. Automated Integration*, 745 So.2d 1046, 1047-48 (Fla. 1st DCA 1999).
REVERSED and REMANDED.

KAHN and BENTON, JJ., concur.

I don't know whether Mr. Thompson won. However, the affidavit was enough to get the case back to the trial court for an evidentiary hearing.

We can use this case for the rules relating to what is and is not a person's usual place of abode and for the rules relating to the burden of proof. The State is going to say that our case is much weaker than this case. While Ms. Olsen was staying with her sister three nights a week, Mr. Thompson hadn't (or says he hadn't) lived with his wife for three years. We are going to have to focus on the language—"actually living at the time of service" to argue that at the time of service Ms. Olsen was not actually living with her sister.

D. EXERCISE

As you read the following case, write in the right-hand margin what you are thinking as you read. After you have finished doing your own "think aloud," compare what you wrote to what one of your classmates wrote.

Text of Opinion	What You Thought as You Read the Opinion
Shurman v. Atlantic Mortg. & Inv. Corp. 795 So.2d 952 Fla., 2001. September 06, 2001 (Approx. 5 pages) Supreme Court of Florida. Gerald R. SHURMAN, Petitioner, v. ATLANTIC MORTGAGE & INVESTMENT CORPORATION, Respondent. No. SC96918. Sept. 6, 2001. Mortgage brought mortgage foreclosure action against inmate. The Circuit Court, Lake County, Don F. Briggs, J., entered final judgment against inmate based on default. Inmate appealed. The District Court of Appeal, 740 So.2d 1221, affirmed. Inmate sought discretionary review. The Supreme Court held that inmate's "usual place of abode" for service of process was prison, not home where inmate had lived with his wife. Quashed and remanded. Wells, C.J., concurred in result only and filed opinion, in which Harding, J., joined. West Headnotes [1] KeyCite Notes 313 Process 313II Service 313II(A) Personal Service in General 313k48 k. Nature and Necessity in General. Most Cited Cases The fundamental purpose of service of process is to give proper notice to the defendant in the case that he is answerable to the claim of plaintiff and, therefore, to vest jurisdiction in the court entertaining the controversy. West's F.S.A. § 48.031.	Florida Supreme court case, therefore mandatory authority. wants foreclosure quashed and remanded.

[2] KeyCite Notes

313 Process
313II Service
313II(A) Personal Service in General
313k49 k. Statutory Provisions. Most Cited Cases

313 Process KeyCite Notes
313II Service
313II(A) Personal Service in General
313k64 k. Mode and Sufficiency of Service. Most Cited Cases

Because of the importance of litigants receiving notice of actions against them, statutes governing service of process are to be strictly construed and enforced. West's F.S.A. § 48.031.

[3] KeyCite Notes

266 Mortgage
266X Foreclosure by Action
266X(E) Parties and Process
266k440 k. Process in General. Most Cited Cases

Inmate's "usual place of abode" for service of process in foreclosure action was prison, not house where prisoner formerly lived with his wife, where inmate actually lived in prison. West's F.S.A. § 48.031.

*952 Gerald R. Shurman, pro se, Orlando, FL, for Petitioner. Anne S. Mason and Jennifer S. Ebanks of Mason & Associates, P.A., Clearwater, FL, for Respondent.

PER CURIAM.
We have for review *Shurman v. Atlantic Mortgage & Investment*, 740 So.2d 1221 (Fla. 5th DCA 1999), which expressly and directly conflicts with *953 *State ex rel. Merritt v. Heffernan*, 142 Fla. 496, 195 So. 145 (1940). We have jurisdiction. *See* art. V, § 3(b)(3), Fla. Const. For the reasons set forth below, we quash the decision of the district court.

FACTS

The record reflects that Gerald Shurman was criminally prosecuted, convicted, and incarcerated in state prison in May of 1997. Subsequently, Shurman was named as a defendant in a mortgage foreclosure action commenced in March of 1998 by Atlantic Mortgage & Investment Corporation (Atlantic). Service of process was effected on Shurman by substituted service on his wife, Emily, at their home where they had resided together before Shurman's incarceration.
At the time of service of process Shurman was incarcerated in state prison. Because no responsive pleadings were filed by Shurman a default was entered against him in May of 1998. Thereafter, the trial

court granted Atlantic's motion for final summary judgment of foreclosure and the property was sold at a foreclosure sale on June 25, 1998, to the second mortgagee.

On January 11, 1999, Shurman filed a motion to set aside the judgment alleging that he was not properly served process in the action and, therefore, the judgment as to his interest in the property was void. Following an evidentiary hearing on Shurman's motion, the trial court concluded that Shurman's "usual place of abode" for purposes of serving process under section 48.031, Florida Statutes (1997), was the residence where he lived with his wife prior to his incarceration and where his wife continued to reside afterward. As such, the trial court found that service was perfected when a copy of the process and complaint was left with Shurman's wife at their marital residence. In light of its finding that service was valid and that Shurman had not demonstrated any meritorious defense to the foreclosure action, the trial court denied Shurman's motion to set aside the judgment.

On appeal, the Fifth District affirmed the trial court's denial of Shurman's motion to set aside the judgment. *See Shurman v. Atlantic Mortgage & Inv.*, 740 So.2d 1221 (Fla. 5th DCA 1999). Relying on *Bull v. Kistner*, 257 Iowa 968, 135 N.W.2d 545 (1965), and *Montes v. Seda*, 157 Misc.2d 895, 599 N.Y.S.2d 401, 403 (Sup.Ct.1993), *aff'd,* 208 A.D.2d 388, 626 N.Y.S.2d 61 (1994), the district court agreed with the trial court's conclusion that service was made at Shurman's "usual place of abode." *Shurman*, 740 So.2d at 1222. The district court noted that Shurman and his wife had resided at the subject property for years prior to his incarceration and his family continued to reside there afterward. *See id.* at 1223. Accordingly, the court held that service was valid. *See id.* Shurman subsequently sought discretionary review in this Court.

ANALYSIS

The issue presented in this case is whether Shurman was properly served at his "usual place of abode" as required under section 48.031, Florida Statutes (1997). Shurman argues that since he was incarcerated at the time of service his "usual place of abode" was prison and, as such, he should have been served there in order to be afforded due process. By contrast, Atlantic asserts that an incarcerated party's "usual place of abode" is where the party resided prior to incarceration if the party's family continues to reside there.

[1] It is well settled that the fundamental purpose of service is "to give proper notice to the defendant in the case that he is answerable to the claim of plaintiff and, therefore, to vest jurisdiction in the court entertaining the controversy." *State ex rel. Merritt v. Heffernan,*

142 Fla. 496, 195 So. 145, 147 (1940); *see also* *954 *Klosenski v. Flaherty*, 116 So.2d 767, 768 (Fla.1959) (quoting *Heffernan*); *Clark v. Clark*, 158 Fla. 731, 30 So.2d 170, 171 (1947) ("The purpose of constructive or substituted service is to bring knowledge of the pending litigation to the defendant in order that he may appear and guard his interests."); *Gribbel v. Henderson*, 151 Fla. 712, 10 So.2d 734, 739 (1942); *Arcadia Citrus Growers Ass'n v. Hollingsworth*, 135 Fla. 322, 185 So. 431, 434 (1938). In other words, the purpose of this jurisdictional scheme is to give the person affected notice of the proceedings and an opportunity to defend his rights.

[2] KC Section 48.031, Florida Statutes (1997), provides in pertinent part:

> (1)(a) Service of original process is made by delivering a copy of it to the person to be served with a copy of the complaint, petition, or other initial pleading or paper or by leaving the copies at his or her usual place of abode with any person residing therein who is 15 years of age or older and informing the person of their contents.

§ 48.031(1)(a), Fla. Stat. (1997). Section 48.031 expressly requires that substituted service be at the person's "usual place of abode." *Id.* Further, because of the importance of litigants receiving notice of actions against them, statutes governing service of process are to be strictly construed and enforced. *See Schupak v. Sutton Hill Assocs.*, 710 So.2d 707, 708 (Fla. 4th DCA 1998); *Aero Costa Rica, Inc. v. Dispatch Servs., Inc.*, 710 So.2d 218, 219 (Fla. 3d DCA 1998); *Hauser v. Schiff*, 341 So.2d 531, 531 (Fla. 3d DCA 1977).

In *Heffernan*, this Court defined the term "usual place of abode" as meaning the place where the defendant is actually living at the time of service. *See Heffernan*, 195 So. at 147. In so doing, we quoted favorably from *Eckman v. Grear*, 14 N.J. Misc. 807, 187 A. 556 (Com. Pl.1936), and *Mygatt v. Coe*, 63 N.J.L. 510, 44 A. 198 (Sup.Ct.1899):

We quote further from the case of *Eckman v. Grear*, 187 A. 556, 558, 14 N.J.Misc. 807:

> "Going one step further, 'usual place of abode' is the place where the defendant is actually living at the time of the service. The word abode means one's fixed place of residence for the time being when the service is made. Thus, if a person have several residences, he must be served at the residence in which he is actually living at the time service is made."

And in *Mygatt v. Coe*, 63 N.J.L. 510, 512, 44 A. 198, 199, the following pertinent statement appears:

> "The statute does not direct service to be made at the 'residence' of the defendant, but at his 'dwelling house' or 'usual place of

abode,' which is a much more restricted term. As was said in *Stout v. Leonard*, 37 N.J.L. 492, many persons have several residences, which they permanently maintain, occupying one at one period of the year and another at another period. Where such conditions exist, a summons must be served at the dwelling house in which the defendant is living at the time when the service is made."

Heffernan, 195 So. at 147. *See also Milanes v. Colonial Penn Ins. Co.*, 507 So.2d 777, 778 (Fla. 3d DCA 1987); *Panter v. Werbel-Roth Securities, Inc.*, 406 So.2d 1267, 1268 (Fla. 4th DCA 1981); *Hauser*, 341 So.2d at 532.

Not surprisingly, in applying the definition of the term "usual place of abode" set forth in *Heffernan*, courts have frequently invalidated substituted service of process in cases where the defendant was not actually living at the place where service was made. *See, e.g.*, *955 *Alvarez v. State Farm Mutual Auto Ins. Co.*, 635 So.2d 131, 132 (Fla. 3d DCA 1994) (invalidating substituted service on defendant's cousin where affidavits and supporting documentation, including a telephone bill and marriage license, established defendant was not living at that address on the date of service); *Milanes*, 507 So.2d at 778 (noting that service of process on the residence of defendant's ex-wife did not satisfy section 48.031); *Stern v. Gad*, 505 So.2d 531, 532 (Fla. 3d DCA 1987) (holding mere ownership of a condominium and service upon the wife of an owner will not suffice to establish "usual place of abode," when defendant submitted affidavit that he was not in the jurisdiction on the date of purported service and did not reside in the United States); *Gonzalez v. Totalbank*, 472 So.2d 861, 864 (Fla. 3d DCA 1985) (invalidating substituted service where wife was separated from husband and no longer living at address where service was attempted); *Panter*, 406 So.2d at 1268 (finding substituted service at home of appellant's father invalid where uncontradicted affidavits stated appellant was living in Michigan when service was made). Notably, several of these cases involved familial relationships where presumably the defendant would be more likely to receive notice, yet the courts still invalidated the service of process because the defendant was not actually living at the place where service was made. *See Alvarez*, 635 So.2d at 132 (substituted service on defendant's cousin); *Stern*, 505 So.2d at 532 (substituted service on wife); *Panter*, 406 So.2d at 1268 (substituted service on appellant's father).

[3] KC In this case it is uncontradicted that Shurman had been incarcerated in prison in May of 1997 and had not been living with his wife for at least nine months prior to the time substituted service was effected. Although Atlantic argues that Shurman's "usual place of abode" was where he lived with his family before being incarcerated, Shurman was "actually living" in prison at the time of service. Thus, under our obligation to strictly construe the statutory notice provisions and our analysis in *Heffernan*, it is apparent that Shurman's

"usual place of abode" was prison, not his prior residence. *See Heffernan*, 195 So. at 147.

We find additional support for our decision in *Heffernan* and our conclusion that prison was Shurman's "usual place of abode" in *Fidelity & Deposit Co. v. Abagnale*, 97 N.J.Super. 132, 234 A.2d 511 (1967), and *Saienni v. Oveide*, 355 A.2d 707 (Del.Super.Ct.1976).[FN1] In *Abagnale*, the court rejected the defendant's argument that he could be reached by substituted service in New Jersey while he was incarcerated out-of-state. The court explained:

FN1. We recognize that the majority of jurisdictions have reached a different conclusion. *See Blue Cross & Blue Shield v. Chang*, 109 F.R.D. 669 (E.D.Mich.1986); *Bohland v. Smith*, 7 F.R.D. 364 (E.D.Ill.1947); *Grant v. Dalliber*, 11 Conn. 234 (1836); *Bull v. Kistner*, 257 Iowa 968, 135 N.W.2d 545 (1965); *Fidelity & Deposit Co. v. Boundy*, 236 Mo.App. 656, 158 S.W.2d 243 (1942); *Walker v. Stevens*, 52 Neb. 653, 72 N.W. 1038 (1897); *Montes v. Seda*, 157 Misc.2d 895, 599 N.Y.S.2d 401 (Sup.Ct.1993), *aff'd*, 208 A.D.2d 388, 626 N.Y.S.2d 61 (1994); *Smith v. Hooton*, 3 Pa.D. 250 (1894). *See generally* Allen E. Korpela, Annotation, *Construction of Phrase "Usual Place of Abode," or Similar Terms Referring to Abode, Residence, or Domicil, as Used in Statutes Relating to Service of Process*, 32 A.L.R.3d 112, § 16 (1970). However, we believe that the better view is that one's "usual place of abode" is where the person is actually living at the time of service, even in cases involving prisoners.

The law in this State has developed in somewhat rigid conformity to the principle that provisions for substituted service, being in derogation of the common law, must be strictly construed. Hence, the rule has been consistently applied *956 that one's "dwelling house or usual place of abode" is limited in its meaning to the place where one is "actually living" at the time when service is made. The expectation that a defendant will normally receive notice of process served through a competent member of his household living at the same place of abode as he, does not, it seems to me, prevail in the setting of familial disorganization frequently ensuing where the head of the household is committed to prison. *Abagnale*, 234 A.2d at 519 (citations omitted). While the court recognized some jurisdictions had concluded that an incarcerated party's usual place of abode continues to be where his family resides, it distinguished those cases on the basis that they were "largely influenced, if not governed, by a hybrid of residence and domicile." *Id.* The Delaware court in *Saienni* followed *Abagnale* and held that the defendant, who was incarcerated in Pennsylvania, was not properly served at his usual place of abode by substituted service on his wife in Delaware. The court noted that in Delaware a person's usual place of abode is not the equivalent of his domicile. *See Saienni*, 355 A.2d at 708. Rather, for purposes of substituted service, a defendant must be served at the place where he is

actually living at the time service is made. *See id.* (citing *Whetsel v. Gosnell*, 181 A.2d 91 (Del.1962)). Relying on *Abagnale* and *Whetsel*, the court concluded that the defendant's usual place of abode was the Pennsylvania State Correctional Institution since that was where the defendant was physically living at the time of service. *See id.* We find the reasoning of the courts in *Abagnale* and *Saienni* persuasive in this case. As stated previously, the object of all process is to impart to the person affected notice of the proceeding and an opportunity to defend his rights. *See Klosenski*, 116 So.2d at 768; *Clark*, 30 So.2d at 171; *Gribbel*, 10 So.2d at 739; *Heffernan*, 195 So. at 147; *Arcadia Citrus Growers Ass'n*, 185 So. at 434. By applying the definition of "usual place of abode" set forth in *Heffernan* to the facts in this case, we are adhering to this underlying principle. Further, it is clear that the Legislature contemplated that people in prison would be sued and served with process. Section 48.051, Florida Statutes (1997), provides that "[p]rocess against a state prisoner shall be served on the prisoner." *Id. Cf. State ex rel. Page v. Hollingsworth*, 117 Fla. 288, 157 So. 887 (1934). Had the Legislature intended the term "usual place of abode" to apply differently to prisoners, it could have so stated. Hence, we see no need to depart from *Heffernan* in cases involving prisoners. In sum, we adhere to *Heffernan* and reaffirm that for purposes of substituted service one's "usual place of abode" is where the person is actually living at the time of service. In this case, it is uncontroverted that Shurman was actually living in prison at the time substituted service was made on his wife at their marital residence. Thus, Shurman was not properly served at his usual place of abode as required under section 48.031(1)(a), Florida Statutes (1997). Accordingly, we quash the decision of the district court of appeal and remand for further proceedings consistent herewith. It is so ordered. SHAW, HARDING, ANSTEAD, PARIENTE, LEWIS, and QUINCE, JJ., concur. WELLS, C.J., concurs with an opinion, in which HARDING, J., concurs. WELLS, C.J., concurring. I concur in result only in this case. I conclude that this decision should be controlled by the plain meaning of *957 section 48.051, Florida Statutes, which states: "Process against a state prisoner shall be served on the prisoner." I would read this to mean that process should be served on the prisoner at the prison. I do not believe reliance on section 48.031(1)(a), Florida Statutes, is appropriate. HARDING, J., concurs. Reprinted with permission.	

CHAPTER

5

Reading Like a Lawyer

Until a few years ago, most law professors and experienced attorneys assumed that law students and new attorneys read statutes and cases in the same way that they read them. While some individuals come to law school reading as experienced attorneys read, most do not. As a consequence, during their first year of law school, many law students have to "unlearn" the reading strategies that they used as undergraduates or in their home countries and learn a new way of reading. For example, many first-year law students have to change their focus from passively reading for information to a much more engaged and critical form of reading.

This chapter tries to speed up the process of learning how to read as lawyers read by identifying both the characteristics of good legal readers and the strategies that good legal readers use. Although you may be tempted to skip this chapter, don't. While the research on legal reading is limited, the research that does exist suggests that there is a strong correlation between reading like a lawyer and doing well on law school exams.

A. GOOD LAWYERS ARE GOOD READERS

Good lawyers are good readers. When they read a document, statute, or case, they read exactly what is on the page. They do not skip words, read in words, or misread words. In addition, they have good vocabularies. They recognize and understand most of the words that they read, and the ones that they do not recognize or understand they look up either in a book or an online dictionary.

PRACTICE POINTER

There are a number of good, free online dictionaries. For example, *Merriam-Webster's Online Dictionary* is at *http://www.m-w.com;* the *Cambridge Dictionaries Online* is at *http://dictionary.cambridge.org; JURIST's Legal Dictionaries* are at *http://jurist.law.pitt.edu/dictionary.htm;* and *FindLaw's Legal Dictionary* is at *http://dictionary.lp.findlaw.com.*

Poor reading skills can significantly affect your ability to understand what you are reading. For instance, in the following example, which is taken from the transcript of a law student reading a case aloud, Jackie, a first-year student, mispronounced and apparently did not recognize the word "palatial."[1]

EXAMPLE **Transcript of Jackie's Think Aloud**

> Some months prior to the alleged imprisonment, the plaintiff, while in Jaffa, announced her intention to leave the sect. The defendant, with the help of the plaintiff's husband, persuaded the plaintiff to return to the United States aboard the sect's [platial] yacht, the Kingdom.

James, another student who read the same case, misread the following sentence. The first example shows how the sentence appears in the casebook. The second sentence shows how James read it when he read the sentence aloud.

EXAMPLE **Sentence as it Appears in the Casebook**

> According to the uncontradicted evidence, at no time did any one physically restrain the plaintiff except for the defendant's refusal, once the plaintiff announced her decision to quit the yacht, to let the plaintiff use a small boat to take herself, her children, and belongings ashore.

EXAMPLE **Sentence as James Read It**

> According to the uncontradicted evidence, at no time did any one physically restrain the plaintiff except for the defendant's (pause) defendant's refusal once (pause) defendant's refusal once (pause) the plaintiff announced her decision to quit the yacht to let the plaintiff use a small boat to take herself, her children, and belongings ashore.

When questioned about what the court was saying in this sentence, James stated that the defendant had, on one occasion, refused to let the plaintiff take the boat. In fact, the court says that the refusal came once the defendant announced her decision to quit the yacht.

Although at first these errors may seem insignificant, in each instance they resulted in the student misunderstanding the case and, thus, the rules and the court's reasoning. In addition, in both instances, the errors were a harbinger of things to come. Both students ended up doing poorly on their exams. At the end of the first year, Jackie was in the bottom 20 percent of her class, and James had flunked out.

To determine whether you may be misreading cases, make two copies of one of the cases in your casebook. Keep one copy for yourself, and give the other to a trusted classmate or teaching assistant. Then read aloud from your copy while your partner follows along on his or her copy, highlighting any words or phrases that you misread and any words that you mispronounce or do not appear to

1. The examples in this section come from Laurel Currie Oates, *Beating the Odds, Reading Strategies of Law Students Admitted Through Special Admissions Programs,* 83 Iowa L. Rev. 139 (1997). See also Laurel Currie Oates, *Leveling the Playing Field: Helping Students Succeed by Helping Them Learn to Read as Expert Lawyers,* 80 St. John's L. Rev. 227 (2006).

understand. After you have finished your reading of the case, compare your understanding of the case with your partner's. Did you both read the case in essentially the same way? If your partner noted more than one or two problems or if your understanding of the case is substantially different from your partner's, try the following. First, try reading more slowly. You may be trying to read the material too quickly. Second, take the time to look up any words that you are not sure that you understand. Third, if the problems appear to be serious, ask your school's learning center if it can provide you with a more thorough evaluation of your reading skills.

B. GOOD LEGAL READERS READ AND REREAD MATERIAL UNTIL THEY ARE SURE THAT THEY UNDERSTAND IT

While in some types of reading you can skip sections that you do not completely understand, such a strategy does not work when you are doing legal reading. If the document, statute, or case is one that is relevant to your problem, you need to read and reread it until you are sure that you understand it.

The following example shows how a first-year student, William, read and reread a case until he was sure that he understood it. The material in the regular typeface is the text of the case. The material in italics is what William said after he had read that section of the text.

EXAMPLE **Excerpt from William's Think Aloud**

Whittaker v. Sanford
110 Me. 77, 88 S. 399 (1912)

Savage, J. Action for false imprisonment. The plaintiff recovered a verdict for $1100. The case comes up on defendant's exceptions and a motion for a new trial.

So the defendant is the appellant and is appealing the verdict of $1100.

The plaintiff had been a member of a religious sect, which had colonies in Maine and in Jaffa, Syria, and of which the defendant was a leader. Some months prior to the alleged imprisonment, the plaintiff, while in Jaffa, announced her intention to leave the sect.

I need to reread this again [rereads sentence]. So just prior to the alleged imprisonment the plaintiff was in Jaffa and expressed an intention to leave the sect. At this point, I am a bit confused about who the parties are. I need to reread this to make sure that I have the facts straight, [rereads from the beginning.]
OK. This is an action for false imprisonment. The plaintiff recovered a verdict for $1100. The case came up on the defendant's exceptions. The plaintiff is a member of the sect and the defendant is the head of the sect so Whittaker is the member of the sect and Sanford is its leader.

Although it took William more time to read the case than it took some of the other students, the payoff was substantial. Although his undergraduate GPA and LSAT placed William in the bottom 10 percent of his entering law school class, at the end of his first year, his law school GPA placed him in the top 10 percent.

There are several things you can do to make sure that you understand the cases that you are reading. First, see if you can diagram the action. At the trial court level, who sued whom and what was the cause of action? Who "won" at trial, who filed the appeal, and what is the issue on appeal?

PRACTICE POINTER

In some instances, you may be able to compare your chart showing the case's prior and subsequent history with the chart that is on KeyCite under Direct History, Graphical View.

Second, do not underestimate the value of preparing your own case briefs. While it may be faster and easier to highlight sections of a statute or case, highlighting does not ensure that you understand the material you are reading. In fact, there is some evidence that students who highlight remember less than students who do not highlight. (In highlighting a section, some students focus their attention on the process of highlighting and not on the material that they are highlighting. As a result, when they are asked to recall what it is that they just highlighted, they are unable to do so.)

Finally, after reading a statute or case, test yourself to make sure you understand what you just read. After reading a statute, diagram that statute. See section 3.D.4. After reading a case, answer the following questions: (1) What issue was before the court? (2) What was the standard of review? (3) What rule did the court apply? (4) In applying the rule, what facts did the court consider? (5) What did the court decide, and why did it decide the case that way? (6) What was the disposition: Did the appellate court affirm, reverse, or remand? See section 3.D.4. If you cannot diagram the statute or answer these questions about the case, keep reading until you can.

C. GOOD LEGAL READERS SYNTHESIZE THE STATUTES AND CASES THAT THEY READ

In addition to reading accurately and until they understand the statutes and cases, good legal readers synthesize the statutes and cases that they read.

Synthesis is the process of putting the pieces together. You take each of the statutory sections and cases you have read and try to make sense of them. Are they consistent? What are the steps in the analysis? How do they fit into your existing conceptual frameworks?

The following example shows the type of synthesis that a law professor did in reading a restatement section and a case. The text is set out in regular type and the professor's comments in italics.

EXAMPLE **Excerpt from Law Professor's Think Aloud**

> There was evidence that the plaintiff had been ashore a number of times, had been on numerous outings and had been treated as a guest during her stay aboard the yacht. According to the uncontradicted evidence, at no time did anyone physically restrain the plaintiff except for the defendant's refusal, once the plaintiff announced her decision to quit the yacht, to let the plaintiff use a small boat to take herself, her children, and her belongings ashore.
>
> *I'm sort of getting a visual image of the boat that she was in and out of... uhm... the plaintiff had been ashore. I'm thinking about the elements that I just read* [a reference to the *Restatement* section that had been set out immediately before the case] *and I'm trying to see how, I guess, frankly how I would decide the case on a certain level before I even want to know what Judge Savage thought.* [pause] *I need to look at the Restatement section* [looks back at the *Restatement* section]. *Is the defendant acting to or with intent to confine the plaintiff? She got off the boat. That kind of bothers me. That results directly or indirectly in confinement. Maybe that's relevant here. The other is conscious of the confinement or is harmed by it. Given the facts, that bothers me too.*

Doing synthesis is time consuming and hard work. You are no longer reading just for information. Instead, as you are reading, you are either placing new information into existing conceptual frameworks or constructing completely new frameworks.

If you are like most law students, at some point you will argue that law school would be a lot easier if your professors put the pieces together for you, if they just gave you their conceptual frameworks. If you had come to law school just to learn the law, you would be right. It would be easier for both you and your professors if they just gave you the law. However, there is a lot more to law school than just learning the law. Although you will learn some law while you are in law school, the real reason that you came to law school was to learn to think like a lawyer. Thus, the primary skills you will need to teach yourself while you are in law school are how to do legal analysis and synthesis. You need to be able to look at a statute and a group of cases and determine what the law is and how it might be applied in a particular situation.

D. GOOD LEGAL READERS PLACE STATUTES AND CASES THAT THEY READ INTO THEIR HISTORICAL, SOCIAL, ECONOMIC, POLITICAL, AND LEGAL CONTEXTS

Good legal readers understand that statutes are usually enacted to solve a problem or to promote certain interests and that judicial decisions reflect, at least in part, the time and place in which they were written. As a consequence, in reading statutes and cases, good legal readers place those statutes and cases in their historical, social, economic, political, and legal contexts. They note the date that the statute was enacted and amended (if applicable) and the year in which the case was decided. They think about the social and economic conditions during those periods and about the political issues that were in the headlines when the statute was enacted or amended or the case was decided. Finally, they place the case in its larger legal context. They determine how the particular issue fits into the broader area of law, they note whether the decision is from an intermediate court of appeals or from the highest court in the jurisdiction, and they read the court's decision in light of the standard of review that the court applied. Was the court deciding the issue *de novo*, or was it simply looking to see whether there was sufficient evidence to support the jury's verdict?

PRACTICE POINTER

If you do not know what the phrase *de novo* means, look it up in a print or online dictionary. When you use the online link on FindLaw, you retrieve the following information:

> [de-'no-vo, da-]
> Medieval Latin, literally, from (the) new
> : over again: as if for the first time: as
> a: allowing independent appellate determination of issues (as of fact or law)
> Example: a de novo review
> b: allowing complete retrial upon new evidence
> (compare abuse of discretion clearly erroneous)
>
> Note: A *de novo* review is an in-depth review. Decisions of federal administrative agencies are generally subject to *de novo* review in the United States District Courts, and some lower state court decisions are subject to *de novo* review at the next level.

Reprinted with permission.

In reading the case that is set out in the examples in this chapter, the professor placed the case in its historical, social, and political context. First, she noted that the case was an old one. It was decided by the Maine Supreme Judicial Court in 1912. Second, she noted that, in 1912, $1,100 would have been a substantial amount of money. Third, she considered the social climate in 1912: the role of women and their rights and the public's attitudes about "religious cults." She knew that in 1912 women had far fewer rights than they do today. For instance, it was often the husband who determined where the couple lived and what religion they practiced. What she did not know was how religious cults were viewed. In 1912 did people view religious cults in the same way that most people view them today? Were cults seen as a problem? How did these factors influence the court's decision and the way it wrote its opinion?

You need to think about the cases that you read in similar ways. When you are reading cases, pay close attention to the dates of the decisions and the courts that issued them. If you read the cases in chronological order, can you discern a trend? Over the last five, twenty-five, or fifty years have the rules or the way the courts apply those rules changed? If the answer is yes, what social, economic, or political events might account for those changes? In contrast, if you arrange the decisions by jurisdiction, does a pattern appear? For example, do industrial states tend to take one approach and more rural states another? Are some jurisdictions more conservative while others more liberal? If you read between the lines, what do you think motivated the judges and persuaded them to decide the case in one way rather than another?

E. GOOD LEGAL READERS "JUDGE" THE STATUTES AND CASES THAT THEY READ

As a beginning law student, you may be tempted to "accept" everything you read. You may be thinking, who am I to judge the soundness of a Supreme Court Justice's analysis or Congress's choice of a particular word or phrase? Do not give in to this temptation. If you are going to be a good legal reader, you need to question and evaluate everything you read.

In judging the cases that you read, make sure you do more than evaluate the facts. Although in the following example William engages in some evaluation, it is the evaluation of a non-lawyer. He evaluates the witness's testimony but not the court's choice of rule, application of the rules to the facts, or reasoning. Once again, the text of the case is set out using a regular typeface and William's thoughts are in italics.

EXAMPLE **Excerpt from William's Think Aloud**

There was evidence that the plaintiff had been ashore a number of times, had been on numerous outings and had been treated as a guest during her stay aboard the yacht.

So at this point I'm getting a picture of what happened . . . I'm not sure though. There is evidence that the plaintiff had been ashore so at this point I'm thinking was she really held against her will. So I have doubts . . . doubts about the plaintiff's story at this point.

According to the uncontradicted evidence, at no time did anyone physically restrain the plaintiff except for the defendant's refusal, once the plaintiff announced her decision to quit the yacht, to let the plaintiff use a small boat to take herself, her children, and her belongings ashore.

Well . . . the defendant by this point isn't really stopping the plaintiff from leaving.

Throughout the entire episode the plaintiff's husband was with her and repeatedly tried to persuade her to change her mind and remain with the sect.

At this point, mentally, I think . . . I don't think the plaintiff's story holds water . . . that's what I am thinking. Because her husband was there so maybe you, there's in my mind that her story doesn't hold water. So I am thinking at this point that the court might end up reversing her position.

In contrast, the professor evaluated the court's conclusion and reasoning. After she finished reading the case, the professor made the following comments. (Note how the professor talks about the elements of the tort and how she poses a hypothetical.)

EXAMPLE **Excerpt from Professor's Think Aloud**

I'm not sure that the plaintiff proved all of the elements of false imprisonment. For example, I'm not sure that the plaintiff proved that the defendant intended to confine the plaintiff. If I remember correctly, [pause] on a number of occasions he allowed her to go ashore. He just wouldn't let her use the small boat to take her children and their things ashore. It would have been interesting to know what would have happened if a boat had come to get the plaintiff. Would the defendant have let her go? If he would have, there wouldn't have been false imprisonment [pause]. The facts may, however, support a finding that the defendant's actions resulted in confinement. In those days, the plaintiff may not have had a way to contact anyone on shore to ask them to come get her. Although the court may have reached the right result, I wish Judge Savage had done more analysis [pause]. I get the feeling that he had made up his mind, maybe he didn't like cults, and then just tried to justify his conclusion.

F. GOOD LEGAL READERS READ FOR A SPECIFIC PURPOSE

The reading you do for your law school classes is very different from the reading you will do in practice. In law school, you read so you will be prepared for class. Consider the following comment made by James.

When I read cases, I usually read them not for briefing cases per se, but more out of fear of being called on in class. I don't want to look like a fool so I just want to know the basic principles.

In contrast, in practice, you will read for a specific purpose. For example, you will read to keep up to date in an area of law, to find the answer to a question a client has posed, to find statutes or cases to support your client's position, or to find holes in your opponent's arguments.

In reading the statutes and cases for your legal writing assignments, read not as a student, but as a lawyer. Initially, read to find out what the law is. Analyze the statutes and cases that you have found, and then put the pieces together. Then read the cases as the parties and the court would read them. Begin by putting yourself in your client's position. How can your client use the statutes and cases to support its position? Put yourself in the other side's shoes. How could the other side use the same statutes and cases to support its position? Finally, put yourself in the court's position. If you were the judge, how would you read the statutes and cases?

G. GOOD LEGAL READERS UNDERSTAND THAT STATUTES AND CASES CAN BE READ IN MORE THAN ONE WAY

Different people have different beliefs about text. While some people believe that there is a right way to read each statute or case, others believe that most statutes and cases can be read in more than one way. For those in the first group, the meaning of a particular text is fixed. For those in the second group, the meaning of a particular text is "constructed" by juries and judges and the attorneys who practice before them.

As a general rule, the students who seem to have the easiest time in their first year of law school are those students who believe that statutes and cases can be read in more than one way, that the meaning of a particular text is socially constructed. These students have an easier time seeing how each side might interpret a particular statute and in stating a rule so it favors their client's position. When they talk about a court's holding, they refer to it as "a holding" and not "the holding."

If you are a student who believes that meaning is fixed, be aware of how your belief system is affecting the way you read statutes and cases and the way you make arguments. In reading cases, can you see how both the plaintiff and the defendant might be able to use the same case to support its argument? In making arguments, are you able to see what the other side might argue and how you might be able to respond to those arguments? Are you spending too much time looking for the correct answer and not enough time creating that answer? In contrast, if you are a student who believes that meaning is socially constructed, be careful that you do not become cynical or only a hired gun. Although there may be many ways of reading a particular statute or case, not all of those readings will lead to a "just" result.

In closing, keep in mind that learning to read, think, and write like a lawyer takes time. There are no crash courses, shortcuts, or magic wands. Instead, you will learn to read and think like a lawyer through trial and error and by observing how real lawyers—not T.V. lawyers—read and think about statutes and cases.

H. EXERCISE

Using the think aloud that you did as an exercise at the end of Chapter 4 (see section 4.D), diagnose your own strengths and weaknesses as a legal reader.

1. Did you read what was on the page? Did you skip words, read in words, or misread words? Did you look up words that you did not know?
2. If you did not understand the opinion, or a part of it, did you read and reread until you did?
3. Did you engage in synthesis? For example, did you compare the court's decision in *Shurman* (the case set out in section 4.D) with the court's decision in *Thompson* (the case set out in Chart 4.3)? Did both cases involve the same

issue? Are the decisions consistent? Did both courts rely on the same authorities? Did both courts employ the same reasoning?

4. Did you put *Shurman* in its historical, political, social, economic, and legal context? Is *Shurman* a relatively old or a relatively new case? Was there anything going on at the time that *Shurman* was decided that might have influenced the court? Have political, social, or economic conditions changed since *Shurman* was decided? How are the issues that were raised in *Shurman* related to other legal issues?
5. Did you evaluate the court's decision? Did the majority apply the rule or rules that it set out? Is the majority's reasoning sound? Is the approach that is set out in the concurring opinion better or worse than the approach set out in the majority opinion? Is the result "just"?
6. In reading the opinion, what role did you assume? Did you think about how you might use the case if you were representing a client who wanted to challenge service of process? If you were representing a client who wanted to argue that service was proper? If you were a trial court judge?
7. Is there more than one way to read the court's opinion? What would be a narrow reading of the court's holding? A broad reading of the court's holding?

CHAPTER 6

Drafting Memos

More likely than not, one of your first assignments as an intern, extern, or associate will be to research a legal issue and prepare a memo for your supervising attorney. Sometimes, your supervising attorney will give you several days to complete the assignment and will want you to prepare a formal memo; at other times, the attorney needs the answer "now," and wants not a formal memo but just an email in which you set out your analysis and conclusion.

So that you are ready for practice, this chapter and the following four chapters walk you through the process of writing both formal memos and shorter memos, which we call e-memos. Because they are an effective tool for teaching you to think like a lawyer, we begin by showing you how to write a formal memo: In Chapter 7, we show you how to write a formal memo using a "script" format, in Chapter 8 [Laurel Currie Oates and Anne Enquist, Just Memos: Preparing for Practice, 4th Ed.,] we show you how to write a formal memo using an "integrated" format, and in Chapter 8 we talk about other types of formal memos. Then, in Chapter 10 [Laurel Currie Oates and Anne Enquist, Just Memos: Preparing for Practice, 4th Ed.,], we explain how you can use what you have learned to write shorter, less formal e-memos.

PRACTICE POINTER

So how difficult can it be to write a memo? Unfortunately, if the memo is a legal memo, it can be very difficult. To write an effective memo, you need to know how to do legal research; how to analyze and synthesize statutes, regulations, and cases; how to construct arguments; how to evaluate the relative merits of different arguments; and how to write about complex issues clearly and concisely.

A. AUDIENCE

For an objective, or office, memo, your primary audience is other attorneys in your office. In most instances, a more experienced attorney asks a law student or newer attorney to research an issue and write a memo setting out not only the law but also how that law applies to a particular situation, for example, how the law might apply in a particular client's case. While sometimes a copy of the memo will be sent to the client, memos are, if appropriate precautions are taken, attorney work product and are not, therefore, discoverable. Consequently, neither an opposing party nor the courts have a right to see these memos.

B. PURPOSE

Your primary purpose in writing an office memo is to give the attorneys in your law office the information they need to evaluate a case, advise a client, or draft another document, for example, a complaint, brief, or contract. Thus, your memo needs to be objective. In drafting the statement of facts, include both the facts that favor your client and the facts that favor the other side. In addition, make sure that your issue statement, your summaries of the general and specific rules, and your descriptions of the analogous cases are neutral. Most importantly, in setting out the arguments, give appropriate weight to each side's arguments and, in setting out your conclusions, be candid.

C. CONVENTIONS

Because objective memos are in-house documents, there are no rules governing their format. As a result, the format used for a memo varies from office to office and even from lawyer to lawyer. In addition, the practice of law is changing. While historically lawyers wanted longer, more formal memos, today many lawyers prefer shorter memos that are either imbedded in or attached to an email. These less formal memos save supervising lawyers time and save clients money, both important efficiencies in today's law firm.

Therefore, before writing a memo, ask the attorney who is assigning the project the following questions:

1. Should I prepare a formal memo or a less formal, shorter "e-memo"?
2. About how much time should I spend on this project?
3. What research resources may I use (e.g., can I use Lexis Advance® and WestlawNextTM)?

PRACTICE POINTER

aAs an intern or clerk, you also need to know what types of questions you should not ask. Do not, for example, ask how many cases you should include in the memo. Writing a memo is not a school assignment. If the attorney knew how many cases were relevant, he or she would not have asked you to do the research and write the memo.

D. SAMPLE MEMOS

In the first two examples set out below, we show the final drafts of the memos that we discuss in Chapters 7 and 8 [Laurel Currie Oates and Anne Enquist, Just Memos: Preparing for Practice, 4th Ed.,]. While both examples involve a single issue that requires an elements analysis, the examples differ in two ways. In the first example, the writer sets out the facts before the issue statement and brief answer and organizes the discussion section using what we call a script format. In contrast, in the second example, the writer sets out the issue statement first, does not include a brief answer, and organizes the discussion section using an integrated format. (For more on organizing the discussion section using a script format, see Chapter 8. For more on organizing the discussion section using an integrated format, see Chapter 8. For a discussion of memos requiring other types of analysis, see Chapter 8.)

The third, fourth, and fifth examples are e-memos that provide the attorney with a "quick" answer to his or her question. Once again, the format varies: Because e-memos are in-house memos, there are no rules governing the format. You do, however, want to present the information in the order in which the attorney expects to see it: rules before examples of how those rules have been applied in analogous cases and rules and analogous cases before your analysis and conclusion.

The first time that you read the examples, focus on the content. What is the issue? What is the law? How does that law apply in the client's situation? The second time that you read the examples, focus on organization. How is the memo organized? How is each subsection organized? The last time that you read the examples, focus on the writing. Have the writers used what is commonly known as legalese? If they haven't, how would you describe the tone and the writing style?

PRACTICE POINTER

More likely than not, once you begin applying for jobs, you will need a writing sample. Because some employers allow first-year students to use a memo that they prepared as part of a class, you may be able to use one of your legal writing memos as a writing sample. Accordingly, make sure that you understand what information needs to go into a memo and why that information needs to be presented in a particular order and in particular ways. In addition, make sure that your analysis is sophisticated and that your writing is clear, concise, and correct.

1. *Sample Formal Memo 1*

For a description of the process involved in writing this memo,[1] see Chapter 7.

1. Because this memo was written for a Florida attorney and involves an issue of Florida law, it uses the Florida citation rules. See Fla. R. Civ. P. 9.800, *available at* http://www.floridasupremecourt.org/decisions/barrules.shtml.

To: Christina Galeano
From: Legal Intern
Date: September 9, 2013
Re: Elaine Olsen, Case No. 13-478
Service of Process, Usual Place of Abode; Notification of Contents

Statement of Facts

Elaine Olsen has contacted our office asking for assistance in overturning an order terminating her parental rights. You have asked me to determine whether the service of process was valid.

On February 1, 2013, Ms. Olsen entered an inpatient drug treatment program in Miami, Florida. She remained in the program until March 27, 2013, when she moved into a residential treatment house for recovering addicts.

During April, May, and June 2013, Ms. Olsen was a full-time resident at the residential treatment house. She had a bedroom in the house, ate her meals there, and had some of her possessions there. In addition, when she applied for jobs, she listed the treatment house address as her address.

Beginning in July 2013, Ms. Olsen began spending less time at the treatment house and more time with her sister, Elizabeth Webster, who is 32. Both Ms. Olsen's sister and the manager of the halfway house will testify that, during July and August 2013, Ms. Olsen spent weeknights at the treatment house and Friday, Saturday, and Sunday nights at her sister's house. Because she was spending time at her sister's house, Ms. Olsen moved some of her clothing and personal effects into her sister's house.

On Wednesday, July 24, 2013, a process server went to Ms. Webster's house and asked for Elaine Olsen. When Ms. Webster told the process server that "Elaine isn't here today," the process server handed the summons to Ms. Webster and told her that Ms. Olsen "needed to go to court."

Ms. Webster will testify that she never gave the summons to her sister. Because she thought that the papers related to some of Ms. Olsen's unpaid bills, she simply put the summons in a shoebox in the kitchen with a stack of Ms. Olsen's other mail. Ms. Olsen says she never received the summons and, as a result, did not respond. The return of service is regular on its face.

Ms. Olsen has been employed since August 1, 2013, and she has lived in her own apartment since September 1, 2013. She has her sister's address on her driver's license.

There is nothing in the record that indicates whether the State tried to personally serve Ms. Olsen or whether it tried to serve her at the halfway house.

Issue

Under Florida's service of process statute, was Ms. Olsen properly served when (1) during the month when service was made, Ms. Olsen spent weeknights at a residential treatment house where she had a room, ate meals, and kept belongings, and spent Friday, Saturday, and Sunday nights at her sister's house, where she had some belongings; (2) Ms. Olsen listed the treatment house address on job applications but her sister's address on her driver's license; (3) service was made on Ms. Olsen's 32-year-old sister on a Wednesday at Ms. Olsen's sister's house; (4) the process server told Ms. Olsen's sister that Ms. Olsen needed to go to court; and (5) Ms. Olsen's sister did not give the summons and petition to Ms. Olsen, and Ms. Olsen states that she did not receive notice?

Brief Answer

Probably not. Because the return is regular on its face, Ms. Olsen has the burden of proving that she was not properly served. Because the petition was left with Ms. Olsen's 32-year-old sister at the sister's house, Ms. Olsen will have to concede that service was made on a person 15 years or older who was living at the house at which the service was made. In addition, because the process server told Ms. Olsen's sister that Ms. Olsen needed to go to court, more likely than not the court will decide that the person served was informed of the contents of the documents. However, because Ms. Olsen can present evidence that establishes that she was staying at the residential treatment house on the day that service was made, the court may decide that the petition was not left at Ms. Olsen's usual place of abode.

Discussion

The Florida courts have repeatedly stated that the fundamental purpose of service of process is to give defendants notice of claims that have been filed against them and to provide them with an opportunity to defend their rights. *E.g., Shurman v. Atl. Mortg. & Inv. Corp.*, 795 So. 2d 952, 953-54 (Fla. 2001). Because these rights are so important, the courts strictly construe and enforce statutes governing service of process. *Id.* at 954.

In the present case, the relevant portion of the statute reads as follows:

> (1) (a) Service of original process is made by delivering a copy of it to the person to be served with a copy of the complaint, petition, or other initial pleading or paper or by leaving the copies at his or her usual place of abode with any person residing therein who is 15 years of age or older and informing the person of their contents. . . .

§ 48.031 (1) (a), Fla. Stat. (2013).

Although the party seeking to invoke the jurisdiction of the court has the burden of proving that service was proper, if the return is regular on its face, the courts presume that the service was valid. *Busman v. State, Dep't of Revenue,* 905 So. 2d 956, 958 (Fla. 3d DCA 2005); *Thompson v. State, Dep't of Revenue,* 867 So. 2d 603, 605 (Fla. 1st DCA 2004). In such instances, the party challenging the service has the burden of presenting clear and convincing evidence that the service was invalid. *Id.*

In this case, Ms. Olsen may be able to present clear and convincing evidence that the petition was not left at her usual place of abode. However, if the court decides that the petition was left at her usual place of abode, Ms. Olsen will have to concede that the summons was left with a person 15 years or older who was residing at the house where service was made. In addition, although Ms. Olsen can argue that her sister was not informed of the contents of the documents, it is unlikely that she can meet her burden of proof.

A. Usual Place of Abode

Although the statute does not define the phrase "usual place of abode," the courts have said that a defendant's usual place of abode is the place "where the defendant was actually living at the time of service." *E.g., Shurman v. Atl. Mortg. & Inv. Corp.*, 795 So. 2d 952, 953-54 (Fla. 2001); *Busman v. State, Dep't of Revenue*, 905 So. 2d 956, 957 (Fla. 3d DCA 2005).

In an early case, and one of the few published decisions in which the court concluded that the defendant had been served at his usual place of abode, the court emphasizes that, at the time of service, defendant's wife and children were living at the apartment where service was made. *State ex rel. Merritt v. Heffernan*, 195 So. 145, 146-47 (Fla. 1940). In that case, the defendant had relocated his family to Florida two months before service was made and had twice visited them while they were in Florida, the second time leaving the apartment to return to Minnesota just an hour before service was made. *Id.* Although the defendant argued that his usual place of abode was Minnesota, where he had an office, paid taxes, and voted, the court disagreed, stating that "[w]e do not hold the view that Florida was the permanent residence of the defendant, but we do feel that in the circumstance reflected in the record, it was his usual place of abode . . . ." *Id.* at 148.

In contrast, in the more recent cases, the courts have emphasized that it is not enough that the complaint or petition is left with a relative. *See, e.g., Busman*, 905 So. 2d at 947; *Torres v. Arnco Const., Inc.*, 867 So. 2d 583 (Fla. 5th DCA 2004). For example, in *Busman*, the court concluded that service of process was not valid even though the summons and complaint had been left with the defendant's half brother. *Id.* at 958. Similarly, in *Torres*, the court concluded that service had not been made at the defendant's usual place of abode when, after trying unsuccessfully to serve the defendant at his New York apartment, the plaintiff served the defendant's mother at her home in Florida. *Id.* at 585, 587. Although the defendant's mother told the process server that her son "would be home soon," the court decided that this statement was, at best, ambiguous. *Id.* at 585; *accord Portfolio Recovery Assocs., LLC v. Gonzalez*, 951 So. 2d 1037, 1038 (Fla. 3d DCA 2007) (service was not made at the defendants' usual place of abode when the summons and complaint were left with a woman who was the mother of one defendant and the mother-in-law of the other defendant, but the defendants had not lived at the residence for five years).

Ms. Olsen can make three arguments to support her assertion that her sister's house was not her usual place of abode. First, Ms. Olsen will argue that, under the plain language of the statute, her sister's house was not her usual place of abode. As the courts have stated, service must be made at the place where the defendant was actually living at the time the summons and complaint were served. In this case, the summons and complaint were served on a weekday, and on weekdays Ms. Olsen was actually living at the residential treatment house.

Second, Ms. Olsen will argue that the facts in her case are more like the facts in *Busman* and *Torres* than the facts in *Heffernan.* Like Mr. Busman, who produced a lease that corroborated his testimony that he was not living with his half brother on the day that the summons and complaint were served, Ms. Olsen can produce evidence that establishes that on the day she was served she was living at the residential treatment house. Both Ms. Olsen's sister and the manager of the residential treatment house have said they will testify that during June and July Ms. Olsen lived at the treatment house during the week and stayed with her sister only on weekends. In the alternative, Ms. Olsen can argue that the facts in her case are even stronger than the facts in *Torres.* While Mr. Torres's mother's statement that Mr. Torres "would be home soon" suggested that Mr. Torres would be returning to his mother's house that day, Ms. Olsen's sister told the process server that Ms. Olsen "isn't here today." In addition, Ms. Olsen can distinguish *Heffernan*: Although Mr. Heffernan had been at his family's apartment only an hour before the summons and complaint were served, Ms. Olsen had not been at her sister's house for several days.

Finally, Ms. Olsen can argue that, as a matter of public policy, the court should decide that the summons and petition were not left at her usual place of abode. The courts have stated that the statute should be narrowly construed, and this policy is particularly important in cases in which the State is seeking to terminate a mother's parental rights. In addition, this is not a case in which the State tried but could not locate Ms. Olsen: There is no evidence that the State tried to serve Ms. Olsen at the residential treatment house.

In response, the State will argue that Ms. Olsen was served at one of her usual places of abode. The courts have not required that the plaintiff be living at the house where the summons and complaint are served on the day on which the service is made. Therefore, while Ms. Olsen may not have been at her sister's house on the day that the summons and complaint were served, she had been there the previous weekend, and she was there the following weekend. In addition, Ms. Olsen had possessions at her sister's house.

Thus, the State will argue that the facts in this case are much stronger than the facts in *Heffernan.* While in *Heffernan,* Mr. Heffernan visited his family only "twice during the season," Ms. Olsen lived at her sister's house on weekends. In addition, while Mr. Heffernan had another permanent residence, Ms. Olsen was staying at a halfway house, which, by definition, is only a temporary residence. Finally, while in *Heffernan* there was no indication that Mr. Heffernan listed the Florida address on any documents, Ms. Olsen listed her sister's address on her driver's license, and there is evidence indicating that Ms. Olsen received other types of mail at her sister's house.

The State will use these same facts to distinguish *Torres.* While in *Torres,* Mr. Torres presented evidence establishing that his permanent residence was in New York, in the present case, Ms. Olsen did not have a permanent residence. In the five months before service, she had been an inpatient in a treatment facility, she had lived at the halfway house, and she had lived with her sister. The plaintiff can also distinguish *Shurman* and *Busman*. While in *Shurman* and *Busman* the record indicated that the defendants had not lived at the house where service had been made for months or years, in this case, Ms. Olsen admits that she stayed at her sister's house on the weekend before her sister was served.

Finally, the State will argue that, because the return was regular on its face, Ms. Olsen has the burden of proving, by clear and convincing evidence, that her sister's house was not her usual place of abode. In this instance, Ms. Olsen has not met that burden. When there is evidence that the defendant was in fact living at the house where service was made, the courts should not require plaintiffs to determine which house the defendant was living at on any particular day.

While both sides have strong arguments, the court will probably conclude that the summons and petition were not left at Ms. Olsen's usual place of abode. In the more recent cases, the courts have emphasized that it is not enough that service is made on a relative and concluded that the service was invalid when the defendant presented evidence establishing that he or she was not actually living at the place where the summons and complaint were left. Therefore, we can argue that it is not enough that the summons and petition were left with Ms. Olsen's sister: Service was invalid because, on the day that service was made, Ms. Olsen was not actually living with her sister. The problem, of course, is that Ms. Olsen stayed with her sister the weekend preceding and following service. Although these facts make this case weaker than the analogous cases, the court may be persuaded by the fact that this case involves termination of parental rights, that there is no evidence that the State tried to serve Ms. Olsen personally or at the treatment house, and that Ms. Olsen did not have actual notice.

B. Person 15 Years Old or Older Residing Therein

In addition to leaving the summons at the defendant's usual place of abode, the process server must leave the summons with a person 15 years old or older residing therein. Because Ms. Webster is 32 and lives at the house where the summons and complaint were left, Ms. Olsen will have to concede that the summons was left with a person residing therein who is at least 15 years old.

C. Informed of Contents

[Not shown]

Conclusion

Because of the strong public policy in favor of ensuring that defendants receive notice of actions that have been filed against them, the court will probably decide that the substituted service of process was not valid and vacate the judgment terminating Ms. Olsen's parental rights.

Ms. Olsen will have to concede that her sister, Ms. Webster, is a person of suitable age and that Ms. Webster was residing at the house where the service was made. In addition, because the process server told Ms. Webster that

Ms. Olsen needed to go to court, it seems unlikely that Ms. Olsen will be able to prove that Ms. Webster was not informed of the contents.

Ms. Olsen may, however, be able to prove that the summons and complaint were not served at her usual place of abode. In the more recent cases, the courts have concluded that service made on a relative was invalid when the defendants produced evidence establishing that they were not actually living with that relative on the day that service was made. While in most of these cases the defendants had not lived at the house where service was made for several months or several years, in the present case the court may be swayed by three facts: This case involves the termination of Ms. Olsen's parental rights; there is no evidence that the State tried to personally serve Ms. Olsen or that it tried to serve Ms. Olsen at the treatment house; and Ms. Olsen states that she did not receive notice.

2. *Sample Formal Memo 2*

For a description of the process involved in writing this memo,[2] see Chapter 8 [Laurel Currie Oates and Anne Enquist, Just Memos: Preparing for Practice, 4th Ed.,].

To:	Julia Fishler
From:	Legal Intern
Date:	November 1, 2013
Re:	Michael Garcia Adverse possession; Washington law

Issue

Whether Doctors and Nurses Who Care (DNWC) has obtained a right to Mr. Garcia's land through adverse possession when (1) it has used Mr. Garcia's land for campouts several nights a week for eight weeks each summer since 1997; (2) to facilitate these campouts, DNWC has maintained the campsites, fire area, outhouse, and dock; (3) in 2001, DNWC sent a letter to Mr. Garcia asking him whether it could continue using the land for campouts, but Mr. Garcia did not respond to the letter; and (4) Mr. Garcia has paid the taxes but did not visit the land from 1999 until August 2013.

Statement of Facts

Michael Garcia has contacted our office regarding property that he owns in Washington State. Mr. Garcia is concerned that the organization that owns the property next to his, Doctors and Nurses Who Care (DNWC), may be able to claim title to his property through adverse possession.

Mr. Garcia's property is on Lake Chelan, which is in the eastern part of Washington State. Mr. Garcia's grandfather, Eduardo Montoya, purchased

2. Because this memo was written for a Washington attorney and involves an issue of Washington law, it uses the Washington citation rules. *See* Wash. Courts, Style Sheet (Dec. 28, 2010), *available at* http://www.courts.wa.gov/appellate_trial_courts/supreme/?fa=atc_supreme.style.

the two-acre waterfront parcel in 1958, and the Montoya family used the land every summer from 1958 until Eduardo Montoya became ill in the early 1990s. When it used the land, the family would camp on the site and use a small dock for swimming, fishing, and boating. In 1999, Mr. Garcia's grandfather died and left the property to Mr. Garcia. Although Mr. Garcia spent one weekend at the property in fall of 1999, he moved to California in 2000 and did not visit the property until last August. He has, however, continued to pay all of the taxes and assessments.

In 1996, DNWC purchased the five-acre parcel that adjoins Mr. Garcia's property. Since 1997, DNWC has used its land as a summer camp for children with serious illnesses or disabilities. In a typical summer, the DNWC runs two one-week camps for children with cancer, two one-week camps for children who are blind, two one-week camps for children with autism, and two one-week camps for children with diabetes.

Most of the time the children stay in cabins located on the DNWC property. However, DNWC uses Mr. Garcia's property for "campouts." On one night, one group of about 10 children will camp out in tents on Mr. Garcia's property, the next night another group of 10 will camp out on the property, and so on. Thus, DNWC has been using the Garcia property four or five nights a week for eight weeks each summer since 1997. During these campouts, the children pitch and stay in tents, cook over a fire, and use the dock. To facilitate these campouts, DNWC has maintained the campsite, the fire area, the outhouse, and the dock.

In February 2001, DNWC sent Mr. Garcia a letter asking him whether it could continue using his land for campouts. Mr. Garcia was busy and did not respond to the letter. Sometime during the summer of 2001, DNWC posted a no trespassing sign on the dock, and the sign is still there.

Last August, Mr. Garcia visited the property with the intent of spending a few days camping on the lake. When he got there, he discovered the children and their counselors on the property.

After discovering the children on his land, Mr. Garcia went to the DNWC camp headquarters and talked to the director, Dr. Liu, who told Mr. Garcia that it was his understanding that the land belonged to DNWC. Although Mr. Garcia did not spend that night at the property, he did spend the next night there after the children left. DNWC did not ask him to leave.

Although over the years the land around the lake has become more and more developed, the area in which the camp is located is still relatively undeveloped. Most of the property owners use their land only during the summer.

Discussion

The doctrine of adverse possession was developed to assure maximum use of the land, to encourage the rejection of stale claims, and to quiet titles. *Chaplin v. Sanders,* 100 Wn.2d 853, 859-60, 676 P.2d 431 (1984); *see also* William B. Stoebuck, *The Law of Adverse Possession in Washington,* 35 Wash. L. Rev. 53, 53 (1960).

To establish title through adverse possession, the claimant must prove that its possession was (1) exclusive, (2) actual and uninterrupted, (3) open and notorious, and (4) hostile for the statutory period. *ITT Rayonier, Inc. v. Bell*, 112 Wn.2d 754, 757, 774 P.2d 6 (1989); *Chaplin v. Sanders*, 100 Wn.2d 853, 857, 676 P.2d 431 (1984). In this case, the statutory period is 10 years. RCW 4.16.020(1).

Adverse possession is a mixed question of law and fact. *Chaplin*, 100 Wn.2d at 863. Whether the essential facts exist is for the trier of fact to decide; but whether the facts, as found, constitute adverse possession is for the court to determine as a matter of law. *Id.*

In this case, DNWC can easily prove that its possession was open and notorious and exclusive. In addition, it can probably prove that its possession is actual and uninterrupted. The only element that it may not be able to prove is that its possession was hostile.

A. Open and Notorious

A claimant can satisfy the open and notorious element by showing either (1) that the title owner had actual notice of the adverse use throughout the statutory period or (2) that the claimant used the land such that any reasonable person would have thought that the claimant owned it. *Riley v. Andres*, 107 Wn.2d 391, 396, 27 P.3d 618 (2001).

In this case, DNWC can prove both that Mr. Garcia had actual notice of its adverse use and that any reasonable person would have thought that DNWC owned the land. To prove that Mr. Garcia had actual knowledge of DNWC's use of the land, DNWC can offer the letter that it sent to Mr. Garcia in 2001 asking for continuing permission to use his land for campouts. To prove that a reasonable person would have thought that DNWC owned the land, DNWC will point out that it not only used the land for campouts but also maintained the campsites, fire area, outhouse, and dock and posted a no trespassing sign.

B. Actual and Uninterrupted

Although the Washington courts have not set out a test for actual possession, the cases illustrate the types of acts that are needed to establish actual possession. 17 *Wash. Prac., Real Estate: Property Law* § 8.10 (2d ed.).

The courts have held that the claimants had actual possession of rural land when the claimants built a fence and cultivated or pastured up to it, *Faubion v. Elder*, 49 Wn.2d 300, 301 P.2d 153 (1956); cleared the land, constructed and occupied buildings, and planted orchards, *Metro. Bldg. Co. v. Fitzgerald*, 122 Wash. 514, 210 P. 770 (1922); or cleared and fenced the land, planted an orchard, and built a road, *Davies v. Wickstrom*, 56 Wash. 154, 105 P. 454 (1909). In contrast, the courts have held that the claimants did not have actual possession of rural land when they maintained a fence intended to be a cattle fence and not a line fence, *Roy v. Goerz*, 26 Wn. App. 807, 614 P.2d 1308 (1980); erected two signboards and a mailbox and ploughed weeds, *Slater v. Murphy*, 55 Wn.2d 892, 339 P.2d 457 (1959); or occasionally used the land for gardening, piling wood, and mowing hay, *Smith v. Chambers*, 112 Wash. 600, 192 P. 891 (1920). *See generally* 17 *Wash. Prac., Real Estate: Property Law* § 8.10 (2d ed.).

If DNWC had used the land only for occasional campouts, it would have been difficult for it to prove that it had actual possession. However, in addition to using the land for campouts, DNWC maintained the campsites, the fire area, the outhouse, and the dock, and it posted a no trespassing sign. Because DNWC maintained permanent structures and posted the no trespassing sign, more likely than not a court will hold that it had actual possession.

In addition, DNWC's use and maintenance of the campsites, fire area, outhouse, and dock are probably enough to establish that its possession was uninterrupted. In all of the cases in which the claimants maintained and used permanent structures, the courts have held that the use was uninterrupted. For instance, in *Howard v. Kunto*, 3 Wn. App. 393, 477 P.2d 210 (1970), the court held that the claimants' use was continuous even though the claimants used the property only during the summer. As the court noted in that case, "the requisite possession requires such possession and dominion 'as ordinarily marks the conduct of owners in general in holding, managing, and caring for property of like nature and condition.'" *Id.* at 397. Consequently, while Mr. Garcia might be able to argue that DNWC's use of the land was not uninterrupted because it used the land only during the summer months, this argument is a weak one. Because the land is recreational land, DNWC's use of the land only in summer is consistent with how the owners of similar land hold, manage, and care for their property.

C. Exclusive

To establish that its possession was exclusive, the claimant must show that its possession was "of a type that would be expected of an owner . . . ." *ITT Rayonier*, 112 Wn.2d 754, 758, 774 P.2d 6 (1989). Therefore, while sharing possession of the land with the true owner will prevent a claimant from establishing that its possession was exclusive, sharing possession with a tenant or allowing occasional use by a neighbor does not. *Id.*

In this case, Mr. Garcia has stated that he did not visit the property between 1999 and 2013. Thus, during that period, DNWC did not share the property with the true owner. Although DNWC "shared" its use of Mr. Garcia's land with its campers, this fact should not prevent a court from finding that its possession was exclusive. Because the campers used the Garcia land under the supervision of DNWC, they are analogous to tenants.

D. Hostile

While before 1984 the Washington courts considered the claimant's subjective intent in determining whether its use of the land was hostile, since 1984 the claimant's subjective intent has been irrelevant. *Chaplin*, 100 Wn.2d at 860-61 (overruling cases in which the courts had considered the claimant's subjective intent). Accordingly, under current Washington law, the claimant must prove only that it used the land as if it were its own for the statutory period. *Id.; Miller v. Anderson*, 91 Wn. App. 822, 828, 964 P.2d 365 (1998). If the claimant proves that it used the land as if it were its own, the use was hostile unless the true owner can prove that it gave the claimant permission to use the land. *Id.*

Permission can be express or implied. *Miller*, 91 Wn. App. at 829 (case dealt with a prescriptive easement and not adverse possession). The courts infer that the use was permissive if, under the circumstances, it is reasonable to assume that the use was permitted. *Id.* If there was permission, the party claiming adverse possession bears the burden of proving that permission terminated because either (1) the servient estate changed hands through death or alienation or (2) the claimant has asserted a hostile right. *Id.*

In deciding whether a claimant was using the land as if it were its own, the courts consider whether the claimant made improvements to the land, whether the claimant maintained the property, and whether the claimant used the land on a regular basis. *See, e.g., Chaplin*, 100 Wn.2d at 855-56; *Timberlane Homeowners Ass'n, Inc. v. Brame*, 79 Wn. App, 303, 310-11, 901 P.2d 1074 (1995). For example, in *Chaplin*, the court held that the claimants were using the land as if it were their own when the claimants built a road across the disputed land, cleared and maintained the disputed land, installed utility lines, and used the area for recreational activities. *Id.* at 855-56. Similarly, in *Timberlane*, the court held that claimants had used land belonging to the homeowners' association as if it was their own when they built and maintained a fence and a concrete patio and the claimants' children played on the land. *Id.* at 310-11.

In deciding whether the claimants' use was permissive, the courts consider whether the parties are related or have a friendly relationship, whether the improvements benefited both the claimants' and the title owners' property, and whether the title owners allowed the claimants to use the land as a neighborly accommodation. *See, e.g., Granston v. Callahan*, 52 Wn. App. 288, 294-95, 759 P.2d 462 (1988); *Miller v. Jarman*, 2 Wn. App. 994, 471 P.2d 704 (1970). For instance, in *Granston*, the court held that the claimants' use was permissive because the original owners of the two parcels were brothers who worked together to build driveways, walkways, and other improvements that benefited both properties. *Id.* at 294-95. Likewise, in *Miller*, the court held that the use was permissive because the title owners had allowed the claimants, who were their neighbors, to use their driveway as a neighborly accommodation. *Id.* at 998. In contrast, in *Lingvall v. Bartmess*, 97 Wn. App. 245, 256, 982 P.2d 690 (1999), the court held that the antagonistic relationship between two brothers negated a finding that the claimant's use of the land was permissive.

In the Garcia case, the court will probably conclude that DNWC's use of Mr. Garcia's land was hostile.

First, the court will probably conclude that DNWC used Mr. Garcia's land as if it were the true owner. Although DNWC did not build any new structures on Mr. Garcia's land, it maintained the campsites, the fire area, the outhouse, and the dock. In addition, although DNWC did not use the property year-round, it did use the property during the summer, which is how a typical owner would have used the land. As a result, this case is similar to *Chaplin* and *Timberlane*, in which the claimants maintained and used the disputed land as a true owner would have used the land. While in *Chaplin* and *Timberlane* the claimants built new structures (in *Chaplin*, the claimants built a road, and in *Timberlane*, they built a fence and a patio), the courts have held that the claimant does not have to do everything that a title owner might do.

Second, the court will probably conclude that DNWC's use of Mr. Garcia's land was not permissive. Unlike *Granston*, in which the parties were related and had a close relationship, there is no evidence that the members of DNWC are related to Mr. Garcia. In addition, unlike *Miller*, in which the title owners allowed their neighbors to use their driveway as a neighborly accommodation, the typical owner of recreational land does not allow a neighboring property owner to use its land several days a week during the peak season.

While Mr. Garcia can argue that the letter that DNWC sent to him establishes that DNWC's use of the land was permissive, the court will probably reject this argument. More likely than not, the court will conclude that, if Mr. Garcia's grandfather gave DNWC permission to use his land, that permission terminated when his grandfather died. In addition, the court will probably conclude that even if DNWC used Mr. Garcia's land with Mr. Garcia's implied permission from the time of his grandfather's death until it sent the letter in February of 2001, that permission terminated in the summer of 2001 when DNWC posted the no trespassing sign and continued to use the property as its own.

Conclusion

More likely than not, DNWC will be able to establish title to Mr. Garcia's land through adverse possession.

To prove that its possession was open and notorious, DNWC needs to show only that Mr. Garcia had actual notice of its use of his land throughout the statutory period or that it used his land in such a way that any reasonable person would have thought that it owned this land. In this case, DNWC can use the letter that it sent to Mr. Garcia to prove that he had actual notice, and it can show that its use of the land for campouts was such that any reasonable person would have thought that DNWC owned the land.

To prove that its possession was actual and uninterrupted, DNWC needs to show only that it actually used the land and that its use was consistent with how the true owner might have used the land. The case law suggests that DNWC's maintenance of the campsites, fire area, outhouse, and dock were sufficient to establish actual possession. In addition, although DNWC used the land only during the summer months, the court is likely to find that such use was uninterrupted because most owners of recreational land use their land only during certain seasons.

To prove that its use of the land was exclusive, DNWC will have to show that it did not share the land with anyone else. Although we could try to argue that DNWC's use was not exclusive because it allowed campers to use the land, this argument is weak because the campers used the land under DNWC's supervision.

Finally, to prove that its use was hostile, DNWC will have to prove that it used the land as if it were its own and that it did not do so with Mr. Garcia's permission. DNWC's maintenance and use of the property is probably sufficient to establish that it used Mr. Garcia's land as if it were its own.

In addition, DNWC will be able to prove that its use was not permissive. Even if DNWC's initial use of the property was with Mr. Garcia's grandfather's permission, that permission terminated when Mr. Garcia's grandfather died. In addition, although in its 2001 letter DNWC asked Mr. Garcia for permission to continue using the land, DNWC has a strong argument that it did a hostile act that terminated permission when, even after Mr. Garcia did not respond, it continued maintaining and using the property and it posted the no trespassing sign.

Because all of these elements have been met for the statutory period, which is 10 years, it is likely that a court will decide that DNWC has established a right to title to the land through adverse possession.

3. *Sample E-Memo*

You asked me to research Illinois law and determine what the statute of limitations is on actions to recover damages to personal property. The applicable statute is 735 ILCS 5/13-205, which states that the statute of limitations is five years:

> [A]ctions on unwritten contracts, expressed or implied, or on awards of arbitration, or *to recover damages for an injury done to property, real or personal,* or to recover the possession of personal property or damages for the detention or conversion thereof, and all civil actions not otherwise provided for, shall be commenced within 5 years next after the cause of action accrued.

(Emphasis added.)

If you need additional research, please let me know.

4. *Sample E-Memo*

You have asked me to determine whether KOSLaw LLP, must provide one of its employees, Melissa Karimi, with parental leave under the Family and Medical Leave Act (FMLA.) Specifically, the issue is whether Ms. Karimi's worksite is the firm's Des Moines insourcing office,[3] which has 12 employees, or the firm's Chicago office, which has approximately 175 employees. If Ms. Karimi's worksite is Des Moines, she would not be entitled to leave under the FMLA; if her worksite is Chicago, she is entitled to FMLA leave.

To be entitled to leave under the FMLA, an employee must work for an employer that has 50 or more employees working at worksites that are within a 75-mile radius of one another (50/75 rule). 29 U.S.C. § 2611(2)(B)(ii) (2012) According to the Act's legislative history, Congress included the

3. Insourcing is similar to outsourcing. However, instead of sending work to individuals in a different country, the work is sent to individuals who live in another part of the United States.

50/75 rule to protect employers who might not have enough employees within a particular geographic area to cover FMLA leaves. *See Harbert v. Healthcare Serv. Grp., Inc.*, 391 F.3d 1140, 1149 (10th Cir. 2004).

As a general rule, an employee's worksite is the site to which the employee reports to *or*, if the employee does not report to a particular site, the site from which the employee's work is assigned. 29 C.F.R. § 825.111(a) (2013). However, the regulations set out a different test for employees who work from home or who telecommute. In those situations, the employee's worksite is the office where the employee reports *and* from which assignments are given. *Id.* § 825.111(a)(2).

In our case, it is not clear which test applies. Although Ms. Karimi works from home the majority of the time, she does go into the Des Moines office once or twice a week to use the Des Moines office's conferencing technology, to review sensitive documents, or to receive assistance from the IT staff. However, her supervising attorney is in the Chicago office, and she receives her assignment from that attorney and sends her completed work to that attorney, usually via email.

In other cases in which the employee had a connection to more than one worksite, the courts have held that the location of the employee's worksite was a question of fact. *See, e.g., Podkovich v. Glazer's Distrib. of Iowa, Inc.*, 446 F. Supp. 2d 982, 1000-02 (N.D. Iowa 2006) (concluding that there was an issue of fact when a traveling saleswoman physically reported to one worksite but received her assignments from another site); *Collinsworth v. Earthlink/Onemain, Inc.*, CIV.A. 03-2299GTV, 2003 WL 22916461, at *4 (D. Kan. Dec. 4, 2003) (concluding that there was an issue of fact when the plaintiff worked from home, sometimes used a branch office with fewer than 50 people within 75 miles, yet received and delivered her work product to the main office with more than 50 people within 75 miles).

Given the courts' decision in the above cases, if Ms. Karimi files a lawsuit, it is unlikely that a court would grant KOSLaw summary judgment. Instead, the case would have to go to trial, and a jury would have to decide whether the Des Moines or the Chicago office is Ms. Karimi's worksite. If the jury decides that Ms. Karimi reports to the Des Moines office because that is the office that she sometimes uses, that office would be her worksite, and she would not be entitled to FMLA leave. If, however, the jury decides that Ms. Karimi reports to the Chicago office because that it is the office from which she receives her assignments, then she would be entitled to FMLA leave. The result is more uncertain if the jury decides that Ms. Karimi works from home. In that situation, Ms. Karimi's worksite would be the place where she reports to *and* from which she receives her assignments.

Although a jury might find that the Des Moines office is Ms. Karimi's worksite because she "reports" to that office once or twice a week, I recommend that the firm grant Ms. Karimi the leave she has requested. Litigation is expensive, the type of leave that Ms. Karimi is requesting is unpaid leave, and the policy underlying the rule does not apply in this case. Because the Des Moines office is an insourcing office, the work does not need to be done by someone in Des Moines. It can be done by someone in the Chicago office or in any of the firm's other offices.

Please let me know whether you have any more questions or need additional research.

5. Sample E-Memo

TO: Supervising Attorney
FROM: Jessica Burns, Intern
RE: Amanda Nickerson, Admissibility of Prior Convictions for Purpose of Impeachment

You have asked me to determine whether any of Ms. Nickerson's prior convictions can be used to impeach her credibility as a witness in our upcoming products liability trial. I have determined that Ms. Nickerson's conviction for the possession of stolen property is admissible for purposes of impeachment.

The Washington Rules of Evidence state that, for the purpose of attacking the credibility of a witness in a civil case, evidence of a prior criminal conviction can be used to impeach the credibility of a witness if the information is elicited from the witness or established by public record during examination of the witness. ER 609(a). However, evidence of a prior conviction can be used for the purpose of impeachment *only if*

> the crime (1) was punishable by death or imprisonment in excess of 1 year under the law under which the witness was convicted, and the court determines that the probative value of admitting this evidence outweighs the prejudice to the party against whom the evidence is offered, or (2) involved dishonesty or false statement, regardless of the punishment.

ER 609(a)(1)-(2).

The Washington Rules of Evidence have also imposed a time limit on the admissibility of criminal convictions for the purposes of impeachment of a witness:

> [E]vidence of a conviction under this rule is not admissible if a period of more than 10 years has elapsed since the date of the conviction or of the release of the witness from the confinement imposed for that conviction, whichever is the later date, unless the court determines, in the interests of justice, that the probative value of the conviction supported by specific facts and circumstances substantially outweighs its prejudicial effect.

ER 609(b).

1. Assault Charge

Ms. Nickerson's assault charge was an offense punishable by more than one year: Assault in the second degree is punishable by no more than 10 years in prison, RCW 9A.36.021. However, because Ms. Nickerson's assault conviction is more than 10 years old, evidence of the conviction is not admissible unless the court determines that the probative value of the conviction *substantially* outweighs the prejudicial effect of admitting the evidence.

In this case, a products liability case, the prior conviction has no probative value. The fact that Ms. Nickerson committed an assault is not relevant to whether she was injured by a defective product. In addition, the admission of the conviction could be prejudicial because if the jury hears about the conviction, it may view Ms. Nickerson in a less favorable light. Consequently, because the probative value does not outweigh the prejudicial effect, the court is unlikely to admit evidence of the assault conviction.

2. DUI Conviction

The courts have held that a DUI conviction is not admissible for the purposes of impeachment. *State v. Kilgore*, 107 Wn. App. 160, 186, 26 P.3d 308 (2001), *aff'd*, 147 Wn.2d 288 (2002).

3. Possession of Stolen Property

Ms. Nickerson's conviction for possession of stolen property in 2009 could be used to impeach her credibility. Although Ms. Nickerson's conviction for possession of stolen property was not punishable by more than one year in jail, the courts have held that possession of stolen property is admissible because it is a crime of dishonesty. *State v. McKinsey*, 116 Wn.2d 911, 912, 801 P.2d 908 (1991).

In conclusion, it is unlikely that a court would allow the defendant to use either Ms. Nickerson's assault charge or DUI charge to impeach Ms. Nickerson. However, the court could admit Ms. Nickerson's conviction for possession of stolen property.

Please let me know whether you have any additional questions or concerns.

CHAPTER 7

Drafting Memo 1

Although you are still a first-year law student, you have just gotten a part-time job at a local law firm. On your first day, your supervising attorney stops by your desk and asks you to help her with one of her cases.

A. THE ASSIGNMENT

Assignments come in different shapes and sizes. While sometimes the attorney will give you the facts orally, at other times you may need to find the facts, pulling them from documents in the client's file or from other sources. In this instance, however, the attorney has set out the facts, and the issue that she wants you to research, in the following memo.

To: Legal Intern

From: Christina Galeano

Date: September 9, 2013

Re: Elaine Olsen, Case No. 13-478

Elaine Olsen has requested our help in overturning an order terminating her parental rights.

- ☐ Ms. Olsen says she never received the summons and, as a result, did not respond.
- ☐ On Wednesday, July 24, 2013, a process server went to Ms. Webster's house and asked for Elaine Olsen. (Ms. Webster is Ms. Olsen's sister.) When Ms. Webster told the process server that "Elaine isn't here today," the process server handed what was probably a summons and complaint to Ms. Webster and told Ms. Webster that Ms. Olsen "needed to go to court."

- ☐ On February 1, 2013, Ms. Olsen entered an inpatient drug treatment program in Miami, Florida. She remained in the program until March 27, 2013, when she moved into a "halfway" house. The residential treatment house was a four-bedroom house in a residential neighborhood. Up to eight women live in the house for three to twelve months while they make the transition from inpatient treatment to living on their own. The house is staffed 24/7; staff members provide counseling; enforce house rules, including no drug or alcohol use; and handle administrative duties.
- ☐ During April, May, and June, Ms. Olsen was a full-time resident at the residential treatment house. She had a bedroom in the house, ate her meals there, and had some of her possessions there.
- ☐ Beginning in July 2013, Ms. Olsen began spending less time at the residential treatment house and more time with her sister, Elizabeth Webster. During July and August 2013, Ms. Olsen usually spent weeknights at the residential treatment house and Friday, Saturday, and Sunday nights at her sister's house. Because she was spending time at her sister's house, Ms. Olsen moved some of her clothing and personal effects into her sister's house.
- ☐ Ms. Webster is 32. She will testify that she never gave the summons to her sister. Because she thought that the papers related to some of Ms. Olsen's unpaid bills, she simply put them in a shoebox in the kitchen with a stack of Ms. Olsen's other mail.
- ☐ During April and May 2013, Ms. Olsen put the residential treatment house address on employment applications. However, her driver's license showed her sister's address as her address.
- ☐ On September 1, 2013, Ms. Olsen moved into her own apartment. Since August 1, 2013, she has worked part-time.
- ☐ I looked at the return on the service of process and everything appears to be in order. Thus, please assume that the return of service is regular on its face.
- ☐ There is nothing in the record that indicates whether the State tried to personally serve Ms. Olsen or whether it tried to serve her at the residential treatment house.

As the first step, I need to determine whether the service of process is valid under the applicable Florida statute or statutes. Therefore, please research the rules relating to substituted service of process in Florida, and prepare an objective memo in which you set out the applicable rules and apply those rules to the facts of this case.

B. RESEARCHING THE LAW

After reading, and rereading, the assignment, your next step is to do the research. See the electronic supplement for step-by-step instructions on how to research an issue governed by a state statute using free sources, Lexis Advance®,

WestlawNext™, Bloomberg Law, Lexis.com®, and Westlaw® Classic. You can access the electronic supplement by going to *http://www.aspenlawschool.com/books/oates_legalwritinghandbook/* and typing in the access code that is on the card that came with this book. One you are on the website, click on the links to Sections 4.C.1-4.3.7.

PRACTICE POINTER

You can often research an issue governed by a state statute using free sources: You can find a copy of the applicable statutory sections on the state legislature's website, and you can find copies of cases on Google® Scholar. You will, however, need to cite check using *Shepard's*®, KeyCite®, or BCite. Before doing other research on a fee-based service, get permission from your supervising attorney.

Do not, however, treat research as a separate stage in the process. As you research, read and analyze the statutes and cases that you find, determining whether they help answer the question or questions that you were asked to research. In addition, as soon as possible, begin creating a research log in which you record and organize the information that you find during your research. This log will help guide your research, reminding you of what types of information you need to find, and will serve as an outline for the discussion section of your memo. See the sample set out in Example 1 below.

PRACTICE POINTER

In your log, be clear about what material is quoted directly and what is paraphrased. Record cites, including pinpoint cites. Finally, come up with a system that tells you when you have cited checked a case.

EXAMPLE 1 **Research Log**

I. GENERAL RULES

A. What are the policies underlying the statute?

☐ ***Torres v. Arnco Constr., Inc.*, 867 So. 2d 583, 586 (Fla. 5th DCA 2004). (Cite checked; still good law.)**

> The purpose of service of process is to advise the defendant that an action has been commenced and to warn the defendant that he or she must appear in a timely manner to state such defenses as are available.

☐ ***Shurman v. Atl. Mortg. & Inv. Corp.*, 795 So. 2d 952, 953-54 (Fla. 2001) (citing *State ex rel. Merritt v. Heffernan*, 142 Fla. 496, 195 So. 145, 147 (1940)). (Cite checked; still good law.)**

> It is well settled that the fundamental purpose of service is "to give proper notice to the defendant in the case that he is answerable to the claim of plaintiff and, therefore, to vest jurisdiction in the court entertaining the controversy.

B. What is the applicable statute?

☐ **§ 48.031(1)(a), Fla. Stat. (2013). (Cite checked; this is the applicable version of the statute.)**

> Service of original process is made by delivering a copy of it to the person to be served with a copy of the complaint, petition, or other initial pleading or paper or by leaving the copies at his or her usual place of abode with any person residing therein who is 15 years of age or older and informing the person of their contents. . . .

C. What are the elements?

a. the usual place of abode of the person being served
b. with any person residing therein
c. who is 15 years of age or older and
d. informing the person of their contents.

D. Who has the burden of proof ?

☐ ***Thompson v. State, Dep't of Revenue*, 867 So. 2d 603 (Fla. 1st DCA 2004). (Cite checked; still good law.)**

> **Quote from page 605:**
> "The burden of proof to sustain the validity of service of process is upon the person who seeks to invoke the jurisdiction of the court and, without proper service of process, the court lacks personal jurisdiction over the defendant." *M.J.W. v. Department of Children and Families*, 825 So. 2d 1038, 1041 (Fla. 1st DCA 2002).
>
> [4] [5] "[A] process server's return of service on a defendant which is regular on its face is presumed to be valid absent clear and convincing evidence presented to the contrary." *Telf Corp. v. Gomez*, 671 So. 2d 818 (Fla. 3d DCA 1996). Although simple denial of service is not sufficient, *id.* at 819, Thompson's motion and affidavit are based on the fact that the service did not comply with section 48.031 and was therefore legally deficient. *National Safety Associates, Inc. v. Allstate Insurance Co.*, 799 So. 2d 316, 317 (Fla. 2d DCA 2001). Thompson's affidavit makes a *prima facie* showing that he was not served at his usual place of abode by valid substituted service. . . . Having raised the issue of personal jurisdiction, Thompson's motion and accompanying affidavit placed the burden on the Department to establish the validity of service of process. M.J.W., 825 So. 2d at 1041.

☐ ***Busman v. State, Dep't of Revenue*, 905 So. 2d 956, 958 (Fla. 3d DCA 2005). (Cite checked; still good law.)**

Quote from page 958:
Although the sheriff's return of service, which is regular on its face, is presumptively valid, [footnote omitted] see *Department of Revenue v. Wright*, 813 So. 2d 989, 992 (Fla. 2d DCA 2002); *Fla. Natl. Bank v. Halphen*, 641 So. 2d 495, 496 (Fla. 3d DCA 1994), Busman presented clear, convincing and uncontradicted evidence that the 327 N.W. 4th Avenue address was not his "usual place of abode."

E. Other general rules

"The statutes regulating service of process are to be strictly construed to assure that a defendant is notified of the proceedings." Torres, 867 So. 2d at 586. "Indeed, because statutes authorizing substituted service are exceptions to the general rule requiring a defendant to be served personally, due process requires strict compliance with their statutory requirements." *Id.*

II. ELEMENTS

A. Usual place of abode (in dispute)

1. Specific rules (what test do the courts use in determining whether a particular place is a person's usual place of abode?)

   ☐ ***Thompson v. State, Dep't of Revenue*, 867 So. 2d 603 (Fla. 1st DCA 2004). (Cite checked; still good law.)**

   Quote from page 605:
   Turning to the merits, "[s]ection 48.031 expressly requires that substituted service be at the person's usual place of abode." *Shurman v. Atl. Mortg. & Inv. Corp.*, 795 So. 2d 952, 954 (Fla. 2001). The requirement "usual place of abode" means "the place where the defendant is actually living at the time of service." *Id., citing State ex rel. Merritt v. Heffernan*, 142 Fla. 496, 195 So. 145, 147 (1940).

   ☐ ***Torres v. Arnco Const., Inc.*, 867 So. 2d 583 (Fla. 5th DCA 2004). (Cite checked; still good law.)**

   Quote from page 586:
   In *State ex rel. Merritt v. Heffernan*, 142 Fla. 496, 195 So. 145, 147 (1940), the Florida Supreme Court defined the term "usual place of abode" as the place where the defendant "is actually living at the time of service." The word "abode" means "one's fixed place of residence for the time being when service is made." *Id.* If a person has more than one residence, he must be served at the residence in which he is actually living at the time of service. *Id.*

   ☐ ***Shurman v. Atl. Mortg. & Inv. Corp.*, 795 So. 2d 952 (Fla. 2001). (Cite checked; still good law.)**

Quote from page 954:
Going one step further, "usual place of abode" is the place where the defendant is actually living at the time of the service. The word abode means one's fixed place of residence for the time being when the service is made. Thus, if a person has several residences, he must be served at the residence in which he is actually living at the time service is made.

2. Analogous cases

☐ ***State ex rel. Merritt v. Heffernan*, 142 Fla. 496, 195 So. 145, 147 (1940). (Cite checked; still good law.)**

Quote from pages 147-48.
The summons was left with the defendant's wife at the family's apartment in Florida an hour after the defendant boarded a train to Minnesota. Although the defendant argued that his usual place of abode was Minnesota, where he had an office, paid taxes, and voted, the court disagreed, noting that the defendant had moved his family to the Florida apartment two months before his wife was served, that the defendant had visited his family at the apartment twice "during the season," and that the defendant's family had remained in Florida for some time after he was served. As the court stated, "We do not hold the view that Florida was the permanent residence of the defendant, but we do feel that in the circumstance reflected in the record, it was his usual place of abode . . . ." *Id.* at 148.

☐ ***Busman v. State, Dep't of Revenue*, 905 So. 2d 956 (Fla. 3d DCA 2005). (Cite checked; still good law.)**

Quote from page 958:
In a paternity action, service was made on the defendant' half-brother on July 16, 2003. Defendant testified that he had moved out of his half-brother's house on July 1, 2002, and presented lease and landlord's testimony. Although the return of service was regular on its face, the court held that Busman had presented clear, convincing, and uncontradicted evidence that service was not made at his usual place of abode. The court stated that the statute must be strictly construed.

☐ ***Thompson v. State, Dep't of Revenue*, 867 So. 2d 603 (Fla. 1st DCA 2004). (Cite checked; still good law.)**

Quote from page 605:
In a child support case service was made with the defendant's wife. The defendant filed an affidavit stating that he had been separated from his wife for three years and that he not lived at the address where service was made. The court reversed and remanded for an evidentiary hearing.

☐ ***Torres v. Arnco Const., Inc.*, 867 So. 2d 583 (Fla. 5th DCA 2004). (Cite checked; still good law.)**

Quote from page 587:
NY process server tried to serve the defendant at his NY address, where he had lived for 12 years. Although NY neighbors told process server that the defendant lived at the house, they also said that he traveled a lot. Service

was then made on the defendant's mother, who lived in Florida. When process server left the papers with defendant's mother, mother said that the defendant "would be home soon, and she would see to it that he received the papers." Majority concluded that the plaintiff had not met its burden of proof and that the mother's statement was ambiguous. The dissent argued that if the defendant spent substantial amounts of time visiting family in Florida the Florida house was his usual place of abode at the time service was made.

3. Ms. Olsen's arguments:
   - ☐ On the day that service was made, Ms. Olsen was living not at her sister's house but at the residential treatment house.
   - ☐ Service on a relative is not sufficient.
   - ☐ Her more permanent address was the residential treatment house address. She had a room, etc., at the residential treatment house.
   - ☐ *Heffernan* is an old case.
   - ☐ In *Torres,* the court held that the defendant's mother's house was not the defendant's usual place of abode even though the mother indicated that the defendant would be home later.
4. The State's arguments:
   - ☐ Ms. Olsen stayed at her sister's house three nights a week.
   - ☐ Ms. Olsen apparently received mail at her sister's house—the shoebox.
   - ☐ Ms. Olsen listed her sister's address on her driver's license.
   - ☐ In *Heffernan,* the court held that the apartment was the defendant's usual place of abode even though the defendant had left the apartment and was on a train back to his permanent residence.
   - ☐ In *Torres,* the defendant had a permanent residence where he had lived for 12 years. He was just visiting his mother.

B. Any person residing therein (not in dispute)

☐ Service was left with Ms. Webster, who is a person, at Ms. Webster's house.

C. 15 years old or older (not in dispute)

☐ Ms. Webster is 32.

D. Informing the person of their contents (in dispute)

1. Specific rules (what test do the courts use in determining whether the process server informed the person being served of the contents of the documents?)
2. Analogous cases
3. Ms. Olsen's arguments
4. State's arguments

C. UNDERSTANDING WHAT YOU HAVE FOUND

1. *Make Sure You Understand the Big Picture*

Your first step should be a step back. Can you place the issue that you were asked to research into the bigger picture? For instance, in the Olsen case, do you understand how service of process relates to jurisdiction and how jurisdiction relates to whether the court had the power to enter a default judgment? If you don't, don't panic. The law is complicated, and neither professors nor employers expect first-, second-, or even third-year students to have a complete understanding of how the system works. However, both professors and employers expect students to look for answers and, if they can't find them, to ask questions.

2. *Make Sure You Understand the Statute*

Once you understand the big picture, make sure you understand the statute. In particular, make sure you understand the requirements, or elements, and that you have looked for statutory sections that explain the statute's purpose and that define terms used in the statute. In addition, if the statute is a complicated one, take the time to diagram the statute.

In the example problem, the applicable statute is Fla. Stat. § 48.031(a)(1) (2013), which reads as follows:

> Service of original process is made by delivering a copy of it to the person to be served with a copy of the complaint, petition, or other initial pleading or paper or by leaving the copies at his or her usual place of abode with any person residing therein who is 15 years of age or older and informing the person of their contents. . . .

A close reading of the statute reveals that service can be accomplished in either of two ways: (1) by delivering a copy of the summons, complaint, petition, or other initial pleading or paper to the person to be served or (2) by leaving a copy of those documents at the person's usual place of abode with a person who resides there who is 15 years old or older and by informing the person with whom the documents are left of their contents.

Note that in this instance there is an "or" between the (1) and the (2) but that there is an "and" between the "c" and the "d." While you can accomplish service of process either by delivering the summons to the person being served or by leaving it at his or her usual place of abode, if you leave it at the person's usual place of abode, you must leave the summons with a person who is residing therein, that person must be 15 years old or older, and you must inform the person with whom you leave the documents of their contents.

Also note that, in some instances, the statutory language will be ambiguous. Some of these ambiguities are the result of poor drafting; some may, however, be intentional. To get enough votes to enact the legislation, the drafters may have intentionally used vague language. Don't despair. You will often be able to use these ambiguities to make an argument on behalf of your client.

PRACTICE POINTER

There is often more than one way to list the elements. For example, you can list "any person residing therein" and "who is 15 years of age or older" as separate elements, or you can combine these two elements and treat them as one: "any person residing therein who is 15 years of age or older." In deciding whether to combine elements, look at how the cases have listed the elements (do they separate or combine them?) and think about whether, in your memo, it make more sense to treat the requirements as separate elements or one element.

3. Make Sure You Understand the General and Specific Rules

In addition to reading the statute carefully, read carefully those portions of the cases that are relevant to the issue you were asked to research.

Begin by focusing on the cases that have set out general rules, that is, the cases that have listed the elements, the cases that have set out the rules relating to the burden of proof, and the cases that have explained the policies underlying the statute. For example, in researching the sample problem, we found several cases that set out the rules relating to the burden of proof.

If all of the cases set out the same rule, all you need to do is make sure that you understand that rule. If, however, different cases set out different rules, you need to determine which of those rules governs. To do this, begin by cite checking the cases. If one or more of the cases have been reversed or overruled on the point of law for which you are looking at the case, do not use those cases. They are no longer good law.

If the remaining cases, that is, the cases that are still good law, set out the same rule, use that rule. If, though, there is still a discrepancy, try to resolve that discrepancy by looking to see if different rules apply in different types of cases (for example, is there a different rule in child custody cases than there is in contract cases?); whether different divisions apply different rules (for example, does the 1st DCA apply one rule and the 3d DCA apply a different rule?); or whether the rule seems to be evolving.

In our example case, all of the cases seem to set out the same rule of law. Although it takes some careful reading to determine what that rule is, the rule seems to be as follows:

1. The party who is seeking to invoke the jurisdiction of the court (the plaintiff) has the burden of proving that the service was valid.
2. If, however, the "return of service" is regular on its face, service is presumed to be valid.
3. Thus, if the "return of service" is regular on its face, the party challenging the validity of the service (the defendant) must present clear and convincing evidence that the service is invalid.

PRACTICE POINTER

When you are not sure what a particular word or phrase means, take a few minutes to look up the definition. For example, if you are not sure what the phrase "return of service" means, look up that phrase. If you are online, the easiest way to find a definition is to go to Bing or Google and type in the word "definition" and the phrase "return of service." When you do, you will be taken to a site like thefreedictionary.com, which provides plain English definitions for legal terms. In this instance, the website sets out the following definition for "return of service": "n. Written confirmation from a process server under oath that declares that the legal documents were served (such as a summons and complaint)." Although you should not cite to this type of dictionary in a memo or brief, you can use this type of dictionary to help you understand terms used in a statute or case.

Accordingly, in our example problem, because the return is regular on its face, Ms. Olsen would have to present clear and convincing evidence that the service was not valid.

PRACTICE POINTER

If several cases set out the same rule, you will usually want to cite a recent case from the jurisdiction's highest court as authority for that rule. For instance, in our sample case, you would want to cite to a recent Florida Supreme Court case. If there is not a recent case from the jurisdiction's highest court, you can cite to an older case from the jurisdiction's highest court and then to a more recent decision from an intermediate court of appeals. The exception to this "rule" is when the rule is known by the name of the case that announced it. For example, if you are setting out the *Miranda* rule, cite to *Miranda v. Arizona,* 384 U.S. 436 (1966), and not to a more recent United States Supreme Court case.

Once you understand the general rules, turn your attention to the specific rules, that is, the rules that the courts apply in determining whether a particular element, or requirement, is met. For instance, in the Olsen case, look at the rules that the courts apply in determining whether the service was made at the defendant's usual place of abode. Do all of the cases set out the same rule? If they do not set out the same rule, are some of the cases no longer good law? If all of the cases are still good law, is there a way of reconciling the various rules?

Once you understand the big picture and have a good understanding of both the general and specific rules, it is time to start writing. As you do this writing, keep two things in mind. First, writing a memo is usually a multi-step process. If you want to do a good job, you will need to do a first draft, a second draft, and maybe even a third or fourth draft. As a consequence, do not put off writing the first draft until the night before the final draft is due. Second, most of the time drafting a memo involves more than recording completely formed ideas and arguments. Most law students and attorneys find that they rethink their analysis and synthesis as they write. Consequently, do not be surprised if, part way through writing the first draft, you have one of those "aha!" moments in which you see the issue, the law, or an argument in a different light.

The rest of this chapter walks you through the process of writing the memo. Although we discuss the sections in the order in which they appear in a formal memo, you do not have to write the sections in order. For example, many law students and attorneys find that it works better to write the first draft of the discussion section before they write the first draft of the statement of facts, issue statement, and brief answer.

Chapter 7 Quiz No. 1

Draft answers for each of the following questions. Make your points clearly and concisely, and write sentences that are easy to read and that are grammatical and correctly punctuated.

1. How will keeping a research log like the one set out in Example 1 help you research and write a memo?
2. What is an element?
3. What is the difference between burden of proof and standard of review?
4. What is the difference between a general rule and a specific rule?
5. If more than one case sets out the applicable rule, what factors should you consider in deciding which case or cases to cite as authority for that rule?

D. DRAFTING THE HEADING

The heading is the easiest section to write. It consists of only four entries: the name of the person to whom the memo is addressed, the name of the person who wrote the memo, the date, and an entry identifying the client and the issue or issues discussed in the memo. Although the first three entries are self-explanatory, the fourth needs some explanation.

In some firms, the memo is filed only in the client's file. For such firms, the "Re:" entry can be quite general.

EXAMPLE 1 **Sample Heading**

To:	Christina Galeano
From:	Legal Intern
Date:	September 9, 2013
Re:	Elaine Olsen, Case No. 13-478

In other firms, the memo is filed not only in the client's file but also in a "memo bank"—that is, a computer or paper file in which all memos are filed by topic. In these offices, the "Re:" section serves two purposes: (1) within the client's file, it distinguishes the memo from other memos that have been or will be written, and (2) in the memo bank, it provides either the database for a word search or topic categories under which the memo will be filed. To serve this last purpose, the heading should include the key terms.

EXAMPLE 2 **Sample Heading**

To:	Christina Galeano
From:	Legal Intern
Date:	September 9, 2013
Re:	Elaine Olsen, Case No. 13-478 Service of Process, Usual Place of Abode; Notification of Contents

E. DRAFTING THE STATEMENT OF FACTS

Just as every case starts with a story, so does every memo. Therefore, in most instances, begin your memo by telling your supervising attorney who did what when.

1. Decide What Facts to Include

In a typical statement of facts, there are three types of facts: the legally significant facts, the emotionally significant facts, and the background facts. In addition, in some instances you will want to identify the facts that are not yet known.

a. Legally Significant Facts

A legally significant fact is a fact that a court would consider in deciding whether a statute or rule is applicable or that a court would use in applying that statute or rule. For instance, in the Olsen case, the legally significant facts are those facts that the court would consider in determining whether service of process was valid. More specifically, the legally significant facts are the facts that the court would consider in determining (1) whether the summons was left at the defendant's usual place of abode, (2) whether the summons was left with a person residing therein who is 15 years old or older, and (3) whether the process server notified the person being served of the contents of the documents. Because a change in one of the legally significant facts could change your analysis and prediction, you should include all of the legally significant facts in your statement of facts.

You can use either of two techniques to determine whether a fact is legally significant. Before you write the discussion section, you can prepare a two-column chart in which you list the elements in the first column and the facts that relate to those elements in the second column. See Exhibit 7.1.

EXHIBIT 7.1 DETERMINING WHICH FACTS ARE LEGALLY SIGNIFICANT

Element	Facts Related to Element
Usual Place of Abode	Ms. Webster told the process server that "Elaine isn't here today."
	On February 1, 2013, Ms. Olsen entered an inpatient drug treatment program in Miami. She remained in the program until March 27, 2013, when she moved into a residential treatment house for recovering addicts.
	During April, May, and June 2013, Ms. Olsen was a fulltime resident at the residential treatment house. She had a bedroom in the house, ate her meals there, and had some of her possessions there.
	Beginning in July 2013, Ms. Olsen began spending less time at the residential treatment house and more time with her sister, Elizabeth Webster.
	During July and August 2013, Ms. Olsen spent weeknights at the residential treatment house and Friday, Saturday, and Sunday nights at her sister's house. Because she was spending time at her sister's house, she moved some of her clothing and personal effects into her sister's house.
	During April and May 2013, Ms. Olsen put the residential treatment house address on employment applications. However, her driver's license showed her sister's address as her address.
	On September 1, 2013, Ms. Olsen moved into her own apartment.

Element	Facts Related to Element
	The return on the service of process appears to be in order.
	The service was made on Wednesday, July 24, 2013.
	At this point there is no evidence indicating that the state tried to serve Ms. Olsen at the treatment house.
Person Residing Therein Who Is 15 Years Old or Older	Ms. Webster lives in the house where the summons was left.
	Ms. Webster is 32.
Element	**Facts Related to Element**
Informing Person of Contents	The process server handed what was probably a summons and complaint to Ms. Webster and told Ms. Webster that Ms. Olsen "needed to go to court."

The second technique is used after the discussion section has been completed. To ensure that you have included all of the legally significant facts in your statement of facts, go through your discussion section, checking to make sure that each of the facts that you used in setting out the arguments is in your statement of facts. If you used a fact in the analysis, that fact is legally significant and should be included in the statement of facts.

PRACTICE POINTER

Remember, writing a memo is a recursive process. Even though you may write the statement of facts first, you may need to revise it after you have completed the discussion section.

b. Emotionally Significant Facts

An emotionally significant fact is one that, while not legally significant, may affect the way the judge or jury decides the case.

For example, in the Olsen case, while it is not legally significant that Ms. Olsen was in a drug treatment program, that fact may color the way the judge views her. Therefore, this fact is an emotionally significant fact and should be included in the statement of facts. In addition, while it is not legally significant that Ms. Olsen got a job, that fact may also color the way in which the judge views her and should, therefore, be included in the statement of facts.

c. Background Facts

In addition to including the legally and emotionally significant facts, also include those facts that are needed to tell the story and that provide the context for the legally and emotionally significant facts.

d. Unknown Facts

Sometimes you are not given all of the facts needed to analyze an issue. For instance, because the attorney did not know the law, he or she may not have asked the right questions, or the documents containing the unknown facts are in the possession of the opposing party. If the unknown facts are legally significant and you can obtain them, try to do so before writing the memo. If, however, the unknown facts are not legally significant or if you cannot obtain them, write the memo, but tell the attorney, either in the statement of facts, the discussion section, or the conclusion what facts are unknown.

PRACTICE POINTER

You may not realize a fact is unknown until you have read the cases. For instance, in the example problem, at the time that she interviewed Ms. Olsen, the attorney did not ask Ms. Olsen whether the process server had tried to serve her at the residential treatment house or on any other occasions. However, after doing the research, you know that these facts may be legally significant.

2. *Select an Organizational Scheme*

As a general rule, begin your statement of facts with an introductory sentence or paragraph that identifies the parties and the issue. Then present the facts using one of three organizational schemes: a chronological organizational scheme, a topical organizational scheme, or a combination of the two, for example, a scheme in which you organize the facts by topic and then, within each topic, you set out the facts in chronological order.

Most of the time, the facts dictate which organizational scheme will work best. If the case involves a series of events related by date, then the facts should be presented chronologically. If, however, there are a number of facts that are not related by date (for example, the description of several different pieces of property) or a number of unrelated events that occurred during the same time period (for example, four unrelated crimes committed by the defendant over the same two-day period), the facts should be organized by topic.

Sometimes, though, the facts can be presented in more than one way. For example, in the Olsen case, the facts can be presented using either a scheme that is primarily chronological or a scheme that is primarily topical. See Examples 1 and 2.

EXAMPLE 1 Statement of Facts with Facts Presented in Chronological Order

Elaine Olsen has contacted our office asking for assistance in overturning a judgment terminating her parental rights. You have asked me to determine whether the service of process was valid.

On February 1, 2013, Ms. Olsen entered an inpatient drug treatment program in Miami, Florida. She remained in the program until March 27, 2013, when she moved into a residential treatment house for recovering addicts.

During April, May, and June 2013, Ms. Olsen was a full-time resident at the treatment house. She had a bedroom in the house, ate her meals there, and had some of her possessions there. In addition, when she applied for jobs, she listed the treatment house address as her address.

Beginning in July 2013, Ms. Olsen began spending less time at the treatment house and more time with her sister, Elizabeth Webster, who is 32. Both Ms. Olsen's sister and the manager of the residential treatment house will testify that, during July and August 2013, Ms. Olsen spent weeknights at the residential treatment house and Friday, Saturday, and Sunday nights at her sister's house. Because she was spending time at her sister's house, Ms. Olsen moved some of her clothing and personal effects into her sister's house.

On Wednesday, July 24, 2013, a process server went to Ms. Webster's house and asked for Elaine Olsen. When Ms. Webster told the process server that "Elaine isn't here today," the process server handed the summons to Ms. Webster and told her that Ms. Olsen "needed to go to court."

Ms. Webster will testify that she never gave the summons to her sister. Because she thought that the papers related to some of Ms. Olsen's unpaid bills, she simply put the summons in a shoebox in the kitchen with a stack of Ms. Olsen's other mail. Ms. Olsen says she never received the summons and, as a result, did not respond. The return of service is regular on its face.

Ms. Olsen has been employed since August 1, 2013, and she has lived in her own apartment since September 1, 2013. She has her sister's address on her driver's license.

There is nothing in the record that indicates whether the State tried to personally serve Ms. Olsen or whether it tried to serve her at the residential treatment house.

EXAMPLE 2 Statement of Facts with Facts Organized by Topic

You have asked me to determine whether the service of process on one of our clients, Elaine Olsen, is valid.

During the past six months, Ms. Olsen has lived in three places. From February 1, 2013, until March 27, 2013, Ms. Olsen was a patient in an inpatient drug treatment program in Miami, Florida. On March 27, 2013, she moved into a residential treatment house for recovering addicts. During April, May, and June, Ms. Olsen was a full-time resident at the treatment house. She had a bedroom in the house, ate her meals there, and had some of her possessions there. In addition, Ms. Olsen listed the treatment house address on job applications. Beginning in July 2013, Ms. Olsen began spending more time at her sister's house. During July and August 2013, Ms. Olsen spent weeknights at the treatment house and Friday, Saturday, and Sunday nights at her sister's house. Because she was spending time at her sister's house, Ms. Olsen moved some of her clothing and personal effects into her sister's house. Ms. Olsen has her sister's address on her driver's license.

On Wednesday, July 24, 2013, a process server went to Ms. Olsen's sister's house and asked for Elaine Olsen. When Ms. Olsen's sister, Ms. Webster, told the process server that "Elaine isn't here today," the process server handed the summons to Ms. Webster and told her that Ms. Olsen "needed to go to court."

Ms. Webster, who is 32, will testify that she never gave the summons to her sister. Because she thought that the papers related to some of Ms. Olsen's unpaid bills, she simply put the summons in a shoebox in the kitchen with a stack of Ms. Olsen's other mail. Ms. Olsen says she never received the summons and complaint, and as a result, she did not respond.

You have asked me to presume that the return of service is regular on its face. There is nothing in the record that indicates whether the State tried to personally serve Ms. Olsen or whether it tried to serve her at the residential treatment house.

PRACTICE POINTER

If you are using a chronological organizational scheme, you can signal that fact to your readers by starting the sentence that follows your introduction with a date. In contrast, if you are using a topical organizational scheme, try to use topic sentences that identify the topics. Do not, however, include law or argue the facts in the statement of facts; save that material for the discussion section.

3. Present the Facts Clearly and Concisely

Most attorneys prefer statements of facts that are short and to the point. This does not, however, mean that they want the facts set out using bullet points. While bullet points are common in some types of business writing, most attorneys want the facts presented in easy-to-read sentences in well-constructed paragraphs.

Well-written sentences and paragraphs have several advantages over bullet points. First, most readers have an easier time understanding what happened when the facts are presented in the form of a "story." The narrative quality of a story helps readers understand who the actors are and the sequence of events. Second, setting out the facts in story form makes it easier to use the statement of facts in the memo to write the summary of facts for a letter to the client or the statement of the case for a brief.

4. Present the Facts Accurately and Objectively

In writing the statement of facts for an objective memorandum, present the facts accurately and objectively. Do not include facts that are not in your file, and do not set out legal conclusions, misstate facts, leave out facts that are legally significant, or present the facts so that they favor one side over the other. In Example 3, the writer has violated all of these "rules."

PRACTICE POINTER

You set out a legal conclusion when you set out as a fact that one of the elements or rules is met or is not met. Whether an element or rule is or is not met is a legal conclusion and not a fact.

EXAMPLE 3 **Writer Has Not Presented the Facts Accurately and Objectively**

> Hoping to obtain a default judgment against Ms. Olsen, the plaintiff had the sheriff serve the summons and petition at Ms. Olsen's sister's house and not at the residential treatment house where Ms. Olsen was actually living. Although Ms. Olsen occasionally visited her sister at her sister's house, she did not keep any of her personal belongings at her sister's house.

In the first sentence, the writer violates the first two rules. First, she sets out facts that are not in the record when she states that the plaintiff hoped to get a default judgment and when she states that the plaintiff had a sheriff serve Ms. Olsen at her sister's house and not at the residential treatment house. Second, she sets out legal conclusions when she states that the defendant was actually living at the residential treatment house. Because a person's usual place of abode is the place where the defendant is actually living, in the context of this case, the statement that the defendant was actually living in the residential treatment house is a legal conclusion.

In the second sentence, the writer violates the last three rules. The writer misstates the facts when she states that Ms. Olsen did not keep any personal belongings at her sister's house; she leaves out legally significant facts when she does not include the fact that Ms. Olsen had her sister's address on her driver's license; and she presents the facts in a light favorable to her client when she states that Ms. Olsen visited her sister only occasionally.

PRACTICE POINTER

As a general rule, do not refer to individuals by their first names only. Instead, use the appropriate title and family name. For instance, instead of referring to Elaine Olsen as "Elaine," use "Elaine Olsen" or "Ms. Olsen."

5. *Checklist for Critiquing the Statement of Facts*

a. Content

- ☐ The writer has included all of the legally significant facts.
- ☐ When appropriate, the writer included emotionally significant facts.
- ☐ The writer included enough background facts that a person not familiar with the case can understand what happened.
- ☐ The writer has identified the unknown facts.
- ☐ The writer presented the facts accurately.
- ☐ The writer presented the facts objectively.
- ☐ The writer has not included legal conclusions in the statement of facts.

b. Organization

- ☐ The writer has included an introductory sentence or paragraph that identifies the parties and the nature of the dispute.
- ☐ The writer has used one of the conventional organizational schemes: chronological, topical, or a combination of chronological and topical.

c. Writing

- ☐ The attorney can understand the facts of the case after reading the statement of facts once.
- ☐ The paragraph divisions are logical, and the paragraphs are neither too long nor too short.
- ☐ Transitions and dovetailing have been used to make the connection between ideas clear.
- ☐ In most sentences, the writer has used the actor as the subject of the sentence, and the subject and verb are close together.
- ☐ The writer has varied the length of the sentences and the sentence patterns so that each sentence flows smoothly from the prior sentence.
- ☐ The writing is concise and precise.
- ☐ The writing is grammatically correct and correctly punctuated.
- ☐ The statement of facts has been proofread.

F. DRAFTING THE ISSUE STATEMENT

It is not unusual for students to ask whether they really need to include an issue statement in their memo. Doesn't the attorney know the issue? The answer to both questions is yes. However, even though your supervising attorney told you what issue to research, you should include an issue statement.

You should include an issue statement, or question presented, because, by convention, formal memos have an issue statement. While at first it may seem as if writing a formal statement of the issue is a waste of time, the opposite is often true. Writing an issue statement provides you the opportunity to do more sophisticated analysis: Given your research, what is the applicable law? What is the legal question? What are the most important facts?

As a general rule, you should have the same number of issue statements as you have "parts" to the discussion section. Accordingly, if you have three issue statements—(1) whether service of process was valid, (2) whether the statute of limitations has run, and (3) whether the defendant is entitled to judgment as a matter of law—you should also have three parts to the discussion section, one corresponding to each of the three issues. If, however, you have only one issue statement, for example, whether service of process is valid, your discussion section will have only one part.

> **PRACTICE POINTER**
>
> As a general rule, do not treat each element as a separate issue. For example, if the issue is whether the service of process was valid, do not treat the first element, usual place of abode, as one issue; the second element, person residing therein who is 15 or older, as a second issue; and the third element, informing about the contents, as a third issue.

Convention also dictates that in a multi-issue memo you list the issues in the same order in which you discuss those issues in the discussion section. The first issue statement will correspond to the first part of the discussion section, the second will correspond to the second part, and so on.

In this chapter we describe how to write an issue statement using the "under-does-when" format. In the next chapter, we describe the "whether" format.

1. *Select a Format: The "Under-Does-When" Format*

The under-does-when format is easy to use because the format forces you to include all of the essential information. After the "under," insert a reference to the applicable law; after the verb (for example, "does," "is," or "may"), insert the legal question; and after "when," insert the most important of the legally significant facts. Because the format is written as a question, place a question mark at the end.

Under [insert reference to applicable law]
does/is/may [insert legal question]
when [insert the key facts]?

a. Reference to the Applicable Law

To be useful to the reader, the reference to the rule of law cannot be too specific or too general. For example, a reference to "Florida law" is too broad; hundreds of cases are filed each year in which the issue is governed by Florida law.

EXAMPLE 1 **Reference to the Rule of Law Too General**

Under Florida law, . . .

EXAMPLE 2 **Appropriate References**

Under Florida's service of process statute, . . .
Under Florida's service of process statute, § 48.031 Fla. Stat. (2013), . . .

If you identify the statute in your statement of the legal question, you can refer to the statute by number in your reference to the rule of law. For example, in some instances, the following format works well: "Under § 48.031 Fla. Stat. (2013), was service of process valid when . . . ."

b. Statement of the Legal Question

After identifying the applicable law, set out the legal question. In doing so, make sure that your statement of the legal question is neither too narrow nor too broad. If stated too narrowly, your statement of the legal question will not cover all of the issues and subissues; if stated too broadly, the question does not serve its function of focusing the reader's attention on the real issue.

PRACTICE POINTER

Although we refer to this format as the "under-does-when" format, you do not need to use "does" as the verb. As the following examples illustrate, a number of different verbs can work.

EXAMPLE 3 **Legal Questions that Are Too Narrow**

- ☐ Was the summons left at Ms. Olsen's usual place of abode when . . . ?
- ☐ Was the summons left at the place where Ms. Olsen was actually living when . . . ?
- ☐ Did the process server inform Ms. Webster about the contents of the summons when . . . ?

EXAMPLE 4 **Legal Questions that Are Too Broad**

☐ Did the court properly terminate Ms. Olsen's parental rights when . . . ?
☐ Were Ms. Olsen's rights violated when . . . ?

EXAMPLE 5 **Legal Questions that Are Properly Framed**

☐ Was service valid when . . . ?
☐ Was Ms. Olsen properly served when . . . ?
☐ Was service at Ms. Olsen's sister's house valid when . . . ?
☐ Was the substituted service on the defendant's sister at the sister's house valid when . . . ?

c. The Key Facts

Unless the issue that you have been asked to research involves only a question of law, end your issue statement by setting out the key facts. How will the court apply the rule of law to the facts in your client's case?

How many facts you include depends on how many facts are legally significant. If there are only a few legally significant facts, you will usually want to include all of them. If, however, there are a large number of legally significant facts, be selective. Either list only the most important of the legally significant facts, or list only the facts that relate to the disputed element or elements.

In Example 6, the writer has not included enough facts: While he has included the facts that the court would consider in deciding whether the process server informed the person served of the contents of the documents, he has not included facts that the court would consider in deciding whether the summons was left at Ms. Olsen's usual place of abode with a person 15 years or older residing therein.

EXAMPLE 6 **Writer Has Not Included Enough Facts**

> Under Florida's service of process statute, § 48.031, Fla. Stat. (2013), was the service valid when the process server told Ms. Webster that Ms. Olsen "needed to go to court"?

In contrast, in Example 7, the writer has included too many facts. As a result, the issue statement is so long that some attorneys would not read it.

EXAMPLE 7 **Writer Has Included Too Many Facts**

> Under Florida's service of process statute, was substituted service on Ms. Olsen's sister at the sister's house valid when (1) Ms. Olsen was a patient in an inpatient drug treatment program in Miami from February 1, 2013, until March 27, 2013; (2) Ms. Olsen moved into a residential treatment house for recovering addicts on March 27, 2013; (3) during April, May, and June

2013, Ms. Olsen was a fulltime resident at the residential treatment house, where she had a bedroom, where she ate her meals, and where she had some possessions; (4) during April and May 2013, Ms. Olsen listed the residential treatment house address on job applications; (5) beginning in July 2013, Ms. Olsen began spending less time at the residential treatment house and more time with her sister, Ms. Webster; (6) during July and August 2013, Ms. Olsen usually spent weeknights at the residential treatment house and Friday, Saturday, and Sunday nights at her sister's house; (7) on July 24, 2013, a process server went to Ms. Webster's house and asked for Elaine Olsen; (8) when Ms. Webster told the process server that "Elaine isn't here today," the process server handed the summons to Ms. Webster and told her that Ms. Olsen "needed to go to court"; and (9) Ms. Webster is 32 years old and lives at the house where she received the summons?

Examples 8 and 9 are better: They include the key facts without going into too much detail.

EXAMPLE 8 **Better Example**

Under Florida's service of process statute, was Ms. Olsen properly served when (1) during the month when service was made, Ms. Olsen spent weeknights at a residential treatment house and spent Friday, Saturday, and Sunday nights at her sister's house; (2) Ms. Olsen listed the address of the residential treatment house on job applications but her sister's address on her driver's license; (3) service was made on Ms. Olsen's 32-year-old sister on a Wednesday at Ms. Olsen's sister's house; (4) the process server told Ms. Olsen's sister that Ms. Olsen needed to go to court; and (5) Ms. Olsen's sister did not give the summons to Ms. Olsen, and Ms. Olsen states that she did not receive notice?

EXAMPLE 9 **Better Example**

Under Florida's statute authorizing substituted service of process, was service on the defendant's adult sister at the sister's house valid when the defendant spent weeknights at a residential treatment house and weekends at her sister's house; when the service was made on a weekday; when the process server told the defendant's sister that the defendant "needed to go to court"; and when the defendant states that she did not receive notice?

PRACTICE POINTER

While some attorneys will want you to "personalize" your issue statements by using the parties' names, other attorneys will want you to write issue statements that are more generic. Compare Example 8 in which the writer used Ms. Olsen's name with Example 9 in which the writer uses the words, "the defendant."

In setting out the facts, make sure you set out facts and not legal conclusions. While what is a fact and what is a legal conclusion will vary from case to case, saying or implying that an element is or is not met will always be a legal conclusion. In Example 10, the writer has set out legal conclusions. Instead of setting out the facts that the court would consider in deciding whether an element is met, she has simply listed the elements.

EXAMPLE 10 Writer Has Incorrectly Set Out Legal Conclusions Rather Than Facts

> Under Florida's statute authorizing substituted service of process, was the service valid when the process server left the summons with a person of suitable age and discretion at one of the defendant's usual places of abode and told the person about the contents of the notice?

Finally, make sure that you set out the facts accurately and objectively. Do not misstate a fact, and do not include only those facts that favor your client. While in a brief to a court you will want to present the facts in the light most favorable to your client, in an office memo you need to be objective.

EXAMPLE 11 Writer Has Not Set Out Facts Accurately and Objectively

> Under Florida's service of process statute, was the service invalid when (1) at the time that service was made, Ms. Olsen's permanent residence was a residential treatment house where she had a room, ate meals, and kept belongings; (2) Ms. Olsen listed the residential treatment house address on job applications; (3) the process server did not tell Ms. Olsen's sister that the State was planning to terminate Ms. Olsen's parental rights; and (4) Ms. Olsen's sister did not give the summons to Ms. Olsen, and Ms. Olsen states that she did not receive notice?

2. *Make Sure that Your Issue Statement Is Easy to Read*

It is not enough to include the right information in your issue statement. You must also present that information in such a way that your issue statement is easy to read.

The "under-does-when" format helps you write a readable issue statement by forcing you to use the three slots in a sentence: the reference to the rule of law goes into the introductory phrase or clause, the legal question goes into the main clause, and the key facts go into a list of "when" clauses at the end of the sentence.

____________________, ________________ ________________?

introductory phrase or clause,main clause "when" clauses

You can also make your issue statement easier to read by using the active voice and concrete subjects and action verbs. Finally, in listing the key facts, use parallel constructions for each item in the list and, when appropriate, use enumeration.

> **PRACTICE POINTER**
>
> End issue statements written using the "under-does-when" format with a question mark. End issue statements written using the "whether" format, which is discussed in Chapter 8 [Laurel Currie Oates and Anne Enquist, Just Memos: Preparing for Practice, 4th Ed.,], with a period.

3. *Checklist for Critiquing the Issue Statement*

a. Content

☐ The reference to the rule of law is neither too broad nor too narrow.
☐ The legal question is properly focused.
☐ The most significant of the legally significant facts have been included.
☐ Legal conclusions have not been set out as facts.

b. Format

☐ The writer has used one of the conventional formats, for example, the "under-does-when" format or the "whether" format.

c. Writing

☐ The issue statement is easy to read and understand.
☐ In setting out the legal question, the writer has used a concrete subject and an action verb.
☐ In listing the facts, the writer has used parallel constructions for all of the items in the list.
☐ If the list of facts is long, the writer has used enumeration or has repeated key structural cues, for example, words like "when" and "that."

G. DRAFTING THE BRIEF ANSWER

The brief answer serves a purpose similar to that served by the formal conclusion: it tells the attorney how you think a court will decide an issue and why. The brief answer is not, however, as detailed as the formal conclusion.

1. *Select a Format*

Convention dictates that, in a formal memo, you should include a separate brief answer for each issue statement. In addition, convention dictates that you should start each of your brief answers with a one- or two-word short answer. The words that are typically used are "probably," and "probably not." After this one- or two-word answer, briefly explain your answer.

2. *Set Out Your Conclusion and Reasoning*

In writing your brief answers, keep a couple of things in mind. First, remember your audience and purpose. You are writing to an attorney who needs an objective evaluation of the client's case. Second, make sure that you answer the question you set out in your issue statement and that you match the style you used in your issue statement. For example, if you used the parties' names in your issue statement, also use them in your brief answer. Third, be specific. Tell the attorney which elements you or the other side will or will not be able to prove. Finally, make sure that you get the burden of proof right. If you have personalized your issue statement and your client has the burden of proof, talk about what your client can and cannot prove. If, however, the other side has the burden of proof, talk about what it can and cannot prove. In contrast, if you wrote a more generic issue statement, talk about what the court will do.

EXAMPLE 1 **Issue Statement and Brief Answer in Which the Writer Uses the Parties' Names**

Issue

Under Florida's service of process statute, was Ms. Olsen properly served when (1) during the month when service was made, Ms. Olsen spent weeknights at a residential treatment house and spent Friday, Saturday, and Sunday nights at her sister's house; (2) Ms. Olsen listed the address of the residential treatment house on job applications but her sister's address on her driver's license; (3) service was made on Ms. Olsen's 32-year-old sister on a Wednesday at Ms. Olsen's sister's house; (4) the process server told Ms. Olsen's sister that Ms. Olsen needed to go to court; and (5) Ms. Olsen's sister did not give the summons to Ms. Olsen, and Ms. Olsen states that she did not receive notice?

Brief Answer

Probably not. Because the return is regular on its face, Ms. Olsen has the burden of proving that she was not properly served. Because the summons and petition were left with Ms. Olsen's 32-year-old sister at the sister's house, Ms. Olsen will have to concede that service was made on a person 15 years or older who was living at the house at which the service was made. In addition, because the process server told Ms. Olsen's sister that Ms. Olsen needed to go to court, more likely than not the court will decide that the person served was informed of the contents of the documents. However, because Ms. Olsen can present evidence that establishes that she was staying at the residential treatment house on the day that service was made, the court may decide that the summons and petition were not left at Ms. Olsen's usual place of abode.

EXAMPLE 2 Issue Statement and Brief Answer in Which the Writer Does Not Use the Parties' Names

ISSUE

Under Florida's statute authorizing substituted service of process, was service at the defendant's adult sister's house valid when the defendant spent weeknights at a residential treatment house and weekends at her sister's house; the service was made on a Wednesday; the process server told the defendant's sister that the defendant "needed to go to court"; and the defendant states that she did not receive notice?

BRIEF ANSWER

Probably not. The court will conclude that the service was made on a person 15 years old or older living at the place where service was made and that the process server informed the person served of the contents of the documents. However, the court will probably conclude that the service was not made at the defendant's usual place of abode because the defendant was not actually living at her sister's house on the day service was made.

3. Checklist for Critiquing the Brief Answer

a. Content

- ☐ The writer has predicted but not guaranteed how the issue will be decided.
- ☐ The writer has briefly explained his or her prediction, for example, the writer has explained which elements will be easy to prove and which will be more difficult and why.

b. Format

- ☐ The writer has included a separate brief answer for each issue statement.
- ☐ The answer begins with a one- or two-word short answer. This one- or two-word short answer is then followed by a short explanation.

c. Writing

- ☐ The brief answer is easy to read and understand.
- ☐ Most of the sentences have concrete subjects and action verbs.
- ☐ There are no grammatical or punctuation errors.

Chapter 7 Quiz No. 2

Draft answers for each of the following questions. Make your points clearly and concisely, and write sentences that are easy to read and that are grammatical and correctly punctuated.

1. What is a legally significant fact?
2. Why should you include all of the legally significant facts in a statement of facts?
3. How can you determine whether a fact is legally significant?
4. What is a legal conclusion? Why is there a "rule" against including legal conclusions in your statement of facts?
5. Given that your supervising attorney gave you the issue, why should you include an issue statement in a formal memo?

H. DRAFTING THE DISCUSSION SECTION USING A SCRIPT FORMAT

Expectations. We all have them, and we have them about a variety of things. If we go to the symphony, we expect to be handed a program, have an usher show us to our seats, wait until the hall is darkened, hear the orchestra members tuning their instruments, and then applaud the conductor as he or she takes the podium. We expect these things to be in a certain order, and there is a sense of satisfaction when our expectations are met.

We even have expectations about the organization of the most mundane things in our lives. If you walk into a house, you expect to see certain types of rooms (kitchen, bedrooms, bathroom, living or family room), and you expect those rooms to be in specific places. Dining rooms should be near kitchens; bathrooms should be near bedrooms, and so on. We even expect certain things to be in each room. Stoves should be in kitchens, not in dining rooms, and desks are usually in bedrooms, offices, or studies, not in bathrooms.

The same is true of discussion sections. When attorneys read a discussion section, they expect to see specific types of information. For example, in a formal memo, the attorney expects to see the applicable rules, examples of how those rules have been applied in analogous cases, each side's arguments, and a conclusion. In addition, the attorney expects to see each of those types of information in specific places. In most instances, the rules should be before, and not after, the descriptions of the analogous cases, and the descriptions of analogous cases should be before, and not after, the arguments. Finally, the attorney expects to see specific things in each section. Just as you would be surprised to see a dining table in a bedroom, an attorney would be surprised to see arguments in the rules section.

These expectations are not born of whim. Instead, they reflect the way attorneys in the United States think about legal questions. In most instances, attorneys begin their analysis by identifying the applicable statute or common law rule and by determining who has the burden of proof and what that burden is. If this "general rule" sets out a list of elements, most attorneys then go through those elements one by one, determining which elements the party with the burden of proof can easily prove and which elements will be more difficult to prove.

In most situations, the attorney gives relatively little space to the elements that the party with the burden of proof can easily prove: For these "undisputed elements," the attorney simply applies the law to the facts. Instead, the attorney focuses on the elements that will be more difficult to prove. For each of these "disputed elements," the attorney looks at the definitions or tests the courts use in determining whether the element is met, at examples of how those definitions or tests have been applied in analogous cases, and at each side's arguments. What factual arguments will the parties make? How will each side use the analogous cases? Given the purpose and policies underlying the statute or rule, what types of policy arguments might each side make? Finally, most attorneys make a prediction. Given the facts, rules, cases, and arguments, how will a court decide each element?

The discussion section reflects this process. It contains the same components—rules, analogous cases, arguments, and mini-conclusions—in the same order. At its simplest, and at its best, the discussion section analyzes the problem, walking the attorney step by step through the statute, cases, and arguments to the writer's prediction.

1. Modify the Template So that It Works for Your Issue

Just as different people prefer different styles of houses, some attorneys prefer different styles of discussion sections: some prefer discussion sections written using what we call the script format, and others prefer discussion sections written using a more integrated format. Although neither format is inherently better than the other, the script format tends to be a bit easier to use. Thus, in this chapter we show you how to write a discussion section using that format. Then, once you have mastered the script format, turn to the next chapter for a description of how to write a discussion section using a more integrated format.

In studying Example 1 below, note how the template reflects the way attorneys think about problems involving an elements analysis. The first section is an introductory section in which the writer introduces and sets out the applicable statute or common law rule, the burden of proof, and any other general rules. At the end of this introductory section, most writers provide the attorney with a roadmap that tells the attorney which elements the party with the burden of proof can easily prove and which elements will be more difficult to prove. The writer then walks the attorney through the elements one by one. For the elements that the party with the burden of proof can easily prove, the writer simply sets out the specific rules for that element and applies them to the client's case. For the elements that will be more difficult to prove, the writer sets out the specific rules for those elements, provides the attorney with descriptions of analogous cases in which those rules have been applied, and then writes the "script" for the arguments related to that element. If that element were litigated, what would the party with the burden of proof argue? What would the other side argue? How would the court decide the question?

EXAMPLE 1 **Template for Discussion Section Written Using a Script Format**

DISCUSSION

Introductory section *(Note: Do not include this subheading in the memo.)*

☐ If one or both sides will make a policy argument, describe the policies underlying the statute or rule.

- ☐ Introduce and set out the applicable statute(s) or common law rule.
- ☐ Explain which side has the burden of proof and what that burden is.
- ☐ Set out any other rules that apply to all of the elements.
- ☐ End by providing the attorney with a roadmap for the rest of the discussion.

A. First Element *(Note: Include a subheading that identifies the element.)*

- ☐ If the first element is not likely to be in dispute, simply set out and apply applicable rule.
- ☐ If, however, the first element will be in dispute, set out the following information:
  1. Specific rules for the first element
  2. Examples showing how the specific rules have been applied in analogous cases
  3. Arguments
  4. Mini-conclusion for the first element

B. Second Element *(Note: Include a subheading that identifies the element.)*

- ☐ If the second element is not likely to be in dispute, simply set out and apply applicable rule.
- ☐ If, however, the second element will be in dispute, set out the following information:
  1. Specific rules for second element
  2. Examples of how specific rules have been applied in analogous cases
  3. Arguments
  4. Mini-conclusion for the second element

C. Third Element *(Note: Include a subheading that identifies the element.)*

- ☐ If the third element is not likely to be in dispute, simply set out and apply applicable rule.
- ☐ If, however, the third element will be in dispute, set out the following information:
  1. Specific rules for the third element
  2. Examples of how specific rules have been applied in analogous cases
  3. Arguments
  4. Mini-conclusion for the third element

D. Fourth Element *(Note: Include a subheading that identifies the element.)*

- ☐ If the fourth element is not likely to be in dispute, simply set out and apply applicable rule.
- ☐ If, however, the fourth element will be in dispute, set out the following information:
  1. Specific rules for fourth element
  2. Examples of how specific rules have been applied in analogous cases
  3. Arguments
  4. Mini-conclusion for the fourth element

The template set out in Example 1 is, however, only a template. Just as a builder may need to modify a standard blueprint so that the house fits on the lot and satisfies the buyer's preferences, you may need to modify the template set out below in Example 2 so that it works for your issue. For example, if the applicable statute or rule has only two elements, you would need to modify the template so that it has only two subsections. Similarly, if the statute has five elements, you would need to modify the template so that it has five subsections.

In the Olsen case, the statute sets out three elements: (1) the complaint or petition must be left at the usual place of abode of the person being served, (2) the complaint or petition must be left with a person who is 15 years old or older who resides therein; and (3) the process server must inform the person served of the contents. Therefore, we modify the template so that it has three subsections. See Example 2.

PRACTICE POINTER

In the Olsen case, we decided to combine the discussion of "residing therein" and "15 years or older." These two elements are closely related, and neither is in dispute.

EXAMPLE 2 **Revised Template**

Discussion

Introductory section:

Set out policies underlying § 48.031, Fla. Stat. (2013).

- ☐ Introduce and set out § 48.031, Fla. Stat. (2013).
- ☐ Explain which side has the burden of proof and what that burden is.
- ☐ Set out any other rules that apply to all of the elements.
- ☐ End with a roadmap that tells the attorney that the State can easily prove the second element but that it may not be able to prove the first and third elements.

A. Usual Place of Abode *(disputed element)*

1. Specific rules
2. Examples of how specific rules have been applied in analogous cases
3. Arguments
   - ☐ Ms. Olsen's arguments
   - ☐ The State's arguments
4. Mini-conclusion

B. Age and Residing Therein *(undisputed element)*

1. Set out applicable rules
2. Apply applicable rules

C. Informing of Contents *(disputed element)*

1. Specific rules
2. Examples of how specific rules have been applied in analogous cases
3. Arguments
   - ☐ Ms. Olsen's arguments
   - ☐ The State's arguments
4. Mini-conclusion

PRACTICE POINTER

As a general rule, set out the party who has the burden of proof 's arguments first. In the sample problem, Ms. Olsen has the burden of proof because the return of service is regular on its face.

2. *Draft the Introductory, or General Rule, Section*

Drafting the introductory, or general rule, section is a three-step process. Decide what information to include, order that information, and draft the section.

a. Decide What Information You Need to Include

The first step is to list the information that you want to include in your introductory section. In preparing this list, keep two things in mind. First, remember your audience. If the attorney for whom you are preparing the memo knows little or nothing about the area of law, provide the attorney with an overview of the area of law, distinguishing closely related doctrines and defining key terms. If, however, the attorney knows the area of law, do not include this type of information. Second, distinguish between general rules—that is, rules that apply to all of the elements—and specific rules—that is, rules that apply to only one element. Include only general rules in your introductory section. Save the specific rules for the discussion of the element to which they apply.

In the sample problem, you can presume that the attorney will have taken civil procedure as a law student and will, therefore, know the basics. Accordingly, in drafting the introductory section, you do not need to explain the difference between personal service and substituted service or define those terms. You do, though, need to set out the applicable portion of the statute and the rules relating to the burden of proof. In addition, you should set out two other "rules" that apply to all of the elements. First, because Ms. Olsen can make a policy argument, set out the policies underlying the statute. Second, tell your supervising attorney that the courts have said that the statute should be narrowly construed to assure due process. Finally, include a roadmap, which is what the name suggests: a map for the rest of the discussion.

b. Order the Information

The next step is to order the items on the list. Most of the time, you will want to set out more general information before more specific information. Therefore, in drafting the introductory section, you will usually want to use an inverted pyramid: broad rules first, narrower rules next, and exceptions last.

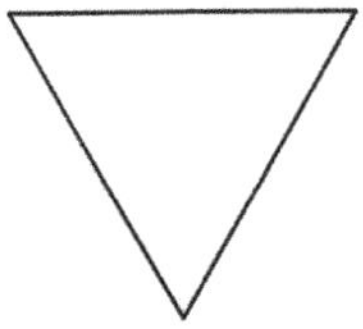

More general information
More specific information
Exceptions

Most attorneys would agree that the policies that underlie the statute are the most general piece of information, that the applicable portion of the statute is the next most general piece of information, and that the rules relating to the burden of proof are the most specific. Consequently, in our sample problem, you would want to set out the policies underlying the statute first, the applicable portions of the statute next, and the rules relating to the burden of proof last.

PRACTICE POINTER

If you are not sure which rules are the more general rules and which rules are the more specific rules, look at the cases. In most instances, the courts set out more general rules before more specific rules.

The approach is similar when there is more than one applicable statutory section: Instead of setting out the statutes in the order in which they appear in the code, set out the more general statutory sections first. For example, set out the section that explains the statute's purpose before the section that sets out the rule, and set out the section that contains the rule before the section that contains the definitions.

c. Prepare the First Draft

In preparing the first draft, do not do what the writer did in Example 3: String together a series of quotes, some of which set out the same rules using slightly different language.

EXAMPLE 3 **Poor Draft: Writer Has Simply Strung Together a Series of Quotes**

DISCUSSION

"The purpose of service of process is to advise the defendant that an action has been commenced and to warn the defendant that he or she must appear in a timely manner to state such defenses as are available." *Torres v. Arnco Constr., Inc.*, 867 So. 2d 583 (Fla. 5th DCA 2004). It is well settled that the fundamental purpose of service is "to give proper notice to the defendant in the case that he is answerable to the claim of plaintiff and, therefore, to vest jurisdiction in the court entertaining the controversy." *Shurman v. Atl. Mortg. & Inv. Corp.*, 795 So. 2d 952, 953-54 (Fla. 2001) (citing *State ex rel. Merritt v. Heffernan*, 142 Fla. 496, 195 So. 145, 147 (1940)). Therefore, "a judgment entered without due service of process is void." *Torres*, 867 So. 2d at 586.

The statute specifically states:

> Service of original process is made by delivering a copy of it to the person to be served with a copy of the complaint, petition, or other initial pleading or paper or by leaving the copies at his or her usual place of abode with any person residing therein who is 15 years of age or older and informing the person of their contents. Minors who are or have been married shall be served as provided in this section.

§ 48.031(1)(a), Fla. Stat. (2013).

"The statutes regulating service of process are to be strictly construed to assure that a defendant is notified of the proceedings." *Torres*, 867 So. 2d at 586. "Indeed, because statutes authorizing substituted service are exceptions to the general rule requiring a defendant to be served personally, due process requires strict compliance with their statutory requirements." *Id.*

Thus, because Ms. Olsen is challenging the validity of the service, she will have the burden of proof. Ms. Olsen will concede that the summons was left with a person who is 15 years old or older residing therein. In addition, she will probably concede that her sister was informed of the contents of the documents. She may, however, be able to prove that the summons was not left at her usual place of abode.

Instead of just cutting and pasting the rules from your research notes into your first draft, take the time to read, analyze, and synthesize the rules. Once you understand the rules, determine which rules apply to your case, and then set out each of the applicable rules once and only once.

PRACTICE POINTER

Almost all attorneys will want you to quote the relevant portions of statutes. However, when it comes to other rules, for example, common law rules or rules that the courts have set out, different attorneys prefer different things. While some attorneys will want you to quote all of the rules, others find a series of quotes annoying and prefer that you set out close paraphrases of the rules. Therefore, before you do your first draft, check with your supervising attorney to see which style he or she prefers.

EXAMPLE 4 Better Draft: Writer Has Set Out Each Rule Only Once

DISCUSSION

The fundamental purpose of service of process is to give defendants notice of claims that have been filed against them and to provide them with an opportunity to defend their rights. *Shurman v. Atl. Mortg. & Inv. Corp.*, 795 So. 2d 952, 953-54 (Fla. 2001). Because it is important that litigants receive notice of actions against them, courts strictly construe and enforce statutes governing service of process. *Id.* at 954.

In this case, the applicable section of the statute reads as follows:

> Service of original process is made by delivering a copy of it to the person to be served with a copy of the complaint, petition, or other initial pleading or paper or by leaving the copies at his or her usual place of abode with any person residing therein who is 15 years of age or older and informing the person of their contents. Minors who are or have been married shall be served as provided in this section.

§ 48.031(a)(1), Fla. Stat. (2013).

Although the party seeking to invoke the jurisdiction of the court has the burden of proving that service was proper, if the return is regular on its face, the courts presume that the service was valid. *Busman v. State, Dep't of Revenue*, 905 So. 2d 956, 958 (Fla. 3d DCA 2005); *Thompson v. State, Dep't of Revenue*, 867 So. 2d 603, 605 (Fla. 1st DCA 2004). In such instances, the party challenging the service has the burden of presenting clear and convincing evidence that the service was invalid. *Id.*

In this case, Ms. Olsen will have to concede that the summons was left with a person 15 years or older who was residing at the house where the summons and complaint were served. In addition, it is unlikely that Ms. Olsen will be able to prove that her sister was not informed of the contents of the documents. Ms. Olsen may, however, be able to present clear and convincing evidence that the summons was not left at her usual place of abode.

You do not, however, have to quote the entire statute. If only part of the statute is applicable, you can set out only that part.

EXAMPLE 5 Better Draft: Writer Has Quoted Only the Applicable Portion of the Statute

DISCUSSION

The Florida courts have repeatedly stated that the fundamental purpose of service of process is to give defendants notice of claims that have been filed against them and to provide defendants with an opportunity to defend their rights. *E.g., Shurman v. Atl. Mortg. & Inv. Corp.*, 795 So. 2d 952, 953-54

(Fla. 2001). Because these rights are so important, the courts strictly construe and enforce statutes governing service of process. *Id.* at 954.

In the present case, the relevant portion of the statute reads as follows:

> (1)(a) Service of original process is made by delivering a copy of it to the person to be served with a copy of the complaint, petition, or other initial pleading or paper or by leaving the copies at his or her usual place of abode with any person residing therein who is 15 years of age or older and informing the person of their contents. . . .

§ 48.031(a)(1), Fla. Stat. (2013).

Although the party seeking to invoke the jurisdiction of the court has the burden of proving that service was proper, if the return is regular on its face, the courts presume that the service was valid. *Busman v. State, Dep't of Revenue,* 905 So. 2d 956, 958 (Fla. 3d DCA 2005); *Thompson v. State, Dep't of Revenue,* 867 So. 2d 603, 605 (Fla. 1st DCA 2004). In such instances, the party challenging the service has the burden of presenting clear and convincing evidence that the service was invalid. *Id.*

In this case, Ms. Olsen may be able to present clear and convincing evidence that the summons was not left at her usual place of abode. However, if the court decides that the summons was left at her usual place of abode, Ms. Olsen will have to concede that the summons was left with a person 15 years or older who was residing at the house where the summons and complaint were served. In addition, although Ms. Olsen can argue that her sister was not informed of the contents of the summons and complaint, it is unlikely that she can meet her burden of proof.

PRACTICE POINTER

If your quotation has fifty words or more, you need to set it out as a block quote, indenting five spaces on the left and five spaces on the right and omitting the quotation marks. In contrast, if the quote has fewer than fifty words, you can include it in the text of your sentence. See Rule 38 in the *ALWD Guide to Legal Citation* and Rule 5.1 in *The Bluebook.*

PRACTICE POINTER

Read other lawyers' memos, briefs, wills, contracts, and other documents to learn how experienced attorneys organize their arguments and craft their writing. Do not just copy those documents, however: What worked in one situation may not work in another situation. Instead, adapt the examples so that they reflect the law that applies in your case.

d. Include a Citation to Authority for Each Rule

You must include a citation to authority for each rule that you set out in your memo. This authority may be a constitutional provision, a statute, a regulation, a court rule, or a case.

> **PRACTICE POINTER**
>
> In drafting your memo, use the applicable citation rules. For example, if you are writing a memo to a Florida attorney about an issue governed by Florida law, use the Florida citation rules.

In choosing a citation for a rule, always choose mandatory, or binding, authority over persuasive authority. See section 2.C. For example, in choosing a case, always choose cases from your jurisdiction over cases from other jurisdictions. In addition, as a general rule, choose decisions from higher courts over decisions from lower courts and more recent decisions over older decisions. The exception might be when the decisions of the jurisdiction's highest court, for example, your state's highest court, are quite old and there are more recent decisions from your state's intermediate court of appeals. If the decisions from both your state's highest court and intermediate court are mandatory authority, you can choose to cite the more recent decision from the state intermediate court of appeals. Although there may be times when you want to list more than one case to show the attorney that the rule is well established, avoid long string cites, that is, listing more than two or three cases.

> **PRACTICE POINTER**
>
> As a general rule, do not cite unpublished or unreported decisions as authority for a rule. Instead, cite a published decision, for example, the case or cases that the unpublished or unreported decision cited as authority for the rule.

3. *Draft the Discussion of the Undisputed Elements*

More likely than not, one or more of the elements will not be in dispute. Although you cannot ignore these undisputed elements, you do not need to devote much space to them.

a. Decide Where to Put Your Discussion of the Undisputed Elements

While some attorneys choose to raise and dismiss the undisputed elements at the end of their introductory section, others choose to discuss all of the elements in order. Compare the following examples. In Example 6, the writer has raised and dismissed the undisputed element in her roadmap at the end of her introductory section. In contrast, in Example 7, the writer has raised and dismissed the undisputed elements in their own subsections.

EXAMPLE 6 Undisputed Elements Raised and Dismissed at the End of the Introductory Section

[Note: The text of the first part of the introductory section is not shown.]

In this case, Ms. Olsen may be able to present clear and convincing evidence that the petition was not left at her usual place of abode. However, if the court decides that the petition was left at her usual place of abode, Ms. Olsen will have to concede that the summons was left with a person 15 years or older who was residing at the house where service was made. In addition, although Ms. Olsen can argue that her sister was not informed of the contents of the documents, it is unlikely that she can meet her burden of proof.

EXAMPLE 7 Undisputed Elements Raised in Separate Subsections

Introductory section

[Note: The first part of the introductory section is not shown.]

In this case, the second element is not in dispute: The summons was left with Ms. Webster at her home, and Ms. Webster is over the age of 15. In addition, more likely than not, a court would conclude that the process server told Ms. Webster about the contents of the document. Ms. Olsen may be able to prove, however, that service was not made at her usual place of abode.

A. USUAL PLACE OF ABODE

[Disputed element; text not included in this example.]

B. PERSON 15 YEARS OLD OR OLDER RESIDING THEREIN

In addition to leaving the complaint or petition at the defendant's usual place of abode, the process server must leave the complaint or petition with a person 15 years old or older residing therein. If the court concludes that Ms. Olsen's sister's house was Ms. Olsen's usual place of abode, Ms. Olsen will have to concede that the petition was left with a person residing therein who is at least 15 years old: Ms. Webster is 32 years old, and the petition was left with her at her house.

C. NOTIFIED OF CONTENTS

[Disputed element; text not included in this example]

To see the full text of this example, see the memo set out in section 6.D.1.

b. Prepare the First Draft of Your Discussion of the Undisputed Elements

In most instances, your discussion of an undisputed element will be very short: Identify the element, set out any applicable specific rules, and apply those rules to the facts of your case. While in some instances you will need to include brief case descriptions, in most instances such descriptions are not necessary. Compare the following examples.

> **PRACTICE POINTER**
>
> As a general rule, in a criminal case a defendant does not "concede" that an element is met. He or she makes the government prove each element of the crime. Accordingly, in a criminal case, do not state that the defendant will concede that an element is met. Instead, frame the sentence in terms of what the government can prove.

EXAMPLE 8 **Poor Draft of Undisputed Element: Writer Has Set Out Conclusion Without Setting Out Facts that Support that Conclusion**

Ms. Olsen should concede that the second element, that the complaint or petition be left with a person 15 years or older residing therein, is met.

EXAMPLE 9 **Poor Draft of Undisputed Element: Writer Has Gone into Too Much Depth on Undisputed Element**

For substitute service of process to be valid at a defendant's "usual place of abode," the complaint or petition must be left with a person residing therein who is 15 years of age or older. § 48.031, Fla. Stat. (2013). Although the statute does not specify the period of time an individual must occupy a home to be regarded as "residing therein," the courts do not require extended habitation. *Compare Magazine v. Bedoya*, 475 So. 2d 1035 (Fla. 3d DCA 1985) (six-week stay long enough to establish residency), *with Gamboa v. Jones*, 455 So. 2d 613 (Fla. 3d DCA 1985) (ten-day visit not sufficient to establish residency). Because she is 32, Ms. Webster satisfies the age requirement. From the facts given, it is unclear how long Ms. Webster has lived at the home in question; however, the memo indicated that she was served at "her house." Consequently, unless other facts are presented, Ms. Webster appears to be the owner and a resident of the house, and she has lived there long enough to establish residency. Therefore, the residing therein requirement is met.

EXAMPLE 10 **Better Draft of Undisputed Element**

In addition to leaving the complaint or petition at the defendant's usual place of abode, the process server must leave the documents with a person 15 years old or older residing therein. If the court concludes that Ms. Olsen's sister's house was Ms. Olsen's usual place of abode, Ms. Olsen will have to concede that the summons was left with a person residing therein who is at least 15 years old: Ms. Webster is 32 years old, and the summons and complaint were left with her at her house.

EXAMPLE 11 **Better Draft of Undisputed Element**

A court will find that the second element is met. Because the summons and complaint were left with Ms. Olsen's 32-year-old sister, the age requirement is met. In addition, because Ms. Olsen's sister lives at the house where the summons and complaint were left, the residing therein requirement is met.

PRACTICE POINTER

While some elements are clearly not in dispute and some are clearly in dispute, there will be elements that fall somewhere in between these two categories.

________________________ X ________________________

Not in dispute In dispute

When you have an element that falls into this "in between" category, you will usually do more than raise and dismiss the element but less than a full analysis. Alert the attorney to the fact that one side might have a weak argument, set out that argument, explain why the argument is weak, and then move on.

4. *Draft the Discussion of the Disputed Elements*

You will usually want to create a separate subsection for each disputed element. Include a subheading that identifies the element and then set out, in paragraph form, the following information:

a. the specific rules for that element;
b. cases that illustrate how those specific rules have been applied;
c. each side's arguments; and
d. your prediction about how the court is likely to decide the element.

a. Set Out the Specific Rules

Begin your discussion of a disputed element by setting out the rules that relate to that element. For example, if the courts apply a particular test in determining whether the element is met, set out that test. Similarly, if the courts have defined any terms, set out those definitions.

In drafting your specific rule paragraphs, use the same process that you used in drafting the introductory section. Begin by listing all of the information that you want to include in your specific rule paragraph, and then order that information, setting out more general information before more specific information. Finally, draft the specific rule paragraph or paragraphs.

In drafting these paragraphs, keep the following in mind. First, include only those rules that apply to the element that you are currently discussing. Do not repeat general rules that you set out in your introductory section, and do not set out rules that apply to other elements. Second, do not simply cut and paste the rules from your research notes into your draft. Instead, determine what the rules are, and then set out each rule once, and only once, using clear and concise language. Finally, remember to include a citation to authority for each rule that you set out. Compare Examples 12 and 13, both of which are examples of the specific rule paragraph for the usual place of abode element.

EXAMPLE 12 **Poor Draft: Writer Has Simply Cut and Pasted Rules from Research Notes into Draft**

> The Florida courts have defined "usual place of abode" as "the fixed place of residence for the time being when the service is made." *Shurman v. Atl. Mortg. & Inv. Corp.*, 795 So. 2d 952, 953-54 (Fla. 2001). "If a person has more than one residence, a summons must be served at the residence at which the defendant is actually living at the time of service." *Id.* at 954. As the Florida Supreme Court noted in *Torres v. Arnco Const., Inc.*, 867 So. 2d 583, 586 (Fla. 5th DCA 2004), "the courts have frequently invalidated substituted service of process in cases where the defendant was not actually living at the place where service was made, even though process might have been delivered to a relative."

EXAMPLE 13 **Better Draft: Writer Has Identified the Rules and Then Set Out Each Rule Once, Using Language that Is Clear and Concise**

> Although the statute does not define the phrase "usual place of abode," the courts have said that a defendant's usual place of abode is the place "where the defendant was actually living at the time of service." *E.g., Shurman v. Atl. Mortg. & Inv. Corp.*, 795 So. 2d 952, 953-54 (Fla. 2001); *Busman v. State, Dep't of Revenue*, 905 So. 2d 956, 957 (Fla. 3d DCA 2005).

b. Describe the Analogous Cases

When an element is in dispute, most attorneys want to see not only the specific rules but also examples of how those specific rules have been applied in analogous cases. Therefore, if an element is in dispute and there are analogous cases, you will usually want to describe at least some of those cases.

In drafting the analogous case section, always keep in mind why you are including cases. Do not include analogous case descriptions just to show your supervising attorney that you found and read cases. The analogous case section is not there so that you can prove that you did a lot of work. Instead, include analogous case descriptions because the case descriptions will help the attorney understand the rules or because either your side or the other side is likely to use the cases to support its position.

Step 1: Identify the Analogous Cases

The first step is to go back through your research notes and identify the cases in which the court discussed the disputed element. In the Olsen case, there are about a dozen cases that discuss usual place of abode. (For a list of the Florida cases that discuss usual place of abode, see subheading 9 in the notes of decision following section 48.031 in Florida Statutes Annotated.)

> **PRACTICE POINTER**
>
> In looking for analogous cases, look first for cases from your jurisdiction. If you do not find any, you can then look for analogous cases from other jurisdictions. However, before deciding to use an out-of-state case, make sure that the other state's specific rules are the same as your state's specific rules.

Step 2: Sort the Analogous Cases

Once you have identified the analogous cases, sort those cases. Put the cases in which the court held that the element was met in one stack and the cases in which the court held that the element was not met in another stack.

EXAMPLE 14 **Chart Listing Cases**

Cases in Which Element Was Not Met	Cases in Which Element Was Met
• *Shurman v. Atl. Mortg. & Inv. Corp.*, 795 So. 2d 952 (Fla. 2001) • *Heck v. Bank Liberty*, 86 So. 3d 1281) (Fla. 1st DCA 2012) • *Portfolio Recovery Assocs., LLC v. Gonzalez*, 951 So. 2d 1037 (Fla. 3d DCA 2007) • *Cordova v. Jolcover*, 942 So. 2d 1045 (Fla. 2d DCA 2006) • *Gilbert v. Storey*, 920 So. 2d 1173 (Fla. 3d DCA 2006) • *Busman v. State, Dep't of Revenue*, 905 So. 2d 956 (Fla. 3d DCA 2005) • *Thompson v. State, Dep't of Revenue*, 867 So. 2d 603 (Fla. 1st DCA 2004) • *Torres v. Arnco Const., Inc.*, 867 So. 2d 583 (Fla. 5th DCA 2004) [other entries not included]	• *State ex rel. Merritt v. Heffernan*, 195 So. 145 (Fla. 1940) • *Johnston v. Hudlett*, 32 So. 3d 700 (Fla. 4th DCA 2010)

Step 3: Analyze and Synthesize the Cases

It is at this step that the real work begins. Because you want to do more than provide the attorney with "book reports" on the cases that you have read, you need to analyze each of the cases and then synthesize the group of cases.

Analysis requires you to read the cases carefully and critically, identifying the issue that was before the court, the standard of review that the court applied, the facts that the court considered, the court's holding, and the court's reasoning.

> **PRACTICE POINTER**
>
> The standard of review is the standard that an appellate court uses in reviewing a trial court's decision. If the standard of review is *de novo*, the appellate court does not defer to the trial court. Instead, the appellate court reviews the issue on the merits and can substitute its judgment for the judgment of the trial court. In contrast, if the standard of review is abuse of discretion, the appellate court defers to the trial court. When the standard of review is abuse of discretion, the appellate court will overturn the trial court only when the trial court abused its discretion.
>
> In general, the standard of review is *de novo* when the issue is an issue of law—for example, whether the trial court properly instructed the jury. In contrast, the standard of review is usually abuse of discretion if the issue is an issue of fact—for example, whether a particular expert is qualified.

If there is more than one case, you also need to do synthesis. When the cases are read as a group, what principle or principles can you draw from them? For example, in the Olsen case, what principle or principles can you draw from the group of cases in which the courts have held that the summons was not left at the defendant's usual place of abode?

One way of doing this analysis and synthesis is to prepare a chart in which, for each case, you identify the court, the date of the decision, the key facts, and the court's reasoning. Note that in Examples 15 and 16 there is not a column for the holding. This column is not necessary because the cases are grouped based on their holdings. Example 15 analyzes the cases in which the element was met, and Example 16 is an excerpt from the chart that analyzes cases in which the element was not met.

> **PRACTICE POINTER**
>
> There is more than one way to list the cases: You can list them in chronological order; in reverse chronological order; by court; or within a court, by district or division. In Example 15, we set out decisions from the Florida Supreme Court first. We then list the decisions from the Court of Appeals in reverse chronological order.

EXAMPLE 15 **Excerpt from Chart Analyzing Cases in Which the Court Held that Service Was Not Made at the Defendant's Usual Place of Abode**

Case	Court	Date	Facts	Reasoning
Shurman v. Atl. Mortg. & Inv. Corp.	Florida Suprem-e Court	2001	• Mortgage fore-closure action • Service left with D's wife. • D had been incarcerated for at least 9 months.	• D was actually living in the prison. • Substituted serv-ice, being in derogation of the common law, must be strictly construed. • In general, the courts presume that the defend-ant will receive notice of proc-ess if the sum-mons is left with a competent member of his household who lives in his house. This pre-sumption is not, however, valid when the head of the house-hold is in prison.
Portfolio Recovery Assocs., LLC v. Gon-zalez	Fla. 3d DCA	2007	• Summons left with the woman who was mother of one D and mother-in-law of the other D. • Undisputed affi-davit estab-lished that neither D had lived at resi-dence for five years.	• DCA affirmed trial court because undis-puted affidavit established that neither defend-ant had lived at residence for five years. Thus, residence was not their usual place of abode.

Case	Court	Date	Facts	Reasoning
				• It does not describe the underlying cause of action.
Cordova v. Jolcover	Fla. 2d DCA	2006	• P sued D to enforce real estate contract. Summons was left with D's estranged wife, who told process server that the D was not in the country. D submitted his passport and police report that showed that he was living in Peru. Estranged wife also submitted affidavit saying that she and husband were estranged and that process server did not notify her of content.	• DCA reversed trial court because defendant presented clear and convincing evidence that service was not left at the defendant's usual place of abode. The return of service raised doubts and the defendant submitted proof that he was living in Peru.
Busman v. State, Dep't of Revenue	Fla. 3d DCA	2005	• Action to establish paternity. • Service was left with the defendant's half brother on July 16, 2003 • D testified that he had moved out of half brother's house on July 1, 2003, and presented	• Although the sheriff's return of service was regular on its face, Busman presented clear, convincing, and uncontradicted evidence that the summons was not left at his "usual place of abode."

Case	Court	Date	Facts	Reasoning
			lease and landlord's testimony.	• Statute must be strictly construed.
Thompson v. State, Dep't of Revenue	Fla. 1st DCA	2004	• Child support action. • Summons left with wife. • D filed affidavit stating that he had been separated from wife for three years, that he had not lived at the address where the summons was left for three years, and he did not authorize anyone to accept service on his behalf.	• DCA reversed and remanded for an evidentiary hearing. • Thompson's motion and affidavit are based on the fact that the service did not comply with § 48.031 and was, therefore, legally deficient.
Torres v. Arnco Const., Inc.	Fla. 5th DCA	2004	• Summons left with D's mother. • D had resided in NY for 57 years and at NY address for 12 years. • NY neighbors verified that D lived in house but that he traveled a lot. • Mother said that D would be home soon.	• Although standard of review is gross abuse of discretion, no live testimony. • P has the burden of proof. • P did not meet burden. • Mother's statement was ambiguous. • Dissent argues that D had burden of proof and that his statements were not sufficient. If D were visiting his family in

Case	Court	Date	Facts	Reasoning
				Florida for substantial periods of time, the Florida house was his "usual abode" when he was served in Florida. It would also be consistent with the affidavit of the Florida process server who said that D's mother remarked that Torres "would be home soon, and she would see to it that he received the papers."
Alvarez v. State Farm	Fla. 3d DCA	1994	• Service was left with D's cousin at cousin's residence. • Affidavits, telephone bill, and marriage license established that D was not living with cousin at time of service and that D had not lived there for some time.	• Uncontradicted evidence established that D was not living at that address on the date of service or for some time before. Therefore, service of process was ineffective as a matter of law.

EXAMPLE 16 **Case in Which the Court Held that Service Was Made at the Defendant's Usual Place of Abode**

Case	Court	Date	Facts	Reasoning
State ex rel. Merritt v. Heffernan, 195 So. 145 (Fla. 1940)	Florida Suprem-e Court	1940	• Wife served one hour after D left to go back to Minnesota. • D had an office, voted, and paid taxes in Minnesota. • D had moved family to Florida two months earlier. • D had visited family twice "during season." • Summons was left with D's wife and, apparently, D received actual notice.	• Ct acknowl-edges that D's permanent resi-dence was in Minnesota. • However, ct seems to think that it was more important that his family was in Florida, that D was on a train and not in Min-nesota at the time of service, and that the evi-dence sug-gested that D intended to return to Minnesota.

PRACTICE POINTER

Just as it is unlikely that anyone other than you will see your research notes, it is also unlikely that anyone other than you will see your charts. Therefore, use the format and abbreviations that make sense to you. Do not waste time creating charts that "look nice."

In creating and examining your chart, you might discover that the cases in which the element was met (or not met) have one of the following in common:

- ☐ that all of the cases in which the element is met (or not met) have a particular fact or set of facts in common;
- ☐ that in all of the cases in which the element is met (or not met) the courts seem to focus on a particular policy underlying the rule;
- ☐ that different courts or different divisions of the same court seem to take a particular approach;
- ☐ that the rules seem to be evolving; or
- ☐ that the decisions seem to be result oriented.

When you determine what the cases have in common, or that they do not have anything in common, you have done synthesis.

Step 4: Write the Sentences Introducing Your Description of the Analogous Cases

Do not make your supervising attorney guess about how a case or group of cases contributes to the overall analysis. Instead, use topic sentences to introduce each case or group of cases. The language you use will depend on a number of factors, including the number of analogous cases and what you discovered in analyzing and synthesizing those cases.

In the Olsen case, the writer wants to illustrate how the courts have interpreted the phrase "usual place of abode" by providing her supervising attorney with examples of the types of fact situations in which the courts have concluded that service was made at the defendant's usual place of abode and with examples of the types of fact situations in which the courts have held that the service was not made at the defendant's usual place of abode. While the writer could introduce the first case with a sentence that says, "In State ex rel. Merritt v. Heffernan, 195 So. 145, 146 (Fla. 1940), service was made on the defendant's wife at the defendant's apartment in Florida," most attorneys expect more. They want to know why the case is important and why you included the case in your memo.

In charting the first group of cases, the writer discovered that there was only one analogous case, one from 1940, in which the court held that the service was made at the defendant's usual place of abode. In addition, in analyzing and synthesizing both the 1940 case and the more recent cases, the writer concluded that, although the 1940 case had never been overruled, in the more recent cases the courts have changed the way in which they view service on a relative. As a consequence, the writer begins her description of the 1940 case by placing the old case in its historical context, by telling the attorney that the case is one of the few published decisions, and by setting out the court's conclusion. See Example 17.

EXAMPLE 17 Sentence Introducing Analogous Cases

In an early case, and one of the few published decisions in which the court concluded that the defendant had been served at his usual place of abode, the court reasoned that, at the time of service, defendant's wife and children were living at the apartment where service was made. *State ex rel. Merritt v. Heffernan*, 195 So. 145, 146-47 (Fla. 1940). In that case, the defendant had relocated his family to Florida two months before service was made and had twice visited them while they were in Florida, the second time leaving the apartment to return to Minnesota just an hour before service was made. *Id.* Although the defendant argued that his usual place of abode was Minnesota, where he had an office, paid taxes, and voted, the court disagreed, stating that "[w]e do not hold the view that Florida was the permanent residence of the defendant, but we do feel that in the circumstance reflected in the record, it was his usual place of abode . . . ." *Id.* at 148.

However, when there is more than one analogous case, you want to do more than just tell your readers that there are two, three, or four cases. In these instances, draft a principle-based topic sentence.

A principle-based topic sentence is a sentence that tells your reader what "principle" you are using the cases to illustrate. Sometimes, the courts set out these principles. For instance, in our sample problem the courts have explicitly said that the phrase "usual place of abode" should be narrowly construed and, in fact, in their decisions they do construe the language narrowly. At other times, you will "discover" the principle while synthesizing the cases. In charting the cases, you may discover (1) that all or most of cases have a particular set of facts in common; (2) that in all or most of the cases the courts seem to focus on a particular policy underlying the rule; (3) that different courts or different divisions of the same court seem to take a particular approach; (4) that the rules seem to be evolving; or (5) that the decisions seem to be result oriented.

While in some situations the case law is so consistent that everyone who reads a group of cases draws the same principle or principles from those cases, in other situations there is more than one way to read the cases or, depending on the arguments that you think the parties are likely to make, you may want to emphasize different points. See Examples 18, 19, and 20. In each example, the principle-based topic sentence is in bold.

EXAMPLE 18 **Principle-Based Topic Sentence Used to Introduce a Group of Analogous Cases**

In contrast, in the more recent cases, the courts have emphasized that it is not enough that the complaint or petition is left with a relative. *See, e.g., Busman,* 905 So. 2d at 947; *Torres v. Arnco Const., Inc.,* 867 So. 2d 583 (Fla. 5th DCA 2004). For example, in *Busman,* the court concluded that service of process was not valid even though the summons and complaint had been left with the defendant's half brother. *Id.* at 958. Similarly, in *Torres,* the court concluded that service had not been made at the defendant's usual place of abode when, after trying unsuccessfully to serve the defendant at his New York apartment, the plaintiff served the defendant's mother at her home in Florida. *Id.* at 585, 587. Although the defendant's mother told the process server that her son "would be home soon," the court decided that this statement was, at best, ambiguous. *Id.* at 585; *accord Portfolio Recovery Assocs., LLC v. Gonzalez,* 951 So. 2d 1037, 1038 (Fla. 3d DCA 2007) (service was not made at the defendants' usual place of abode when the summons and complaint were left with a woman who was the mother of one defendant and the mother-in-law of the other defendant, but the defendants had not lived at the residence for five years).

EXAMPLE 19 **Principle-Based Topic Sentence Used to Introduce a Group of Analogous Cases**

In the most recent cases, the courts have held that the service was invalid or remanded the case for an evidentiary hearing when the defendant presented evidence that he was not actually living at the house where service was made. *See, e.g., Busman,* 905 So. 2d at 958; *Thompson,* 867 So. 2d at 605. For example, in *Busman,* the Third District Court of Appeals held that service was invalid when the defendant presented a lease agreement that corroborated his testimony that he had moved out of his half brother's house two and one-half months before his half brother was served. Likewise, in *Thompson,* the First District Court of Appeals reversed and remanded the case for an evidentiary hearing when the defendant submitted an affidavit in which he stated that he was separated from his wife, that he had not resided at that address for over three years, and that he did not authorize anyone to accept service of process on his behalf. *Id.* at 605.

EXAMPLE 20 **Principle-Based Topic Sentence Used to Introduce a Group of Analogous Cases**

In most of the cases in which the courts have held that the summons was not left at the defendant's usual place of abode, the defendant had not lived at the house where service was made for a substantial period of time. *See, e.g., Shurman v. Atl. Mortg. & Inv. Corp.*, 795 So. 2d 952 (Fla. 2001); *Portfolio Recovery Assocs. LLC v. Gonzalez,* 951 So. 2d 1037 (Fla. 3d DCA 2007). For instance, in *Shurman,* the defendant was incarcerated and had not lived at the family home for at least nine months, 795 So. 2d at 953, and in *Portfolio Recovery Assocs.*, the defendants had not lived at the house where service was made for five years, 951 So. 2d at 1038.

PRACTICE POINTER

When you have difficulty coming up with a good topic sentence (and there will be times when you do), try asking yourself the following questions:

1. Why am I including these cases in my memo?
2. What is the common thread that runs through this group of cases?
3. If the client's case is litigated, how will each side use these cases?

Step 5: Draft Your Descriptions of the Cases

Once you have drafted the topic sentence, the next step is to draft the case descriptions.

If there are only two or three analogous cases, you can describe all of them. If, however, there are a number of cases, describe only the "best" cases. In selecting these cases, use the following criteria:

- ☐ Select cases from your jurisdiction over cases from other jurisdictions.
- ☐ Select cases with published decisions over cases with unpublished, or unreported, decisions.
- ☐ Select more recent cases over older cases.
- ☐ Select cases from higher courts over cases from lower courts.

In addition, most of the time you will be using the cases to see where your case falls along the continuum of decided cases. Is your case more like the cases in which the court held that the element was met or more like the cases in which the court held that the element was not met? Accordingly, select cases that are more factually analogous over cases that are less factually analogous.

??←my case→??

Cases in which element met   Cases in which element not met

How much you say about a case will depend on the point that you are using the case to illustrate. If you are using the case to illustrate a small point, then a sentence or even a clause, phrase, or word may be enough. In contrast, if you expect that one or both sides will rely heavily on the case, your description will be longer. The bottom line is that you need to include only that information that is relevant to the principle that you are using the case to illustrate and to set up the arguments based on that case.

Compare Examples 21, 22, and 23. In Example 21, the case descriptions are very short because the writer is using the cases to illustrate a small point. In contrast, in Example 22, the case description is longer because the writer wants to use the case to illustrate several points and because the writer expects that both sides will use the case. In Example 23, the writer sets out two medium-length case descriptions.

EXAMPLE 21 **Short Descriptions of Two Cases**

Although the statute does not specify how long the person who received the service must have been "residing therein," the courts do not require extended habitation. While in *Gamboa,* the court determined that a ten-day visit was not sufficient to establish residency, *id.* at 614, in *Magazine,* the court determined that a six-week stay was sufficient, *id.* at 1035.

EXAMPLE 22 **Longer Description in Which the Writer Sets Out Facts and the Court's Holding and Reasoning**

In an early case, and one of the few published decisions in which the court concluded that the defendant had been served at his usual place of abode, the summons was left with the defendant's wife at the family's apartment in Florida an hour after the defendant boarded a train to Minnesota. *State ex rel. Merritt v. Heffernan,* 195 So. 145, 146 (Fla. 1940). Although the defendant argued that his usual place of abode was Minnesota, where he had an office, paid taxes, and voted, the court disagreed, noting that the defendant had moved his family to the Florida apartment two months before his wife was served, that the defendant had visited his family at the apartment twice "during the season," and that the defendant's family had remained in Florida for some time after the defendant was served. *Id.* at 147. As the court stated, "We do not hold the view that Florida was the permanent residence of the defendant, but we do feel that in the circumstance reflected in the record, it was his usual place of abode . . . ." *Id.* at 148.

EXAMPLE 23 Two Descriptions in Which the Writer Sets Out Facts and the Courts' Holdings and Reasoning

In recent cases, the courts have either held that the service was invalid or remanded the case for an evidentiary hearing when the defendant produced evidence establishing that he was not actually living at the house where the summons was served. *See, e.g., Busman*, 905 So. 2d at 958; *Thompson*, 867 So. 2d at 605. For example, in *Busman*, the Third District Court of Appeals held that the service was not valid when the defendant presented a lease agreement that corroborated his testimony that he had moved out of his half brother's house two and one-half months before his half brother was served. *Id.* at 958. Likewise, in *Thompson*, the First District Court of Appeals reversed and remanded the case for an evidentiary hearing when the defendant submitted an affidavit in which he stated that he was separated from his wife, that he had not resided at that address for over three years, and that he did not authorize anyone to accept service of process on his behalf. *Id.* at 605.

Occasionally, you will not need to include a full description of an analogous case. For instance, you may not need to include a full description of a case if you are using the case to illustrate a single point or if you have already given full descriptions of one or two cases but want to tell the attorney about a third or fourth case, or when you simply want to illustrate one aspect of a rule. In these situations you can use parentheticals.

EXAMPLE 24 Cases Described in Parentheticals

Although the statute does not specify the period of time an individual must occupy a home to be regarded as "residing therein," the courts do not require extended habitation. *Compare Magazine v. Bedoya*, 475 So. 2d 1035 (Fla. 3d DCA 1985) (six-week stay sufficient to establish residency), *with Gamboa v. Jones*, 455 So. 2d 613 (Fla. 3d DCA 1985) (ten-day visit not sufficient to establish residency).

EXAMPLE 25 Additional Cases Described in Parentheticals

In contrast, in the more recent cases, the courts have emphasized that it is not enough that the complaint or petition is left with a relative. *See, e.g., Busman*, 905 So. 2d at 947; *Torres v. Arnco Const., Inc.*, 867 So. 2d 583 (Fla. 5th DCA 2004). For example, in *Busman*, the court concluded that service of process was not valid even though the summons and complaint had been left with the defendant's half brother. *Id.* at 958. Similarly, in *Torres*, the court concluded that service had not been made at the defendant's usual place of abode when, after trying unsuccessfully to serve the defendant at his New York apartment, the plaintiff served the defendant's mother at her home in Florida. *Id.* at 585, 587. Although the defendant's mother told the process server that her son "would be home soon," the court decided that this statement was, at best, ambiguous. *Id.* at 585; *accord Portfolio Recovery Assocs., LLC v. Gonzalez*, 951 So. 2d 1037, 1038 (Fla. 3d DCA 2007) (service was not made at the defendants' usual place of abode when the summons and complaint were left with a woman who was the mother of one defendant and the mother-in-law of the other defendant, but the defendants had not lived at the residence for five years).

PRACTICE POINTER

In most instances, when you refer to a case by only one party's name, you should use the plaintiff 's name. For example, when you refer to *Thompson v. State, Dep't of Revenue,* you would say "in *Thompson,*" and when you refer to *Cordova v. Jolcover,* you would say, "in *Cordova.*" There are, however, some exceptions to this general rule. When the plaintiff is the state, you will refer to the case using the defendant's name: "*State v. Smith*" becomes "*Smith,*" and "*Commonwealth v. Jones*" becomes "*Jones.*" In addition, if the courts typically refer to a case using the defendant's name, you should use that name. For more on short cites, see Rule 12.19 in the *ALWD Guide to Legal Citation* and Rule 10.9 in *The Bluebook.*

c. Draft the Arguments

At this point your role changes dramatically. No longer are you just a "reporter" telling the attorney what you found in doing your research. To do a good job presenting each side's arguments, you must become an advocate, using your training, intellectual abilities, and creativity to construct the arguments each side is likely to make. You must think like the plaintiff's attorney and then like the defendant's attorney.

When you use the script format, you are, in effect, writing a "script" for the oral arguments on the issue. You begin by putting yourself in the shoes of the party with the burden of proof, setting out the arguments that side might make. You then step into the other side's shoes and set out that side's arguments. Finally, you assume the role of the judge, predicting how the court would decide the element and how it would justify its decision.

EXAMPLE 26 **"Script" for Arguments**

- ☐ Party with the burden of proof's arguments
- ☐ Responding party's arguments
- ☐ Party with the burden of proof's rebuttal (optional)
- ☐ Court's decision + rationale

Step 1: Identify Each Side's Arguments

The first step is to identify each side's arguments. If you wrote down possible arguments as you did your research, start with that list.

EXAMPLE 27 List of Arguments from Research Notes

Ms. Olsen's arguments

- ☐ On the day that she was served, Ms. Olsen was living at the residential treatment house.
- ☐ Service on a relative is not sufficient.
- ☐ Her more permanent address was the residential treatment house address. She had a room, etc., at the residential treatment house.
- ☐ *Heffernan* is an old case.
- ☐ In *Torres*, the court held that the defendant's mother's house was not the defendant's usual place of abode even though the mother indicated that the defendant would be home later.
- ☐ There is no indication that the State tried to serve Ms. Olsen at the residential treatment house.

The State's arguments

- ☐ Ms. Olsen stayed at her sister's house three nights a week.
- ☐ Ms. Olsen apparently received mail at her sister's house—the shoebox.
- ☐ Ms. Olsen listed her sister's address on her driver's license.
- ☐ In *Heffernan*, the court held that the apartment was the defendant's usual place of abode even though the defendant had left the apartment and was on a train back to his permanent residence.
- ☐ In *Torres*, the defendant had a permanent residence where he had lived for twelve years. He was just visiting his mother.

Do not, however, stop with the list that you came up with while researching the issue. Push yourself further, asking yourself whether the parties can make any of the other standard types of arguments. For example, can one or both of the parties make plain language arguments, arguments based on the analogous cases, or policy arguments?

i. Plain Language Arguments

A plain language argument is an argument in which you apply the plain language of a statute or rule to the facts of your case. For instance, in the service of process problem, you would make a plain language argument if you argued that, under the plain language of the statute, the service was not made at Ms. Olsen's "usual" place of abode because her sister's house was not the place where she "usually" stayed. During the month in which service was made, Ms. Olsen spent four nights a week at the residential treatment house and only three nights a week at her sister's house. Similarly, you would be making a plain language argument if you argued that, under the plain language of the rule that the courts have set out, Ms. Olsen was not "actually living" at her sister's house because the summons and complaint were served on a weekday and, during the week, Ms. Olsen "actually lived" at the residential treatment house. Note that a plain language argument has two components: a word or phrase from the statute or rule and facts that show that that element is or is not met.

PRACTICE POINTER

To make sure that you have considered all the plain language arguments, do two things. First, think about each word or phrase in the applicable part of the statute and/or rules, asking yourself what the plain meaning of that word or phrase requires. Second, go through each of your facts, asking yourself how each side might be able to use that fact.

ii. Analogous Case Arguments

Under our system of law, judges usually decide like cases in a like manner. Therefore, if the analogous cases support the conclusion that you want the court to reach, you need to argue, first, that your case is like the analogous cases and, second, because your case is like the analogous cases, the court should reach the same result as the courts reached in those decisions. In contrast, if the analogous cases do not support the conclusion that you want the court to reach, you need to distinguish those cases. For example, in Ms. Olsen's case, she will want to argue that her case is like *Busman* and *Torres*, and she will want to distinguish *Heffernan.* Conversely, the State will want to distinguish *Busman* and *Torres* and argue that its case is more like *Heffernan.*

To make sure that you have considered all analogous case arguments, think about rules and the principles you drew from the cases and how the parties might be able to use those rules and principles to support their respective positions. In addition, go through the analogous cases one by one, thinking about how each side might be able to use that case.

PRACTICE POINTER

In constructing analogous case arguments, ask yourself the following questions:

- ☐ In what ways is the analogous case similar to my case?
- ☐ In what ways is it different?
- ☐ Is the case a relatively old case? If it is, how can each side use that fact?
- ☐ Is the case from an intermediate court of appeals or from the state's highest court? How can each side use that fact?
- ☐ Is the case well reasoned or poorly reasoned? How can each side use that fact?
- ☐ How have other cases used or distinguished the case?

iii. Policy Arguments

In making a policy argument, look at the reasons why the legislature enacted a particular statute or a court adopted a particular rule and use those underlying reasons to support your client's position. For example, in the Olsen case you could use the policy behind the service of process statutes—to ensure that defendants have notice of actions filed against them—to argue that service was invalid because Ms. Olsen did not receive notice.

When your issue is one that is governed by a statute, you may be able to find the policies underlying the statute in a "finding" or "purpose" section of the act of which your statute is a part, or a legislative history may tell you what the legislature intended when it enacted the statute. In addition, in applying a statute, the courts frequently set out what they believe are the policies underlying the statutes. Therefore, to come up with policy arguments, look at the text of the statute, the statute's legislative history, and those parts of other courts' decisions that discuss the policies underlying the statute. Once you identify the various policies, determine how each side might be able to use those policies to support its position.

In situations in which the underlying reason for the statute is not explicitly laid out in the act, in its legislative history, or in court decisions, use common sense to determine why the statute was enacted. Ask yourself "what good was the legislature trying to promote" or "what harm was the legislature trying to prevent" when it enacted the statute.

PRACTICE POINTER

At this initial stage, list all of the arguments (plain language, analogous case, and policy), no matter how weak they may seem. Later, you can go through these arguments, weeding out those that don't pass "the giggle test," that is, those that you could not make to a court without laughing.

You can use a chart like the one set out in Example 28 to keep track of the arguments that each side makes.

EXAMPLE 28 **List of Arguments**

Element	Olsen's Arguments	State's Arguments
Usual Place of Abode (in dispute)	Plain language arguments: Analogous case arguments: Policy arguments:	Plain language arguments: Analogous case arguments: Policy arguments:
Age and Residing Therein (not in dispute)		
Informing of Contents (in dispute)	Plain language arguments: Analogous case arguments: Policy arguments:	Plain language arguments: Analogous case arguments: Policy arguments

PRACTICE POINTER

If you find yourself staring at your computer screen unable to come up with more than one or two arguments, find an empty room and then stand up and make Ms. Olsen's arguments. After you have made all of her arguments, take a few steps to your right and make the State's arguments. In most instances, this process will trigger more ideas about what each side can argue. Thus, keep going to back and forth, making and then countering each side's arguments and "answering" questions that you think that a judge might ask you. While at first this exercise may feel a little silly, it will help you come up with additional arguments and it will help you develop the oral skills that you will need as a lawyer.

Step 2: Present the Arguments

After you have identified each side's arguments, you are ready to move to the second step: deciding how you want to present those arguments. Once again, you have some choices. For instance, you can do what we do in this chapter and set out the arguments using a script format, or you can do what we do in the next chapter and set out the rules using an integrated format.

Even under the script format, you have choices. One way to organize the arguments is by type of argument. If you choose this organizational scheme, set out the party with the burden of proof's plain language arguments in one paragraph, its analogous cases arguments in another paragraph or block of paragraphs, and its policy arguments in a third paragraph. Then set out the other side's arguments: Set out the other side's plain language arguments in one paragraph, its analogous case arguments in another paragraph or block of paragraphs, and its policy arguments in a third paragraph.

PRACTICE POINTER

If you organize your arguments around types of arguments, you will usually want to set out the plain language arguments first, analogous cases arguments second, and policy arguments third. This ordering reflects the weight that courts typically give to the different types of arguments. If a court can decide an issue by applying the plain language of the statute or common law to the facts of the case, it will usually do so. If, however, the court cannot decide the issue based on the plain language, it will look to the cases to see how the cases have applied the rules. If the cases do not resolve the issue, the court will then look to the policies underlying the statute.

In the alternative, organize the arguments around the principles that you identified when you analyzed and synthesized the cases. For example, if you determined that all of the cases have three facts in common, you could organize your arguments around those three facts. In setting out the party with the burden of proof's arguments, you would discuss the first fact in one paragraph or block of paragraphs, the second fact in a second paragraph or block of paragraphs, and the third fact in a third paragraph or block of paragraphs. Similarly, in setting out the other side's arguments, you would discuss the first fact in one paragraph or block of paragraphs, the second fact in a second paragraph or block of paragraphs, and the third fact in a third paragraph or block of paragraphs. Within the paragraphs discussing these facts, you would set out any plain language, analogous case, and/or policy arguments that relate to that fact.

A third, and more sophisticated, approach is to organize your arguments around "lines of argument." For example, if you have a burden of proof argument and an argument on the merits, you could organize the arguments around these two lines of argument. In setting out your arguments, set out the party with the burden of proof's arguments relating to the first line of argument in one paragraph or block of paragraphs and its arguments relating to the second line of argument in a second paragraph or block of paragraphs. Then set out the other side's arguments, putting the other side's points relating to the first line of argument in one paragraph and its points relating to the second line of argument in a second paragraph or block of paragraphs. In setting out these lines of argument, include the plain language, analogous case, or policy arguments that relate to that line of argument.

PRACTICE POINTER

If you use the second option—organizing your arguments around the principles you identified when you analyzed and synthesized the cases—you will usually want to discuss the principles in the same order that you set them out and illustrated them in your analogous case section. If you use the third approach—organizing your arguments around "lines of argument"—you should discuss threshold arguments first. In other words, if one argument builds upon another argument, set out the foundational argument first.

Example 29 illustrates the differences between these three organizational schemes.

EXAMPLE 29 **Three Ways of Organizing the Arguments**

Arguments Organized by Type of Argument	Arguments Organized by Principles	Arguments Organized by Lines of Argument
Party with burden of proof's arguments	**Party with burden of proof's arguments**	**Party with burden of proof's arguments**
• Plain language arguments	• Arguments relating to first principle (include any plain language, analogous case, and policy arguments)	• First line of argument (include any plain language, analogous case, and policy arguments)
• Analogous case arguments	• Arguments relating to second principle (include any plain language, analogous case, and policy arguments)	• Second line of argument (include any plain language, analogous case, and policy arguments)
• Policy arguments	• Arguments relating to third principle (include any plain language, analogous case, and policy arguments)	
Responding party's arguments	**Responding party's arguments**	**Responding party's arguments**
• Plain language arguments	• Arguments relating to first principle (include any plain language, analogous case, and policy arguments)	• First line of argument (include any plain language, analogous case, and policy arguments)
• Analogous case arguments	• Arguments relating to second principle (include any plain language, analogous case, and policy arguments)	• Second line of argument (include any plain language, analogous case, and policy arguments)
• Policy arguments	• Arguments relating to third principle (include any plain language, analogous case, and policy arguments)	

Step 3: Draft the Arguments

In most instances, you should start your discussion of each side's arguments by setting out that side's general assertion. For example, in the Olsen case, start the usual place of abode arguments by setting out Ms. Olsen's general assertion: that her sister's house was not her usual place of abode. Similarly, start your discussion of the State's arguments by setting out the State's assertion: Ms. Olsen's sister's house was Ms. Olsen's usual place of abode or it was one of her usual places of abode. In addition, if you are going to make a number of different arguments, you may want to alert the attorney to that fact.

EXAMPLE 30 **Three Ways of Setting Out Ms. Olsen's General Assertion Relating to Usual Place of Abode**

1. Ms. Olsen will argue that her sister's house was not her usual place of abode.
2. Ms. Olsen will argue that she was not actually living at Ms. Webster's house and that, therefore, Ms. Webster's house was not her usual place of abode.
3. Ms. Olsen can make three arguments to support her assertion that her sister's house was not her usual place of abode. First, ...

EXAMPLE 31 **Three Ways of Setting Out the State's General Assertion Relating to Usual Place of Abode**

1. In response, the State will argue that Ms. Webster's house was Ms. Olsen's usual place of abode.
2. The State will counter by arguing that Ms. Olsen was actually living at her sister's house.
3. The State can make three arguments to support its assertion that the service was made at Ms. Olsen's usual place of abode.

In addition to setting out each side's general assertion, you should also introduce and set out each side's subassertions. For example, if you have decided to organize the arguments around types of arguments, introduce each of these types of arguments, asserting that the plain language, the analogous cases, and the policies underlying the statute or rule support your general assertion. Likewise, if you are organizing your arguments around lines of arguments, include a sentence introducing each line of argument.

EXAMPLE 32 **Sentences Introducing Subassertions**

- ☐ First, Ms. Olsen can argue that under the plain language of the statute her sister's house was not her usual place of abode.
- ☐ Second, Ms. Olsen can argue that her case is more like [case names] than it is like [case names].
- ☐ Third, Ms. Olsen can argue that, as a matter of public policy, the court should hold that service was not left at Ms. Olsen's usual place of abode.

It is not, however, enough to just set out general assertions and subassertions. You also need to show the attorney how each side will support those assertions.

One way to do this is to picture yourself standing in front of a judge. If you are making a plain language argument, what facts would you use, and how would you characterize those facts? If you are making an analogous case argument, what cases would you use, and how would you characterize and use those cases? If you are making a policy argument, what policies would you rely on, and how would you use those policies? Similarly, picture the other side presenting its arguments. How would its attorney use the facts, cases, and policies to support its position?

The following example, Example 33, is ineffective because the writer has not supported her assertions. For instance, in the first paragraph, the writer asserts that Ms. Olsen's sister's house was not Ms. Olsen's usual place of abode because the residential treatment house was her usual place of abode. The writer does not, however, back up this assertion with facts: She does not point out that Ms. Olsen had been a full-time resident of the residential treatment house for several months and that she was still spending four nights a week there. Similarly, although the writer asserts that Ms. Olsen's case is more like *Busman* and *Torres* than it is like *Heffernan*, she does not support this assertion by comparing and contrasting the facts in those cases to the facts in the Olsen case. Finally, although the writer sets out a rule relating to the burden of proof, she does not explain why or how that rule will produce a just result.

PRACTICE POINTER

While almost every attorney wants citations to authority in the rule and analogous case sections of memos, not all attorneys want them in the argument sections. Thus, before you draft your memo, determine which approach the attorney that you are working for prefers. (In the following examples, citations are not included in the argument section.)

EXAMPLE 33 **Poor Example: The Writer Has Set Out Assertions but Has Not Supported Those Assertions**

General assertion
First subassertion
Second subassertion
Third subassertion

In this case, Ms. Olsen can make three arguments to support her assertion that the summons and complaint were not left at her usual place of abode. First, she can argue that her sister's house was not her usual place of abode because the residential treatment house was her usual place of abode. Second, she can use the cases to support her position: her case is more like *Busman* and *Torres* than *Heffernan*. Finally, she can argue that as a matter of public policy the party seeking to invoke the jurisdiction of the court has the burden of proving that the service was valid.

General assertion
First subassertion
Second subassertion
Third subassertion

In response, the State will argue that the summons and complaint were left at Ms. Olsen's usual place of abode. The facts establish that Ms. Olsen was, in fact, living at her sister's house at the time the summons and complaint were served. Accordingly, this case is like *Heffernan*. In addition, the State will distinguish *Busman* and *Torres* on the basis that, in those cases, the defendant was not spending any time at the house where the service was made. Finally, the State can argue that the service was valid because the defendant's sister's house was the place where she was most likely to receive notice.

Example 34, while not perfect, is much better. In addition to setting out his assertions, the writer has supported those assertions.

EXAMPLE 34 Better Example: The Writer Has Set Out Assertions and Support for Those Assertions

Ms. Olsen's general assertion
Ms. Olsen's first subassertion
Facts that support Ms. Olsen's first subassertion

Ms. Olsen can make three arguments to support her assertion that her sister's house was not her usual place of abode. First, Ms. Olsen will argue that, under the plain language of the statute, her sister's house was not her usual place of abode. As the courts have stated, service must be made at the place where the defendant was actually living at the time service is made. In this case, the summons and petition were served on a weekday, and on weekdays Ms. Olsen was actually living at the residential treatment house.

Ms. Olsen's second subassertion
Explanation of how cases support Ms. Olsen's second subassertion

Second, Ms. Olsen will argue that the facts in her case are more like the facts in *Busman* and *Torres* than the facts in *Heffernan.* Like Mr. Busman, who produced a lease that corroborated his testimony that he was not living with his half brother on the day that the summons and complaint were served, Ms. Olsen can produce evidence that establishes that on the day she was served she was living at the residential treatment house. Both Ms. Olsen's sister and the manager of the residential treatment house have said that they will testify that, during June and July, Ms. Olsen lived at the treatment house during the week and only visited her sister on weekends. In the alternative, Ms. Olsen can argue that the facts in her case are even stronger than the facts in *Torres.* While Mr. Torres's mother's statement that Mr. Torres "would be home soon" suggested that Mr. Torres would be returning to his mother's house that day, Ms. Olsen's sister told the process server that Ms. Olsen "isn't here today." In addition, Ms. Olsen can distinguish *Heffernan:* Although Mr. Heffernan had been at his family's apartment only an hour before the summons and complaint were served, Ms. Olsen had not been at her sister's house for several days.

Ms. Olsen's third subassertion
Policies supporting Ms. Olsen's third subassertion

Finally, Ms. Olsen can argue that, as a matter of public policy, the court should decide that the summons and petition were not left at her usual place of abode. The courts have stated that the statute should be narrowly construed, and this policy is particularly important in cases in which the State is seeking to terminate a mother's parental rights. In addition, this is not a case in which the State tried but could not locate Ms. Olsen: There is no evidence that the State tried to serve Ms. Olsen at the residential treatment house.

State's main assertion

In response, the State will argue that Ms. Olsen was served at one of her usual places of abode.

State's first subassertion
Facts that support State's first subassertion

The courts have not required that the plaintiff be living at the house where the summons and complaint are served on the day on which the service is made. Therefore, while Ms. Olsen may not have been at her sister's house on the day that the summons and complaint were served, she had been there the previous weekend, and she was there the following weekend. In addition, Ms. Olsen had possessions at her sister's house.

State's second subassertion
Cases that support

Therefore, the State will argue that the facts in this case are much stronger than the facts in *Heffernan.* While in *Heffernan,* Mr. Heffernan visited his family only "twice during the season," Ms. Olsen lived at her sister's house on weekends. In addition, while Mr. Heffernan had another permanent

State's second subassertion

residence, Ms. Olsen was staying at a halfway house, which, by definition, is only a temporary residence. Finally, while in *Heffernan* there was no indication that Mr. Heffernan listed the Florida address on any documents, Ms. Olsen listed her sister's address on her driver's license, and there is evidence indicating that Ms. Olsen received other types of mail at her sister's house.

Cases that support State's second subassertion

The State will use these same facts to distinguish *Torres*. While in *Torres*, Mr. Torres presented evidence establishing that his permanent residence was in New York, in the present case, Ms. Olsen did not have a permanent residence. In the five months before service, she had been an inpatient in a treatment facility, she had lived at the treatment house, and she had lived with her sister. The State can also distinguish *Busman*. While in *Busman* the record indicated that the defendant had not lived at the house where service had been for several weeks, Ms. Olsen admits that she stayed at her sister's house on the weekend before her sister was served.

State's third subassertion

Policies supporting State's third subassertion

Finally, the State will argue that, because the return was regular on its face, Ms. Olsen has the burden of proving, by clear and convincing evidence, that her sister's house was not her usual place of abode. In this instance, Ms. Olsen has not met that burden. When there is evidence that the defendant was in fact living at the house where service was made, the courts should not require plaintiffs to determine which house the defendant was living at on any particular day.

While in the prior example, the writer organized the arguments by type of argument, in the following example, the writer organized the arguments by lines of argument. Once again, the writer has not included pinpoint citations.

EXAMPLE 35 Arguments Organized Around Lines of Argument

Ms. Olsen's strongest argument is that service was not made at the place where she was actually living. Although Ms. Olsen stayed at her sister's house on weekends, on the day that service was made, she was actually living at the residential treatment center. Consequently, this case is more like *Busman* and *Torres* than it is like *Heffernan*. Like Mr. Busman, who was not actually living with his half brother on the day that the summons and complaint were served, Ms. Olsen was not living with her sister on July 24. Both Ms. Olsen's sister and the manager of the residential treatment house have said that they will testify that, during June and July, Ms. Olsen lived at the treatment house during the week and visited her sister only on weekends. This testimony makes this case stronger than *Torres*, in which the defendant's mother's statement that Mr. Torres "would be home soon" suggested that Mr. Torres would be returning to his mother's house that day. Ms. Olsen can also distinguish *Heffernan*: While Mr. Heffernan had been at his family's apartment only an hour before the summons and complaint were served, Ms. Olsen had not been at her sister's house for several days.

Ms. Olsen also has strong policy arguments. The courts have repeatedly said that the purpose of the statute is to ensure that defendants receive notice and that, to that end, the statute should be narrowly construed. In this case, the defendant will testify that she did not receive notice. Her sister states that instead of giving the summons to Ms. Olsen, she put the summons in a shoebox in the kitchen. Moreover, Ms. Olsen can argue that in cases involving the termination of parental rights, the courts should err on the side of ensuring that the parent receives notice. At a minimum, the State should have tried to serve Ms. Olsen at the residential treatment house.

The State can counter this policy argument with its own policy argument. When a defendant has two or more places of abode, the State should not have to determine which one the defendant is staying at on the day that service is actually made. Service can be made at any of the defendant's usual places of abode.

The State can also argue that Ms. Olsen has not met her burden of proving by clear and convincing evidence that she was not actually living at her sister's house on the day when service was made. Unlike Mr. Busman, who had proof that he had moved out of his half brother's house three weeks before service was attempted, Ms. Olsen had not moved out of her sister's house. In fact, she stayed at her sister's house both on the weekend before and the weekend after service was made. The State can also distinguish *Torres.* As the majority in that case noted, the mother's statement was ambiguous; in addition, there was nothing in Mr. Torres's affidavit that established where he was living on the date service was made. In contrast, in this case Ms. Olsen does not deny that she was living at her sister's house three nights a week during the month of July, the month during which service was made. Finally, the State can argue that this case is similar to *Heffernan* in that, as in that case, Ms. Olsen was moving back and forth between two residences. While in *Heffernan* there was no indication that Mr. Heffernan planned to return to the family home the next weekend, in this case Ms. Olsen did, in fact, go back to her sister's house.

d. Predict How the Court Will Decide the Element

The final piece of information you need to include is your prediction about how a court is likely to decide the element. Is it more likely that the court will find that the element is met, or is it more likely that the court will decide that the element is not met?

In writing this section, you must once again change roles. Instead of playing the role of the reporter describing the rules and analogous cases or of the advocate making each side's arguments, you must play the role of judge. You must put yourself in the position of the particular court that will decide the issue—trial court, appellate court, state court, federal court—and decide how that court is likely to decide that element.

At least initially, you may be uncomfortable making such predictions. How can you predict what a court might do? The good news is that with time, and experience, you will get better and better at making predictions. In the meantime, read the statutes and cases carefully, and critically evaluate each side's arguments. Careful reading and careful consideration of arguments—plus common sense—will help you make reliable predictions. Remember, too, that you are predicting, not guaranteeing, an outcome.

In drafting your mini-conclusion, do two things: First, set out your prediction. Second, briefly explain why you believe the court will decide the element as you have predicted. As a general rule, do not include phrases like "I think" or "in my opinion."

In Example 36, the writer has set out his prediction but not his reasoning. As a consequence, the reader has to guess about why the writer reached the conclusion that he reached. Example 37 is better: In it, the writer has set out both his prediction and his reasoning.

EXAMPLE 36 **Poor Draft: The Writer Has Set Out the Prediction but Not the Reasoning**

> While both sides have strong arguments, the court will probably conclude that the summons was not left at Ms. Olsen's usual place of abode.

EXAMPLE 37 **Better Draft: The Writer Has Set Out Both the Prediction and Reasoning**

> While both sides have strong arguments, the court will probably conclude that the summons was not left at Ms. Olsen's usual place of abode. In the more recent cases, the courts have strictly construed the statute, holding that the service was not made at the defendant's usual place of abode when the defendant had a more permanent place of abode. Thus, because the residential treatment house was Ms. Olsen's more permanent residence, the court will probably conclude that it was Ms. Olsen's usual place of abode. In addition, the court may be influenced by two key facts: The record does not indicate that the State tried to serve Ms. Olsen at the residential treatment house, and Ms. Olsen states that she did not receive notice.

5. *Checklist for Critiquing a Discussion Section Written Using a Script Format*

a. Content

Introduction

- ☐ The writer has included a sentence or paragraph introducing the governing statute or common law rule.
- ☐ The writer has set out the general rule, quoting the applicable statutory sections and quoting or paraphrasing the common law rule.
- ☐ The writer has set out any other general rules.
- ☐ When appropriate, the writer has briefly described the policies underlying the statute or common law rule.
- ☐ The writer has included a roadmap.
- ☐ The writer has not included rules or information that the attorney does not need.
- ☐ The rules are stated accurately and objectively.
- ☐ For each rule stated, the writer has included a citation to authority.

Discussion of Undisputed Elements

- ☐ The writer has identified the element and, when there are specific rules, set out those specific rules.
- ☐ The writer has applied the rules to the facts of the client's case, explaining why the element is not in dispute.

Discussion of Disputed Elements

- ☐ For each disputed element, the writer has set out the specific rules, described cases that have interpreted and applied those rules, set out each side's arguments, and predicted how the court will decide the element.
- ☐ The writer has included all of the applicable specific rules and set out those rules accurately and objectively.
- ☐ The writer has introduced each group of analogous cases, telling the attorney what rule or principle the cases illustrate.
- ☐ The case descriptions illustrate the rule or principle and are accurate and objective.
- ☐ In setting out the arguments, the writer has set out both assertions and support for those assertions.
- ☐ The analysis is sophisticated: the writer has set out more than the obvious arguments.
- ☐ The writer has predicted how each element will be decided and given reasons to support those predictions.

b. Large-Scale Organization

- ☐ The writer has presented the information in the order in which the attorney expects to see it. For example, the writer begins the discussion section with an introductory section in which he or she sets out the general rules. The writer then walks the attorney through each of the elements, raising and dismissing the undisputed elements and doing a more complete analysis of the disputed elements.

c. Writing

- ☐ The attorney can understand the discussion with just one reading.
- ☐ The paragraph divisions are logical, and the paragraphs are neither too long nor too short.
- ☐ Transitions and dovetailing have been used to make the connection between ideas clear.
- ☐ In most sentences, the writer has used the actor as the subject of the sentence, and the subject and verb are close together.
- ☐ The writer has varied the length of the sentences and the sentence patterns so that each sentence flows smoothly from the prior sentence.
- ☐ The writing is concise and precise.
- ☐ The writing is grammatically correct and correctly punctuated.
- ☐ The discussion section has been proofread.

I. DRAFTING THE FORMAL CONCLUSION

You are not doing anything wrong. In drafting a formal memo, you do set out your conclusions in more than one place. If you included a brief answer, you set out your conclusion there. In addition, if your problem required an elements analysis, you set out mini-conclusions for each disputed element. And yes, you will now, once again, set out your conclusion, this time in a formal conclusion.

While some attorneys think that the typical memo has too many conclusions, other attorneys believe that each conclusion serves a useful purpose. The brief answer is exactly that: a brief answer. If the client is on the phone and the attorney has not had time to read the full memo, he or she can read the brief answer. The mini-conclusions serve a different purpose. They are part of the analysis and help the attorney understand which elements will be easy to prove and which may be more difficult to prove. The formal conclusion serves still a different purpose. It is the place where you pull all of the pieces together.

1. Summarize Your Conclusions

In a one-issue memo, the formal conclusion is used to summarize the analysis of that one issue. For example, in the Olsen memo, you would use the formal conclusion to tell the attorney whether you think Ms. Olsen was properly served. In Example 1 below, the writer begins by answering the question set out in the issue statement. The writer does not, however, stop there. In addition to answering the question, she goes through the elements, element by element. In the second paragraph, the writer tells the attorney that Ms. Olsen will have to concede that the summons was left with a person of suitable age and discretion and that, more likely than not, the court will conclude that the process server told Ms. Olsen's sister about the contents. In the third paragraph, the writer discusses usual place of abode, briefly explaining why she thinks that Ms. Olsen can prove that the summons was not left at her usual place of abode.

Notice that in Example 1, the writer has not included citations to authority. Most legal readers do not expect citations in a formal conclusion.

EXAMPLE 1 **Formal Conclusion**

CONCLUSION

Because of the strong public policy in favor of ensuring that defendants receive notice of actions that have been filed against them, the court will probably decide that the substituted service of process was not valid and vacate the judgment terminating Ms. Olsen's parental rights.

Ms. Olsen will have to concede that her sister, Ms. Webster, is a person of suitable age and that Ms. Webster was residing at the house where the service was made. In addition, because the process server told Ms. Webster that Ms. Olsen needed to go to court, it seems unlikely that Ms. Olsen will be able to prove that Ms. Webster was not informed of the contents.

Ms. Olsen may, however, be able to prove that the summons and complaint were not served at her usual place of abode. In the more recent cases, the courts have concluded that service made on a relative was invalid when the defendants produced evidence establishing that they were not actually living with that relative on the day that service was made. While in most of these cases the defendants had not lived at the house where service was made for several months or several years, in the Olsen case the court may be swayed by three facts: This case involves the termination of Ms. Olsen's parental rights; there is no evidence that the State tried to personally serve Ms. Olsen or that it tried to serve Ms. Olsen at the residential treatment house; and Ms. Olsen states that she did not receive notice.

2. *Present Your Advice*

While some attorneys just want conclusions, others may want you to go one step further and offer advice. What are the client's options? What action should the attorney take next? Is this the type of case that the firm should, or wants to, handle? When you are asked to include this type of information in the conclusion, add a paragraph like the one in Example 2.

EXAMPLE 2 **Paragraph Setting Out Advice**

Because Ms. Olsen has some strong arguments, I recommend that we move to quash the service of process and vacate the order terminating her parental rights.

3. *Checklist for Formal Conclusion*

a. Content

- ☐ In a one-issue memorandum, the conclusion is used to predict how the issue will be decided and to summarize the reasons supporting that prediction.
- ☐ When appropriate, the writer includes not only the conclusion but also strategic advice.

b. Organization

- ☐ The information is organized logically.

c. Writing

- ☐ The attorney can understand the conclusion with just one reading.
- ☐ The paragraph divisions are logical, and the paragraphs are neither too long nor too short.
- ☐ Transitions and dovetailing have been used to make the connection between ideas clear.

- ☐ In most sentences, the writer has used the actor as the subject of the sentence, and the subject and verb are close together.
- ☐ The writer has varied the length of the sentences and the sentence patterns so that each sentence flows smoothly from the prior sentence.
- ☐ The writing is concise and precise.
- ☐ The writing is grammatically correct and correctly punctuated.
- ☐ The conclusion has been proofread.

Chapter 7 Quiz No. 3

Draft answers for each of the following questions. Make your points clearly and concisely, and write sentences that are easy to read and that are grammatical and correctly punctuated.

1. What is the difference between a disputed element and an undisputed element?
2. When should you include descriptions of analogous cases?
3. Why should you begin your descriptions of a group of analogous cases with a principle-based topic sentence?
4. In drafting the analogous case section, when might you use a parenthetical?
5. What distinguishes a good argument section from a weak one?

J. REVISING, EDITING, AND PROOFREADING THE MEMO

Yes, there are occasions when, because of time or money constraints, you will have to turn in a first draft of an in-house memo. You should not, however, get in the habit of submitting first drafts to your supervising attorney, and you should never submit a first draft to a court, to opposing counsel, or to your client. Unlike speech, which disappears as soon as the words are spoken, written words remain: While well-written documents can enhance your reputation, poorly written ones can damage it

As a consequence, whenever possible, do what we do in this section, and treat revising, editing, and proofreading as three separate processes.

1. Revise Your Draft

Revising is the process of "re-visioning" what you have drafted. During this re-visioning process, step back from your draft, and look at it through the eyes of your reader. Have you given the attorney all of the information that he or she needs? Have you presented that information in the order that the attorney expects to see it?

During the revising stage, you need to be willing to make major changes. If, in revising the draft, you realize that you did not need to include one part of your discussion, delete that part, no matter how many hours you spent drafting it. Similarly, if in revising the draft, you realize that you did not research or discuss a major point, go back and do that research, analysis, and writing. Finally, if in revising your draft, you realize that your organizational scheme just does not work, start over, reorganizing one section or even the entire statement of facts or discussion section.

> **PRACTICE POINTER**
>
> Many writers do a better job revising when they print out a draft and lay out the pages side by side.

a. Check Content

In revising a draft, look first at its content. If there are problems with content, solving those problems must be your first priority.

In checking content, the first question to ask yourself is whether you have given the attorney the information that he or she requested. Did you research the assigned issue or issues? Did you locate all of the applicable statutes and cases? Did you identify and present the arguments that each side is likely to make? Did you evaluate those arguments and predict how the court is likely to rule?

b. Check to Make Sure that the Information Is Presented Accurately

In law, small errors can have serious consequences. The failure to cite check to make sure that a case is still good law, an omitted "not," or an "or" that should have been "and" can make the difference between winning and losing, between competent lawyering and malpractice.

Consequently, in writing the memo, exercise care. Because the attorney is relying on you, your research must be thorough. Make sure that you have located the applicable statutes and cases and that you have checked to make sure that those statutes and cases are still good law. In addition, make sure your analysis is sound. Did you read the statutes and cases carefully? Is the way in which you have put the pieces together sound? Finally, make sure you have presented the statutes and cases accurately and fairly. Did you correctly identify the issue in the analogous cases? Did you take a rule out of context? Did you misrepresent the facts or omit a key fact? Unless the attorney reads the statutes and cases you cite, he may not see an error until it is too late.

c. Check to Make Sure that the Discussion Section Is Well Organized

The next step is to check the discussion section's large-scale organization. Has the information been presented in the order that the attorney expects to see it?

One way to check large-scale organization is to prepare an after-the-fact outline. This is done either by labeling the subject matter of each paragraph and then listing those labels in outline form or by summarizing what each paragraph says.

d. Check to Make Sure that the Connections Are Explicit

Once you have revised for content and organization, look at your use of roadmaps, signposts, topic sentences, and transitions.

i. Roadmaps

A roadmap is just what the term implies: a "map" providing the reader with an overview of the document. For example, in our sample problem, the writer put a roadmap at the end of the introductory section that tells readers which elements will be easy to prove and which elements will be more difficult to prove.

EXAMPLE 1 **Roadmap Telling the Attorney Which Elements Will Be in Dispute and Which Elements Will Not Be in Dispute**

> In this case, Ms. Olsen will have to concede that the summons was left with a person 15 years or older who was residing at the house where the summons and complaint were served. In addition, it is unlikely that Ms. Olsen will be able to prove that her sister was not informed of the contents of the documents. Ms. Olsen may, however, be able to present clear and convincing evidence that the summons was not left at her usual place of abode.

Note that in Example 1 above, the roadmap is substantive in nature. Instead of saying, "First I will discuss this and then I will discuss that," the writer has talked about what Ms. Olsen can and cannot prove.

ii. Topic Sentences, Signposts, and Transitions

Topic sentences, signposts, and transitions serve the same function that directional signs serve on a freeway. They tell readers where they are, what to expect, and how the pieces are connected. While these directional signs may not be particularly important in some types of writing, they are essential in legal writing. Without them, the connections between paragraphs and between sentences may not be clear, making the analysis difficult to follow.

Compare Example 2 below, in which the writer has not included topic sentences, signposts, or transitions, with Example 3. In Example 3, the topic sentences, signposts, and transitions are in boldface type.

EXAMPLE 2 The Writer Has Not Included Topic Sentences, Signposts, or Transitions

When a defendant has more than one residence, the service must be made at the place where the defendant was actually living at the time the summons and complaint were served. Ms. Olsen had more than one residence: During the week she lived at the treatment house, and on weekends she visited her sister. Because the summons and complaint were served on a Wednesday, a weekday, the service was not made at the place where Ms. Olsen was actually living.

Like Mr. Torres, who only visited his mother and who was not at his mother's house when service was made, Ms. Olsen only visited her sister and was not at her sister's house when the summons and complaint were served. While Mr. Torres's mother's statement that Mr. Torres "would be home soon" suggested that Mr. Torres would be returning to his mother's house that day, Ms. Olsen's sister told the process server that Ms. Olsen "isn't here today." While the plaintiff in *Torres* had tried on a number of occasions to serve Mr. Torres at his New York house, we do not know whether the defendant tried to serve Ms. Olsen personally or at the treatment house. While Mr. Heffernan had been at his family's apartment only an hour before the summons and complaint were served, Ms. Olsen had not been at her sister's house for several days and, while in *Heffernan* the summons and complaint were served on the defendant's wife, in the present case the summons and complaint were served on Ms. Olsen's sister. Since *Heffernan*, the courts have interpreted the service process statutes more narrowly.

The courts have repeatedly held that the service of process statutes should be strictly construed and that service on a relative is not, by itself, enough. *Shurman v. Atl. Mortg. & Inv. Corp.*, 795 So. 2d 952, 953-54 (Fla. 2001). Ms. Olsen did not receive notice.

EXAMPLE 3 The Writer Has Included Topic Sentences, Signposts, and Transitions

Ms. Olsen can make three arguments to support her assertion that her sister's house was not her usual place of abode. First, Ms. Olsen will argue that, under the plain language of the statute, her sister's house was not her usual place of abode. As the courts have stated, service must be made at the place where the defendant was actually living at the time the summons and complaint were served. **In this case,** the summons and complaint were served on a weekday, and on weekdays Ms. Olsen was actually living at the residential treatment house.

Second, Ms. Olsen will argue that the facts in her case are more like the facts in *Busman* and *Torres* than the facts in *Heffernan*. Like Mr. Busman, who produced a lease that corroborated his testimony that he was not living with his half brother on the day that the summons and complaint were served, Ms. Olsen can produce evidence that establishes that on the day she was served she was living at the residential treatment house. Both Ms. Olsen's sister and the manager of the residential treatment house have said they will testify that during June and July Ms. Olsen lived at the treatment house during the week and only stayed with her sister on weekends. **In the alternative,** Ms. Olsen can argue that the facts in her case are even stronger than the facts in *Torres.* While Mr. Torres's mother's statement that Mr. Torres "would be home soon" suggested that Mr. Torres would be returning to his mother's house that day, Ms. Olsen's sister told the process server that Ms. Olsen "isn't here today." **In addition,** Ms. Olsen can distinguish *Heffernan*: Although Mr. Heffernan had been at his family's apartment only an hour before the summons and complaint were served, Ms. Olsen had not been at her sister's house for several days.

Finally, Ms. Olsen can argue that, as a matter of public policy, the court should decide that the summons and petition were not left at her usual place of abode. The courts have stated that the statute should be narrowly construed, and this policy is particularly important in cases in which the State is seeking to terminate a mother's parental rights. **In addition,** this is not a case in which the State tried but could not locate Ms. Olsen: There is no evidence that the State tried to serve Ms. Olsen at the residential treatment house.

iii. Dovetailing

Another technique that you can use to make the connections between ideas clear is dovetailing. You use dovetailing when you refer back to a point made in the prior sentence or paragraph.

A	B	Reference to B	C

In Examples 4 and 5, the writer has used dovetailing to make clear the connections between the first and second sentences. The language that is in bold is the dovetail.

EXAMPLE 4 Dovetailing Used to Connect First and Second Sentences

During April, May, and June 2013, Ms. Olsen usually spent weeknights at the treatment house and Friday, Saturday, and Sunday nights at her **sister's house. Because she was spending time at her sister's house,** she moved some of her clothing and personal effects into her sister's house.

EXAMPLE 5 Dovetailing Used to Connect First and Second Sentences

Although the party seeking to invoke the jurisdiction of the court has the burden of proving that service was proper, if the return is regular on its face, the courts presume that the service was valid. *Busman v. State, Dep't of Revenue,* 905 So. 2d 956, 958 (Fla. 3d DCA 2005); *Thompson v. State, Dep't of Revenue,* 867 So. 2d 603, 605 (Fla. 1st DCA 2004). **In such instances,** the party challenging the service has the burden of presenting clear and convincing evidence that the service was invalid. *Id.*

While in Examples 4 and 5 dovetailing was used to make clear the connections between sentences, in Example 6 it is used to make clear the connections between paragraphs. The first sentence in the second paragraph refers back to the information at the end of the first paragraph.

***EXAMPLE 6* Dovetailing Used to Connect Paragraphs**

> Thus, the plaintiff will argue that the facts in this case are much stronger than the facts in *Heffernan.* While in *Heffernan,* Mr. Heffernan visited his family only "twice during the season," Ms. Olsen lived at her sister's house three days a week. In addition, while Mr. Heffernan had another permanent residence, Ms. Olsen was staying at a treatment house, which by definition, is only a temporary residence. Finally, while in *Heffernan* there was no indication that Mr. Heffernan listed the Florida address on any documents, Ms. Olsen listed her sister's address on her driver's license.
>
> **The plaintiff will use these same facts to distinguish *Torres.*** While in *Torres,* Mr. Torres presented evidence establishing that his permanent residence was in New York, in our case, Ms. Olsen did not have a permanent residence. In the five months prior to service, she had been an . . .

PRACTICE POINTER

While roadmaps, topic sentences, signposts, transitions, and dovetailing are more important in legal writing than in many other types of writing, do not overuse them. For example, do not use dovetailing to connect all of your sentences or all of your paragraphs.

The work is now almost done. When you step back from the memo and look at it through the attorney's eyes, you are pleased with its content and organization. You do, however, still need to edit and proofread your memo.

Although some writers mistakenly believe that revising, editing, and proofreading are the same, they are not. While during the revision process you "revision" your creation, during the editing process you make that vision clearer, more concise, more precise, and more accessible. Proofreading is different yet again. It is the search for errors. When you proofread, you are not asking yourself, "Is there a better way of saying this?" Instead, you are looking to see if what you intended to have on the page is in fact there.

Although the lines between revising and editing and between editing and proofreading blur at times, the distinctions among these three skills are important to keep in mind, if for no other reason than to remind you that there are three distinct ways of making changes to a draft and that the best written documents undergo all three types of changes.

2. *Edit Your Draft*

Like revising, editing requires that you look at your work through fresh eyes. At this stage, however, the focus is not on the larger issues of content and organization but on sentence structure, precision and conciseness, grammar, and punctuation. The goal is to produce a professional product that is easy to read and understand. In this chapter, we focus on writing effective sentences and writing correctly; in Chapter 8 [Laurel Currie Oates and Anne Enquist, Just Memos: Preparing for Practice, 4th Ed.,], we focus on writing precisely and concisely.

a. Writing Effective Sentences

Most writers can substantially improve their sentences by following four simple pieces of advice about writing:

1. Use the actor as the subject of most sentences.
2. Keep the subject and verb close together.
3. Put old information at the beginning of the sentence and new information at the end.
4. Vary sentence length and pattern.

i. Use the Actor as the Subject of Most Sentences

By using the actor as the subject of most of your sentences, you can eliminate many of the constructions that make legal writing hard to understand: overuse of the passive voice, most nominalizations, expletive constructions, and many misplaced modifiers.

I. Passive Constructions

In a passive construction, the actor appears in the object rather than the subject slot of the sentence, or it is not named at all. For instance, in Example 7, although the jury is the actor, the word "jury" is used as the object of the preposition "by" rather than the subject of the sentence.

EXAMPLE 7 **Passive Voice**

A verdict was reached by the jury.

In the following example, the actor, "jury," is not named at all.

EXAMPLE 8 **Passive Voice**

A verdict was reached.

To use the active voice, simply identify the actor (in this case, the jury) and use it as the subject of the sentence.

EXAMPLE 9 **Active Voice**

The jury reached a verdict.

Now read each of the sentences in Example 10, marking the subject and verb and deciding whether the writer used the actor as the subject of the sentence. If the writer did not use the actor as the subject of the sentence, decide whether the sentence should be rewritten. As a general rule, the active voice is better unless the passive voice improves the flow of sentences or the writer wants to de-emphasize what the actor did.

If the return is regular on its face, there is a presumption that the service was valid. *Thompson v. State, Dep't of Revenue*, 867 So. 2d 603, 605 (Fla. 1st DCA 2004); *Magazine v. Bedoya*, 475 So. 2d 1035, 1035 (Fla. 3d DCA 1985). In such instances, the defendant must prove that the service was invalid. *Thompson*, 867 So. 2d at 605; *Magazine*, 475 So. 2d at 1035.

Sentence 1

If the return is regular on its face, there is a presumption that the service was valid.

In writing Sentence 1, the writer used the passive voice. Instead of using the actor (the court) as the subject of the sentence, the writer has used an expletive construction: "there is." Because the writer did not have a good reason for using the passive voice, we have rewritten the sentence using the active voice.

EXAMPLE 10 **Rewrite Using the Active Voice**

However, if the return is regular on its face, the courts presume that the service was valid.

Sentence 2

In such instances, the burden of presenting clear and convincing evidence that the service was invalid is on the defendant.

Sentence 2 is also written in the passive voice. Instead of using the actor (the defendant) as the subject of the sentence, the writer has placed the actor in a prepositional phrase. Because the writer did not have a good reason for using the passive voice, we have shown three ways to rewrite the sentence.

EXAMPLE 11 **Edits Using the Active Voice**

In such instances, the party challenging the service has the burden of presenting clear and convincing evidence that the service was invalid.

In such instances, the party challenging the service must prove that the service was invalid by clear and convincing evidence.

In such instances, the party challenging the service must prove, by clear and convincing evidence, that the service was invalid.

> **PRACTICE POINTER**
>
> Be sure to distinguish between the passive voice and past tense. A sentence written in the past tense may or may not use the passive voice.

II. Nominalizations

You create a nominalization when you turn a verb or an adjective into a noun.

Verb		Nominalization
apply	→	application
conclude	→	conclusion
decide	→	decision

Although there are times when you will want to use a nominalization, overusing nominalizations can make your writing harder to read and understand. In the following sentence, "presumption" is a nominalization.

***EXAMPLE 12* Nominalization**

> If the return is regular on its face, there is a presumption that the service is valid.

To make this sentence better, identify the real actor (in this instance, the court) and then, in the verb, specifically state what action that actor has taken or will take. Note that "presumption" becomes "presume."

***EXAMPLE 13* Edit Without Nominalization**

> If the return is regular on its face, the courts presume that the service is valid.

III. Expletive Constructions

In an expletive construction, phrases such as "it is" or "there are" are used as the subject and verb of the sentence. Although it is sometimes necessary to use such a construction (note the use of an expletive construction in this sentence), such a construction gives the reader almost no information. Therefore, when possible, use a concrete subject and verb—that is, a subject and verb that describe something the reader can "see" in his or her mind.

***EXAMPLE 14* Expletive Constructions**

> However, if the return is regular on its face, there is a presumption that the service was valid.
>
> It is Ms. Olsen's argument that . . .

EXAMPLE 15 **Edits Without Expletive Constructions**

If the return is regular on its face, the courts presume that the service was valid.

Ms. Olsen will argue that . . .

PRACTICE POINTER

Note that expletive constructions and nominalizations often go hand in hand. Because you use a expletive construction, you are forced into using a nominalization:

If the return is regular on its face, there is a presumption that the service is valid.

IV. Dangling Modifiers

A dangling modifier is a modifier that does not reasonably modify anything in the sentence. For example, in the following sentence, the modifying phrase "Applying this test" does not reasonably modify anything in the sentence. It is not "it was held" that is doing the applying.

EXAMPLE 16 **Dangling Modifier**

Applying this test, it was held that the summons and complaint were not left at the defendant's usual place of abode.

The dangling modifier can be eliminated if the actor is used as the subject of the sentence.

EXAMPLE 17 **Edit Without Dangling Modifier**

Applying this test, the **court** held that the summons and complaint were not left at the defendant's usual place of abode.

Now the phrase "Applying this test" modifies something in the sentence: the court.

PRACTICE POINTER

When you see a word ending in "ing" (a participle) in a phrase or clause near the beginning of a sentence, ask yourself who is doing the action. For example, in the preceding sentence, ask who is doing the "applying." Then look at the subject of the sentence. If the subject does not identify who is doing the action, then you have a dangling modifier.

ii. Keep the Subject and Verb Close Together

Researchers have established that readers cannot understand a sentence until they have located both the subject and the verb. In addition, readers have difficulty remembering the subject if it is separated from the verb by more than seven or eight words: If there are more than seven or eight words, after finding the verb, many readers must go back and relocate the subject.

The lesson to be learned from this research is that, as a writer, you should try to keep your subject and verb close together. In Examples 18 and 19, the subject and verb are underlined.

EXAMPLE 18 **Subject and Verb Too Far Apart**

In such instances, the burden of presenting clear and convincing evidence that the service was invalid is on the party challenging the service.

EXAMPLE 19 **Edits with Subject and Verb Closer Together**

In such instances, the party challenging the service has the burden of presenting clear and convincing evidence that the service was invalid.

In such instances, the defendant must prove by clear and convincing evidence that the service was invalid.

iii. Put Old Information at the Beginning of the Sentence and New Information at the End

Sentences, and the paragraphs they create, make more sense when the old information is placed at the beginning and the new information is placed at the end. When this pattern is used, the development progresses naturally from left to right without unnecessary backtracking.

EXAMPLE 20 **Old Information Is at the Beginning of the Sentence, and New Information Is at the End**

The only Florida case in which the summons was left with a relative with whom the defendant was visiting is *Torres*. *Id.* at 585. In that case, the plaintiff tried for more than a month to serve Mr. Torres at the New York apartment where Mr. Torres had lived for 12 years. *Id.* Although all attempts at service were unsuccessful, the New York process server indicated in his affidavit that he had "verified" with a neighbor that "Mr. Torres lived at the New York address, but that he was often out of town, and was expected to return in two weeks." *Id.* Because it could not serve the defendant in New York, the plaintiff served Mr. Torres's mother at her residence in Florida. In his affidavit, the Florida process server stated that Mr. Torres mother told him that "he (presumably Mr. Torres) would be home soon." *Id.* Mr. Torres stated that he never received notice. In holding that the service was not valid, the court noted that while the standard of review was gross abuse of discretion, the trial court had not heard live testimony and the plaintiff had the burden of establishing that the service was valid. *Id.* at 587. It then went on to note that the evidence tended to support Mr. Torres's position that his usual place of abode was in New York and that Mr. Torres's mother's statement that Mr. Torres would be home soon was, at best, ambiguous. *Id.*

In the paragraph set out above, the first sentence, which is in bold, acts as a topic sentence, telling the attorney that there is only one Florida case that has facts similar to the facts in the client's case. That first sentence ends with a reference to the new information, which is the name of the case: "*Torres.*" In the second sentence, the name of the case is now the old information, and the second sentence begins with a reference back to that old information. The second sentence then ends with the new information: that the plaintiff had tried, on a number of occasions, to serve the defendant in New York. In the third sentence, the old information is that the plaintiff had tried to serve the defendant in New York. Thus, the author uses this old information to start the third sentence, putting the new information, that the neighbor had told the process server that the defendant was out of town, at the end of the third sentence.

PRACTICE POINTER

Note how putting "old" information at the beginning of the sentence allows you to use dovetailing.

iv. Vary Sentence Length and Pattern

Even if writing is technically correct, it is not considered good if it is not pleasing to the ear. Read Example 21 aloud.

EXAMPLE 21 **All the Sentences Are About the Same Length and Use the Same Pattern**

A process server went to Ms. Webster's house on Wednesday, July 24, 2013. The process server asked for Elaine Olsen. Ms. Webster told the process server that "Elaine isn't here today." The process server then handed the summons and complaint to Ms. Webster. The process server told Ms. Webster that Ms. Olsen "needed to go to court."

In Example 21, the writing is not pleasing because the sentences are similar in length and all follow the same pattern. Although short, uncomplicated sentences are usually better than long, complicated ones, the use of too many short sentences results in writing that sounds choppy and sophomoric. As Example 22 illustrates, the passage is much better when the writer varies sentence length and pattern.

EXAMPLE 22 **The Writer Has Varied the Length of the Sentences and the Sentence Pattern**

On Wednesday, July 24, 2013, a process server went to Ms. Webster's house and asked for Elaine Olsen. When Ms. Webster told the process server that

"Elaine isn't here today," the process server handed the summons to Ms. Webster and told her that Ms. Olsen "needed to go to court."

b. Writing Correctly

For a moment, imagine that you have received the following letter from a local law firm.

EXAMPLE 23 **Sample Letter**

Dear Student:

Thank you for submitting an application for a position as a law clerk with are firm. Your grades in law school are very good, however, at this time we do not have any positions available. Its possible, however, that we may have a opening next summer and we therefore urge you to reapply with us then.

Sincerely,
Senior Partner

No matter how bad the market is, most students would not want to be associated with a firm that sends out a three-line letter containing three major errors and several minor ones. Unfortunately, the reverse is also true. No matter how short-handed they are, most law firms do not want to hire someone who has not mastered the basic rules of grammar and punctuation. Most firms cannot afford an employee who makes careless errors or one who lacks basic writing skills.

Consequently, at the editing stage you need to go back through your draft, correcting errors. Look first for the errors that potentially affect meaning (misplaced modifiers, incorrect use of "which" and "that") and for errors that educated readers are likely to notice (incomplete sentences, comma splices, incorrect use of the possessive, lack of parallelism). Then look for the errors that you know from past experience that you are likely to make.

3. Proofreading

Most writers learn the importance of proofreading the hard way. A letter, brief, or contract goes out with the client's name misspelled, with an "or" where there should have been an "and," or without an essential "not." At a minimum, these errors cause embarrassment; at worst, they result in a lawsuit.

To avoid such errors, treat proofreading as a separate step in the revising process. After you have finished revising and editing, go back through your draft, looking not at content, organization, or sentence style, but for errors. Proofreading is most effective when it is done on hard copy several days (or, when that is not feasible, several hours) after you have finished editing. Force yourself to read slowly, focusing not on the sentences but on the individual words in the sentences. Is a word missing? Is a word repeated? Are letters transposed? You can force yourself to read slowly by using a clean piece of paper to cover up all but the line you are reading, by reading from right to left, or by reading from the bottom of the page to the top.

Also, force yourself to begin your proofreading by looking at the sections that caused you the most difficulty or that you wrote last. Because you were concentrating on content or were tired, these sections probably contain the most errors.

Finally, when you get into practice, don't rely on just your spelling and grammar checkers. Instead, make it a habit to have a second person proofread your work. Not only will someone else see errors that you missed, he or she is also less likely than you to "read in" missing words.

4. *Citations*

As a legal writer, you have an extra burden. In addition to editing and proofreading the text, you must also edit and proofread your citations to legal authorities.

At the editing stage, focus on selection and placement of citations. Is the authority you cited the best authority? Did you avoid string cites (the citing of multiple cases for the same point)? Have you included a citation to authority for every rule stated? Did you include the appropriate signal? Have you over- or under-emphasized the citation? (You emphasize a citation by placing it in the text of a sentence; you de-emphasize it by placing it in a separate citation sentence.)

In contrast, at the proofreading stage, focus on the citation itself. Are the volume and page numbers correct? Are the pinpoint cites accurate? Have you included the year of the decision and any subsequent history? Is the spacing correct?

Chapter 7 Quiz No. 4

Draft answers for each of the following questions. Make your points clearly and concisely, and write sentences that are easy to read and that are grammatical and correctly punctuated.

1. What is the difference between revising, editing, and proofreading?
2. In the following sentences, has the writer used dovetailing? If your answer is yes, what is the dovetail?

   The State will use these same facts to distinguish *Torres*. While in *Torres*, Mr. Torres presented evidence establishing that his permanent residence was in New York, in the present case, Ms. Olsen did not have a permanent residence.

3. Rewrite the following sentence using the active voice.

   There are three arguments that the State can make to support its assertion.

4. Rewrite the following sentence eliminating the nominalization.

   The court's conclusion was that the plaintiff had not met its burden of proof.

5. Rewrite the following sentence eliminating the dangling modifier.

   Weighing these arguments, it is likely that the court will conclude that Ms. Olsen has met her burden of proving that service was not made at her usual place of abode.

CHAPTER 8

Drafting Memos Requiring Other Types of Analysis

In Chapters 7 and 8 [Laurel Currie Oates and Anne Enquist, Just Memos: Preparing for Practice, 4th Ed.,], we showed you one of the most common types of legal analysis, an elements analysis. There are, however, other types of analysis, and this chapter provides you with templates for three of those types: section 8.A provides you with a template for issues that require the analysis of a set of factors; section 8.B, with a template for issues that require the balancing of competing interests, and section 8.C, with templates for issues of first impression.

A. FACTOR ANALYSIS

While in an elements analysis the party with the burden of proof must prove all of the elements, in a factor analysis no one factor is determinative. The court can find for a party even when one or more of the factors favor the other side. For example, in most states, the legislature has set out a list of factors that the courts must consider in deciding child custody cases. Although the statutes may state that a particular factor, or set of factors, should be given the most weight, the courts can find for a parent even when the majority of the factors favor the other parent.

1. Templates for Issues Involving a Factor Analysis

The templates for issues involving a factor analysis are very similar to the templates for issues involving an elements analysis. In both instances, you begin the discussion section with an introductory section, and in both instances you then walk your reader through the analysis step by step: In an elements analysis you walk the reader through the elements, and in a factor analysis you walk the reader through the factors. The primary difference is that, in a factor analysis, you need to add a section in which you weigh the factors. Taken as a group, do the factors weigh in favor of the plaintiff, or do they weigh in favor of the defendant?

In the following examples, Example 1 sets out the templates for an elements and factor analysis using the script format, and Example 2 sets out the templates for an elements and factor analysis using a more integrated format. For the purposes of both examples, presume that, for the issue involving an elements analysis, there are three elements, one of which is not likely to be in dispute and two that will be in dispute. Likewise, for the issue involving a factors analysis, presume that there are three factors: Even though the first factor is not "in dispute," the second and third factors are.

PRACTICE POINTER

When you use a script format, you use inductive reasoning and organize the analysis around the parties' arguments: You set out all of one side's arguments and then all of the other side's arguments. See section 8.7 [Laurel Currie Oates and Anne Enquist, Just Memos: Preparing for Practice, 4th Ed.,]. On the other hand, when you use a more integrated format, you use deductive reasoning: You set out your conclusion and then your reasoning. For more on the script and integrated formats, see section 8.7 [Laurel Currie Oates and Anne Enquist, Just Memos: Preparing for Practice, 4th Ed.,].

EXAMPLE 1 **Templates for an Elements and Factor Analysis Using a Script Format**

Elements Analysis	**Factor Analysis**
Discussion	**Discussion**
Introductory Section	**Introductory Section**
☐ If one or both sides will make a policy argument, describe the policies underlying the statute, common law rule, or court rule. ☐ Introduce and set out the applicable statute, common law rule, or court rule. ☐ If one of the parties has the burden of proof, explain which side has the burden of proof and what that burden is. ☐ Set out any other rules that apply to all of the elements. ☐ End the introductory section by providing the attorney with a roadmap for the rest of the discussion.	☐ If one or both sides will make a policy argument, describe the policies underlying the statute, common law rule, or court rule. ☐ Introduce and set out the applicable statute, common law rule, or court rule. ☐ If one of the parties has the burden of proof, explain which side has the burden of proof and what that burden is. ☐ Set out any other rules that apply to all of the factors. ☐ End the introductory section by providing the attorney with a roadmap for the rest of the discussion.

Elements Analysis	Factor Analysis
A. First Element (not in dispute)	**A. First Factor (not in dispute)**
☐ Set out and apply the applicable rule and/or definitions.	☐ Set out and apply the applicable rule and/or definitions.
B. Second Element (in dispute)	**B. Second Factor (in dispute)**

☐ Set out the specific rules or definitions for the second element.
☐ If there are analogous cases that discuss the second element and descriptions of those analogous cases would help your supervising attorney understand how the courts have interpreted this element, include descriptions of analogous cases.
☐ Set out arguments:
    ☐ Party with burden of proof's arguments
    ☐ Responding party's arguments.
☐ Evaluate each side's arguments and set out mini-conclusion for the second element.
	☐ Set out the specific rules or definitions for the second factor.
	☐ If there are analogous cases that discuss the second factor and descriptions of those analogous cases would help your supervising attorney understand how the courts have interpreted this factor, include descriptions of analogous cases.
	☐ Set out arguments:
	    ☐ Party with burden of proof's arguments
	    ☐ Responding party's arguments.
	☐ Evaluate each side's arguments and set out mini-conclusion for the factor.

C. Third Element (in dispute)	**C. Third Factor (in dispute)**

☐ Set out the specific rules or definitions for the third element.
☐ If there are analogous cases that discuss the second element and descriptions of those analogous cases would help your supervising attorney understand how the courts have interpreted this element, include descriptions of analogous cases.
☐ Set out each side's arguments:
    ☐ Party with burden of proof's arguments
    ☐ Responding party's arguments.
☐ Evaluate each side's arguments and set out mini-conclusion for the third element.
	☐ Set out the specific rules or definitions for the third factor.
	☐ If there are analogous cases that discuss the second factor and descriptions of those analogous cases would help your supervising attorney understand how the courts have interpreted this factor, include descriptions of analogous cases.
	☐ Set out each side's arguments:
	    ☐ Party with burden of proof's arguments
	    ☐ Responding party's arguments.
	☐ Evaluate each side's arguments and set out mini-conclusion for the third factor.

Elements Analysis	Factor Analysis
Conclusion	**Evaluation of Factors**
☐ Set out your conclusion and advice.	☐ Using either a script or an integrated format, weigh the factors and set out your mini-conclusion. Note: if doing so would help your reader, describe how the courts have weighed the factors in analogous cases, and then show how the parties would use those cases to support their arguments (script format) or how the court might use those cases in making its decision (integrated format).
	Conclusion
	☐ Set out your conclusion and advice.

EXAMPLE 2 **Templates for an Elements and Factor Analysis Using a More Integrated Format**

Elements Analysis	Factor Analysis
Discussion	**Discussion**
Introductory Section	**Introductory Section**
☐ If one or both sides will make a policy argument, describe the policies underlying the statute, common law rule, or court rule. ☐ Introduce and set out the applicable statute, common law rule, or court rule. ☐ If one of the parties has the burden of proof, explain which side has the burden of proof and what that burden is. ☐ Set out any other rules that apply to all of the elements. ☐ End the introductory section by providing the attorney with a roadmap for the rest of the discussion.	☐ If one or both sides will make a policy argument, describe the policies underlying the statute, common law rule, or court rule. ☐ Introduce and set out the applicable statute, common law rule, or court rule. ☐ If one of the parties has the burden of proof, explain which side has the burden of proof and what that burden is. ☐ Set out any other rules that apply to all of the factors. ☐ End the introductory section by providing the attorney with a roadmap for the rest of the discussion.

Elements Analysis	Factor Analysis
A. First Element (not in dispute)	**A. First Factor (not in dispute)**
☐ Set out and apply the applicable rule and/or definitions.	☐ Set out and apply the applicable rule and/or definitions.
B. Second Element (in dispute)	**B. Second Factor (in dispute)**
☐ Set out the specific rules or definitions for the second element. ☐ If there are analogous cases that discuss the second element and descriptions of those analogous cases would help your supervising attorney understand how the courts have interpreted this element, include descriptions of analogous cases. ☐ Set out your conclusion. ☐ Set out your reasoning, summarizing and evaluating each side's arguments.	☐ Set out the specific rules or definitions for the second factor. ☐ If there are analogous cases that discuss the second factor and descriptions of those analogous cases would help your supervising attorney understand how the courts have interpreted this factor, include descriptions of analogous cases. ☐ Set out your conclusion. ☐ Set out your reasoning, summarizing and evaluating each side's arguments.
C. Third Element (in dispute)	**C. Third Factor (in dispute)**
☐ Set out the specific rules or definitions for the third element. ☐ If there are analogous cases that discuss the third element and descriptions of those analogous cases would help your supervising attorney understand how the courts have interpreted this element, include descriptions of analogous cases. ☐ Set out your conclusion. ☐ Set out your reasoning, summarizing and evaluating each side's arguments.	☐ Set out the specific rules or definitions for the third factor. ☐ If there are analogous cases that discuss the third factor and descriptions of those analogous cases would help your supervising attorney understand how the courts have interpreted this factor, include descriptions of analogous cases. ☐ Set out your conclusion. ☐ Set out your reasoning, summarizing and evaluating each side's arguments.
Conclusion	**Evaluation of Factors**
☐ Set out your conclusion and advice.	Using an integrated format, weigh the factors and set out your mini-conclusion. Note: if doing so would help your reader, describe how the courts have weighed the factors in

Elements Analysis	Factor Analysis
	analogous cases, and then show how the court might use those cases in making its decision.
	Conclusion
	Set out your conclusion and advice.

You must, of course, modify the templates so that they work for your issue and your readers. For instance, if there are four and not three factors, discuss each of those four factors. However, if there are more than three or four factors, think about whether you need a separate subsection for each factor. Can you raise and dismiss some of the factors at the end of your introductory section? If some of the factors are closely related, can you combine your discussions of the related factors?

In addition, modify your template so that it is consistent with your supervising attorney's preferences. While some attorneys love subheadings and will want you to use lots of them, others don't. Likewise, while in a factor analysis some attorneys will want you to include both a section in which you weigh the factors and a formal conclusion, others will say that the formal conclusion is repetitive and that you can either (1) delete the formal conclusion or (2) keep the formal conclusion but move the weighing of the factors out of the discussion section and into that formal conclusion. When in doubt, use common sense or ask your supervising attorney what he or she prefers.

2. *Draft the Introductory or General Rule Section*

In both a memo involving an elements analysis and a memo involving a factor analysis, the introductory section serves the same function. It places the issue in context, it sets out the general rules, and it provides the reader with a roadmap for the rest of the discussion.

In deciding what to include in your introductory section, think about how much your supervising attorney knows about the area of law. If the area is one that she knows well, the section can be short. In most instances, include only the following information:

- ☐ a sentence introducing the applicable law;
- ☐ the applicable law, for example, the applicable portions of the statute, common law rule, or court rule;
- ☐ any other rules that apply to all of the factors; and
- ☐ a roadmap that tells your supervising attorney which factors appear to be in dispute and which factors are not in dispute.

If, however, the area of law is not one that your supervising attorney knows, you will usually want to include at least some background information.

Depending on the issue and the types of arguments that you expect that the parties may make, explain how the law developed, the policies underlying the law, and the rules relating to the burden of proof.

PRACTICE POINTER

While most attorneys will want you to quote the applicable portions of statutes and regulations, you can paraphrase common law and other rules.

As a general rule, set out more general rules before more specific rules. Thus, set out the policies underlying the rules before the rules themselves and the rules before the exceptions to the rules. Also remember to include a citation to authority for each rule that you set out. Finally, in most instances, keep the focus on the rule by putting the citation not at the beginning of the sentence, but in a separate citation sentence after the rule.

3. *Draft the Discussion of the Undisputed Factors*

Most likely, not all of the factors will be in dispute. Sometimes the factor will favor one side but not the other side; at other times, the factor helps—or hurts—both sides equally.

For these undisputed factors, you have a choice. You can either raise and dismiss these factors at the end of the introductory section, or you can discuss them in separate, but very short, subsections. For example, if you are working on a child custody case and both parents want custody of their 3-year-old child, you could raise and dismiss the factor that relates to the parents' and child's preferences either at the end of the general rule section or in a separate subsection.

PRACTICE POINTER

Even if the factor is not in dispute, you need to discuss it, both initially and in the section where you weigh the various factors.

4. *Draft the Discussion of the Disputed Factors*

Just as disputed elements require more analysis, so do disputed factors. In some instances, the dispute will be a purely factual dispute. For example, in a custody case, the mother might argue that she has the more flexible work schedule while the father argues that his schedule is the more flexible schedule. In this situation, you do not need to include descriptions of the analogous cases. Simply set out the facts and each side's arguments based on those facts using either a script or integrated format.

There will, of course, be times when you will need to do more than just set out the factual arguments. If the rules are ambiguous and there are analogous cases, set out the rules, provide the attorney with the examples of how those rules have been applied in analogous cases, and then set out each side's arguments and your mini-conclusion using either a script or an integrated format. For more on drafting the descriptions of analogous cases, and in particular, drafting the description of analogous cases using a principle-based analysis, see sections 7.H.4.b and 7.H.4.b.

5. *Draft the Paragraph or Block of Paragraphs in Which You Weigh the Factors*

Unlike an elements analysis in which your discussion section is done once you have discussed each of the elements, in a factor analysis you need to go one step further. You need to weigh the factors.

There are several ways to organize this part of the discussion section. If you use a script format, set out the rules first, the descriptions of any analogous cases second, the plaintiff's arguments third, the defendant's arguments fourth, and your mini-conclusion at the end. If you use a more integrated format, begin by setting out the rules, then set out the description of any analogous cases, and end by setting out your conclusion and reasoning.

EXAMPLE 3 **Organizational Schemes for Section Weighing the Factors**

Script Format	Integrated Format

☐ Set out the rules or tests that the courts use in weighing the factors.
☐ If there are analogous cases that illustrate how the courts have weighed the factors in situations that are analogous to your situation, include descriptions of those analogous cases.
☐ Set out each side's arguments:
  ☐ Party with burden of proof's arguments
  ☐ Responding party's arguments.
☐ Evaluate each side's arguments and set out your conclusion.
	☐ Set out the rules or tests that the courts use in weighing the factors.
	☐ If there are analogous cases that illustrate how the courts have weighed the factors in situations that are analogous to your situation, include descriptions of those analogous cases.
	☐ Set out your conclusion.
	☐ Set out your reasoning, summarizing and evaluating each side's arguments.

Whichever organizational scheme you choose, take the time to think critically and carefully about each side's arguments and about how a court might view those arguments. If there is a statute, begin by reviewing the statute. Has the legislature stated that one factor or one set of factors should be given the most weight? Similarly, if the issue is governed by a common law or court rule, review the cases. Do the courts give one factor or set of factors more weight? In creating and applying the rules, what policies have the courts emphasized or tried to promote?

Do not, however, stop there. Push yourself to construct each side's story. For example, in a custody case, how will the mother use the factors to tell her story and persuade the court that it would be in the best interests of the children to grant her custody? How will the father use the factors to construct his story? Then ask yourself which story a court is likely to find most compelling.

EXAMPLE 4 Block of Paragraphs in Which the Writer Weighs the Factors

> In this case, even though three of the four factors favor Ms. Morris, the court will probably find in favor of Ms. Springer. The three factors that favor Ms. Morris are position of authority, susceptibility, and the public nature of the comment. As Ms. Morris's basketball coach, Ms. Springer was in a position of authority over Ms. Morris, and given that Ms. Morris cried during her meeting with Ms. Springer, Ms. Springer knew that Ms. Morris was susceptible to statements about her weight. In addition, Ms. Springer made the comments about Ms. Morris's weight publicly on the basketball court in front of players, parents, and scouts.
>
> The factor that favors Ms. Springer is that the case involves a single statement. Given that there are no cases in which the courts have held that a single statement by a defendant constituted extreme and outrageous conduct, the court is likely to find that Ms. Springer's comment, although inappropriate behavior for a coach, does not rise to the level of extreme and outrageous conduct. Other factors that are likely to contribute to the decision that the conduct was not extreme and outrageous are that the statement was made at the end of an emotionally charged basketball game between two elite teams, no racial slurs were involved, and Ms. Morris was almost 18 and not a young child.

B. BALANCING OF COMPETING INTERESTS

Another common type of analysis is an analysis that requires the balancing of competing interests. For example, in a criminal case, the trial court will balance the probative value of admitting particular evidence against the prejudicial value of allowing the jury to view that evidence, and in a nuisance case, the court will balance one individual's right to use his or her land against the rights of adjoining landowners.

1. Templates for Issues Requiring the Balancing of Competing Interests

As with an elements analysis and factor analysis, there is more than one way to organize the discussion of an issue that requires the balancing of competing interests. However, regardless of which organizational scheme you choose to use, you need to do two things: identify the competing interests, and do the balancing.

Example 1 sets out two templates: The template in the left-hand column shows how to organize the discussion section using a script format while the template in the right-hand column shows how to organize the discussion section using a more integrated format. As you look at these templates, note that there is no one "right place" for the descriptions of analogous cases. While sometimes it will make more sense to put the descriptions of the analogous cases in a separate section, at other times it will make more sense to integrate them into the parties' arguments or into your reasoning.

In making the decision about where to put the cases, think about how you are going to use the cases. If you are going to use a case or set of cases extensively, showing how both sides would use the cases or how the court would treat the cases, it will probably make more sense, and be more efficient, to put the descriptions of those cases in a separate analogous case section. If, however, you are using the case to illustrate only a small point, it will probably make more sense to integrate your description of the case into your discussion of that point. For more on drafting the descriptions of analogous cases, and in particular, drafting the description of analogous cases using a principle-based analysis, see sections 7.H.4.b and 8.8.2 [Laurel Currie Oates and Anne Enquist, Just Memos: Preparing for Practice, 4th Ed.,].

EXAMPLE 1 **Templates for an Issue Requiring the Balancing of Competing Interests**

Script Format	Integrated Format
Discussion	**Discussion**
Introductory Section	**Introductory Section**
☐ If one or both sides will make a policy argument, describe the policies underlying the general rule (constitutional provision, statute, common law rule, or court rule). ☐ Introduce and set out the general rule, identifying the competing interests and explaining the burden of proof. ☐ Set out any other general rules or exceptions.	☐ If one or both sides will make a policy argument, describe the policies underlying the general rule (constitutional provision, statute, common law rule, or court rule). ☐ Introduce and set out the general rule, identifying the competing interests and explaining the burden of proof. ☐ Set out any other general rules or exceptions.

Script Format	Integrated Format
[If appropriate, descriptions of analogous cases]	**[If appropriate, descriptions of analogous cases]**
Plaintiff's or Moving Party's Arguments	**Conclusion**
☐ Set out the plaintiff's or moving party's assertion. ☐ Summarize the plaintiff's arguments, including any plain language, analogous case, and policy arguments.	☐ Set out your conclusion. (In this case, which interest outweighs the other interest?)
Defendant's or Responding Party's Arguments	**Reasoning**
☐ Set out the defendant's or responding party's assertion. ☐ Summarize the defendant's or responding party's arguments, including any plain language, analogous case, and policy arguments. ☐ Set out your mini-conclusion (in this case, which interest outweighs the other interest?) and explain your reasoning.	☐ Set out your first reason, incorporating and evaluating each side's arguments. (Often this will be a discussion of the first interest.) ☐ Set out your second reason, incorporating and evaluating each side's arguments. (Often, this will be a discussion of the second interest.) ☐ Set out your third reason, incorporating and evaluating each side's arguments. (Often, this will be where you balance the competing interests.)
Conclusion	**Conclusion**
[Put your formal conclusion here. In this conclusion, explain why one party's interests outweigh the other party's interests.]	**[Put your formal conclusion here.]**

2. *Draft the Introductory or General Rule Section*

In a memo involving the balancing of competing interests, the introductory section serves the same function that the introductory section serves in memos involving other types of analysis. It introduces and sets out the applicable law, and it provides the reader with a roadmap for the rest of the discussion.

However, for issues involving the balancing of competing interests, the introductory section serves an additional function. While there are always exceptions, in most instances, you will want to use the introductory section to explain the competing interests and describe the policies that underlie them. How much you say will, of course, depend on the issue and what your supervising attorney knows about that issue. At one end of the continuum are those instances in which your supervising attorney knows the area of law and the application of the law to your client's facts is relatively easy. In these situations, your description of the competing interests and the underlying policies can be very short. At the other end of the continuum are cases in which your supervising attorney is not familiar with the area of law, the rules are evolving, the application of the law to the facts of your case is nuanced, and/or a lot is at stake. While you never want to turn a memo into a law review article, in these situations, your descriptions of the interests and the underlying policies needs to be more thorough.

PRACTICE POINTER

Remember to include a citation to authority for each rule that you set out. In addition, when possible, cite to mandatory authority.

3. *Draft the Discussion of the Competing Interests*

In most instances, your discussion of the competing interests will have three components: an analysis of each interest; an analysis of how a court, or other decision maker, is likely to balance those competing interests; and a conclusion. How you organize those components depends on whether you use a script format or a more integrated format.

If you use the script format, begin by setting out one side's arguments in a paragraph or, more likely, a block of paragraphs. In setting out your client's arguments, begin by setting out your assertion, which will usually consist of a statement that your client's interests outweigh the other side's interests. Then set out your support for your assertion, showing your supervising attorney how you can use the facts, analogous cases, and underlying policies to support that assertion. While sometimes you will want to organize these arguments by type of argument—for example, putting your plain language arguments first, your analogous case arguments second, and your policy arguments last—it is usually better to organize the arguments around lines of argument, showing your supervising attorney how you can weave together the facts, analogous cases, and policies to make a particular point. After you have set out your client's arguments, then set out the other side's arguments using the same format: Set out the other side's assertion and the arguments that it can make to support that assertion. Finish by setting out your prediction and your reasoning. How do you think the court will balance the competing interests? What reasons do you think that the court will give for finding that one party's interests are stronger than the other party's interests?

PRACTICE POINTER

Sometimes there are more than two competing interests. For instance, in a land use case, the court, or another decision maker, may not only have to balance the interests of two parties but also the interests of the public at large. In such situations, discuss and balance all of the competing interests.

If you use a more integrated format, begin by setting out your conclusion. How do you think that the court will balance the competing interests? Then, in a paragraph or block of paragraphs, walk your supervising attorney through your reasoning. If you have several reasons, you will usually want to start your discussion of each reason by setting out a subassertion that builds on a rule, the cases interpreting that rule, or one of the underlying policies. You will then want to set out your reasoning in much the same way that a court might discuss its reasoning in a judicial decision. Just make sure that you do not omit or give short shrift to the losing side's arguments. To do her job well, your supervising attorney needs thorough analysis of each side's potential arguments.

PRACTICE POINTER

In moving from a script to an integrated format, you should not lose any arguments. For more on avoiding the common problems, see section 8.8.5 [Laurel Currie Oates and Anne Enquist, Just Memos: Preparing for Practice, 4th Ed.,].

Depending on the format that you use, your supervising attorney's preferences, and whether your memo discusses just one issue or several issues, you may or may not need a formal conclusion. If you are analyzing a single issue using a script format, you may be able to use your mini-conclusion, that is, the paragraph or block of paragraphs in which you predict how the court will balance the interests and how it will explain its decision, as your formal conclusion. On the other hand, if your memo has more than one issue statement and, thus, more than one part to the discussion section, include a formal conclusion.

C. ISSUE OF FIRST IMPRESSION

Some of the most interesting, and most challenging, issues that you will work on are issues of first impression, that is, issues that have not been decided by the courts in your jurisdictions.

Issues of first impression have two things in common: They require you to predict what rule the court is likely to apply, and they require you to apply that rule, and in some instances, alternative rules, to the facts of your case. Unfortunately, though, that is about all that issues of first impression have in common. You will, therefore, need to use the following templates as starting, and not ending, points for determining what types of information you need to include in your discussion section and the best way of organizing that information.

1. *Circuit Split*

One of the most common scenarios is one in which there is a "circuit split." In the federal system, a circuit split occurs when one or more of the federal circuits adopt one rule or approach while one or more of the other circuits adopt a different rule or approach. In the state systems, a "split" occurs when one or more of the divisions of a state's intermediate court of appeals adopt one rule or approach and one or more of the other divisions adopt a different rule or approach. Until the United States Supreme Court or the state's highest court resolves the split, other circuits or divisions are free to adopt whichever rule or approach that they choose.

In discussing an issue in which there is a circuit split, you need to do the following:

☐ You need to tell your supervising attorney that your jurisdiction has not decided the issue and that there is a circuit split, with other circuits taking two or more different approaches.

☐ You need to describe the different approaches, telling your supervising attorney which circuits have taken which approach and the reasons that the courts have given for selecting one approach over other approaches. If different courts have adopted the same approach for different reasons, make that point clear.

☐ You need to evaluate the different approaches, predict which approach your jurisdiction is likely to take, and explain your reasoning.

☐ You need to apply the rules to the facts of your case. If you are confident that your jurisdiction will adopt a particular rule, just apply that rule to the facts of your case. If, however, it is not clear which rule your jurisdiction will adopt, you should do an alternative analysis, applying the various rules to the facts of your case.

Example 1 shows two templates for organizing this information.

EXAMPLE 1 **Templates for Organizing a Discussion of First Impression Involving a Circuit Split Using the Script and a More Integrated Format**

Script Format	Integrated Format
Introductory Section ☐ Introduce the issue and explain (1) that in your jurisdiction the issue is an issue of first impression and (2) that in other jurisdictions the courts have adopted different rules or taken different approaches.	**Introductory Section** ☐ Introduce the issue and explain (1) that in your jurisdiction the issue is an issue of first impression and (2) that in other jurisdictions the courts have adopted different rules or taken different approaches.
Majority Rule ☐ If the majority of jurisdictions have adopted a particular rule or approach, begin by introducing that rule or approach, telling your supervising attorney which jurisdictions have adopted that rule or approach, and summarizing the courts' reasons for adopting that rule or approach.	**Majority Rule** ☐ If the majority of jurisdictions have adopted a particular rule or approach, begin by introducing that rule or approach, telling your supervising attorney which jurisdictions have adopted that rule or approach, and summarizing the courts' reasons for adopting that rule or approach.
Minority Rule ☐ Set out the minority rule, telling your readers which jurisdiction or jurisdictions have adopted that rule or approach and explaining the court's or courts' reasons for adopting that rule or approach.	**Minority Rule** ☐ Set out the minority rule, telling your readers which jurisdiction or jurisdictions have adopted that rule or approach and explaining the court's or courts' reasons for adopting that rule or approach.
Arguments ☐ Set out the plaintiff's or moving party's assertion about which rule or approach the court should adopt and the arguments that the plaintiff or moving party is likely to make.	**Conclusion and Reasoning** ☐ Tell your supervising attorney which rule or approach you think the court is likely to adopt. ☐ Set out your reasoning, incorporating into your reasoning a discussion and evaluation of each side's arguments.

Script Format	Integrated Format
☐ Set out the defendant's or responding party's assertion about which rule or approach the court should adopt and the arguments that the defendant or responding party is likely to make. **Conclusion and Reasoning** ☐ Tell your supervising attorney which rule you think the court is likely to adopt and why you think that the court will adopt that rule. **Application of Rule or Approach to Facts** • Apply the rule or approach that you predict the court will adopt to the facts of your case. If the application of the rule or approach will be in dispute, set out the plaintiff or moving party's assertion and arguments, the defendant's or responding party's assertion and arguments, and your mini-conclusion. Note: If that rule or approach requires an elements analysis, a factor analysis, or the balancing of competing interests, do that analysis using the templates set out in Chapters 7 and 8 [Laurel Currie Oates and Anne Enquist, Just Memos: Preparing for Practice, 4th Ed.,] and sections 8.A and 8.B. • If you think that there is a possibility that the court will adopt a different rule or approach, do an alternative analysis. If the application of the other rule or approach will be in dispute, set out the plaintiff's or moving party's assertion and arguments, the defendant's or responding party's arguments, and your mini-	**Application of Rule or Approach to Facts** • Apply the rule or approach that you predict the court will adopt to the facts of your case. If the application of the rule will be in dispute, set out the plaintiff's or moving party's assertion and arguments, the defendant's or responding party's assertion and arguments, and your mini-conclusion using either a script or integrated format. Note: If that rule or approach requires an elements analysis, a factor analysis, or the balancing of competing interests, do that analysis using the templates set out in Chapters 7 and 8 [Laurel Currie Oates and Anne Enquist, Just Memos: Preparing for Practice, 4th Ed.,] and sections 8.A and 8.B. • If you think that there is a possibility that the court will adopt a different rule or approach, apply that different rule or approach to the facts of your case. If the application of the rule will be in dispute, set out the plaintiff or moving party's assertion and arguments, the defendant's or responding party's assertion and arguments, and your mini-conclusion using a script or an integrated format. Note: If that rule or approach requires an elements analysis, a factor analysis, or the balancing of competing interests, do that analysis using the templates set out in Chapters 7 and 8 [Laurel Currie Oates and Anne Enquist, Just Memos: Preparing for Practice, 4th Ed.,] and sections 8.A and 8.B.

Script Format	Integrated Format
conclusion. Note: If that rule or approach requires an elements analysis, a factor analysis, or the balancing of competing interests, do that analysis using the templates set out in Chapters 7 and 8 [Laurel Currie Oates and Anne Enquist, Just Memos: Preparing for Practice, 4th Ed.,] and sections 8.A and 8.B.	

2. *The Statute Is Ambiguous, and There Are No Regulations or Cases that Have Interpreted that Statute*

Another common scenario is one in which the statute is ambiguous and there are no regulations or cases that have resolved that ambiguity.

In this situation, you will usually want to start your discussion section by introducing and quoting the relevant statutory language, identifying the ambiguity, and telling your supervising attorney that there are no regulations or cases that have resolved the ambiguity. What else you include, and how you order that other information, will depend on what you found in doing your research and what arguments you think the parties are likely to make.

3. *Arguments Based on Agency Decisions*

If, in doing your research, you located administrative memos or decisions that interpret the statute, you will need to do a *Chevron* analysis[1] to determine whether the courts will defer to the agency's interpretation. Because the courts sometimes do the Step Zero analysis first and sometimes they do it last, Example 2 shows two ways of organizing a *Chevron* analysis.

---

1. In *Chevron U.S.A., Inc. v. Natural Resources Defense Council, Inc.*, 67 U.S. 837 (1984), the United States Supreme Court set out a two-part test to determine whether courts should defer to an administrative agency's interpretation of a statute. Under the first part of this test, the courts look to see whether the statute is ambiguous or whether there is a "gap" in the statute that Congress intended the agency to fill. If the statute is ambiguous, the courts then look to see whether the agency's interpretation of the statute is reasonable. If the agency's decision is reasonable, the courts will defer to the agency; if the agency's decision is not reasonable, the courts will substitute their judgment for the agency's. In more recent cases, some courts have added a "Step Zero," in which they look to see if an agency's interpretation has the force of law, for example, whether the agency followed the notice and comment provisions of § 553 of the Administrative Procedure Act. See Cass R. Sunstein, *Chevron Step Zero*, 92 Va. L. Rev. 187 (2006). While the courts do not have to defer to agency interpretations that do not have the force of law, the courts often give these interpretations substantial weight.

***EXAMPLE 2* Templates for Doing a *Chevron* Analysis**

Option 1	Option 2
A. *Chevron* Analysis ☐ Explain *Chevron,* including a brief description of the two-part test. ☐ Do a *Chevron* Step Zero analysis, using a script or integrated format to discuss whether the agency's decision has the force of law. ☐ Do a *Chevron* Step One analysis, discussing whether the statutory language is, in fact, ambiguous. (If this step of the analysis is not in dispute, you can simply raise and dismiss this issue.) ☐ Do a *Chevron* Step Two analysis, using a script or integrated format to discuss whether the agency's interpretation of the statute is reasonable.	**A. *Chevron* Analysis** ☐ Explain *Chevron,* including a brief description of the two-part test. ☐ Do a *Chevron* Step One analysis, discussing whether the statutory language is, in fact, ambiguous. (If this step of the analysis is not in dispute, you can simply raise and dismiss this issue.) ☐ Do a *Chevron* Step Two analysis, using a script or integrated format to discuss whether the agency's interpretation of the statute is reasonable. ☐ If, given your facts, there is an issue about whether the agency's decision has the force of law, do a *Chevron* Step Zero analysis.

4. Policy Arguments

If there are no agency decisions interpreting a statute, or if you believe that the courts will find that an agency's decision is unreasonable or does not have the force of law, think policy. In doing your research, did you locate a "findings" or "purpose" section in which Congress or the state legislature explained why it enacted the statute and/or what its purpose or goal was in enacting that statute? (These sections are often set out in a separate section or sections at the beginning of the act or of the chapter in which your statute has been placed.) If there isn't a findings or purpose section, is there anything in the legislative history that the parties might use to support their assertions about how the statute should be interpreted? Last, but certainly not least, take a step back. Given the facts of your case, and the larger social, political, and economic context in which that case is being decided, what will each side argue is the "right" or "just" way to interpret the statute?

If there is a finding and/or purposes section, make those arguments first. Then move to any arguments based on the legislative history and, if you think the parties will use them, any broader policy arguments. See Example 3.

PRACTICE POINTER

If you did a legislative history but did not find any relevant information, include that fact in your discussion section.

EXAMPLE 3 Templates for Organizing Policy and Legislative History Arguments Using the Script and a More Integrated Format

Script Format	Integrated Format
B. Policy Arguments	**B. Policy Arguments**
If you are going to include more than one type of policy argument, include a roadmap that alerts your supervising attorney to that fact.	If you are going to include more than one type of policy argument, include a roadmap that alerts your supervising attorney to that fact.
1. Arguments based on a findings and/or purpose section ☐ Introduce and quote the relevant portions of any findings or purpose sections. ☐ Set out the plaintiff's or moving party's assertion and support for those assertions. ☐ Set out the defendant's or responding party's assertion and support for those assertions. ☐ Set out your mini-conclusion.	1. Arguments based on a findings and/or purpose section ☐ Introduce and quote the relevant portions of any findings or purpose sections. ☐ Set out your prediction. ☐ Set out your first reason, summarizing and evaluating the arguments that each side is likely to make. ☐ If you have additional reasons, set out those additional reasons, summarizing and evaluating the arguments that each side is likely to make.
2. Arguments based on legislative history ☐ Describe and, if appropriate, quote, relevant portions of legislative history. ☐ Set out the plaintiff's or moving party's assertions and support for those assertions. ☐ Set out the defendant's or responding party's assertion and support for those assertions. ☐ Set out your mini-conclusion.	2. Arguments based on legislative history ☐ Describe and, if appropriate, quote, relevant portions of legislative history. ☐ Set out your conclusion ☐ Set out your first reason, summarizing and evaluating the arguments that each side is likely to make. ☐ If you have additional reasons, set out those additional reasons, summarizing and evaluating the arguments that each side is likely to make.

Script Format	Integrated Format
3. Broader policy arguments ☐ Set out the plaintiff's or moving party's assertions and support for those assertions. ☐ Set out the defendant's or responding party's assertion and support for those assertions. ☐ Set out your mini-conclusion.	3. Broader policy arguments ☐ Set out your conclusion. ☐ Set out your first reason, summarizing and evaluating the arguments that each side is likely to make. ☐ If you have additional reasons, set out those additional reasons, summarizing and evaluating the arguments that each side is likely to make.

CHAPTER 9

Drafting Letters

Some clients love their attorney and recommend him or her to their business associates, friends, relatives, and people they meet at the gym and on the golf course. Unfortunately, other clients do not give their attorneys the same rave reviews. As a new attorney, how do you make it more likely that you fall into the first and not the second category? While "by winning" seems like the obvious answer, it is not the only answer. Even though clients tend to like attorneys who win or who tell the clients what they want to hear better than attorneys who lose or who have to give them bad news, many clients are looking for more: They want an attorney who listens to them, who explains the law to them in language they can understand, who gives them good advice, and who does not make promises that are not kept. In addition, they want an attorney who is professional. They want someone who dresses professionally, who has a professional demeanor, and who creates professional documents.

Thus, in writing a letter to a client, keep in mind that you are doing more than just telling the client what the law is or what you think your client should do. You are establishing a relationship with your client and building, or destroying, your professional reputation.

A. THE ASSIGNMENT

As an attorney, you will write many different types of letters to clients. You will, for example, write letters confirming that you have agreed to represent a particular individual, letters updating your client about the status of his or her case, demand letters, and letters like the ones that we describe in this chapter: opinion letters that explain the law and your client's options.

> **PRACTICE POINTER**
>
> Before you write your first demand letter, read Bret Rappaport's article, *A Shot Across the Bow: How to Write an Effective Demand Letter*, 5 JALWD 32 (2008).

For the purposes of this chapter, assume that you are an attorney in Austin, Texas, and that you represent Mary Corner, who has just purchased a restaurant in a historic building in the Austin Historic District. On September 13, 2013, Ms. Corner filed an application for a permit to install two six-foot by four-foot painted signs on the front of her new restaurant, the Corner Café, which is located in the corner of a building that has been designated as a Historic Landmark. One sign would be on the north side of the building, and the other sign would be on the west side of the building. Each sign would extend eighteen inches above the roof line and would have a beige background and green lettering. At night, the signs would be lit by a small light installed under the signs. On October 1, 2013, the Historic Landmark Commission denied Ms. Corner's application and gave her fourteen days to appeal its decision. Ms. Corner is thinking about appealing and has asked for our advice.

B. KNOW YOUR AUDIENCE AND YOUR PURPOSE

Before you begin writing, ask yourself two questions: Who is my audience? What is my purpose?

1. *The Audience for an Opinion Letter*

Although the primary audience for an opinion letter is the client, there may be a secondary audience. The letter may be read not only by the client but also by an interested third party. Consequently, in writing the letter, write both for the client and for anyone else who may read the letter.

In the Corner Café sign case, the primary audience for your opinion letter will be Mary Corner. Ms. Corner may, however, show the letter to another small business owner, to friends and relatives, or even to a city official.

2. *The Purpose of an Opinion Letter*

Assume for a moment that the audience is the client and no one else. In writing to that client, what is your purpose? Is it to inform? To persuade? To justify your bill? Should you be giving the client only your conclusions, or should you include the information that the client needs to reach his or her own conclusions?

Your role is determined, at least in part, by your state's Rules of Professional Conduct. For example, in Texas attorneys are bound by the following rule and comments.

EXAMPLE 1 **Texas Disciplinary Rules of Professional Conduct**

1.03 COMMUNICATION

(a) A lawyer shall keep a client reasonably informed about the status of a matter and promptly comply with reasonable requests for information.

(b) A lawyer shall explain a matter to the extent reasonably necessary to permit the client to make informed decisions regarding the representation.

COMMENT:

1. The client should have sufficient information to participate intelligently in decisions concerning the objectives of the representation and the means by which they are to be pursued, to the extent the client is willing and able to do so. For example, a lawyer negotiating on behalf of a client should provide the client with facts relevant to the matter, inform the client of communications from another party and take other reasonable steps to permit the client to make a decision regarding a serious offer from another party. A lawyer who receives from opposing counsel either an offer of settlement in a civil controversy or a proffered plea bargain in a criminal case should promptly inform the client of its substance unless prior discussions with the client have left it clear that the proposal will be unacceptable. See Comment 2 to Rule 1.02.

2. Adequacy of communication depends in part on the kind of advice or assistance involved. For example, in negotiations where there is time to explain a proposal the lawyer should review all important provisions with the client before proceeding to an agreement. In litigation a lawyer should explain the general strategy and prospects of success and ordinarily should consult the client on tactics that might injure or coerce others. . . . The guiding principle is that the lawyer should reasonably fulfill client expectations for information consistent with the duty to act in the client's best interests, and the client's overall requirements as to the character of representation.

Accordingly, under the Texas rules, your primary purpose in writing the letter would be to give Ms. Corner the information that she needs to make an informed decision about whether to appeal the Historic Landmark Commission's decision.

C. PREPARE THE FIRST DRAFT OF THE LETTER

Just as convention dictates the content and form of the objective memorandum, convention also dictates the content and form of the opinion letter. Most opinion letters have (1) an introductory paragraph identifying the issue and, most often, the attorney's opinion; (2) a summary of the facts on which the opinion is based; (3) an explanation of the law; (4) the attorney's advice; and (5) a closing sentence or paragraph. Note the similarities between a formal memorandum and the opinion letter.

Objective Memorandum	Opinion Letter
Heading	Name Address File Reference Salutation
Question presented	Introductory paragraph
Brief answer	Opinion
Statement of facts	Summary of facts on which opinion is based
Discussion section	Explanation
Conclusion	Advice
	Closing

1. *The Introductory Paragraph*

In writing the introductory paragraph, you have two objectives: to establish the appropriate relationship with your client and to define the issue or goal. In addition, you will often include substantive information. For example, when the news is favorable, you will usually set out your opinion in the introductory paragraph.

Because the introductory paragraph is so important, avoid "canned" opening sentences. For instance, do not begin all of your letters with "This letter is in response to your inquiry of . . . " or "As you requested . . . ." Instead of beginning with platitudes, begin by identifying the issue or goal. Compare Examples 1, 2, and 3.

EXAMPLE 1 **Canned Opening Sentence**

> This letter is in response to your inquiry of October 3, 2013. The information that you requested is set out below.

EXAMPLE 2 **Better Opening Sentence**

> After our meeting yesterday, I researched the Austin ordinances governing signs in the Austin Historic Districts.

EXAMPLE 3 **Even Better Opening Sentence**

> During our meeting yesterday, you asked me whether you should appeal the Historic Landmark Commission's decision denying your request for a permit to install two signs above the entrance to your new restaurant, the Corner Café. To answer your question, I have reviewed the facts and the Austin ordinances on signs in Historic Landmark Districts.

Because Example 1 could be used to open almost any letter, it subtly suggests to the reader that he or she is just one more client to whom the attorney is cranking out a response. Consequently, most successful attorneys avoid opening sentences like the one in Example 1 and, like the authors of Examples 2 and 3, personalize their openings.

2. *Statement of the Issue*

Although you need to identify the issue, you do not want to include a formal issue statement. In most instances, the "under-does-when" and the "whether" formats used in formal memos are inappropriate in an opinion letter.

In deciding how to present the issue, keep in mind your purpose, both in including a statement of the issue and in writing the letter itself. In most letters, your purpose is twofold: You want the client to know that you understand the issue, and you want to protect yourself. Consequently, you include a statement of the issue for both rhetorical and practical reasons. You use it to establish a relationship with the client and to limit your liability.

In the Corner Café sign case, there are a number of different ways and places to set out the issue: You can incorporate your issue statement into your introductory paragraph; you can combine your statement of the issue with your statement of your opinion; or you can set out the issue at the beginning of your explanation of the law.

EXAMPLE 4 **Issue Statement Incorporated into the Introductory Paragraph**

> During our meeting on Tuesday, you asked whether you should appeal the City's decision denying your request to install two signs above the entrance to your new restaurant, the Corner Café.

EXAMPLE 5 **Issue Statement Combined with Your Opinion**

> I have completed my review of the ordinances governing business signs in the Austin Historic Districts. Based on this review, I recommend that you appeal the City's decision denying your request to install two signs above the entrance to your new restaurant, the Corner Café.

EXAMPLE 6 **Issue Used to Introduce Explanation of the Law**

> [Introductory paragraph and facts go here.]
>
> Before deciding whether to appeal the City's denial of your application for a permit to install two signs above the entrance to your new restaurant, you should consider the following ordinances and the procedures and costs that are involved in appealing a decision. [Explanation of the law goes here.]

3. *Opinion*

When the client has asked for your opinion, set out your opinion in the letter. When the news is good, you will usually put your opinion in the introductory paragraph; having had his or her question answered, the client can then concentrate on the explanation. You may, however, want to use a different strategy when the news is bad. Instead of putting your opinion "up front," you may choose to put it at the end, in the hope that having read the explanation, the client will better understand your opinion.

Whatever your opinion, present it as your opinion. Because you are in the business of making predictions and not guarantees, never tell clients that they will or will not win. Instead, present your opinion in terms of probabilities: "It is unlikely that you would win on appeal." "It is unlikely that the City Council will overturn the decision of the Historic Landmark Commission and grant your application for a permit."

4. *Summary of the Facts*

There are two reasons for including a summary of the facts. As with the statement of the issue, the first is rhetorical. You want the client to know that you heard his or her story. The second is practical. You want to protect yourself. Your client needs to know that your opinion is based on a particular set of facts and that, if the facts turn out to be different, your opinion might also be different.

Just as you do not include all of the facts in the statement of facts written for an objective memorandum, you do not include all of the facts in an opinion letter. Include only those facts that are legally significant or that are important to the client. Because the letter itself should be short, keep your summary of facts as short as possible. For instance, in the Corner Café sign case, your statement of facts might look like this.

EXAMPLE 7 **Summary of Facts**

> You submitted your original application on September 13, 2013. In that application, you requested a permit that would have allowed you to install two six-foot by four-foot painted wood signs on the front of your building. One of the signs would have been installed on the north side of the building, and the other would have been installed on the west side of the building. Both signs would extend about eighteen inches above the top of the building and would be beige with green lettering. At night, the signs would be lit by a light installed under the signs. The Historic Landmark Commission denied your application on October 1, 2013, giving you fourteen days to appeal its decision to the City Council.

5. *Explanation*

Under the rules of professional responsibility, you must give the client the information that he or she needs to make an informed decision. It is essential, therefore, that you give not only your opinion but also the basis for your opinion. The explanation section is not, however, just a repeat of the discussion section from an objective memorandum. It is usually much shorter and much more client-specific.

When the explanation requires a discussion of more than one or two issues, you will usually want to include a roadmap. Having outlined the steps, you can then discuss each step in more detail. The amount of detail will depend on the question, the subject matter, and the client. Although there are exceptions, as a general rule, do not set out the text of ordinances or statutes or include references to specific cases. Instead, just tell the client what the ordinances, statutes, and cases say, without citations to authority.

After explaining the law, apply the law to the facts of your client's case. If a particular point is not in dispute, explain why it is not in dispute; if it is in dispute, summarize each side's arguments. The difference between the analysis in an objective memorandum and in an opinion letter is a difference in degree, not kind. In each instance, give the reader what he or she needs—nothing more and nothing less. For examples of explanations, see the sample letters set out at the end of this chapter.

6. *Advice*

When there is more than one possible course of action, include an advice section in which you describe and evaluate each option. For example, if there are several ways in which your client could change its business operations to avoid liability, describe and evaluate each of those options. Similarly, if your client could choose negotiation over arbitration or arbitration over litigation, describe and evaluate each option. Having described the options, you can then advise the client as to which option you think would be in his or her best interest.

7. *Concluding Paragraph*

Just as you should avoid canned openings, also avoid canned closings. Instead of using stock sentences, use the concluding paragraph to cement the relationship that you have established with the client and to confirm what, if anything, is to happen next. What is the next step and who is to take it?

8. *Warnings*

Some firms will want you to include explicit warnings. They will want you to tell the client that your opinion is based on current law and on the facts currently available and that your opinion might be different if the facts turn out to be different. Other firms believe that these warnings, when set out explicitly, set the wrong tone. Because practice varies, determine which approach your firm takes before writing the letter.

In writing your letter, you can use any of the standard formats for business letters. For examples of accepted formats, see the sample letters at the end of this chapter.

D. REVISING, EDITING, AND PROOFREADING THE OPINION LETTER

It is not enough that the law be stated correctly and that your advice be sound. Your letter must be well written and the tone must be the one that you intend.

1. *Drafting a Well-Written Letter*

Like other types of writing, a well-written letter is well organized. As a general rule, present the information in the order listed above: an introductory paragraph in which you identify the issue and give your opinion followed by a summary of the facts, an explanation of the law, your advice, and a concluding sentence or paragraph. You will also want to structure each paragraph carefully, identifying the topic in the first sentence and making sure that each sentence builds on the prior one.

In addition, take care in constructing your sentences. You can make the law more understandable by using concrete subjects and action verbs and relatively short sentences. When longer sentences are needed, manage those sentences by using punctuation to divide the sentences into shorter units of meaning.

Finally, remember that you will be judged by the letter you write. Although clients may not know whether you have the law right, they will know whether you have spelled their names correctly. In addition, many will notice other mistakes in grammar, punctuation, or spelling. If you want to be known as a competent lawyer, make sure that your letters provide the proof.

2. *Using an Appropriate Tone*

In addition to selling competence, you are selling an image. As you read each of the following letters, picture the attorney who wrote it.

EXAMPLE 1

Dear Mr. and Mrs. McDonald:

This letter is to acknowledge receipt of your letter of February 17, 2013, concerning your prospects as potential adoptive parents. The information that you provided about yourselves will need to be verified through appropriate documentation. Furthermore, I am sure that you are cognizant of the fact that there are considerably more prospective adoptive placements than there are available adoptees to fill those placement slots.

Nonetheless, I will be authorizing my legal assistant to keep your correspondence on file. One can never know when an opportunity may present itself and, in fact, a child becomes unexpectedly available for placement. If such an opportunity should arise, please know that I would be in immediate contact with you.

Very sincerely yours,
Kenneth Q. Washburn III
Attorney at Law

EXAMPLE 2

Dear Bill and Mary,

Just wanted you to know that I got your letter asking about adopting a baby. I can already tell that you two would make great parents. But, as you probably know, there are far more "would be" parents out there than there are babies.

But I don't want you to lose hope. You might be surprised. Your future little one may be available sooner than you think. It has happened before! And you can be sure that I'll call you the minute I hear of something. Until then, I'll have Marge set up a file for you.

All the best,
Ken Washburn

EXAMPLE 3

Dear Mr. and Mrs. McDonald:

Your letter about the possibility of adopting a baby arrived in my office yesterday. Although the information in your letter indicates that you would be ideal adoptive parents, I am sure that you realize that there are more couples who wish to adopt than there are adoptable babies. For this reason, you may have to wait for some time for your future son or daughter.

Even so, occasionally an infant becomes available for adoption on short notice. For this reason, I will ask my legal assistant to open a file for you so that we can react quickly if necessary. Because we do not know exactly when an infant will become available, I recommend that we begin putting together the appropriate documentation as soon as possible. In the meantime, please know that I will call you immediately if I learn of an available infant who would be a good match for you.

Sincerely,
Kenneth Washburn

3. *Checklist for Critiquing the Opinion Letter*

I. Organization

☐ The information has been presented in a logical order: The letter begins with an introductory sentence or paragraph that is followed, in most instances, by the attorney's opinion, a summary of the facts, an explanation, the attorney's advice, and a concluding paragraph.

II. Content

☐ The introductory sentence identifies the topic and establishes the appropriate relationship with the client.

☐ The attorney's opinion is sound and is stated in terms of probabilities.

- ☐ The summary of the facts is accurate and includes both the legally significant facts and the facts that are important to the client.
- ☐ The explanation gives the client the information that he or she needs to make an informed decision.
- ☐ The options are described and evaluated.
- ☐ The concluding paragraph states who will do what next and sets an appropriate tone.

III. Writing

- ☐ The client can understand the letter after reading it once.
- ☐ The paragraph divisions are logical, and the paragraphs are neither too long nor too short.
- ☐ Transitions and dovetailing have been used to make the connections between ideas clear.
- ☐ In most sentences, the writer has used the actor as the subject of the sentence, and the subject and verb are close together.
- ☐ The writer has varied the length of the sentences and the sentence patterns so that each sentence flows smoothly from the prior sentence.
- ☐ The writing is concise and precise.
- ☐ The writing is grammatically correct and correctly punctuated.
- ☐ The letter has been proofread.

Chapter 9 Quiz

Draft answers for each of the following questions. Make your points clearly and concisely, and write sentences that are easy to read and that are grammatical and correctly punctuated.

1. In writing an opinion letter, what is your purpose?
2. As a general rule, what types of information should be included in an opinion letter and in what order should that information be presented?
3. In general, what is the appropriate tone for an opinion letter?

E. SAMPLE CLIENT LETTERS

EXAMPLE 1 **Sample Client Letter**

Confidential
Attorney-Client Communication

Mary Corner
101 Main Street
Austin, Texas 73344

Dear Ms. Corner:

During our meeting yesterday, you asked me whether you should appeal the Historic Landmark Commission's decision denying your request for a permit to install two signs above the entrance to your new restaurant, the Corner Café. To answer your question, I have reviewed the facts and the Austin ordinances on signs in Historic Landmark Districts.

You submitted your original application on September 13, 2013. In that application, you requested a permit that would have allowed you to install two six-foot by four-foot painted wood signs on the front of your building. One of the signs would have been installed on the north side of the building, and the other would have been installed on the west side of the building. Both signs would extend about eighteen inches above the top of the building and would be beige with green lettering. At night, the signs would be lit by a light installed under the signs. The Historic Landmark Commission denied your application on October 1, 2013, giving you fourteen days to appeal its decision to the City Council.

City of Austin ordinances prohibit certain types of signs in Historic Landmark Districts. For example, the ordinances specifically prohibit roof signs and any sign, or any portion of a sign, that rotates. Although your signs would not rotate, they might fall within the definition of a roof sign, which is defined as a sign that is "installed over or on the roof of a building." In determining whether to grant a permit for other types of signs, the Historic Landmark Commission considers a number of other factors, including the following:

1. the proposed size, color, and lighting of the sign;
2. the material from which the sign is to be constructed;
3. the proliferation of signs on a building or lot;
4. the proposed orientation of the sign with respect to structures; and
5. other factors that are consistent with the Historic Landmark Preservation Plan, the character of the National Historic Register District, and the purpose of historic landmark regulations.

If the Commission denied your application for a permit because your proposed signs fall within the definition of a roof sign, it is unlikely that the City Council would overturn the Commission's decision. Our only hope would be to persuade the City Council that a sign that extends above the top of the building does not fall within the definition of a roof sign.

If, however, the Commission denied the permit for some other reason, the City Council might overturn the Commission's decision, particularly if your proposed signs are consistent in size, color, lighting, and material with other signs in the area and if there are not already a number of other signs on the building.

To preserve your right to appeal, I recommend that you file a notice of appeal within the time limits set out in the letter that you received from the Commission. I would then schedule a meeting with a member of the Commission to determine the reason that the Commission denied your application. If the Commission denied your application because your signs would extend beyond the roof line, the Commission may be willing to approve your application for a permit if you agree to change the size and/or locations of your signs so that they do not extend beyond the roof line. Similarly, if the Commission denied your application because of the signs' size, color, or lighting, you may be able to work with the Commission to modify your application so that your proposed signs meet the Commission's criteria. If, however, you cannot find out from the Commission why it denied your application or you cannot reach an agreement with the Commission about an application that would meet its criteria, you can then proceed with your appeal to the City Council.

Although you do not need an attorney to file an appeal with the City Council or to schedule meetings with the Commission, I would be glad to assist you with either or both actions. If you would like me to act on your behalf, please call me by Wednesday, October 9, 2013, so that I can submit the appeal before the deadline. If you would like to file the appeal without my assistance, please see the instructions that are set out in the letter that you received from the Commission. In addition, you can request an appointment with a Commissioner by calling the following number: (512) 974-2680. If you have any further questions or concerns, please feel free to call me. Please keep in mind that you must file your appeal no later than Monday, October 14, 2013.

Very truly yours,
Your name

***EXAMPLE 2* Sample Client Letter**

Confidential
Attorney-Client Communication

September 30, 2013

Ms. Marian Walter
1234 Main Street
Wichita, KS 67218

File No. 0192002

Dear Ms. Walter:

Thank you for contacting me about whether you can vacate your current location before the expiration of your lease. After researching the issues, I have determined that, if you decide to move out before the end of your lease and your landlord, Valley Antiques, files a lawsuit to collect the unpaid rent, you can probably win the lawsuit. You should, however, consider some of your other options.

Because my opinion is based on the following facts, please contact me if I have left out a fact or misstated a fact.

In June 2012, you received a brochure advertising an "elegant antiques mall" that was certain to attract "the most discriminating clients." When you met with the leasing agent, Joann Carter, she told you that the mall would house antique stores and that the mall was designed to attract adults, not children. In August 2012, you signed a five-year lease. The lease stated that the remaining spaces would be rented to antique stores or other retail businesses.

Between August 2012 and November 2012, five other upscale antique stores moved into the mall. The landlord was, however, unable to rent the remaining eight spaces to antique dealers. As a result, between February and April 2013, the landlord leased four of the remaining spaces to other types of businesses. It leased one of the spaces to a video arcade and three others to secondhand stores. Since these stores moved into the mall, there have been children with skateboards in the mall area, and you have experienced a 20 percent decrease in profits. In addition to making oral complaints, on April 30, 2013, you sent a letter to the landlord notifying it that you believe that it violated the terms of your lease when it leased spaces in the mall to the video arcade and secondhand stores.

If you vacate the premises and default on the lease, Valley Antiques may file a lawsuit against you to recover the rent due for the remaining months of the lease. If this happens, you can argue that Valley Antiques "constructively evicted" you when it leased to the arcade and secondhand stores. A constructive eviction is different from an actual eviction: While an actual eviction occurs when the landlord literally takes the premises away from the tenant, a constructive eviction occurs when the landlord interferes with a tenant's right to use the premises for their intended purpose. It would be up to the jury to decide whether the circumstances surrounding your case constitute constructive eviction.

To establish that you have been constructively evicted, you will need to prove four things. First, you must prove that Valley Antiques violated the lease agreement. Valley Antiques will argue that, under the lease, it had the right to lease to retail stores and that an arcade and thrift shops are retail stores. Although the lease does allow Valley Antiques to lease to retail stores, you can argue that both parties understood the language in the lease to mean that Valley Antiques could lease to antique stores and other "upscale" retail establishments, for example, an upscale jewelry store or restaurant. Based on the language in the brochure and the statements made by the leasing agent, a jury should conclude that the landlord violated the lease by leasing the other spaces to the video arcade and secondhand stores.

Second, you must prove that when Valley Antiques leased the vacant spaces to a video arcade and secondhand stores it substantially interfered with your ability to use your leased space. Although there have been cases in which the courts have found that a landlord substantially interfered with a tenant's use of its leased space when the landlord rented to an incompatible business, there are other cases in which the court found that the landlord did not substantially interfere. The key seems to be whether the landlord's act caused a loss of profits. As a consequence, to prove substantial interference, we will have to show that Valley Antiques caused your loss of profits when it leased the vacant spaces to the arcade and the secondhand stores. Even though we should be able to do this, Valley Antiques will try to prove that your losses are the result of other factors, such as the seasonal nature of your business, the current economic climate, or your own business practices.

Third, you must prove that you gave Valley Antiques notice of the problem and an opportunity to correct it. You should be able to meet this requirement: in addition to making oral complaints, you also sent a letter, and you have given Valley Antiques several months to correct the problem.

Finally, you must prove that you vacated the premises within a reasonable amount of time after complaining to the landlord. If you vacate the premises by November 1, 2013, the jury will most likely find that you have met this requirement.

Although you should be able to prove that you have been constructively evicted, litigation is expensive and stressful, and there are no guarantees. As a result, you should consider some of your other options.

One option is to stay and pay rent. Although this option avoids the expense and stress of litigation, you may lose your right to claim that you have been constructively evicted. As I indicated earlier in this letter, one of the requirements for constructive eviction is that you move out within a reasonable time. In addition, if your loss in profits continues, it may be impractical to stay in business.

A second option would be to try to sublease your space to another business. Even though your lease requires that you obtain Valley Antiques' approval before you sublet your space, the courts have said that a landlord cannot withhold approval except for good cause. The risk associated with this option is that you may be liable for unpaid rents if the new tenant fails to make payments.

A third option is to try to negotiate an early termination of the lease on the grounds that Valley Antiques has violated the lease by leasing to the arcade and secondhand stores. I can do this for you or, if you want to minimize your costs, you can do it on your own.

A fourth option would be to file a lawsuit against Valley Antiques for breach of contract. Although you should be able to win this lawsuit and recover your lost profits, such a lawsuit would be expensive and, once again, there are no guarantees.

Unfortunately, none of these options is very good. As a result, you need to balance your desire to move out of the mall against the potential costs. Although there is a good chance that your landlord will not sue you, under our state's statute of limitations it has six years to file a lawsuit. Therefore, you would have to live under the cloud of potential litigation for a number of years.

Please contact my office to schedule an appointment to talk in more detail about your options. I look forward to meeting with you.

Sincerely,
Name
Attorney at Law

EXAMPLE 3 Sample Client Letter

Confidential
Attorney-Client Communication

September 20, 2013

Onlinebooks.com
6524 Industrial Parkway South
Tampa Bay, Florida 33607

Dear Mr. Brooks:

You have asked if Onlinebooks may ask job applicants whether they have back problems or have used more than five days of sick leave during the past year. My research indicates that the Americans with Disabilities Act (ADA) prohibits the asking of such questions. You can, however, ask questions that will help you determine whether an applicant can perform the essential job requirements. Because my opinion is based on current law and my understanding of the facts, I have set out those facts so that you can review them for accuracy. Please note that a change in the facts might change my opinion.

Onlinebooks employs "pickers," that is, individuals who pick books off shelves, place them in a box, and then place the box on a conveyor belt. Pickers must be able to climb, reach, and lift boxes weighing up to thirty pounds. In the past, some of the individuals you have hired as pickers have not been able to do all parts of the job or have used substantial amounts of sick leave for back or other health problems. Thus, you want to ask job applicants about whether they have back problems and about how they use sick leave.

The ADA prohibits employers from discriminating against qualified job applicants who are disabled. More specifically, the ADA prohibits employers from asking applicants questions that are designed to "weed out" individuals who have a disability or who suffer from a chronic illness. As a result, Onlinebooks cannot ask job applicants about whether they have back problems or about their use of sick leave.

The ADA does not, however, prohibit an employer from asking job applicants whether they can, with or without reasonable accommodations, perform the essential functions of the job for which they are applying. Therefore, Onlinebooks may describe the essential functions of the job and then ask applicants whether they can perform those functions. For example, you may tell applicants that pickers must be able to climb, reach, and lift thirty-pound boxes and then ask them whether they can perform each of these tasks. In addition, Onlinebooks may ask applicants to demonstrate that they can do each of these tasks.

If an applicant asks for a reasonable accommodation, Onlinebooks must grant that accommodation unless doing so would impose an unreasonable burden on Onlinebooks. For example, if an applicant asks to be allowed to wear a back support or to use a handcart to move heavy boxes longer distances, you should grant the request unless doing so would create an unreasonable burden on the company. You would not, however, need to grant an employee's request to be exempted from carrying boxes weighing over, for example, ten pounds.

In addition, the ADA does not prohibit employers from asking applicants about their work histories. Consequently, although you may not ask applicants how much sick leave they used in the last year, you may ask them about their attendance records. In doing so, you just need to make sure that the questions are designed to collect information about the applicants' work records, not to determine whether the individual is disabled or suffers from a chronic illness.

To summarize then, although you may not ask applicants whether they have back problems, you may ask them whether they can, with or without reasonable accommodations, perform the essential functions of the job. In addition, although you may not ask applicants about their use of sick leave, you may ask them about their attendance records as long as your questions are not designed to collect information about whether the person is disabled or suffers from a chronic illness.

If you have any additional questions, please feel free to contact me.

Sincerely,
Name
Attorney at Law

CHAPTER 10

Writing a Motion Brief

A. MOTION BRIEFS

Much of litigation is motions practice. For example, as a trial attorney, you may file motions for temporary relief, to compel discovery, to suppress evidence, to dismiss, or for summary judgment. Although not all of these motions will be supported by briefs, many will.

> **PRACTICE POINTER**
>
> The names of these briefs vary from jurisdiction to jurisdiction. In some jurisdictions, they are called "briefs in support of a motion" or "motion briefs," while in other jurisdictions they are called "memoranda of law," "memoranda of points of authority" or "P and A memos," for short. Check your court rules and with local attorneys to see what these briefs are called in your jurisdiction.

1. Audience

In writing a brief in support of or in opposition to a motion, your primary audience is the trial judge.

Sometimes you will know which judge will read your brief. either the brief has been requested by a specific judge, or you know which judge will hear the motion. At other times, though, you will not know who will read your brief. the brief will be read by whichever judge is hearing motions on the day that your motion is argued.

If you know which judge will read your brief, write your brief for that judge. Learn as much as you can about that judge, and then craft a brief that he or she will find persuasive. If you do not know which judge will read your brief, write a brief that will work for any of the judges who might hear your motion.

In whichever situation you find yourself, keep the judge's schedule in mind. It is not uncommon for a judge hearing civil motions to hear twenty motions in a single day. If in each of these cases each party has filed a twenty-page brief, the judge would have 800 pages to read. given this workload, it is not surprising that for most judges the best brief is the short brief. Know what you need and want to argue, make your argument, and then stop.

Also keep in mind the constraints placed on trial judges. Because trial judges must apply mandatory authority, they need to know what the law is, not what you think it should be. Whenever possible, make the easy argument: set out and apply existing law.

2. *Purpose*

In writing to a trial judge, you have two goals: to educate and to persuade. You are a teacher who teaches the judge both the applicable law and the facts of the case. You are not, however, *just* a teacher; you are also an advocate. As you teach, you will be trying to persuade the court to take a particular action.

3. *Conventions*

The format of a particular brief will vary from jurisdiction to jurisdiction and, even within a jurisdiction, from court to court. Consequently, check both the general and the local rules. Is there a rule that prescribes the types of information that should be included in the brief, the order in which that information should be presented, and the particular format? If there is, follow that rule. If there is no rule, check with other attorneys or with the court clerk to see if there is a format that is typically used.

B. STATE V. PATTERSON

In this chapter, the example case is *State v. Patterson,* a criminal case in which the defendant has filed a motion to suppress the identifications obtained at a show-up held shortly after an assault and at a line-up held one day later. the facts of the case are as follows. At about 4:00 p.m. on Monday, August 13, 2012, Beatrice Martinez left her apartment and began walking down residential streets to her place of employment, a restaurant located about one mile from her apartment. As she was walking, Ms. Martinez noticed an older model red station wagon with a chrome luggage rack as it drove by her. A few minutes later, the same car drove by once again. this time, the driver pulled in front of Ms. Martinez, blocking the sidewalk. the driver then got out of the car; walked toward Ms. Martinez; and when he was about five feet from Ms. Martinez, pulled a gun from his coat pocket and pointed it at her.

At about 4:15 p.m. Chester Clipse was walking home when he saw a man in a red station wagon driving slowly down the street. Because it appeared that the driver was going to pull into Mr. Clipse's private parking spot, Clipse's attention was drawn to the car. As a result, Clipse was watching when the driver got out of the station wagon and pulled a gun. As soon as he saw the gun, Clipse shouted, "Hey!" Startled, the man turned and went back to his car, got in it, and drove away. Crying, Ms. Martinez ran across the street.

Mr. Clipse then took Ms.Martinez, who was visibly shaken, to his land-lady's apartment, where they called the police. While the landlady comforted Ms. Martinez, Mr. Clipse went back out to the street to wait for the police, where he saw a parking enforcement officer. Mr. Clipse told the parking enforcement officer what had happened and gave him a description of the vehicle. About ten minutes later, the parking enforcement officer found a red station wagon with a chrome luggage rack parked on the street. A license check showed that the vehicle was registered to Dean Patterson.

As the parking enforcement officer was looking for the vehicle, officer Yuen and officer Cox arrived at Mr. Clipse's apartment building and interviewed Mr. Clipse. Because he had been down the street when the incident occurred, Clipse was only able to tell the officers that the man was a white man in his late thirties or early forties and that he was of average height and weight. While Mr. Clipse was talking to the officers, officer Cox received a radio message indicating that the parking enforcement officer had located a car that matched the one that Clipse had described. While officer Cox took Mr. Clipse in his car to see if he could identify the car, officer Yuen went inside to interview Ms. Martinez.

Ms. Martinez told officer Yuen that her assailant was a white male who was about 5'7" tall; that he weighed between 165 and 170 pounds; that he had wavy blondish-brown hair; that he appeared to be in his early forties; and that at the time of the assault, her assailant was wearing a dark jacket and glasses. neither Mr. Clipse nor Ms. Martinez had been able to give the license plate numbers on the man's vehicle.

After completing the interview, officer Yuen asked Ms. Martinez if she wanted a ride home or to work. Ms. Martinez accepted the offer of a ride home and got into the back seat of officer Yuen's vehicle. About four blocks later, officer Yuen asked Ms. Martinez whether a man who was on the sidewalk in front of them looked like her assailant. Because she could not see the man's face, Ms. Martinez did not respond. As the police car drew nearer, officer Yuen again asked Ms. Martinez whether the man looked like her assailant. this time, Ms. Yuen answered, "Yes, I think so." on hearing this response, officer Yuen pulled up next to the man, got out of his vehicle, and talked to the man, who was wearing a green jacket and glasses.

As officer Yuen was questioning the man, officer Cox drove up with Mr. Clipse. While Martinez and Clipse watched, officers Cox and Yuen continued to question the man. officer Cox then returned to Ms. Martinez and Mr. Clipse and walked them back to Mr. Clipse's apartment. While he did so, officer Yuen arrested the man, who was identified as Dean e. Patterson, for assault with a deadly weapon. Later that day, the police searched Mr. Patterson's apartment and found a gun issued to Patterson by his employer. At a line-up held the next day, Ms. Martinez identified Mr. Patterson as the man who assaulted her. Mr.Clipse was not able to make an identification.

In his statement to the police, twenty-two-year-old Dean Patterson stated that, on the day in question, he finished his shift as a security guard at 7:30 a.m. and walked to his apartment. After having breakfast with his wife, Patterson went to bed and slept until about 1:00 p.m. At about 2:30 p.m., Patterson's wife received a phone call asking her to cover for a co-worker, a nurse who was ill. After about 3:00 p.m., Patterson drove his wife the three-quarters of a mile to the hospital. When he returned home, Patterson could not find a parking place close to his apartment and had to park several blocks away.

At about 3:30 p.m., Patterson called his wife to find out how long she would have to work. they had plans to go to a movie that evening, and he wanted to know whether he should change those plans. At about 3:50 p.m., Patterson took a load of laundry to the apartment complex's laundry room. When he returned to his apartment, Patterson watched part of an old movie. At about 4:20 p.m., Patterson went back to the laundry room to put the clothes in the dryer. By this time, it was 4:30 p.m., and Patterson decided to phone his wife again. He arranged to meet her at 5:15 p.m. for her dinner break. Patterson picked up the laundry and then left the apartment a little before 5:00 p.m. to meet his wife.

While Mr. Patterson was walking to the hospital, a police car pulled up behind him, and a police officer got out of his car and began questioning him. Patterson was then arrested and charged with assault with a deadly weapon.

Mr. Patterson has no prior convictions and has volunteered to take a lie detector test.

C. CONSTRUCTING A "THEORY OF THE CASE"

While different people use different labels, all good advocates understand the importance of having a theory of the case. For some, constructing the "theory of the case" means selecting the lens through which you want the court to view your client's case. there is almost always more than one way to view the law and the facts.

For others, constructing a theory of the case means selecting a theme, which might or might not be summed up in a single sentence or phrase. For instance, in the example problem, defense counsel might select the theme, "wrong place, wrong time." Mr. Patterson just happened to be at the wrong place at the wrong time.

No matter which label resonates for you, keep in mind that, to be a good advocate, it is not enough that you know the facts and the law. You must also be a good storyteller. Your statement of facts should read like a well-written short story and, in your arguments, you must do more than just mechanically set out the law and apply that law to the facts of your case. Instead, you must weave the law and facts in such a way that you present legally sound arguments that appeal both to the judge's head and heart.

There are at least two ways of coming up with a good theory of the case. the first is to look at the case through your client's eyes. According to your client, what happened? Why did the other people involved do what they did? Why did your client act as he or she did? Why does your client think that what he or she did was legally right? Justified? Is there law that supports your client's view of what happened?

The second way is to look at the cases involving the same issue in which the court reached the result that you want the court to reach in your case. In those cases, what was the winning party's theory of the case? What legal arguments did that party make? How did it characterize what happened? What was the court's reaction? Did the trial court "buy" the winning party's theory of the case or come up with its own theory of the case?

In the example case, Patterson says that he did not commit the crime. He was simply at the wrong place at the wrong time. At the time the crime was committed, Patterson was doing laundry, moving his car, and getting ready to meet his wife for dinner. Although Martinez has identified him as her assailant, she did so only because police pointed him out to her and suggested to her that he was the man who had assaulted her. In addition, Patterson does not match Martinez's and Clipse's descriptions of the assailant. Although both Martinez and Clipse told the police that the assailant was in his late thirties or early forties, Patterson is only twenty-two.

In contrast, the State says that Patterson is the person who assaulted Martinez. Martinez has identified Patterson as her assailant, his car matches the one that Martinez and Clipse have described, and a gun was found in his apartment.

D. THE CAPTION

While in some jurisdictions, motion briefs are printed on pleading, or numbered, paper in other jurisdictions they are printed on regular paper. In addition, the rules about where the caption is placed and what information should be included can vary from jurisdiction to jurisdiction. In the example case, we have used the Washington rules: the caption is set out on the first page beginning on about line 5. the parties' names are set out on the left-hand side, and the case number and the title of the document are set out on the right-hand side. See document samples on page 52.

PRACTICE POINTER

Many jurisdictions now allow, or even require, that the parties file their pleadings and briefs electronically. Thus, before filing your brief, check your local rules.

E. INTRODUCTORY PARAGRAPH/PRAYERF OR RELIEF

In many, but not all, jurisdictions the first paragraph after the caption is an introductory paragraph. Most of the time, these paragraphs are very "matter of fact." the attorney simply identifies the motion and sets out the relief that he or she is requesting. At other times, the introductory paragraph is more "colorful": the attorney uses the introductory paragraph in the same way that a motion picture company uses a trailer. In such instances, the attorney uses the introductory paragraph to "hook" the judge, enticing him or her to read further. In deciding which approach to take, consider the conventional practices in your jurisdiction, the nature and importance of your cases, and your own personal style.

EXAMPLE 1 **Introductory Paragraph From Defendant's Brief**

> Mr. Patterson asks the Court to suppress Ms. Martinez's show-up and line-up identifications and to prohibit both Ms. Martinez and Mr. Clipse from making in-court identifications. The show-up was impermissibly suggestive and, because she viewed her assailant for only a few seconds, Ms. Martinez's identifications are unreliable. Mr. Patterson was simply at the wrong place at the wrong time.

EXAMPLE 2 **State's Introductory Paragraph/Prayer for Relief**

> The State asks the Court to deny the defendant's motion to suppress the victim's show-up and line-up identifications and to allow both the victim and the witness to make in-court identifications. The show-up was not suggestive, and the victim's and the witness's identifications are reliable.

EXAMPLE 3 **Alternative Introductory Paragraph**

> August 13, 2012, started out as a normal day for Dean Patterson. After finishing his shift as a security guard, he slept, had breakfast with his wife, and then, after his wife left for work, watched a movie and did the laundry. Everything changed, however, when Patterson decided to walk to the hospital where his wife worked to have dinner with her. As he was walking down the street, a police car pulled up behind him, and while a young woman who had been assaulted watched, questioned him. Although Patterson was twenty years younger than the man the victim said had assaulted her, the police arrested Patterson and charged him with the assault. Because Patterson's only "crime" was being at the wrong place at the wrong time, Patterson respectfully requests that the Court grant his motion to suppress.

PRACTICE POINTER

Capitalize "court" when referring to the court to which your brief is addressed or the United States Supreme Court or when you are setting out the full name of the court. In all other instances, do not capitalize "court."

F. THE STATEMENT OF FACTS

Never underestimate the importance of the facts. Particularly at the trial court level, it is usually the facts that determine the outcome.

1. *Select the Facts*

In drafting your statement of facts, you will, typically, include three types of facts: background facts, legally significant facts, and emotionally significant facts.

a. Background Facts

Background facts play a different role in persuasive writing than they do in objective writing. In an objective statement of facts, the writer includes only those background facts that are needed for the story to make sense. In contrast, in drafting a persuasive statement of facts, you can also use background facts to create a favorable context. See section 10.F.3.a.

b. Legally Significant Facts

Because most courts require that the statement of facts be "fair," in writing the statement of facts you must include all of the legally significant facts, both favorable and unfavorable. thus, in the example case, both the State and the defendant must include all of the facts that will be relevant in determining whether the identifications obtained at the show-up and at the line-up should be suppressed and whether Martinez and Clipse should be allowed to make in-court identifications.

c. Emotionally Significant Facts

While you must include all of the legally significant facts, you do not need to include all of the facts that are emotionally significant. Although as a defensive move you may sometimes include an emotionally significant fact that is unfavorable, recharacterizing it or minimizing its significance, most of the time you will not. It is more common to include only those emotionally significant facts that favor your client.

The harder question is how to handle emotionally significant facts that are unfavorable to the other side. Should you sling mud, or should you take a higher road and omit any reference to those facts? the answer is that it depends: it depends on the case and on the attorney. If the fact's connection to the case is tenuous, most attorneys will not include it. If, however, the case is weak and the fact's connection is closer, many attorneys will include it, some using it as a sword, others using it much more subtly.

2. *Select an Organizational Scheme*

In selecting an organizational scheme, consider two factors. First, decide which organizational scheme makes the most sense. Does it make more sense to use a chronological organizational scheme, a topical organizational scheme, or a topical organizational scheme with the facts within each topic set out in chronological order? Second, decide which organizational scheme will allow you to set out the facts in such a way that you are able to present your story and your theory of the case most effectively.

In the example case, it makes sense to set out the facts in chronological order. In deciding whether to suppress the evidence, the trial judge will want to know what happened first, second, and third. A chronological organizational scheme will also allow each side to tell its story. the only difference will be that Patterson will start his story with his activities on the day in question, while the State will start its story where it started for the victim: with the assault.

PRACTICE POINTER

If your statement of facts is long or if you are setting out the facts for two unrelated issues, think about adding subheadings. While the argumentative headings should be in the form of positive assertions (see section 10.H.2), the subheading in the statement of facts can be in the form of labels.

3. *Present the Facts in a Light Favorable to Your Client*

In writing the statement of facts for an objective memo, you set out the facts accurately and objectively. You do not present the facts in the light most favorable to your client.

In writing the statement of facts for a motion brief, you still need to set out the facts accurately. One of the fastest ways to lose a case is to leave out legally significant facts or to misrepresent either the legally significant or emotionally significant facts. Being accurate does not mean, however, that you need to set out the facts objectively. You are permitted and, in fact, are expected to present the facts in such a way that they support your theory of the case.

In presenting the facts, attorneys use a number of different techniques. they create a favorable context, they tell the story from their client's point of view, they emphasize the facts that support their theory of the case and de-emphasize those that do not, and they select their words correctly.

TECHNIQUES FOR PRESENTING THE FACTS IN A LIGHT FAVORABLE TO YOUR CLIENT

a. Create a favorable context
b. Tell the story from your client's point of view
c. Emphasize favorable facts and de-emphasize unfavorable facts
   i. Airtime
   ii. Detail
   iii. Positions of emphasis
   iv. Short sentences
   v. Main and dependent clauses
d. Select facts both for their denotation and their connotation

a. Create a Favorable Context

People tend to view a fact differently depending on the context in which that fact is presented. Judges are no different.

One way to create a favorable context is to start the story where it favors your client. Look for instance at example 1 below. Instead of starting the statement of facts with the assault or Patterson's arrest, defense counsel starts it by describing what Patterson was doing on the day of the assault. By starting with these facts, she is able to start the story with facts that support her theory of the case: Patterson is an innocent pedestrian who happened to be in the wrong place at the wrong time. note how defense counsel works in the fact that Patterson is married, that he has a job, and that he does nice things, for instance, he takes his wife to work, does the laundry, and arranges to meet his wife during her dinner break.

EXAMPLE 1 **The First Three Paragraphs of the Defendant's Statement of Facts**

At 7:30 on Monday morning, August 13, 2012, twenty-two-year-old Dean Patterson finished his shift as a security guard and walked to his apartment. After having breakfast with his wife, Patterson went to bed and slept until about 1:00 p.m. At about 2:30 p.m., Patterson's wife received a phone call asking her to work at the local hospital, where she is employed as a nurse. She got ready, and Patterson dropped her off at the hospital at about 3:10 p.m. When he returned, Patterson could not find a parking place close to his apartment and had to park several blocks away.

At about 3:30 p.m., Patterson called his wife to find out how long she would have to work. They had plans to go to a movie that evening, and he wanted to know whether he should change those plans. At about 3:50 p.m., Patterson took a load of laundry to the apartment complex's laundry room. When he returned to his apartment, Patterson watched part of an old movie. At about 4:20 p.m., Patterson went back to the laundry room to put the clothes in the dryer. On his way back, he walked to where his car—an older model red station wagon—was parked to see if he needed to get gas. As he did so, Patterson noticed a parking spot much closer to his apartment and, after checking his gas gauge, moved his car to that spot. After parking his car, Patterson got out of the car and, because the driver's side door does not lock from the outside, walked to the passenger side to lock the doors. As he did so, he nodded to a parking enforcement officer who was driving by.

By this time, it was 4:30 p.m., and Patterson decided to phone his wife again. He arranged to meet her at 5:15 p.m. for her dinner break. Patterson picked up the laundry and then left the apartment a little before 5:00 p.m. to meet his wife.

The State also creates a favorable context. However, instead of starting its statement of facts by describing Patterson's actions, it begins the story where it started for the victim. In the first paragraph of its statement of facts, the State describes the assault and then the show-up and line-up.

EXAMPLE 2 **The First Paragraph of the State's Statement of Facts**

> On Monday, August 13, 2012, Beatrice Martinez was assaulted with a deadly weapon. At a show-up held thirty to forty minutes after the attack, Martinez positively identified the defendant, Dean E. Patterson, as her assailant. Four days after the assault, Martinez picked Patterson out of a line-up, once again positively identifying him as her assailant.

b. Tell the Story from the Client's Point of View

One of the most powerful persuasive devices is point of view. In most cases, you will want to tell the story as your client would tell it.

One way of telling the story from your client's point of view is to make your client the "actor" in most of your sentences. note how in the defendant's statement of facts, the writer has made Patterson or his wife the subject in most of the main clauses, while in the State's statement of facts, the writer has made Martinez the subject in most of the main clauses.

In the following examples, the subject of each sentence is in bold.

EXAMPLE 1 **Excerpt from Defendant's Statement of Facts**

> At 7:30 on Monday morning, August 13, 2012, twenty-two-year-old **Dean Patterson** finished his shift as a security guard and walked to his apartment. After having breakfast with his wife, **Patterson** went to bed and slept until about 1:00 p.m. At about 2:30 p.m., **Patterson's wife** received a phone call asking her to work at the local hospital where she is employed as a nurse. **She** got ready, and **Patterson** dropped her off at the hospital at about 3:10 p.m. When he returned, **Patterson** could not find a parking place close to his apartment and had to park several blocks away.
>
> At about 3:30 p.m., Patterson called his wife to find out how long she would have to work. They had plans to go to a movie that evening, and he wanted to know whether he should change those plans. At about 3:50 p.m., Patterson took a load of laundry to the apartment complex's laundry room. When he returned to his apartment, Patterson watched part of an old movie. At about 4:20 p.m., Patterson went back to the laundry room to put the clothes in the dryer. On his way back, he walked to where his car—an older model red station wagon—was parked to see if he needed to get gas. As he did so, Patterson noticed a parking spot much closer to his apartment and, after checking his gas gauge, moved his car to that spot. After parking his car, Patterson got out of the car and, because the driver's side door does not lock from the outside, walked to the passenger side to lock the doors. As he did so, he nodded to a parking enforcement officer who was driving by.
>
> By this time, **it** was 4:30 p.m., and **Patterson** decided to phone his wife again. **He** arranged to meet her at 5:15 p.m. for her dinner break. **Patterson** picked up the laundry and then left the apartment a little before 5:00 p.m. to meet his wife.

EXAMPLE 2 **Excerpt from the State's Statement of Facts**

> On Monday, August 13, 2012, **Beatrice Martinez** was assaulted with a deadly weapon. At a show-up held thirty to forty minutes after the attack, **Martinez** positively identified the defendant, Dean E. Patterson, as her assailant. Four days after the assault, **Martinez** picked Patterson out of a line-up, once again positively identifying him as her assailant.

c. Emphasize the Facts That Support Your Theory of the Case, and De-emphasize Those That Do Not

In addition to presenting the facts from the client's point of view, good advocates emphasize those facts that support their theory of the case and de-emphasize those that do not. they do this by using one or more of the following techniques.

i. Airtime

Just as listeners remember best the songs that get the most airtime, readers remember best the facts that get the most words. Consequently, favorable facts should be given considerable "airtime," and unfavorable ones should be given little or no "play." In the example case, if Patterson is going to persuade the court that the identifications are unreliable, he needs to deemphasize the fact that Martinez saw the car twice. Although he cannot omit this fact, he does not need to give this fact very much airtime. In contrast, if the State is going to persuade the court that Martinez's identifications are reliable, it needs to emphasize the fact that she saw the car twice. thus, the State wants to give this fact as much airtime as possible. In the following examples, the relevant facts are in bold.

EXAMPLE 1 **Excerpt from the Defendant's Statement of Facts**

> Martinez has stated that she was walking down Belmont **when a car that had driven by earlier** pulled in front of her. The man got out of his car, took one or two steps toward Martinez, and then pulled a gun from his pocket. As soon as she spotted the gun, Martinez screamed, looked away, and then, crying, ran across the street. The entire encounter was over in a second or two.

EXAMPLE 2 **Excerpt from the State's Statement of Facts**

> **As she was walking north on Belmont, Martinez observed an older model red station wagon with a chrome luggage rack as it passed slowly by her. Moments later, the same car came down the street again.** This time, the driver pulled his car in front of Martinez, stopping his car so that it blocked her path. As Martinez watched, the driver got out of his car and walked toward her. The man then took a gun from his coat pocket and pointed it

at Martinez. Martinez looked at the gun, looked back up at her assailant, and then, crying, ran back across the street to safety.

ii. Detail

Just as readers tend to remember best those facts that get the most airtime, they also tend to remember best those facts that are described in the most detail. the more detail, the more vivid the picture; the more vivid the picture, the more likely it is that the reader will remember the particular facts. thus, airtime and detail work hand in hand. In contrast, to de-emphasize unfavorable facts, good advocates describe them in general terms.

Look again at the following examples, this time comparing the way in which the defendant and the State describe the assailant's car. By leaving out the description of the car, is the defendant setting out all of the legally significant facts? What inference does the State want the judge to draw from the fact that Ms. Martinez provided the police with a detailed description of her assailant's car?

EXAMPLE 1 **Excerpt from the Defendant's Statement of Facts**

Martinez has stated that she was walking down Belmont when **a car** that had driven by earlier pulled in front of her. The man got out of his car, took one or two steps toward Martinez, and then pulled a gun from his pocket. As soon as she spotted the gun, Martinez screamed, looked away, and then, crying, ran across the street. The entire encounter was over in a second or two.

EXAMPLE 2 **Excerpt from the State's Statement of Facts**

As she was walking north on Belmont, Martinez observed **an older model red station wagon with a chrome luggage rack as it passed slowly by her. Moments later, the same car came down the street again.** This time, the driver pulled his car in front of Martinez, stopping his car so that it blocked her path. As Martinez watched, the driver got out of his car and walked toward her. The man then took a gun from his coat pocket and pointed it at Martinez. Martinez looked at the gun, looked back up at her assailant, and then, crying, ran back across the street to safety.

iii. Positions of Emphasis

Because readers tend to remember best information that is placed in a position of emphasis (the beginning or end of a section, the beginning or end of a paragraph, and the beginning or end of a sentence), whenever possible, place the facts that you want to emphasize in one of these positions. Conversely, if you want to de-emphasize a fact, bury it in the middle—in the middle of a sentence, in the middle of a paragraph, or in the middle of a section.

In the following examples, the defendant wants to emphasize that Martinez told the police that her assailant was in his early forties. As a consequence, defense counsel places that fact near the end of the paragraph. In contrast, because the State wants to de-emphasize that fact, it places it in the middle of a sentence in the middle of a paragraph.

EXAMPLE 1 **Excerpt from the Defendant's Statement of Facts**

> Because she was upset, Martinez was able to give the police only a general description of her assailant. She described him as being a short, white male with blondish-brown hair who was wearing glasses and a dark jacket. In addition, **she told the police that her assailant was in his early forties. Patterson is twenty-two.**

EXAMPLE 2 **Excerpt from the State's Statement of Facts**

> Martinez told the police that her assailant was a white male who was about 5'7" tall; that her assailant had wavy blondish-brown hair; **that her assailant appeared to be in his early forties**; and that at the time of the assault, her assailant was wearing a dark jacket and glasses.

In the next set of examples, the defendant wants to de-emphasize that he owns an older model red station wagon, while the State wants to emphasize that fact. In addition, because the State wants to de-emphasize that the gun found in Patterson's apartment was issued to him by his employer, it has placed that fact in the middle of a paragraph.

EXAMPLE 3 **Excerpt from the Defendant's Statement of Facts**

> At about 3:50 p.m., Patterson took a load of laundry to the apartment complex's laundry room. When he returned to his apartment, Patterson watched part of an old movie. At about 4:20 p.m., Patterson went back to the laundry room to put the clothes in the dryer. On his way back, he walked to where his car—**an older model red station wagon**—was parked to see if he needed to get gas. As he did so, Patterson noticed a parking spot much closer to his apartment and, after checking his gas gauge, he moved his car to that spot. After parking his car, Patterson got out of the car and, because the driver's side door does not lock from the outside, he walked to the passenger side to lock the doors. As he did so, he nodded to a parking enforcement officer who was driving by.

EXAMPLE 4 **Excerpt from the State's Statement of Facts**

> Later that day, **the police searched Patterson's car—an older model red station wagon with a chrome luggage rack—and his apartment.** In the apartment, the police found the gun issued to Patterson by his employer. Four days later, the police held a line-up. Although Clipse did not identify Patterson, Martinez identified Patterson as the man who had approached her.

iv. Sentence Length

Just as airtime and detail work together, so do positions of emphasis and sentence length. Because readers tend to remember information placed in shorter sentences better than information placed in longer sentences, good advocates place favorable facts in short sentences in a position of emphasis. For instance, in example 1, not only did defense counsel place the favorable fact in a position of emphasis, but she also put that fact in a short sentence. In example 2, the State not only buried the unfavorable fact in the middle of the paragraph, it also placed that fact in the middle of a long sentence.

EXAMPLE 1 **Excerpt from the Defendant's Statement of Facts**

Because she was upset, Martinez was able to give the police only a general description of her assailant. She described him as being a short, white male with blondish-brown hair who was wearing glasses and a dark jacket. In addition, she told police that her assailant was in his early forties. **Patterson is twenty-two**.

EXAMPLE 2 **Excerpt from the State's Statement of Facts**

Martinez told the police that her assailant was a white male who was about 5'7" tall; that her assailant had wavy blondish-brown hair; **that her assailant appeared to be in his early forties**; and that at the time of the assault, her assailant was wearing a dark jacket and glasses.

PRACTICE POINTER

Another way to emphasize a favorable fact is by highlighting discrepancies. For instance, in Example 1, defense counsel places the fact that the defendant is twenty-two next to fact that Ms. Martinez told police that her assailant appeared to be in his early forties. By juxtaposing these two facts, defense counsel is able to highlight the discrepancies. In contrast, the prosecutor creates space between these two facts by putting the fact that the Mr. Patterson is twenty-two in one paragraph and the fact that Ms. Martinez told police that her assailant was in his early forties in a different paragraph.

v. Active and Passive Voice

Good advocates use the active voice when they want to emphasize what the actor did and the passive voice when they want to draw the reader's attention away from the actor's actions. Consider the following examples.

EXAMPLE 1 **Active Voice**

Patterson assaulted Martinez.

***EXAMPLE 2* Passive Voice**

Martinez was assaulted.

Because the State wants to emphasize that it was Patterson who assaulted Martinez, the prosecutor would use the language in example 1. In contrast, because defense counsel states that Patterson is not the person who assaulted Martinez, she would use the language set out in example 2. For more on the active and passive voice, see section 5.1 in *Just Writing, Fourth Edition.*

vi. Dependent and Main Clauses

Another technique is to put favorable facts in the main clause and unfavorable facts in a dependent clause. While the defendant wants to emphasize the fact that the bystander, Clipse, was unable to make an identification and de-emphasize the fact that Martinez was able to make an identification, the State wants to do the opposite. Compare the following examples.

***EXAMPLE 1* Excerpt from the Defendant's Brief**

Later that day, the police searched Patterson's car and apartment. In the apartment, the police found the gun issued to Patterson by his employer. Four days later, the police held a line-up at the police station. **Although Martinez identified Patterson as the man who had approached her, Clipse did not pick Patterson out of the line-up.**

***EXAMPLE 2* Excerpt from the State's Brief**

A line-up was held four days later. **Although Clipse was unable to identify the man who had assaulted Martinez, Martinez identified Patterson as her assailant.**

d. Select Words Both for Their Denotation and Their Connotation

Words are powerful. not only do they convey information (denotation), but they also create images (connotation). Consider, for example, the labels that might be used to describe Mr. Patterson:

Mr. Dean Patterson
Dean Patterson
Patterson
Dean
the suspect
the accused
the defendant

While defense counsel would probably want to use "Mr. Patterson," "Dean Patterson," or "Patterson" in referring to her client, the prosecutor might use "the defendant." By using his name, defense counsel reminds the judge that her client is a real person. the title "Mr. Patterson" makes Patterson seem less like a person charged with a felony and more like an average, respectable citizen. In contrast, by using the label "the defendant," the State suggests that Patterson is guilty.

PRACTICE POINTER

Because legal proceedings are formal proceedings, as a general rule, do not refer to parties or to witnesses by just their first names. The only times that you might want to break this "rule" are when referring to a child (for example, the child in a juvenile case), or when there are two or more individuals with the same last name.

Other word choices can also subtly persuade the court. For instance, in the following paragraph the defendant wants to set up his argument that officer Yuen's actions tainted the identifications. thus, he uses "agreed" to suggest that Martinez's identification was prompted by officer Yuen's questions, "questioned" to suggest that the officers' actions would have indicated to Martinez and Clipse that Patterson was guilty, and "watched" to remind the court that Martinez and Clipse may have been influenced by the officers' actions.

EXAMPLE 1 **Excerpt from the State's Statement of Facts**

> Even though Martinez was unable to see the man's face, she **agreed** with the officer that the man looked like her assailant. At this point, Officer Yuen stopped the car, got out, and approached Patterson. As Officer Yuen was **questioning** Patterson, Officer Cox drove up with the witness, Clipse. While Martinez and Clipse **watched**, Officers Cox and Yuen **continued questioning** Patterson. Officer Cox then returned to Martinez and Clipse and walked them back to Clipse's apartment. While Officer Cox did so, Officer Yuen placed Patterson under arrest.

4. Checklist for Critiquing the Statement of Facts

I. ***Organization***

- The facts have been presented in a logical order (chronologically or topically or a combination of the two).
- When possible, the facts have been presented in an order that favors the client.

II. ***Content***

- All of the legally significant facts have been included.
- The emotionally significant facts that favor the client have been included.
- An appropriate number of background facts have been included.

III. *Persuasiveness*

- The writer has presented the facts so that they support the writer's theory of the case.
- The writer has presented the facts in a favorable context.
- The writer has presented the facts from the point of view that favors the client. (In telling the client's story, the writer has used the client as the subject of most sentences.)
- The writer has emphasized favorable facts and de-emphasized unfavorable ones.
  - Favorable facts have been given more airtime than unfavorable facts.
  - Favorable facts have been described in detail; unfavorable facts have been described more generally.
  - The positions of emphasis have been used effectively. When possible, favorable facts have been placed at the beginning or end of the statement of facts, at the beginning or end of a paragraph, and at the beginning or end of a sentence.
  - Short sentences and short paragraphs have been used to emphasize favorable facts; unfavorable facts have been placed in longer sentences in longer paragraphs.
  - Active and passive voices have been used effectively.
  - Favorable information has been emphasized by placing it in the main, or independent, clause; unfavorable facts have been placed in dependent, or subordinate, clauses.
  - Words have been selected not only for their denotation but also for their connotation.
  - The writing is grammatically correct, correctly punctuated, and proofread.

G. DRAFTING THE ISSUE STATEMENT

While you may not include an issue statement in all of your briefs, when you do include one, think carefully about how you want to frame the legal question. By asking the right question, you improve your chances of getting the result that your client wants.

1. *Select the Lens*

The issue statement is the lens through which the judge views the case. Select the correct lens, and you improve your chances that the court will see the case as you see it and decide the motion in your client's favor. the difficulty, of course, is in selecting that lens. How do you select just the right one? Unfortunately, there is no easy answer. Because selecting the lens is, at least in part, a creative act, there is no foolproof formula.

There are, however, some strategies that you can use. First, think about your theory of the case. given your theory, how should you frame the issue? Second, look at how the court framed the issues in cases that are similar to yours. In the cases in which the courts suppressed the evidence, how did the court frame the issue? then look at the cases in which the courts did not suppress the evidence.

Finally, brainstorm. From what other angles can you view the case? What other labels can you attach? think outside the box.

2. *Select a Format*

Most courts do not prescribe a format for an issue statement. Although you should have the same number of issue statements as you have main argumentative headings, you can state the issue using the under-does-when format, the whether format, or the multi-sentence format. See sections 8.2 and 8.3 in *Just Memos, Third Edition.* In addition, in some jurisdictions and for some types of briefs, you can just set out the legal or factual question that you want the court to decide.

EXAMPLE 1 **"Under-Does-When" Format**

> Under the Fourteenth Amendment, should the Court grant Mr. Patterson's motion to suppress Martinez's show-up, line-up, and in-court identifications and Patterson's in-court identification when (1) a police officer pointed out Patterson to Martinez, repeatedly asking the shaken Martinez whether Patterson looked like her assailant; (2) the police questioned Patterson in front of Martinez and Clipse; (3) during the second or two that Martinez had to view her assailant, her attention was focused on his gun and not his face; and (4) Martinez told police that her assailant was in his forties, and Mr. Patterson is twenty-two?

EXAMPLE 2 **"Whether" Format**

> Whether the Court should grant Mr. Patterson's motion to suppress Martinez's show-up, line-up, and in-court identifications and Patterson's in-court identification when (1) a police officer pointed out Patterson to Martinez, repeatedly asking the shaken Martinez whether Patterson looked like her assailant; (2) the police questioned Patterson in front of Martinez and Clipse; (3) during the second or two that Martinez had to view her assailant, her attention was focused on his gun and not his face; and (4) Martinez told police that her assailant was in his forties, and Mr. Patterson is twenty-two.

EXAMPLE 3 **Multi-Sentence Format**

> On August 13, 2012, a man jumped out of his car, approached Martinez, and pointed a gun at her. As soon as she saw the gun, Martinez screamed and, crying, ran across the street. Shortly after the assault, a police officer twice asked Martinez whether a pedestrian looked like her assailant. Although Martinez could not see the pedestrian's face, she agreed. The police then questioned the pedestrian, Dean Patterson, while Martinez and another witness watched. Both Martinez and the witness told the police that

Martinez's assailant was in his late thirties or early forties. Patterson is twenty-two. Under these circumstances, should the Court suppress Martinez's show-up and line-up identifications and prevent Martinez and Clipse from making in-court identifications?

EXAMPLE 4 **Issue Statement that just Sets Out the Legal Question**

Whether the Court should suppress Ms. Martinez's show-up and line-up identifications and prevent Martinez and Clipse from making in-court identifications.

EXAMPLE 5 **Issue Statement that just Sets Out the Legal Question**

Should the court grant Mr. Patterson's motion to suppress?

PRACTICE POINTER

Once you select a format, use that format for each of your issue statements. Do not write one issue statement using the under-does-when format, a second issue statement using the whether format, and a third using the multi-sentence format. Also remember that you are not bound by opposing counsel's choices. You do not need to use the same format that he or she used, and you do not need to have the same number of issue statements. Do not let your opponent dictate your strategy.

3. Make Your Issue Statement Subtly Persuasive

Your issue statement should be subtly persuasive. After reading it, the judge should be inclined to rule in your client's favor.

There are two techniques that you can use to make your issue statements persuasive. First, state the legal question so that it suggests the conclusion you want the court to reach. For example, if you want the court to grant the motion, ask whether the court should grant the motion. In contrast, if you want the court to deny the motion, ask whether the court should deny the motion. Second, when you include facts, present those facts in the light most favorable to your client.

For instance, in the example case, the defendant wants to state the legal question so that it suggests that the court should grant his motion to suppress. In contrast, the State wants to frame the question so that it suggests that the court should deny the defendant's motion.

EXAMPLE 1 **The Defendant's Statement of the Legal Question**

"Whether the Court should grant the motion to suppress when. . . . "

EXAMPLE 2 **The State's Statement of the Legal Question**

"Whether the Court should deny the motion to suppress when. . . . "

The defendant also wants to set out the facts so that they suggest that the police procedures were unnecessarily suggestive and that Martinez's identifications are unreliable. Accordingly, the defendant wants to set out the facts that establish that the procedure was suggestive. (Instead of allowing Martinez to identify Patterson independently, a police officer pointed out Patterson and repeatedly asked the shaken Martinez whether he looked like her assailant.) In addition, the defendant wants to set out facts that establish that Martinez had a limited opportunity to view her assailant and that her description was inaccurate. note that in both instances the writers set out the facts related to the first part of the test first and then the facts related to the second part of the test.

EXAMPLE 3 **The Defendant's Issue Statement**

> Under the Fourteenth Amendment, should the Court grant Mr. Patterson's motion to suppress Martinez's show-up identification (1) when a police officer pointed out Patterson to Martinez, repeatedly asking the shaken Martinez whether Patterson looked like her assailant; (2) when, during the second or two that Martinez had to view her assailant, her attention was focused on his gun and not his face; and (3) when Martinez told the police that her assailant was in his early forties, and Patterson is only twenty-two years old?

While the defendant wants to set out the facts that indicate that the police procedures were unnecessarily suggestive and that Martinez's identifications are unreliable, the State wants to downplay the police officer's questions and emphasize instead that Martinez had a good opportunity to view her assailant.

EXAMPLE 4 **The State's Issue Statement**

> Should the Court deny the defendant's motion to suppress when the police merely asked the victim whether a pedestrian looked like her assailant and when the victim observed her assailant on two occasions for several seconds in broad daylight?

Thus, writing a persuasive issue statement is a three-step process. You must select the appropriate lens, choose a format, and then craft your issue statement so that it is subtly persuasive.

4. *Checklist for Critiquing the Issue Statement*

I. *Format*

- There are the same number of issue statements as there are main argumentative headings.
- The writer has used one of the conventional formats: for example, the under-does-when format, the whether format, or the multisentence format.
- The same format has been used for each issue statement.

II. *Content*

- The issue statement states the legal question and includes references to the legally significant facts. In addition, when appropriate, it also includes a reference to the rule of law.
- The legal questions have been framed so that they support the writer's theory of the case.

III. *Persuasiveness*

- The legal question has been framed so that it suggests an answer favorable to the client.
- Favorable facts have been emphasized, and unfavorable ones de-emphasized.
- Words have been selected for both their denotation and their connotation.

IV. *Writing*

- The judge can understand the issue statement after reading it through once.
- Punctuation has been used to divide the issue statement into manageable units of meaning.
- When appropriate, parallel constructions have been used.
- In both the main and subordinate clauses, the subjects and verbs are close together.
- The issue statement is grammatically correct, correctly punctuated, and proofread.

H. ORDERING THE ISSUES AND ARGUMENTS

1. *Present the Issues and Arguments in a Logical Order*

In many cases, logic dictates the order of both the issues and, under each issue, the arguments. threshold questions (for example, issues relating to whether the court has jurisdiction or to the statute of limitations) must be discussed before questions relating to the merits of the case. Similarly, the parts of a test must be discussed in the correct order and, when one argument builds on another, the foundation argument must be presented first.

Although in the example case there is only one issue—whether the court should grant the defendant's motion to suppress—under that issue are several subissues. the court must decide (1) whether to suppress Martinez's show-up identification, (2) whether to suppress Martinez's line-up identification, and (3) whether to suppress any in-court identifications that Martinez or Clipse might make.

Logic dictates, at least in part, the order in which these three subissues should be discussed. Because an impermissibly suggestive show-up would taint the line-up and in-court identifications, the attorneys would discuss the show-up before the line-up and both the show-up and the line-up before the in-court identifications.

Logic also dictates the order of the arguments. Before it can suppress an identification, the court must find (1) that the police procedures were impermissibly suggestive and (2) that, under the totality of the circumstances, the resulting identifications are unreliable. Consequently, the defendant must discuss suggestiveness first.

In deciding whether an identification is reliable, the court considers five factors: (1) the witness's opportunity to see her assailant, (2) the witness's degree of attention, (3) the accuracy of the witness's description, (4) the witness's level of certainty, and (5) the length of time between the crime and the confrontation. Does logic dictate that these factors be discussed in any particular order?

2. *Decide Which Issues and Arguments Should Be Presented First*

First impressions count. As a consequence, when logic does not dictate the order of your issues or arguments, put your strongest issues and your strongest arguments first. In addition, some attorneys like to end their brief with a strong argument. Although this strategy allows you to take advantage of the positions of emphasis, it also creates a risk. If the judge does not finish your brief or starts skimming, he or she might not see one of your strongest arguments.

I. DRAFTING THE ARGUMENTATIVE HEADINGS

1. *Use Your Argumentative Headings to Define the Structure of the Argument*

Just as posts and beams define the form of a building, argumentative headings define the form of the argument. When drafted properly, they provide the judge with an outline of the argument.

EXAMPLE 1 **Defendant's Argumentative Headings**

I. THE COURT SHOULD GRANT MR. PATTERSON'S MOTION TO SUPPRESS MARTINEZ'S SHOW-UP AND LINE-UP IDENTIFICATIONS AND MARTINEZ'S AND CLIPSE'S IN-COURT IDENTIFICATIONS.

[Put general rules here.]

A. <u>Martinez's show-up identification should be suppressed because the police procedures were impermissibly suggestive and because Martinez's identification is unreliable.</u>

[Set out test.]

1. The police procedures were impermissibly suggestive because the police officer repeatedly asked Martinez whether Patterson looked like her assailant and because the officers questioned Patterson in Martinez's presence.

[Set out argument.]

1. Martinez's identification is unreliable because Martinez was able to view her assailant for only a few seconds, her attention was focused

on the gun and not his face, and her description of her assailant does not match the description of Patterson.

[Set out argument.]

A. Martinez's line-up identification should be suppressed because it was tainted by the show-up.

[Set out argument.]

B. Martinez and Clipse should not be permitted to make an in-court identification because those identification would be tainted by the impermissibly suggestive show-up and the line-up.

[Set out argument.]

In addition to defining the structure of the argument, argumentative headings also act as locators. By using the headings and subheadings, a judge can locate a particular argument.

PRACTICE POINTER

Argumentative headings also help the writer. As a practicing attorney, you will seldom have large blocks of time available for writing. Instead, you will have to squeeze in an hour here and two hours there. If you prepare your argumentative headings first, you can use those blocks to write a section at a time.

Argumentative headings also help the writer. As a practicing attorney, you will seldom have large blocks of time available for writing. Instead, you will have to squeeze in an hour here and two hours there. If you prepare your argumentative headings first, you can use those blocks to write a section at a time.

2. *Use Your Argumentative Headings to Persuade*

In addition to using argumentative headings to define the structure of your argument, use the headings to persuade.

Begin your heading by setting out a positive assertion. If you want the court to grant your motion to suppress, make that assertion: "The Court should grant the motion to suppress. . . . " In contrast, if you want the court to deny the motion to suppress, make that assertion: "The Court should deny the motion to suppress. . . . "

EXAMPLE 1 **Not Effective: Not a Positive Assertion**

The Court should not grant the motion to suppress. . . .

The Court should not suppress Martinez's show-up identification. . . .

EXAMPLE 2 **Effective: Positive Assertion**

The Court should deny the motion to suppress. . . .
The Court should admit Martinez's show-up identification. . . .

After setting out your assertion, you will usually want to set out the facts or reasons that support your assertion. the most common format is as follows:

Assertion	**because**	**facts or reasons that support your assertion**
Martinez's line-up identification should be suppressed	because	it was tainted by the impermissibly suggestive show-up.

In those instances in which you do not set out the reasons in your heading, use subheadings or sub-subheadings to set out the reasons. Look again at the headings and subheadings in the defendant's argumentative headings. Although the writer has not included a "because" clause in the main heading, she has included them in the subheadings and sub-subheadings.

EXAMPLE 3 **Defendant's Argumentative Headings**

I. THE COURT SHOULD GRANT THE DEFENDANT'S MOTION TO SUPPRESS MARTINEZ'S SHOW-UP AND LINE-UP IDENTIFICATIONS AND MARTINEZ'S AND CLIPSE'S IN-COURT IDENTIFICATIONS.

[Put general rules here.]

A. Martinez's show-up identification should be suppressed because the police procedures were impermissibly suggestive and because Martinez's identification is unreliable.

[Set out test.]

2. The police procedures were impermissibly suggestive because the police officer repeatedly asked Martinez whether Patterson looked like her assailant and because the officers questioned Patterson in Martinez's presence.

[Set out argument.]

3. Martinez's identification is unreliable because Martinez was able to view her assailant for only a few seconds, her attention was focused on the gun and not his face, and her description of her assailant does not match the description of Patterson.

[Set out argument.]

B. Martinez's line-up identification should be suppressed because it was tainted by the show-up.

[Set out argument.]

C. Martinez should not be permitted to make an in-court identification because such an identification would be tainted by the impermissibly suggestive show-up and the line-up.

[Set out argument.]

3. *Make Your Headings Readable*

If the judge does not read your headings, they do not serve either of their functions: they do not provide the judge with an outline of your argument, and they do not persuade. to make sure that your headings are read by the judge, keep them short and make them easy to read. As a general rule, your headings should be no more than three typed lines.

In the following example, the writer has tried to put too much information in her heading. As a result, the heading is too long, and the sentence is difficult to understand.

EXAMPLE 1 **Heading is too Long**

A. The police procedures were impermissibly suggestive because the witness viewed only one person, the police repeatedly asked the witness whether that person looked like her assailant, and the police questioned the person in front of the witness, and because the person was simply walking down the street and not trying to escape, and the witness was not likely to die or disappear, there was no reason to conduct a one-person show-up.

The following heading is much better. Instead of trying to put her entire argument into her heading, the writer has included only her most important points.

EXAMPLE 2 **Heading is Shorter and Easier to Understand**

A. The police procedures were impermissibly suggestive because the police officer repeatedly asked Martinez whether Patterson looked like her assailant and because the officers questioned Patterson in Martinez's and Clipse's presence.

4. *Follow the Conventions: Number, Placement, and Typefaces*

By convention, you should have one, and only one, main argumentative heading for each issue statement. You set out the question in your issue statement and answer the question in your main heading. Although subheadings and sub-subheadings are optional, if you include one, you should have at least two. You might or might not elect to include text between the main heading and the first subheading or between a subheading and the first sub-subheading.

PRACTICE POINTER

Historically, only three typefaces were used. When briefs were prepared using typewriters, the main headings were set out using all capital letters, the subheadings were underlined, and the sub-subheadings were set out using regular typeface. Although many attorneys still use this system, others have adopted different systems, for example, setting out the main headings in bold rather than all capitals. Check with your local court and firm to see what is commonly done in your jurisdiction.

EXAMPLE 1 **Typefaces for Main Heading, Subheadings, and Sub-Subheadings**

I. FIRST MAIN HEADING [Answers question set out in first issue statement.]
[If appropriate, set out paragraph and general rules here.]
  A. First subheading
    [If appropriate, set out test here.]
    1. First sub-subheading
      [Set out argument here.]
    2. Second sub-subheading
      [Set out argument here.]
  B. Second subheading
    [Set out argument here.]

II. SECOND MAIN HEADING [If you had two issue statements, answers question set out in the second issue statement.]
  A. First subheading
    [Set out argument here.]
  B. Second subheading
    [Set out argument here.]
  C. Third subheading
    [Set out argument here.]

5. *Checklist for Critiquing the Argumentative Headings*

I. *Content*

- When read together, the headings provide the judge with an outline of the argument.

II. *Persuasiveness*

- Each heading is in the form of a positive assertion.
- Each assertion is supported, either in the main heading or through the use of subheadings.
- The headings are case-specific—that is, they include references to the parties and the facts of the case.
- Favorable facts are emphasized, and unfavorable facts are de-emphasized or omitted if not legally significant.
- Favorable facts have been placed in the positions of emphasis.
- Favorable facts have been described in detail.
- Words have been selected both for their denotation and their connotation.

III. *Conventions*

- The writer has used different typefaces for main headings, subheadings, and sub-subheadings.
- There is never just one subheading or just one sub-subheading in a section.

IV. *Writing*

- The judge can understand the heading after reading it through once. (Headings are not more than two or three lines long.)
- Punctuation has been used to divide the heading into manageable units of meaning.
- When appropriate, parallel constructions have been used.
- In both the main and subordinate clauses, the subject and verb are close together.
- The headings are grammatically correct, correctly punctuated, and proofread.

J. DRAFTING THE ARGUMENTS

Most of us have had arguments. As children, we fought with our parents over cleaning our rooms or over how late we could stay out. As adults, we have fought with friends, roommates, spouses, and partners over household chores, budgets, and world events.

Although most of us have had arguments, very few of us have been taught how to make arguments. We know how to express our anger and frustration; we do not know how to set out an assertion and then systematically walk our listener through our "proof." even fewer of us have been taught how to set out our proofs persuasively.

It is, however, exactly these skills—the ability to set out an assertion, to walk your reader through your proof, and to present that proof persuasively—that you will need to develop if you are going to write an effective brief. good advocates have the mental discipline of a mathematician. they think linearly, identifying each of the steps in the analysis, and then walk the judge through those steps in a logical order. they also have the creativity and insight of an advertising executive. they know their "market," and they know both the image they want to create and how to use language to create it. In short, they have mastered both the science and the art of advocacy.

1. Identify Your Assertions and Your Support for Those Assertions

An argument has two parts: an assertion and the support for that assertion.

a. Setting Out Your Assertion

An assertion can take one of two forms. It can be procedural—setting out the procedural act you want the court to take—or it can be substantive—setting out the legal conclusion you want the court to reach.

EXAMPLE 1 **Types of Assertions**

Procedural
The court should grant the motion to suppress.

The court should deny the motion to suppress.
Substantive
The police procedures were impermissibly suggestive.
The witness's identification is reliable.

b. Supporting Your Assertion

Although your assertion is an essential part of your argument, it is not, by itself, an argument. How many judges would be persuaded by the following exchange?

Defense counsel:	Your Honor, the Court should grant the Defendant's motion to suppress.
Prosecutor:	Your Honor, we respectfully disagree. the Court should deny the motion.
Defense counsel:	No, Your Honor, the Court should grant the motion.
Prosecutor:	No. The Court should deny the motion.

An exchange in which the defendant asserts that the police procedures were impermissibly suggestive and the prosecutor asserts that they were not is equally unpersuasive. Standing alone, assertions do not persuade. they must be supported.

In law, that support can take one of several forms. You can support an assertion by citing to the constitution; by applying a statute or common law rule to the facts of your case; by comparing or contrasting the facts in your case to the facts in analogous cases; or by explaining why, as a matter of public policy, the court should rule in your client's favor.

In example 1 below, defense counsel supports her assertion by applying the rule to the facts of Mr. Patterson's case. In example 2, the defense counsel supports her assertion by comparing the facts in Mr. Patterson's case to the facts in the analogous cases, and in example 3, she supports her assertion by using public policy.

EXAMPLE 1 **Defendant Supports his Assertion by Applying the Rules to the Facts of his Case**

Assertion:	The police procedures were impermissibly suggestive.
Support:	Rule: One-person show-ups are inherently suggestive. *See Neil v. Biggers,* 409 U.S. 188, 199, 93 S. Ct. 375, 34 L. Ed. 2d 401 (1972).[1] When the police present the witness with a single suspect, the witness usually infers that the police believe

1. Because the briefs will be filed in a Washington court, the attorneys have used Washington's citation rules. See http://www.courts.wa.gov/appellate_trial_courts/supreme/?fa=atc_supreme.style.

	that the person being presented committed the crime. *Id.*
Application:	In this case, the police presented Martinez with a single suspect: Dean Patterson. In doing so, the police suggested to Martinez that Patterson was the man who had assaulted her.

EXAMPLE 2 **Defendant Supports his Assertion by Comparing the Facts in his Case with the Facts in an Analogous Case**

Assertion:	The police procedures were impermissibly suggestive.
Support:	Analogous case: In *State v. Booth,* 36 Wn. App. 66, 67-68, 671 P.2d 1218 (1983), the police brought the witness to the scene of the arrest and showed him a single suspect, who was sitting with his back to the witness in the back seat of the police car. The court held that the police procedures were impermissibly suggestive. *Id.* at 70.
Application:	As in *Booth,* in our case the police showed the witness a single suspect and asked her to identify him before she had an opportunity to see his face. The only difference between the two cases is the identity of the person in the police car. While in *Booth* it was the suspect who was in the car, in our case it was the witness.

EXAMPLE 3 **The Defendant Supports his Assertion by using Public Policy**

Assertion:	The police procedures were impermissibly suggestive.
Support:	Policy: To protect the rights of defendants, the courts should suppress unreliable identifications.
Application:	Because Martinez's identifications are unreliable, Patterson will be denied his right to a fair trial if Martinez's show-up and line-up identifications are admitted.

If there is only one argument that supports your assertion, make that argument. If, however, you can make several different arguments, think about whether you want to include all of those arguments. Will your brief be more persuasive if you set out only one strong argument, or will it be more persuasive if you set out three, four, or five arguments? Identifying the arguments is the science; deciding which arguments to include is the art.

2. *Select an Organizational Scheme*

In making their arguments, most advocates use one of two types of reasoning: deductive or inductive. When you use deductive reasoning, you set out your assertion and then the support for that assertion. In contrast, when you use inductive reasoning, you set out your support first, and then walk the judge through your support to your conclusion.

EXAMPLE 1 **Deductive Reasoning**

Assertion:	The identification is not reliable.
Support:	The identification is not reliable because Martinez viewed her assailant for only two or three seconds. The identification is not reliable because Martinez's attention was focused on the gun and not on her assailant's face. The identification is not reliable because Martinez's description of her assailant was inaccurate. The identification is not reliable because, at least initially, Martinez was not certain that Patterson was her assailant.

EXAMPLE 2 **Inductive Reasoning**

Support:	Martinez viewed her assailant for only two or three seconds. Martinez's attention was focused on the gun and not on her assailant's face. Martinez's description of her assailant was inaccurate. At least initially, Martinez was not certain that Patterson was her assailant.
Conclusion:	Because Martinez viewed her assailant for only two or three seconds, because her attention was focused on the gun and not on her assailant's face, because her description of her assailant was inaccurate, and because, at least initially, she was not certain that Patterson was her assailant, Martinez's identification is not reliable.

If you use deductive reasoning, you will usually use a version of the following blueprint. note the similarities between this blueprint and the blueprints that you use to organize the discussion section in an objective memo. Also note that the following example shows two different ways of setting out the arguments. Under the first subheading, the assertion is set out first. Under the second subheading, the assertion is set out after the rules and the descriptions of the cases. You should use whichever format is, in your case, most likely to be effective.

EXAMPLE 1 Blueprint for an Argument using Deductive Reasoning

I. MAIN HEADING
   [Test set out in the light most favorable to your client.]
   A. First subheading
      1. Assertion
      2. Rules set out in the light most favorable to your client
      3. Descriptions of the analogous cases
      4. Your arguments
      5. Your response to your opponent's arguments
   B. Second subheading
      1. Rules set out in the light most favorable to your client
      2. Descriptions of the analogous cases
      3. Assertion
      4. Your arguments
      5. Your response to your opponent's arguments

When you use inductive reasoning, you will usually integrate the rules, the descriptions of the cases, and your response to the other side's arguments into each of your arguments.

EXAMPLE 2 Blueprint for an Argument using Inductive Reasoning

I. MAIN HEADING
   A. First subheading
      1. First argument
      2. Second argument
      3. Third argument
      4. Fourth argument
      5. Conclusion
   B. Second subheading
      1. First argument
      2. Second argument
      3. Third argument
      4. Conclusion

There are also several other organizational schemes that you may use. For example, if in your case the facts are your best argument, start by setting out the facts. then show how those facts are similar to the facts in cases in which the court reached the conclusion you want the court to reach.

EXAMPLE 3 **Facts Set out First**

I. MAIN HEADING
[Test set out in the light most favorable to your client.]
. First subheading
1. Facts of your case
2. Comparison of the facts in your case to the facts in analogous cases
3. Courts' holdings in analogous cases
4. Response to other side's arguments
5. Conclusion

In the following example, defense counsel used the "facts-first" strategy in arguing that the show-up was impermissibly suggestive. Because none of the cases supported her position, defense counsel began her argument by setting out her assertion and the facts that support that assertion.

EXAMPLE 4 **Excerpt from the Defendant's Brief**

A. The police procedures were unnecessarily suggestive because the police showed Martinez a single suspect, asked Martinez whether the suspect looked like her assailant, and questioned the suspect in front of Martinez.

In this case, Officer Yuen's actions suggested to Martinez that he believed Patterson was her assailant.

While driving Martinez home, Officer Yuen pulled up behind Patterson and asked Martinez whether Patterson looked like her assailant. When Martinez did not respond, Officer Yuen repeated his question, asking "Does that look like your assailant?"

Although Martinez could not see Patterson's face, after hesitating, she agreed with Officer Yuen that Patterson looked like her assailant. At that point, Officer Yuen pulled up behind Patterson, got out of the police car, and began questioning him. A few minutes later, Officer Cox and Clipse arrived, and both Officer Yuen and Officer Cox questioned Patterson while Martinez and Clipse watched.

Thus, this case can be distinguished from *State v. Kraus*, 21 Wn. App. at 392, in which the show-up identification occurred during a prompt search for the robber. In this case the show-up did not occur while the police were searching for Martinez's assailant. Instead, it occurred while the officer was driving Martinez home. In addition, unlike *Stovall*, 388 U.S. at 302, in which the police held the show-up because they were concerned that the suspect might die, in this case, there were no exigent circumstances. In fact, because the police had located a car that matched the description of the one driven by the assailant, they could have identified the owner of the car and any individuals who had driven it and placed them in a line-up.

In contrast, if your best argument is an argument based on an analogous case, start by describing that case.

EXAMPLE 5 **Excerpt from the State's Brief**

A. Merely asking the victim whether a pedestrian looks like her assailant does not make a permissible show-up impermissibly suggestive.

There are no published Washington cases in which the courts have held that a show-up was impermissibly suggestive. Instead, in a Division I case, the court held that the show-up was not impermissibly suggestive when the police picked up the witness at a tavern and told him that they wanted to take him back to his apartment to see if he could identify his assailant. *State v. Rogers,* 44 Wn. App. 510, 515-16, 722 P.2d 1249 (1986). When the witness, an elderly individual who was not wearing his glasses, arrived back at his apartment, he identified the defendant when the defendant came out of the building. *Id.* There was a uniformed police officer in front of the defendant and another uniformed police officer following behind him. *Id.*

Similarly, in *State v. Booth,* 36 Wn. App. 66, 70-71, 671 P.2d 1218 (1983), the court held that the show-up was not impermissibly suggestive when the police asked the witness to accompany them to the place where the defendant had been arrested, and the witness identified the defendant after seeing him in the back of a police car. *Id.* at 67-68; *accord State v. Guzman-Cuellar,* 47 Wn.2d 326, 734 P.2d 966 (1987) (show-up not impermissibly suggestive when the defendant was shown to three of the four eyewitnesses while he was in handcuffs standing next to a police car).

Although you want to set out the pieces of your argument in the order that the judge expects to see them, you also want to emphasize your best arguments. therefore, instead of using a format mechanically, use it creatively to accomplish your purpose.

PRACTICE POINTER

Initially, you may be frustrated by the fact that there are no rules for selecting issues or arguments or set formats for organizing your arguments. However, with time, you will learn to enjoy exercising your judgment and creativity.

3. *Present the Rules in the Light Most Favorable to Your Client*

Although the structure of the argument section is similar to the structure of the discussion section, the way in which you present the rules is very different. While in an objective memo you set out the rules objectively, in a brief you set them out in the light most favorable to your client. Without misrepresenting the rules, you want to "package" them so that they support your assertion.

To set out the rules in the light most favorable to your client, use one or more of the techniques set out in the following box.

TECHNIQUES FOR PRESENTING THE RULES IN A LIGHT FAVORABLE TO YOUR CLIENT

A. Create a favorable context.
B. State favorable rules as broadly as possible and unfavorable rules as narrowly as possible.
C. Emphasize favorable rules and de-emphasize unfavorable rules.
   1. Emphasize the burden of proof if the other side has the burden; de-emphasize the burden of proof if you have the burden.
   2. Give favorable rules more airtime and unfavorable rules less airtime.
   3. Place favorable rules in a position of emphasis and bury unfavorable ones.
   4. Place favorable rules in short sentences or in the main clause, and place unfavorable rules in longer sentences or in dependent clauses.
D. Select your words carefully.

Compare the following examples, identifying the techniques that the writers used.

EXAMPLE 1 **Objective Statement of the Rule**

In deciding whether identification testimony is admissible, the courts apply a two-part test. Under the first part of the test, the defendant must prove that the police procedures were impermissibly suggestive. If the court finds that the procedure was impermissibly suggestive, the State then has the burden of showing that, under the totality of the circumstances, the reliability of the identification outweighs the suggestive police procedure. *Manson v. Braithwaite,* 432 U.S. 98, 108, 97 S. Ct. 2243, 53 L. Ed. 2d 140 (1977).

EXAMPLE 2 **Rules Stated in the Light most Favorable to the Defendant**

The United States Supreme Court has developed a two-part test to ensure a criminal defendant the procedural due process guaranteed to every individual by the Fourteenth Amendment. *Manson v. Braithwaite,* 432 U.S. 98, 108, 97 S. Ct. 2243, 53 L. Ed. 2d 108 (1977).

Under the first part of the test, the defendant need show only that the identification that he seeks to suppress was obtained through the use of unnecessarily suggestive police procedures. *Id.* Once this has been established, the onus shifts to the State to prove that, under the totality of the circumstances, the witness's identification is so reliable that it should be admitted even though it was obtained through unnecessarily suggestive means. *Id.*

EXAMPLE 3 **Rules Stated in the Light most Favorable to the State**

Identifications should not be kept from the jury unless the procedures used in obtaining the identifications were so suggestive and unreliable that a substantial likelihood of irreparable misidentification exists. *Perry v. New Hampshire*, ____ U.S.___, 132 S. Ct. 716, 720, 181 L. Ed. 2d 694 (2012); *Simmons v. United States*, 390 U.S. 377, 384, 89 S. Ct. 1127, 22 L. Ed. 2d 402 (1969).

In deciding whether identification evidence is admissible, the courts employ a two-part test. Under the first part of the test, the defendant has the burden of proving that the identification evidence that he or she seeks to suppress was obtained through impermissibly suggestive procedures. *Manson v. Braithwaite*, 432 U.S. 98, 113, 97 S. Ct. 2243, 5 L. Ed. 2d 140. Only if the defendant satisfies this substantial burden is the second part of the test applied. *Id.*

Even if the court determines that the police procedures were impermissibly suggestive, the evidence is admissible if, under the totality of the circumstances, the identifications are reliable. *Perry v. New Hampshire*, 132 S. Ct. at 720; *Simmons v. United States*, 390 U.S. at 384. Due process does not compel the exclusion of an identification if it is reliable. *Id.* Identifications should not be kept from the jury unless the procedures used in obtaining the identifications were so suggestive and unreliable that a substantial likelihood of irreparable misidentification exists. *Simmons v. United States*, 390 U.S. at 384.

Let's begin by comparing the opening sentences of all three examples. In example 1, the writer simply states that the court applies a two-part test. there is no attempt to create a favorable context.

EXAMPLE 1 **Objective Statement of the Rule**

In deciding whether identification testimony is admissible, the courts apply a two-part test.

In contrast, in examples 2 and 3, the writers package the rule, using policy to create a context that favors their respective clients. the key language is in boldface type.

EXAMPLE 2 **Rules Stated in the Light most Favorable to the Defendant**

The United States Supreme Court has developed a two-part test to ensure a criminal **defendant the procedural due process guaranteed to every individual by the Fourteenth Amendment.**

EXAMPLE 3 **Rules Stated in the Light most Favorable to the State**

Identifications should not be kept from the jury unless the procedures used in obtaining the identifications were so suggestive and unreliable that a substantial likelihood of irreparable misidentification exists.

In addition to creating a favorable context, the parties have emphasized or de-emphasized the burden of proof depending on whether they have the burden or the other side has the burden. Compare the highlighted passages.

EXAMPLE 4 **Objective Statement of the Rule**

> Under the first part of the test, **the defendant must prove** that the police procedures were impermissibly suggestive.

EXAMPLE 5 **Rules Stated in the Light most Favorable to the Defendant**

> Under the first part of the test, **the defendant need show** only that the identification that he seeks to suppress was obtained through the use of unnecessarily suggestive police procedures.

EXAMPLE 6 **Rules Stated in the Light most Favorable to the State**

> Under the first part of the test, **the defendant has the burden of proving** that the identification evidence he seeks to suppress was obtained through impermissibly suggestive procedures.

Similarly, both sides try to lead the court to the desired conclusions. Defense counsel presumes that the defendant will meet his burden; the State presents the second part of the test as an alternative. even if the State loses on the first part of the test, it wins on the second. once again, in excerpts from earlier examples 2 and 3 the key language is in boldface type.

EXAMPLE 7 **Rules Stated in the Light most Favorable to the Defendant**

> **Once this has been established**, the onus shifts to the State to prove that, under the totality of the circumstances, the witness's identification is so reliable that it should be admitted even though it was obtained through unnecessarily suggestive means.

EXAMPLE 8 **Rules Stated in the Light most Favorable to the State**

> In deciding whether identification evidence is admissible, the courts employ a two-part test. Under the first part of the test, the defendant has the burden of proving that the identification evidence that he or she seeks to suppress was obtained through impermissibly suggestive procedures. *Manson v. Braithwaite,* 432 U.S. 98, 113, 97 S. Ct. 2243, 5 L. Ed. 2d 140. **Only if the defendant satisfies this substantial burden is the second part of the test applied.** *Id.*
>
> **Even if the court determines that the police procedures were impermissibly suggestive, the evidence is admissible if, under the totality of the circumstances, the identifications are reliable.** *Perry v. New Hampshire,* 132 S. Ct. at 720; *Simmons v. United States,* 390 U.S. at 384. Due process does not compel the exclusion of an identification if it is reliable. *Id.*

Finally, look at the words that each side uses:

Defendant	*State*
ensure	so suggestive
guaranteed	burden
onus shifts	substantial burden
so reliable	compel

Instead of using the language they saw in the cases or the first word that came to mind, each side selected its words carefully, with the goal of subtly influencing the decision-making process.

PRACTICE POINTER

If you are having a hard time coming up with just the right word, look for alternative words using the thesaurus that is on your computer.

4. Present the Cases in the Light Most Favorable to Your Client

When you use analogous cases to support your argument, present those cases in the light most favorable to your client. If a case supports your position, emphasize the similarities between the facts in the analogous case and the facts in your case. on the other hand, if a case does not support your position, emphasize the differences.

In the example case, both sides use *State v. Booth,* 36 Wn. App. 66, 671 P.2d 1218 (1983), a case in which the court held that the identification was reliable. the relevant portion of the court's opinion is set out in Example 1.

EXAMPLE 1 **Excerpt from *State v. Booth***

"The facts provide several indicia of reliability. Ms. Thomas was driving slowly, it was a clear day, and she observed Booth for approximately forty-five seconds. Her attention was greater than average because he had money in his hands and was running. In addition, her attention was particularly drawn to the car with Missouri plates because she had lived in Missouri. Finally, the identification took place thirty to forty minutes later and was unequivocal. On the basis of these facts we find that reliability outweighed the harm of suggestiveness and the identification was properly admitted."

Because the court found that the identification was reliable, the defendant wants to distinguish *Booth.* As a consequence, in discussing opportunity to view, the defendant wants to emphasize that in *Booth* the witness viewed the defendant for almost a minute, while in our case the witness viewed her assailant for only a few seconds.

EXAMPLE 2 **Excerpt from the Defendant's Brief**

An identification will not be found to be reliable unless the witness had an adequate opportunity to view the defendant. This was the situation in *Booth.*

> In that case, a bystander was able to view the defendant for almost a minute. *Id.* at 70. Because she was able to view the defendant for an extended period of time under good conditions, the court concluded that her identification was reliable. *Id.* In contrast, in our case Martinez viewed her assailant for only two or three seconds.

Conversely, the State wants to emphasize the similarities between the facts in its case and the facts in *Booth.* thus, it tries to minimize the amount of time that the witness had to view the defendant.

EXAMPLE 3 **Excerpt from the State's Brief**

> The courts do not require that the witness have viewed the defendant for an extended period of time. For example, in *Booth,* the court found the witness's identification was reliable even though the witness had viewed the defendant for less than a minute. *Id.* at 70.

5. *Present the Arguments in the Light Most Favorable to Your Client*

In addition to presenting the rules and analogous cases in the light most favorable to your client, you also want to set out the arguments in the light most favorable to your client. As a general rule, set out your own arguments first, give your own arguments the most airtime, and use language that strengthens your arguments and undermines the other side's arguments.

a. Present Your Own Arguments First

You should almost always set out your own arguments first. By doing so, you can take advantage of the position of emphasis, emphasizing your argument and de-emphasizing the other side's arguments.

The following example shows what you do *not* want to do. By setting out the defendant's assertions, the State gives the defendant's arguments extra airtime. the court gets to read the defendant's argument in the defendant's brief and then again in the State's brief.

EXAMPLE 1 **Excerpt from the State's Brief: Ineffective**

> The defendant argues that the police procedures were impermissibly suggestive because the police showed Martinez a single suspect, Patterson, and because they asked Martinez whether Patterson looked like her assailant.
>
> It is our contention that the police procedures were not impermissibly suggestive. One-person show-ups are not per se impermissibly suggestive; if the show-up occurs shortly after the commission of the crime during a search for the suspect, it is permissible. *See State v. Booth,* 36 Wn. App. 66, 70-71, 671 P.2d 1218 (1983).

The following example is substantially better. Instead of starting its arguments by setting out the defendant's assertions, the State starts by setting out a favorable statement of the rule. It then sets out its own argument, integrating its responses to the defendant's arguments into its own arguments.

EXAMPLE 2 **Excerpt from the State's Brief: More Effective**

One-person show-ups are not per se impermissibly suggestive: a show-up is permissible if it occurs shortly after the commission of a crime during a search for the suspect. *See State v. Booth,* 36 Wn. App. 66, 70-71, 671 P.2d 1218 (1983).

In this case, the show-up occurred within forty-five minutes of the assault. It also occurred before the police officers had completed their investigation: Officer Yuen saw Patterson as he was leaving the crime scene to take Martinez home.

Under these circumstances, Officer Yuen would not have been doing his job if, upon seeing a man who matched the assailant's description, he had not asked Martinez whether the man looked like her assailant. The officer's question, "Is that the man?" was not enough to turn a permissible show-up into one that was impermissibly suggestive.

b. Give the Most Airtime to Your Own Arguments

Most of the time, you will want to give more airtime to your own arguments than you do to the other side's arguments. Your goal is to respond to or counter the other side's arguments without giving them too much airtime. Compare the following examples. In the first example, the State gives too much airtime to the defendant's age. In the second, the State counters the defendant's arguments without overemphasizing them.

EXAMPLE 1 **Excerpt from the State's Brief: Ineffective**

On the whole, Martinez's description was accurate. When she was interviewed, Martinez told the police that her assailant was a white male, that he was approximately 5'7"tall, that he weighed between 165 and 170 pounds, that he had blondish-brown hair, that he was wearing a dark jacket, and **that he appeared to be in his early forties. In fact, the defendant is twenty-two.**

This discrepancy in age is insignificant. It is often difficult to guess a person's age: some people appear older than they are, and others appear younger. Thus, the court should give little weight to the fact that Martinez misjudged the defendant's age. On the basis of the other information Martinez gave to the police, the police were able to identify the defendant as the assailant.

EXAMPLE 2 **Excerpt from the State's Brief: More Effective**

Martinez was able to give the police a detailed description of her assailant. When she was interviewed, she told the police that her assailant was a white male with blondish-brown hair, that he was approximately 5'7"tall and weighed between 165 and 170 pounds, **that he appeared to be in his early forties**, and that he was wearing a dark green jacket.

This description is accurate in all but one respect. **Although Martinez misjudged the defendant's age**, she accurately described his hair, his height and weight, and his clothing.

c. Use Language That Strengthens Your Arguments and Undermines the Other Side's Arguments

In setting out your own arguments, do not use phrases such as "We contend that . . . ," "It is our argument that . . . ," "We believe that . . . ," or "We feel that. . . . " Just set out your assertions. the following examples from the defendant's brief demonstrate this.

EXAMPLE 1 **Excerpt from the Defendant's Brief**

Ineffective

It is our contention that the police procedures were impermissibly suggestive.

More Effective

The police procedures were impermissibly suggestive.

On the other hand, when it is necessary to set out the other side's argument, use an introductory phrase that reminds the court that the statement is just the other side's assertion or argument.

EXAMPLE 2 **Excerpt from the Defendant's Brief**

Although the State contends that Martinez's identification is reliable, Martinez had only a second or two to view her assailant.

d. Use the Same Persuasive Techniques You Used in Setting Out the Facts, Issues, Rules, and Analogous Cases

Finally, when appropriate, use the same persuasive techniques that you used in writing the other parts of your brief. For instance, use the positions of emphasis to your best advantage. Place your best points at the beginning or end of a section or paragraph. In addition, whenever possible, put your strong points in short sentences or, in a longer sentence, in the main clause. Finally, select your words carefully. Choose words that convey not only the right denotation but also the right connotation.

Also remember that persuasive arguments are not written; they are crafted. In first drafts, concentrate on content and organization; in subsequent drafts, work on writing persuasively.

6. *Checklist for Critiquing the Argument*

I. *Content*

- Has the writer set out his or her assertions?
- Has the writer supported his or her assertions?
  - If appropriate, has the writer applied the constitutional provision, applicable statute, or common law rule to the facts of his or her case?
  - If appropriate, has the writer compared and contrasted the facts in the analogous cases to the facts in his or her case?
  - If appropriate, has the writer explained why, as a matter of public policy, the court should rule in his or her client's favor?
- Has the writer cited to the key relevant authorities?
- Are the writer's statements of the rules and descriptions of the cases accurate?

II. *Organization*

- Has the writer used one of the conventional organizational schemes—for example, deductive or inductive reasoning?
- Has the writer used an organizational scheme that allows him or her to emphasize the strongest parts of his or her arguments?

III. *Persuasiveness*
Rules

- Has the writer presented the rules in the light most favorable to his or her client?
  - Did the writer create a favorable context?
  - Did the writer state favorable rules as broadly as possible and unfavorable rules as narrowly as possible?
  - Did the writer emphasize favorable rules and de-emphasize unfavorable ones?
  - Did the writer select words both for their denotation and for their connotation?

Analogous Cases

- Has the writer presented the cases in the light most favorable to his or her client?
  - Did the writer create a favorable context?
  - Did the writer state favorable holdings as broadly as possible and unfavorable holdings as narrowly as possible?
  - Did the writer emphasize favorable facts and de-emphasize unfavorable ones?
  - Did the writer select words both for their denotation and for their connotation?

Arguments

- Did the writer present his or her own arguments first?
- Did the writer give his or her own arguments the most airtime?
- Did the writer use language that strengthens his or her arguments and weakens his or her opponent's arguments?

K. THE PRAYER FOR RELIEF

The final section of the brief is the prayer for relief or the conclusion. In some jurisdictions, the prayer for relief is very short. the attorney simply sets out the relief that he or she wants.

EXAMPLE 1 **Excerpt from the Defendant's Brief**

> **Prayer for Relief**
>
> For the reasons set out above, Mr. Patterson respectfully requests that the Court grant his motion and suppress Martinez's show-up and line-up identifications and any in-court identifications that Martinez or Clipse might make.

In other jurisdictions, the attorney sets out the relief that he or she is requesting and summarizes the arguments.

EXAMPLE 2 **Excerpt from the Defendant's Brief**

> **Conclusion**
>
> The Court should suppress Martinez's show-up identification because the police officer's questions were impermissibly suggestive and because, given Martinez's limited opportunity to view her assailant and the inaccuracies in her description, her identification is unreliable.
>
> The Court should also suppress Martinez's line-up identification and any in-court identifications that Martinez or Clipse might make. Both the line-up and the in-court identifications have been tainted by the impermissibly suggestive show-up.

L. SIGNING THE BRIEF

Before the brief is submitted to the court, it must be signed by an attorney licensed to practice law in the state. the following format is used in many jurisdictions.

EXAMPLE **Standard Format for Dating and Signing a Brief**

Submitted this______day of_____, 20_____.

____
Attorney for the Defendant

1. Sample Briefs

In this section, we set out two sets of briefs: the briefs from the *Patterson* case, which is used as the example case in this chapter, and the briefs from a civil case in which defense counsel has asked the court to grant defendant's Motion for Summary Judgment. Because the briefs were filed in a Washington trial court, the attorneys used the Washington court rules and the Washington citation rules.

The King County rules, which govern the brief in example 3, are as follows:

> (B) Form of Motion and of responsive Pleadings.
>
> The motion shall be combined with the memorandum of authorities into a single document, and shall conform to the following format:
>
> (i) Relief requested. the specific relief the court is requested to grant or deny.
>
> (ii) Statement of Facts. A succinct statement of the facts contended to be material.
>
> (iii) Statement of Issues. A concise statement of the issue or issues of law upon which the Court is requested to rule.
>
> (iv) Evidence relied Upon. the evidence on which the motion or opposition is based must be specified with particularity. Deposition testimony, discovery pleadings, and documentary evidence relied upon must be quoted verbatim or a photocopy of relevant pages must be attached to an affidavit identifying the documents. Parties should highlight those parts upon which they place substantial reliance. Copies of cases shall not be attached to original pleadings. responsive pleadings shall conform to this format.
>
> (v) Authority. Any legal authority relied upon must be cited. Copies of all cited non-Washington authorities upon which parties place substantial reliance shall be provided to the hearing Judge and to counsel or parties, but shall not be filed with the Clerk.

LCR 7(b)(5)(b).

EXAMPLE 1 Defendant's Brief in Support of Motion to Suppress

THE SUPERIOR COURT OF
KING COUNTY, WASHINGTON (1)(2)

STATE OF WASHINGTON,)	Case No.: 12-01-2226
Plaintiff,)	DEFENDANT'S BRIEF IN SUPPORT OF MOTION TO SUPPRESS
v.)	
DEAN E. PATTERSON,)	
Defendant.)	

(3) Mr. Patterson asks the Court to suppress Ms. Martinez's show-up and line-up identifications and to prevent both Ms. Martinez and Mr. Clipse from making in-court identifications. The show-up was impermissibly suggestive and, because she viewed her assailant for only a few seconds, Ms. Martinez's identifications are unreliable. Mr. Patterson was simply at the wrong place at the wrong time. (4)

Defendant's Brief
in Support of
Motion to Suppress - 1

Defense Counsel's Name
Defense Counsel's Address
Defense Counsel's
Phone Number

(1) The Washington Rules of Criminal Procedure state that the Civil Rules govern the format of briefs submitted in criminal cases. Thus, the following references to "CR" are references to the Washington Rules of Civil Procedure.

(2) Under the Washington rules, you must include a caption that sets out the name of the court, the names of the parties, the file number, and a title that identifies the nature of pleading or document. See CR 10(a).

(3) In this example, defense counsel has included an introductory paragraph in which she sets out her request for relief: She wants the court to suppress Ms. Martinez's show-up and line-up identifications, and she wants to prohibit both the victim and the witness from making in-court identifications. Under the Washington rules, this type of introductory paragraph is optional.

(4) Because the record was not transcribed, defense counsel cannot and has not included citations to that record. However, if you have a record, you should include references to that record. (See your local rules.)

Statement of Facts

[5]At 7:30 a.m. on Monday, August 13, 2012, twenty-two-year-old Dean Patterson finished his shift as a security guard and walked to his apartment. After having breakfast with his wife, he went to bed and slept until about 1:00 p.m. At about 2:30 p.m., Patterson's wife received a phone call asking her to work at the local hospital where she is employed as a nurse. Patterson's wife got ready, and Patterson[6] dropped her off at the hospital at about 3:10 p.m.

At about 3:30 p.m., Patterson called his wife to find out how long she would have to work[7]; they had plans to go to a movie that evening, and he wanted to know whether he should change those plans. At about 3:50 p.m., Patterson took a load of laundry to the apartment complex's laundry room. When he returned to his apartment, Patterson watched part of an old movie. At about 4:20 p.m.,[8] Patterson went back to the laundry room to put the clothes in the dryer. On his way back, he walked to where his car—an older model red station wagon—was parked to see if he needed to get gas. As he did so, Patterson noticed a parking spot much closer to his apartment and, after checking his gas, moved his car to that spot. After parking his car, Patterson got out of the car and, because the driver's side door does not lock from the outside, walked to the passenger side to lock the

Defendant's Brief
in Support of
Motion to Suppress - 2

Defense Counsel's Name
Defense Counsel's Address
Defense Counsel's
Phone Number

[5]To create a favorable context, defense counsel starts the statement of facts by describing Mr. Patterson's activities on the morning of the assault. Note how she works in the fact that Mr. Patterson is married and employed as a security guard, which would explain why Mr. Patterson owns a gun.

[6]Note how defense counsel has used Mr. Patterson or his wife as the subject of most sentences. This is one technique that can be used to tell the story from the client's point of view.

[7]Defense counsel has included the facts set out in this paragraph to paint her client in a favorable light, to explain what Mr. Patterson was doing at the time of the assault, and to explain why the parking enforcement officer saw Mr. Patterson near his car shortly after the assault.

[8]Because defense counsel is setting out the facts in chronological order, she sets out the time at the beginning of some of the sentences.

doors. As he did so, he nodded to a parking enforcement officer who was driving by.

By this time, it was 4:30 p.m., and Patterson decided to phone his wife again. He arranged to meet her at 5:15 p.m. for her dinner break. Patterson retrieved the laundry and then left the apartment a little before 5:00 p.m. to meet his wife.

At about 4:30 p.m. on the same day, seventeen-year-old Beatrice Martinez left her apartment to walk to work. As she was walking southbound on Belmont, a car[9] that had driven by earlier pulled in front of her. The man got out of his car, took one or two steps toward Martinez, and then pulled a gun from his pocket. As soon as she spotted the gun, Martinez screamed, looked away, and then, crying, ran across the street.[10] The entire encounter was over in three or four seconds.

The assault was witnessed by Chester Clipse, who was walking home when he saw a man in a red station wagon driving slowly down the street. When the man started to pull into Clipse's parking space, Clipse began walking towards him to tell him that he could not park there. As he did so, Clipse saw the man get out of his car and walk toward a girl who was on the sidewalk. He then heard the girl scream, and as she screamed, Clipse saw that the man had a gun. Clipse yelled "Hey," and the man turned and ran to his car, putting the gun under his coat. As the

Defendant's Brief
in Support of
Motion to Suppress - 3

Defense Counsel's Name
Defense Counsel's Address
Defense Counsel's
Phone Number

[9] Because Mr. Patterson owns a car that matches the description of the car that the assailant drove, defense counsel describes the car using a generic term: "car." In addition, she has tried to minimize the fact that the car drove by twice.

[10] Because she wants to argue that Martinez's identification is not reliable, defense counsel uses language that suggests that Ms. Martinez did not have a good opportunity to view her assailant. By putting the facts in short clauses in a single sentence, defense counsel creates the impression that events happened quickly.

girl ran across the street, the man got back into his car, backed out, and drove away.[11]

A few seconds later, a parking enforcement officer drove down the street. Clipse flagged him down, told him what had happened, and described the car and the man. The parking enforcement officer called 911 and then left to try to locate the car. Because the girl was still crying, Clipse took her to his landlady's apartment. He then went back outside and waited for the police.

When the police arrived,[12] Clipse told Officers Yuen and Cox what had happened. Clipse told the police that the man was white, about 5′10″ tall, and about 180 to 185 pounds. He also told the officers that the man was wearing a green outfit and that he was in his late thirties or early forties.[13]

While Clipse was talking to the police, Officer Cox received a radio message indicating that the parking enforcement officer had located a car that matched the one Clipse had described. While Officer Cox took Clipse in his car to see if Clipse could identify the car, Officer Yuen went inside to interview Martinez.

Because she was still upset, Martinez was able to give Officer Yuen only a general description of her assailant. She described him as being a short, white male with blondish-brown hair who was wearing glasses and a dark

Defendant's Brief
in Support of
Motion to Suppress - 4

Defense Counsel's Name
Defense Counsel's Address
Defense Counsel's
Phone Number

[11] Once again, defense counsel tries to give the impression that events happened quickly by setting out the facts in short clauses in a single sentence.

[12] Defense counsel has used dovetailing to make clear the connection between the information in this paragraph and the information in the prior paragraph.

[13] Defense counsel has placed a favorable fact, that Clipse said the assailant was in his late thirties or early forties, in a position of emphasis.

jacket.[14] In addition, she told police that her assailant was in his early forties. Patterson is twenty-two.[15]

After interviewing Martinez, Officer Yuen took the still-shaken Martinez to his car to take her home. When they had traveled less than a block, Officer Yuen noticed a white male wearing a dark jacket. As he drove up behind him, Yuen asked Martinez, "Is that the man?" When Martinez did not immediately answer, Yuen asked the question again: "Is that the man who assaulted you?"[16]

Even though Martinez was unable to see the man's face,[17] she agreed with the officer that the man looked like her assailant. At this point, Officer Yuen stopped the car, got out, and approached Patterson. As he was questioning[18] Patterson, Officer Cox drove up with Clipse. While Martinez and Clipse watched, Officers Cox and Yuen continued questioning Patterson. Officer Cox then returned to Martinez and Clipse and walked them back to Clipse's apartment. While he did so, Yuen placed Patterson under arrest.

Later that day, the police searched Patterson's car and apartment. In the apartment, the police found the gun issued to Patterson by his employer.[19] Four days later, the police held a line-up. Although Martinez identified Patterson as the man who had approached her, Clipse did not identify Patterson.[20]

Defendant's Brief
in Support of
Motion to Suppress - 5

Defense Counsel's Name
Defense Counsel's Address
Defense Counsel's
Phone Number

[14] Defense counsel has "buried" the unfavorable facts, the part of Martinez's description that is accurate, in the middle of the paragraph. She then places the favorable fact, that Martinez said that her assailant was in his forties, in the position of emphasis, juxtaposed with the fact that Patterson is only twenty-two.

[15] Defense counsel has placed a favorable fact in the position of emphasis in a short sentence.

[16] Defense counsel has used quotations to emphasize that the police officer used language that suggested to Martinez that Patterson was the person who had assaulted her. Note how defense counsel places the second quote in a position of emphasis.

[17] Defense counsel has placed a favorable fact, that Martinez was not able to see Patterson's face, in a position of emphasis.

[18] Instead of using a word like "talking," defense counsel has used "questioning," which suggests that the police officer was treating Patterson as if he had committed a crime.

[19] Defense counsel has tried to convert an unfavorable fact to a favorable one by emphasizing that the gun had been issued to Patterson by his employer.

[20] Defense counsel has placed the favorable fact, that Clipse did

Issue

Under the Fourteenth Amendment, should the Court grant Mr. Patterson's motion to suppress[21] Martinez's show-up and line-up identifications and Martinez's and Clipse's in-court identification when (1) a police officer pointed out Patterson to Martinez, repeatedly asking the shaken Martinez whether Patterson looked like her assailant; (2) the police questioned Patterson in front of Martinez and Clipse; (3) during the second or two that Martinez had to view her assailant, her attention was focused on his gun and not his face; and (4) both Martinez's and Clipse's descriptions were inaccurate?[22]

Argument

I. THE COURT SHOULD GRANT MR. PATTERSON'S MOTION TO SUPPRESS MARTINEZ'S SHOW-UP AND LINE-UP IDENTIFICATIONS AND MARTINEZ'S AND CLIPSE'S IN-COURT IDENTIFICATIONS.[23]

The United States Supreme Court has developed a two-part test to ensure a criminal defendant the procedural due process guaranteed to every individual by the Fourteenth Amendment. *Manson v. Braithwaite*,[24] 432 U.S. 98, 113, 97 S. Ct. 2243, 53 L. Ed. 2d 140 (1977).[1]

[1] Note: Because the brief is to a Washington court, defense counsel uses the Washington Citation Rules. See http://www.courts.wa.gov/appellate_trial_courts/supreme/?fa = atc_supreme.style. These rules require parallel cites for decisions of the United States Supreme Court.

Defendant's Brief
in Support of
Motion to Suppress - 6

Defense Counsel's Name
Defense Counsel's Address
Defense Counsel's
Phone Number

not identify Patterson as the assailant, in the main clause in the position of emphasis. The unfavorable fact, that Martinez did identify Patterson, is in the dependent clause.

[21] Defense counsel sets out the question so that it suggests the conclusion that she wants the court to reach.

[22] Defense counsel sets out the key facts in a light favorable to her client. Note that she sets out the facts that go to the first part of the test (whether the show-up was suggestive), before the facts that go to the second part of the test (whether the identifications were reliable).

[23] This heading answers the question set out in the issue statement. Although defense counsel would have liked to have included a "because" clause, doing so would have made the heading too long. As a consequence, defense counsel sets out her support for this assertion in the subheadings.

[24] Defense counsel has started the argument by setting out the general rules in a light favorable to Patterson. By doing so, she tries to create a favorable context.

Under the first part of the test,[25] the defendant need show only[26] that the identification that he seeks to suppress was obtained through the use of unnecessarily suggestive police procedures. *Id.* Once the defendant has established that the procedure was suggestive,[27] the onus shifts to the State to prove that, under the totality of the circumstances, the witness's identification is so reliable that it should be admitted even though it was obtained through suggestive means.[28] *Id.*

In this case, the Court should suppress Martinez's show-up identification both because the police procedures were impermissibly suggestive and because, under the totality of the circumstances, Martinez's identification is not reliable. In addition, the Court should suppress Martinez's line-up identification because that line-up was tainted by the show-up. Finally, the Court should rule that neither Martinez nor Clipse should be allowed to make in-court identifications: like Martinez's line-up identification, any in-court identifications would be tainted by the show-up.[29]

A. <u>Martinez's show-up identification should be suppressed because the police procedures were impermissibly suggestive and Martinez's identification is not reliable.</u>[30]

The courts have repeatedly condemned the practice of showing a witness a single suspect.[31] *See, e.g.,*[32] *Stovall v. Denno*, 388 U.S. 293, 302, 87 S. Ct. 1967, 18 L. Ed.

Defendant's Brief
in Support of
Motion to Suppress - 7

Defense Counsel's Name
Defense Counsel's Address
Defense Counsel's
Phone Number

[25] Defense counsel starts the paragraph with a transition that lets the attorney know that she is setting out the first part of a two-part test.

[26] Defense counsel uses language that minimizes Patterson's burden.

[27] Defense counsel uses language that suggests that Patterson can meet his burden.

[28] Defense counsel uses language that suggests that the State's burden is a high burden.

[29] After setting out the general rules, defense counsel sets out a roadmap for the rest of her arguments.

[30] In this heading, defense counsel uses the "traditional" format for an argumentative heading: she set out her assertion and then a "because" clause. Note that the because clause is very general: It simply repeats the two parts of the test. Defense counsel uses the sub-subheadings to provide the facts that support her assertions.

[31] Defense counsel has set out this rule in a light favorable to Patterson.

[32] Although as a general rule you should not include "string cites"—that is, a string of citations—in this case the signal "see, e.g.," and the three cites make the point that the courts have repeatedly condemned the practice of showing a witness a single suspect.

2d 1199 (1967); *State v. Rogers*, 44 Wn. App. 510, 515, 722 P.2d 1349 (1986); *State v. Kraus*, 21 Wn. App. 388, 391-92, 584 P.2d 946 (1978). Although such show-ups are not per se impermissibly suggestive,[33] identifications following such a show-up should be admitted only if the show-up occurs during the prompt search for the suspect and if the State proves that the witness's identification is reliable.[34] *State v. Rogers*, 44 Wn. App. at 515.

1. The police procedures were unnecessarily suggestive because the police showed Martinez one suspect, asked Martinez whether that suspect looked like her assailant, and questioned the suspect in front of Martinez.[35]

In this case,[36] Officer Yuen's actions suggested to Martinez that he believed that Patterson was her assailant. While driving Martinez home, Officer Yuen pulled up behind Patterson and asked Martinez whether Patterson looked like her assailant. When Martinez did not respond, Officer Yuen repeated his question, asking "Is that the man who assaulted you?"[37] Although Martinez could not see Patterson's face, after hesitating, she agreed[38] with Officer Yuen that Patterson looked like her assailant. At that point, Officer Yuen pulled up behind Patterson, got out of the police car, and began questioning him. A few minutes later, Officer Cox and Clipse arrived, and both Officer Yuen and Officer Cox questioned Patterson while Martinez and Clipse watched.

Defendant's Brief
in Support of
Motion to Suppress - 8

Defense Counsel's Name
Defense Counsel's Address
Defense Counsel's
Phone Number

[33] Defense counsel has placed an "unfavorable rule" in a dependent clause in the middle of a paragraph.

[34] Defense counsel has placed the favorable rule in the main clause at the end of the paragraph, which is a position of emphasis. In addition, by using the word "only," she has stated the rule narrowly.

[35] In drafting this heading, defense counsel sets out her assertion (that the police procedures were unnecessarily suggestive) and then includes a because clause in which she sets out the facts that support this assertion.

[36] While in most situations you will start your discussion of a test by setting out the applicable rules, in this case defense counsel decided to start with the facts. If your best argument is a factual argument, you can start with the facts; similarly, if your best argument is an analogous case argument, you can start with an analogous case argument. Just make sure that the judge will be able to follow your argument.

[37] Defense counsel has emphasized this favorable fact by using a quotation and placing that quotation in a position of emphasis.

[38] Once again, defense counsel has selected words that carry not only the right denotation but also the right

Thus, this case can be distinguished from *State v. Kraus*, 21 Wn. App. at 392, in which the show-up identification occurred during a prompt search for the robber.[39][40] In this case, the show-up did not occur while the police were searching for Martinez's assailant. Instead, it occurred while the officer was driving Martinez home. In addition, unlike *Stovall*, 388 U.S. at 302, in which the police held the show-up because they were concerned that the suspect might die, in this case, there were no exigent circumstances. In fact, because the police had located a car that matched the description of the one driven by the assailant, they could have identified the owner of the car and any individuals who had driven it and placed them in a line-up.[41]

2. <u>Martinez's identification is unreliable because Martinez was able to view her assailant for only a few seconds, her attention was focused on the gun and not his face, and her description of her assailant does not match the description of Patterson.</u>[42]

[43]The key inquiry in determining the admissibility of a witness's identification is its reliability. *Manson v. Braithwaite*, 432 U.S. 98, 114, 97 S. Ct. 2243, 53 L. Ed. 2d 140 (1977). In[44] determining whether an identification is reliable, the courts consider the witness's opportunity to view the person who committed the crime, the witness's degree of attention, the time between the crime and the confrontation, the witness's level of certainty, and the

Defendant's Brief
in Support of
Motion to Suppress - 9

Defense Counsel's Name
Defense Counsel's Address
Defense Counsel's
Phone Number

connotation. In particular, note defense counsel's use of the words "agreed," "watched," and "questioned."

[39]Instead of setting out the other side's argument—for example, instead of saying that the State will argue that this case is like Kraus—defense counsel sets out her own positive assertion, which is that Patterson's case can be distinguished from Kraus.

[40]Note that defense counsel does not go into detail in describing *Kraus*: she sets out only the key fact.

[41]Defense counsel ends this section with a strong argument: that the police had another way of locating the assailant.

[42]Defense counsel has used the same format for this sub-subheading as she did for the prior sub-subheading: she sets out her assertion and then the facts that support that assertion.

[43]Unlike the prior subsection in which defense counsel began the section by setting out the key facts, in this section defense counsel uses the more traditional format: she sets out the specific rules and then she applies these rules to the facts of her case.

[44]In this instance, defense counsel re-ordered the list of factors so that the two most favorable factors are in the positions of emphasis.

accuracy of the witness's prior description. *Neil v. Biggers*, 409 U.S. 188, 93 S. Ct. 375, 34 L. Ed. 2d 401 (1972); *State v. Birch*, 151 Wn. App. 505, 514 (2009).

[45]First, in this case, Martinez did not have a good opportunity to view her assailant. Unlike[46] the witness in *Rogers*, who was with his assailant for almost twenty minutes, and the witness in *Booth*, who observed the robber for at least forty-five seconds, Martinez was able to view her assailant for only a few seconds. During the pretrial hearing, Martinez testified that she had seen her assailant for two or three seconds before she turned and ran. In addition, although Martinez testified that she had noticed the car on a prior occasion,[47] she did not testify that she had noticed the driver. In a similar case, the court held that the witness had not had a good opportunity to view the robber when the witness was with the robber for five to six minutes and viewed him for two or three minutes. *State v. McDonald*, 40 Wn. App. 743, 747, 700 P.2d 327 (1985).

Second, Martinez's attention was not focused on her assailant.[48] Unlike the witness in *Booth*, whose attention was focused on the robber because he was running and carrying money and got into a car with license plates from the witness's home state, Martinez's attention was focused on the car and then on the gun that her assailant

Defendant's Brief
in Support of
Motion to Suppress - 10

Defense Counsel's Name
Defense Counsel's Address
Defense Counsel's
Phone Number

[45]Note defense counsel's use of signposts and topic sentences. For example, defense counsel starts this paragraph with "First," and then she sets out her assertion, which is that Martinez did not have a good opportunity to view her assailant.

[46]Defense counsel uses the cases to support her assertion. She sets out the key facts from each of the cases and then distinguishes those cases.

[47]In this sentence, defense counsel anticipates and responds to an argument that she believes the State will make. Note that she does not set out the State's argument. She simply sets out her own argument. Also note that the unfavorable fact, that Martinez testified that she had noticed the car on a prior occasion, is in a dependent clause in the middle of the paragraph. Finally, note defense counsel's word choices: for example, defense counsel states that Martinez had "noticed" the car.

[48]Once again, defense counsel starts the paragraph with a signpost and a topic sentence that sets out her assertion.

was holding. As Martinez has testified, she looked at the gun, glanced at the man holding it, and then ran.[49]

Third, although the show-up occurred within about forty-five minutes of the assault, Martinez's level of certainty was low. The first time that Officer Yuen asked Martinez whether Patterson looked like the man who had assaulted her, she did not respond.[50] In addition, the second time that Officer Yuen asked her the same question, she said only that Patterson looked like him. She did not say, "Yes, that is him."

Finally, Martinez's description was inaccurate. Although Martinez told the police that her assailant was in his early forties, Patterson is twenty-two.[51] While sometimes an individual will believe that an individual is two, three, or even five years older than the individual actually is, it is extremely uncommon for someone to be off by twenty years.[52]

[53]In this case, Martinez identified Patterson as her assailant only because Officer Yuen suggested to her that Patterson was the man who had assaulted her. In addition, the State cannot prove that Martinez's identification is reliable. Martinez did not have a good opportunity to view her assailant, her attention was not focused on her assailant, her identification was uncertain, and her description was inaccurate. As a consequence, Patterson's

Defendant's Brief
in Support of
Motion to Suppress - 11

Defense Counsel's Name
Defense Counsel's Address
Defense Counsel's
Phone Number

[49]Defense counsel has placed the favorable facts at the end of the paragraph in a position of emphasis.

[50]In discussing this factor, defense counsel does not cite to any cases: there are not any cases that specifically discuss this factor. Instead, defense counsel uses the facts. Note how defense counsel ends the paragraph: Sometimes you can use what a party did not do or did not say to support an argument.

[51]While defense counsel would have liked to give this factor more airtime, there was not a good way of doing so. Thus, she makes her point and moves on.

[52]While you will usually provide support for your assertions, sometimes you can make a "common sense" argument.

[53]Defense counsel uses this paragraph to do three things. First, she discusses the first part of the two-part test, arguing that the show-up was suggestive. She then discusses the second part of the test. In doing so, she reminds the court that the State has the burden of proof, and then she summarizes her arguments relating to the factors. Finally, she goes back to the general rule, reminding the court of the constitutional issues.

due process rights would be violated if Martinez's identification is admitted.

B. <u>Martinez's line-up identification should be suppressed because it was tainted by the show-up.</u>[54]

When the initial identification is obtained through impermissibly suggestive procedures, subsequent identifications must also be suppressed unless the State can prove that the subsequent identifications are reliable.[55] *State v. Birch*, 151 Wn. App. 505, 513-14 (2009); *State v. McDonald*, 40 Wn. App. 746. In *McDonald*,[56] the court reversed the defendant's conviction, concluding that the procedures used at the line-up were impermissibly suggestive and that the State had not proved that the witness's subsequent in-court identification was reliable. *Id.*

Similarly, in this case the procedures were impermissibly suggestive, and the State cannot prove that Martinez's subsequent identifications are reliable. See section 1A(2), *supra*.[57] Martinez picked Patterson out of the line-up, not because she remembered him as her assailant, but because the police had suggested to her that he was her assailant.[58]

Defendant's Brief
in Support of
Motion to Suppress - 12

Defense Counsel's Name
Defense Counsel's Address
Defense Counsel's
Phone Number

[54] Defense counsel has set out her assertion and then a "because" clause in which she sets out her support for that assertion.

[55] In setting out this rule, defense counsel has emphasized that the State has the burden of proof.

[56] Defense counsel uses an analogous case to support her argument.

[57] Instead of repeating an argument, you can provide the court with a cross-reference to another part of your brief.

[58] Your arguments do not need to be long. Make your point and then move on.

C. <u>Martinez and Clipse should not be permitted to make an in-court identification because such an identification would be tainted by the impermissibly suggestive show-up and the line-up.</u>

Just as Martinez's line-up identification was tainted by the impermissibly suggestive show-up, any in-court identification by Martinez or Clipse would also be tainted. Although the police did not ask Clipse whether Patterson looked liked the man who had assaulted Martinez, Clipse watched as the police questioned Patterson.[59] In addition, Patterson was with Martinez, who may have told him that Officer Yuen believed that Patterson was her assailant.

[59] Note that defense counsel does not set out the State's argument. She simply counters that argument by setting out her own positive assertion.

Prayer for Relief

For the reasons set out above, the Defendant respectfully requests that the Court suppress Martinez's show-up and line-up identifications and that the Court not permit Martinez or Clipse to make an in-court identification.

Dated this 23rd day of September, 2012.

Signature
Attorney for the Defendant
Name
Bar No. 00000

Defendant's Brief
in Support of
Motion to Suppress - 13

Defense Counsel's Name
Defense Counsel's Address
Defense Counsel's
Phone Number

EXAMPLE 2 State's Brief in Opposition to Motion to Suppress

SUPERIOR COURT OF
KING COUNTY, WASHINGTON[1]

STATE OF WASHINGTON,	)	Case No.: 12-01-2226
Plaintiff,	)	STATES'S BRIEF IN OPPOSITION TO DEFENDANT'S MOTION TO SUPPRESS
v.	)	
DEAN E. PATTERSON,	)	
Defendant.	)	

[1] Under the Washington rules, you must include a caption that sets out the name of the court, the names of the parties, the file number, and a title that identifies the nature of the pleading or document. See CR 10(a).

The State asks the Court to deny the defendant's motion to suppress the victim's show-up and line-up identifications and to allow both the victim and the witness to make in-court identifications. The show-up was not suggestive, and the victim's and the witness's identifications are reliable.[2]

[2] In this example, the prosecutor has included an introductory paragraph in which he sets out his request for relief: Under the Washington rules, this type of introductory paragraph is optional.

Statement of Facts

On Monday, August 13, 2012, Beatrice Martinez was assaulted with a deadly weapon.[3] At a show-up held thirty to forty minutes after the attack, Martinez identified the defendant, Dean E. Patterson, as her assailant. Four days after the assault, Martinez picked Patterson out of a line-up, once again identifying him as her assailant.[4]

[3] The prosecutor starts the story where it started for the victim: with the assault.

[4] The prosecutor uses this paragraph to introduce his theory of the case, which is that the victim has repeatedly identified the defendant as her assailant.

State's Brief in Opposition to Defendant's Motion to Suppress - 1

Name of Prosecutor
Deputy Prosecuting Attorney for King County
Address of Prosecutor's Office

Ms. Martinez left her apartment at about 4:30 p.m. to walk to work at Angelo's, a restaurant. As she was walking north on Belmont, Martinez observed an older model red station wagon with a chrome luggage rack as it passed slowly by her.[5] Moments later, the same car came down the street again. This time, the driver pulled his car in front of Martinez, stopping his car so that it blocked her path. As Martinez watched,[6] the driver got out of his car and walked toward her. The man then took a gun from his coat pocket and pointed it at Martinez. Martinez looked at the gun and then at her assailant. Then, crying, she ran back across the street to safety.[7]

At about the same time,[8] Chester Clipse was walking south on Belmont. As he approached his apartment, Clipse saw a man in a red station wagon pull into the area where he usually parked. Clipse immediately started walking toward the man to tell him that he could not park there. A moment later, Clipse saw the man get out of his car and approach a young woman[9] who had stopped suddenly. As Clipse watched, the man pulled out a gun and pointed it at the woman.

Both Martinez and Clipse screamed, and the man turned and ran to his car, putting the gun under his coat. As the girl ran across the street, the man got back into his car, backed out, and drove away, traveling northbound on Belmont.

State's Brief
in Opposition to
Defendant's
Motion to Suppress - 2

Name of Prosecutor
Deputy Prosecuting Attorney
for King County
Address of Prosecutor's Office

[5] The prosecutor has described the facts related to the car and the victim's opportunity to view that car in detail, giving those facts considerable airtime. The inference that the prosecutor wants the court to draw is that, if the victim's description of the car is accurate, so is her description of her assailant.

[6] The prosecutor uses the word "watched" to suggest that the victim had a good opportunity to view her assailant. In addition, by setting out the facts in three sentences rather than one sentence, the prosecutor "slows down time."

[7] The prosecutor has tried to create the impression that Martinez had a good opportunity to view her assailant by setting out the facts in separate sentences.

[8] Note how the prosecutor put the orienting transitions at the beginning of the sentence.

[9] The prosecutor could have used a number of different words to describe Ms. Martinez: "Ms. Martinez," "the victim," "a girl," "a woman," or "a young woman." In picking a label, the prosecutor had to weigh his desire to paint Ms. Martinez as a victim against his need to establish that her identification was reliable.

Issue

Should the Court deny the defendant's motion to suppress[10] when the police merely asked the victim whether a pedestrian was her assailant and when the victim observed her assailant on two occasions for several seconds in broad daylight?[11]

Argument

I. THE COURT SHOULD DENY THE DEFENDANT'S MOTION TO SUPPRESS BECAUSE THE POLICE PROCEDURES WERE NOT IMPERMISSIBLY SUGGESTIVE AND THE VICTIM'S IDENTIFICATION IS RELIABLE.[12]

Identifications should not be kept from the jury unless the procedures used in obtaining the identifications were so suggestive and unreliable that a substantial likelihood of irreparable misidentification exists.[13] *See Perry v. New Hampshire*, __ U.S. ___, 132 S. Ct. 716, 720, 181 L. Ed. 2d 694 (2012); *Simmons v. United States*, 390 U.S. 377, 384, 89 S. Ct. 1127, 22 L. Ed. 2d 402 (1969).[14]

In deciding whether identification evidence is admissible, the courts employ a two-part test. Under the first part of the test, the defendant has the burden of proving that the identification evidence that he or she seeks to suppress was obtained through impermissibly suggestive procedures. *Manson v. Braithwaite*, 432 U.S. 98, 113, 97 S. Ct. 2243, 5 L. Ed. 2d 140. Only if the defendant

State's Brief
in Opposition to
Defendant's
Motion to Suppress - 3

Name of Prosecutor
Deputy Prosecuting Attorney
for King County
Address of Prosecutor's Office

[10] The prosecutor has framed the legal question so that it suggests the conclusion that he wants the court to reach.

[11] The prosecutor has set out a key fact related to the first part of the two-part test and then a fact related to the second part of the test. In doing so, the prosecutor has presented those facts accurately but in a light favorable to the State.

[12] If you have one issue statement, you should have one main heading. The issue statement sets out the question and the heading answers that question. In this instance, the prosecutor has used the conventional format for a heading: He sets out his assertion and then a "because" clause that provides support for that assertion.

[13] The prosecutor starts his general rule section by creating a favorable context.

[14] Because this brief is a brief to a Washington court, the prosecutor has used the Washington citation rules.

satisfies this substantial burden is the second part of the test applied. *Id.*[15]

Even if the court determines that the police procedures were impermissibly suggestive, the evidence is admissible if, under the totality of the circumstances, the identifications are reliable. *Perry v. New Hampshire*, 132 S. Ct. at 720; *Simmons v. United States*, 390 U.S. at 384. Due process does not compel the exclusion of an identification if it is reliable. *Id.*[16]

A. <u>Merely asking the victim whether a pedestrian was her assailant does not make a permissible show-up impermissibly suggestive.</u>[17]

There are no published Washington cases in which the courts have held that a show-up was impermissibly suggestive.[18] *See, e.g., State v. Rogers*, 44 Wn. App. 510, 722 P.2d 1249 (1986); *State v. Booth*, 36 Wn. App. 66, 671 P.2d 1218 (1983). In *Rogers*,[19] the court held that the show-up was not impermissibly suggestive even though the police had picked up the witness at a tavern, told him that they wanted to take him back to his apartment to see if he could identify his assailant, and then presented the defendant to him while the defendant was standing between two uniformed police officers. *Id.* at 511. Similarly,[20] in *State v. Booth*, 36 Wn. App. 66, 671 P.2d 1218 (1983), the court held that the show-up was not impermissibly suggestive when the police asked the witness to accompany them to

State's Brief
in Opposition to
Defendant's
Motion to Suppress - 4

Name of Prosecutor
Deputy Prosecuting Attorney
for King County
Address of Prosecutor's Office

[15] The prosecutor uses language that emphasizes that it is the defendant who has the burden of proving the first part of the test.

[16] The prosecutor ends the general rule section by responding to Patterson's due process argument. Note, though, that the prosecutor responds to Patterson's argument without saying what Patterson argued.

[17] In drafting this heading, the prosecutor did not use the conventional format. He does, however, make an assertion.

[18] The prosecutor starts this paragraph with a bold, but accurate statement.

[19] The prosecutor uses three cases to support his point: he discusses the first two cases in text and the third case in a parenthetical. Note that the case descriptions are short and to the point. The prosecutor sets out the court's holding and then sets out a short summary of the facts.

[20] The prosecutor uses the transition to tell the court that he is moving to the next case and that case is another case that supports the assertion that he made in the principle-based topic sentence.

the place where the defendant had been arrested and the witness identified the defendant after seeing him in the back of a police car. *Id.* at 67-68; *accord State v. Guzman-Cuellar*, 47 Wn.2d 326, 734 P.2d 966 (1987) (show-up not impermissibly suggestive when the defendant was shown to three of the four eyewitnesses while in handcuffs standing next to a police car).

In our case,[21] the show-up was not nearly as suggestive as the show-ups in *Rogers*, *Booth*, or *Guzman-Cuellar*.[22] Unlike the officers in *Rogers*, *Booth*, and *Guzman-Cuellar*, Officer Yuen did not ask Martinez to go with him to identify her assailant. Instead, the show-up occurred as he was taking Martinez home. In addition, when Martinez made her identification, the defendant was not flanked by police officers, sitting in the back of a patrol car, or in handcuffs standing next to a police car.[23]

If Officer Yuen had not asked Martinez whether the pedestrian looked like her assailant, he would not have been doing his job.[24] If he was going to protect others, Officer Yuen needed to know whether the pedestrian was Martinez's assailant. The officer's question, "Is that the man?" was not enough to turn a permissible show-up into one that was impermissibly suggestive.

State's Brief
in Opposition to
Defendant's
Motion to Suppress - 5

Name of Prosecutor
Deputy Prosecuting Attorney
for King County
Address of Prosecutor's Office

[21] The prosecutor uses a transition to signal that he is moving from a description of the analogous cases to a discussion of his own case.

[22] Instead of discussing the cases one by one, the prosecutor discusses them as a group.

[23] In this sentence, the prosecutor distinguishes all three cases. Note that he distinguishes them in the order in which he discussed them in the preceding paragraph.

[24] In addition to making arguments based on analogous cases, the prosecutor also makes a policy argument.

B. Martinez's identification was reliable: she had observed her assailant on two occasions; her attention was focused on her assailant; and, except for her statement about her assailant's age, her description was accurate.[25]

Even if the police procedures were suggestive,[26] the identification is admissible unless[27] the procedures are "so impermissibly suggestive as to give rise to very substantial likelihood of irreparable misidentifications." *Simmons v. United States*, 390 U.S. 377, 384, 88 S. Ct. 967, 19 L. Ed. 2d 402 (1968); *accord Perry v. New Hampshire*, ___ U.S. ___, 132 S. Ct. 716, 720, 181 L. Ed. 2d 694 (2012). In deciding whether the identification is reliable, the courts consider the witness's opportunity to view the criminal at the time of the crime, the witness's degree of attention, the accuracy of the witness's description, the level of certainty demonstrated by the witness at the confrontation, and the length of time between the crime and the confrontation. *Neil v. Biggers*, 409 U.S. 188, 199-200, 93 S. Ct. 375, 34 L. Ed. 2d 401 (1972).

The courts do not require that the witness view the defendant for an extended period of time.[28] *State v. Booth*, 36 Wn. App. 66, 671 P.2d 1218 (1983). For example, in *Booth*, the court concluded that the witness's identification was reliable when the witness had viewed the defendant for less than a minute.[29] *Id.* at 71. Because the witness's attention had been drawn to the fleeing man and because

State's Brief
in Opposition to
Defendant's
Motion to Suppress - 6

Name of Prosecutor
Deputy Prosecuting Attorney
for King County
Address of Prosecutor's Office

[25] The prosecutor also uses an alternative format for this heading. Instead of using the word "because," he uses a colon. The statement that precedes the colon is the assertion, and the facts set out after the colon are the support for the assertion.

[26] The prosecutor uses language that tells the court that this argument is an alternative argument.

[27] The prosecutor sets out the rule broadly: "the identification is admissible unless . . . ."

[28] After listing the factors, the prosecutor goes through the factors one at a time.

[29] In describing *Booth*, the prosecutor sets out only the key facts and the court's holding.

she viewed him in broad daylight, the court found that the identification was reliable. *Id.* Similarly, in our case, Martinez's attention had been drawn to her assailant.[30] Shortly before the assault, Martinez watched[31] as her assailant drove slowly by her. Consequently, when he drove by her again, her attention was focused on him. She watched as he drove his car in front of her, blocking her path. In addition, she watched as he got out of his car and walked toward her. Thus, although she looked at him for only two or three seconds once he pulled out the gun,[32] before that time, she had a good opportunity to view him and her attention had been focused on him.

The courts also do not require that the witness's description be completely accurate.[33] *State v. Kraus*, 21 Wn. App. 388, 584 P.2d 946 (1978). In *Kraus*, the court held that the witness's identification was reliable despite the fact that the witness had stated that the robber was wearing a dark jacket and the defendant was wearing a light-colored jacket. *Id.* at 393. Similarly, in *State v. Maupin*, 63 Wn. App. 887, 822 P.2d 355 (1992), the court held that the witness's identification was reliable even though the witness was not able to tell the police the rapist's race. *Id.* at 892. In this case, Martinez was able to give the police a detailed description of her assailant. When she was interviewed, she told the police that her assailant was a white male with blondish-brown hair, that he was

State's Brief
in Opposition to
Defendant's
Motion to Suppress - 7

Name of Prosecutor
Deputy Prosecuting Attorney
for King County
Address of Prosecutor's Office

[30] In comparing the facts in *Booth* to the facts in the case before the court, the prosecutor repeats key language from the case: "the witness's attention had been drawn."

[31] The prosecutor has selected words—for example, "watched" and "focused"—that suggest the Ms. Martinez had a good opportunity to view her assailant.

[32] The prosecutor has placed the unfavorable fact in a dependent clause.

[33] The prosecutor organizes the discussion of the second factor in the same way that he organized his discussion of the first factor. First, he sets out a topic sentence that sets out the rule in a light favorable to the State. Second, he uses cases to illustrate how the courts have applied that rule. In setting out his case descriptions, he includes only the key facts, and he sets out those facts in a light favorable to his client. Finally, he applies the rule to the facts of his case.

approximately 5′7″ tall and weighed between 165 and 170 pounds, that he appeared to be in his early forties, and that he was wearing a dark jacket. This description is accurate in all but one respect. Although Martinez misjudged the defendant's age, she accurately described his car, his hair, his height and weight, and his clothing.

In addition, Martinez's identification occurred shortly after the assault, and Martinez was certain in her identification. Although she did not answer Officer Yuen's question the first time that he asked her, as soon as she got a better look at the defendant, she identified him as her assailant.[34] As she stated during the suppression hearing, "Once I got a good look at him I was sure it was him."[35]

Taken together, these facts establish that, even if the show-up was suggestive, Ms. Martinez's identification was reliable.[36] Ms. Martinez had a good opportunity to view her assailant; her attention was focused on her assailant; she accurately identified her assailant's build and clothing; and once she got a good look at the defendant, she was certain that he was her assailant. Accordingly, the Court should not suppress Ms. Martinez's show-up identification.

State's Brief
in Opposition to
Defendant's
Motion to Suppress - 7

Name of Prosecutor
Deputy Prosecuting Attorney
for King County
Address of Prosecutor's Office

[34] In this sentence, the prosecutor responds to defense counsel's argument that the officer's statement influenced Martinez's identification.

[35] The prosecutor ends this section with a favorable quote.

[36] The prosecutor ends this part of the argument by summarizing the points that he made.

C. Because the show-up was not impermissibly suggestive, the Court should not suppress Martinez's line-up identification or prevent Martinez or Clipse from making in-court identifications.[37]

[37] The prosecutor has also used an alternative format for this heading. He has placed the "because" clause at the beginning rather than the end.

The Court should not suppress Martinez's line-up identification, nor should it prevent Martinez or Clipse from making an in-court identification.[38] Because the show-up was not impermissibly suggestive, see subsection IA, it did not taint either the line-up or any potential in-court identifications.

[38] The prosecutor starts this section by setting out his assertion.

Although Clipse may have seen the police talking with the defendant, such an act by itself is not enough to make a show-up impermissibly suggestive.[39] *See State v. Guzman-Cuellar*, 47 Wn. 2d 326, 333, 734 P.2d 966 (1987); *State v. Rogers*, 44 Wn. App. 510, 512, 722 P.2d 1249 (1986); *State v. Booth*, 36 Wn. App. 66, 72, 671 P.2d 1218 (1983). In addition, like Martinez, Clipse had a good opportunity to view Martinez's assailant. His attention was drawn to the assailant because the man was pulling into his parking spot, and, except for his description of the assailant's age, Clipse's description was accurate.

[39] The prosecutor has intentionally kept this argument short. If he wins his first argument, the prosecutor will also win this argument; however, if he loses the first argument, he will, probably, also lose this argument.

Prayer for Relief

For the reasons set out above, the State respectfully requests that the Court deny the defendant's motion to suppress and admit Martinez's show-up and line-up identifications and permit Martinez and Clipse to make in-court identifications.

Dated this 28th day of September, 2012.

____

Assistant Prosecuting Attorney
Washington Bar No. 00000

Name of Prosecutor
Deputy Prosecuting Attorney
for King County
Address of Prosecutor's Office

EXAMPLE 3 Defendant's Brief in Support of a Motion for Partial Summary Judgment

IN THE SUPERIOR COURT OF THE
STATE OF WASHINGTON
IN AND FOR THE COUNTY OF KING[1]

BARBARA DONELY et al.,)) Plaintiffs,)) vs.)) SUNNY ORCHARD) RESTAURANT GROUP, INC.) a Delaware Corporation,)) Defendant.) __________________)	Case No.: 10-1-02399-2 SEA BRIEF IN SUPPORT OF DEFENDANT'S MOTION FOR PARTIAL SUMMARY JUDGMENT

Relief Requested

Sunny Orchard requests that the Court grant its motion for partial summary judgment and dismiss the plaintiffs' strict liability claims because (1) there are no genuine issues of material fact, (2) the relevant product is the orange juice, (3) as a matter of law Sunny Orchard did not manufacture the juice, and (4) as a matter of law Sunny Orchard did not market the orange juice under its trade name or brand name. The defendant is not asking the Court to dismiss the plaintiffs' negligence claims.[2,3]

Brief in Support
of Motion for
Summary Judgment - 1

Attorney for Defendant,
Sunny Orchard Restaurant, Inc.
Address and
Phone Number

[1] The King County Local Rules govern the form of the brief.

[2] In addition to setting out the relief that he wants, the defendant's attorney summarizes his arguments. Each of the listed items are discussed in a separate section of the argument.

[3] In this sentence the defendant's attorney reminds the court that the plaintiffs have set out two causes of action: one for negligence and one for strict liability. The defense attorney's hope is that the court will be more likely to grant this motion if it knows that the plaintiffs will still get "their day in court" on the negligence claims. (Note: the defense attorney thinks the he may be able to win on the negligence claim.)

Statement of Facts

The defendant, Sunny Orchard Restaurant Group (Sunny Orchard), operates 132 family-friendly restaurants in 15 states.[4] Def's Answer to 1st Amended Compl.[5] ¶ 1.3. One of the items that Sunny Orchard[6] serves at its restaurant is orange juice that it purchases from the California Juice Company (California Juice). Def's Responses to Pls' 1st Interr. No. 1.

[7]California Juice delivers the juice in one-gallon containers to Sunny Orchard's distribution center in Tukwila, Washington, which then fill orders from individual restaurants. Def's Resp. to Pls' 1st Interr. No. 3. When a restaurant receives the juice, it places the containers containing the juice in a walk-in cooler. *Id.* As needed, the juice is taken from the walk-in cooler and is poured into a juice dispenser from which servers get the juice that they serve to customers. *Id.*

[8]Sunny Orchard does not refer to the orange juice offered in its restaurants as "Sunny Orchard juices," Def's Responses to Pls' 1st Interr. No. 10, and if asked whether the juice being served was squeezed at the restaurant, the servers are assumed to answer truthfully by saying, "No." Def's Responses to Pls' 1st Interr. No. 15. Although the menu and servers describe the orange juice as "fresh" and "orchard-squeezed,"[9] any use of the name "Sunny Orchard" in conjunction with a description of the juice

Brief in Support of Motion for Summary Judgment - 2

Attorney for Defendant,
Sunny Orchard Restaurant, Inc.
Address and
Phone Number

[4]The defendant's attorney tries to paint his client in a favorable light by including the fact that the restaurants are "family friendly."

[5]The Washington Style Sheet does not prescribe the abbreviations that should be used in referring to documents filed with the court.

[6]In this case, the defendant's attorney has decided to refer to his client as "Sunny Orchard" and to use the label "plaintiffs" for the plaintiffs.

[7]In this paragraph, the defendant for the attorney sets out, in a matter-of-fact way, the distribution process. Ultimately, the attorney wants to establish that the defendant does not alter or change the juice. It is simply a link in the chain of distribution.

[8]In this paragraph the defendant's attorney sets out the facts that he knows he will need in responding to the plaintiffs' arguments. Note that paragraph is not in a position of emphasis.

[9]The attorney has put an unfavorable fact in a dependent clause in the middle of the sentence that is the middle of the paragraph.

refers only to the fact that the juice is served within, at, or by a Sunny Orchard restaurant. Def's Responses to Pls' 1st Interr. No. 11. The orange juice that is sold in the gift shop, which is the same orange juice offered to Sunny Orchard customers, is labeled with the California Juice and not the Sunny Orchard brand name.[10] *Id.*

[11]Sunny Orchard first offered the "Picnic Banquet Breakfast," which included orange juice in a souvenir glass, in 2005. Def's Responses to Pls' 1st Interr. No. 13. While at first the glass was decorated with the Sunny Orchard logo, the logo was removed four years ago. Def's Responses to Pls' 1st Interr. No. 17. Since then, the glasses have featured a seasonal design that changes four times a year. *Id.*

On May 13, 2012, the plaintiffs[12] had breakfast at Sunny Orchard's Seattle restaurant: all six plaintiffs ordered the Picnic Banquet Breakfast, which comes with the orange juice that Sunny Orchard purchases from California Juice. Complaint at ¶ 2.4. The juice was brought to the table in a pitcher that had a kerchief tied on the handle and poured into the decorative glasses, which had been garnished with a slice of orange and a sprig of mint. Def's Responses to Pls' 1st Interr. No. 16. Three days later, the Washington State Department of Community Health (WSDH) issued a warning to consumers not to drink unpasteurized orange juice products distributed under the

Brief in Support of Motion for Summary Judgment - 3

Attorney for Defendant, Sunny Orchard Restaurant, Inc. Address and Phone Number

[10]The attorney ends this paragraph with a favorable fact.

[11]In this paragraph the defense attorney sets out the fact that he will need to respond to the plaintiffs' argument that Sunny Orchard marketed the juice under its brand or trade name. Note that the attorney puts the favorable facts at the end of the paragraph in a position of emphasis and the unfavorable fact in a dependent clause.

[12]While defendant's attorney could have used the phrase "members of the family," he chooses to go with the more "clinical" term, "plaintiffs."

California Juice brand name because the orange juice had the potential to be contaminated with *Salmonella*. Complaint, ¶ 3.1. The plaintiffs allege, Complaint, ¶ 5.4, and the defendant admits, that two of the plaintiffs, Barbara Donely and Daniel Steddic, contracted *Salmonella* from the juice that they drank at the Sunny Orchard restaurant. Requests for Admission, Nos. 13, 14, 16. This has been the only confirmed claim of a foodborne, illness-related injury at a Sunny Orchard restaurant in at least five years. Def's Responses to Pls' 1st Interr. No. 20.[13]

Statement of Issues

Under the Washington Product Liability Act, RCW 7.72, is Sunny Orchard entitled to judgment as a matter of law on the plaintiffs' strict liability claim when (1) the plaintiffs became ill after drinking orange juice at a Sunny Orchard restaurant; (2) Sunny Orchard purchased the contaminated orange juice from California Juice; (3) all Sunny Orchard did was pour the juice from the original containers into a dispenser and then into a pitcher and garnished glasses; and (4) the menu does not represent that Sunny Orchard made the juice and the Sunny Orchard logo is not on the glasses?[14]

Evidence Relied Upon

This motion is based on the First Amended Complaint for Product Liability and Punitive Damages; Defendant's Answer to First Amended Complaint for

Brief in Support of Motion for Summary Judgment - 4

Attorney for Defendant, Sunny Orchard Restaurant, Inc. Address and Phone Number

[13]In this paragraph, the defendant's attorney tries to minimize the process that the servers used in serving the juice. Compare the way in which the plaintiffs' attorney presents these facts with the way in which the defendant's attorney presents them in Example 4.

Although the attorney could have added a paragraph break, he did not do so. Because the facts set out in this paragraph do not favor California Restaurants, he decided to de-emphasize them by putting them in a long paragraph.

By setting out the facts in chronological order, the defendant's attorney highlights the fact that the restaurant did not know about the contamination until after it served the juice.

The defendant's attorney does not give any airtime to the fact that two of the plaintiffs became ill after drinking juice at a Sunny Orchard restaurant. Compare the way in which the plaintiffs' attorney presents these facts with the way in which the defendant's attorney presents them in Example 4.

Defense counsel ends this paragraph, and the statement of facts, with a favorable fact.

Note that the defendant's statement of facts is much shorter than the plaintiffs'. The

Product Liability and Punitive Damages; Plaintiffs' First Requests for Admission, and Defendant's Objections and Responses to the Same; and Plaintiffs' First Interrogatories and Requests for Production, and Defendant's Objections and Responses to the Same.

Authority

I. THE COURT SHOULD GRANT SUNNY ORCHARD'S MOTION FOR PARTIAL SUMMARY JUDGMENT BECAUSE THERE ARE NO ISSUES OF FACT AND, AS A MATTER OF LAW, SUNNY ORCHARD DID NOT MANUFACTURE THE ORANGE JUICE OR MARKET THE JUICE UNDER ITS BRAND NAME.(15)

Summary judgment is appropriate when "the pleadings, depositions, answers to interrogatories, and admissions on file, together with the affidavits, if any, show that there is no genuine issue as to any material fact and that the moving party is entitled to judgment as a matter of law." CR 56(c).(16) In making a decision, the courts must consider all facts submitted and all reasonable inferences from them in the light most favorable to the nonmoving party. *Sanders v. State*, 169 Wn. 2d 827, 844, 240 P.3d 120 (2010). However, the nonmoving party may not rely on speculation, argumentative assertions that unresolved factual issues remain, or on having its affidavits considered at face value. *Seven Gables Corp. v. MGM/UA Entm't Co.*, 106 Wn. 2d 1, 13, 721 P.2d 1 (1986). After

Attorney for Defendant, Sunny Orchard Restaurant, Inc. Address and Phone Number

defendant's attorney wants to suggest that the facts in the case are not in dispute and that the only issues are legal issues.

(14) The defendant's attorney has framed the question so that it suggests the conclusion that he wants the court to reach.

In drafting this issue statement, the defendant's attorney had to decide whether to include the key facts, which makes for a long issue statement, or to set out legal conclusions. The attorney decided to go with the first option and set out the key facts.

(15) Once again, the attorney for defendant had to make a decision. Should he just set out his assertion—THE COURT SHOULD GRANT SUNNY ORCHARD'S MOTION FOR PARTIAL SUMMARY JUDGMENT—or should he include a "because" clause? Including the "because" makes the issue statement much longer.

(16) The defendant's attorney starts the Authority section by setting out the general rules, which in this case are the rules governing summary judgment. However, because judges know the rules governing summary judgment, this section can be very short. The attorney simply sets out the key rules in a light favorable to his client.

the defendant submits adequate affidavits, the burden shifts to the nonmoving party to provide specific facts that sufficiently rebut the moving party's contentions and disclose the existence of a material issue of fact. *Id.* The court should grant the defendant's motion for summary judgment if there are no genuine issues of material fact. *Sanders*, 169 Wn. 2d at 844.

In this case, there are no genuine issues of material fact. Both sides agree that the plaintiffs contracted *Salmonella* after drinking the orange juice that the defendant purchased from California Juice. Requests for Admission, Nos. 13, 14, 16.[17] Because there are no genuine issues of material fact, the questions before the Court are questions of law.[18] *See Almquist v. Finley Sch. Dist.*, 114 Wn. App. 395, 404, 57 P.3d 1191 (2002). In this case, as a matter of law, the relevant product is the orange juice, and Sunny Orchard did not manufacture that orange juice or market that orange juice under its trade or brand name.

A. <u>The relevant product is the orange juice because it was the orange juice that gave rise to the product liability claim</u>.[19]

Under RCW 7.72.010(3), the relevant product is "that product or its component part or parts, which gave rise to the product liability claim."[20] In this case, the plaintiffs allege that their injuries were caused by the orange juice that they drank at one of Sunny Orchard's restaurants.

Brief in Support of Motion for Summary Judgment - 6

Attorney for Defendant, Sunny Orchard Restaurant, Inc. Address and Phone Number

[17] The defendant's attorney starts this paragraph with an assertion: that there are no genuine issues of material fact. He then provides support for this assertion by citing to the Requests for Admission.

[18] At this point, the attorney does not know whether the plaintiffs will argue that there is a question of fact. If they do, he will respond to those arguments in a reply brief or in oral argument.

[19] The attorney uses the conventional format for this argumentative heading. He sets out his assertion and then a "because" clause in which he provides support for that assertion.

[20] In this brief, the attorney does not include a general rule section in which he provides the judge with an overview of the Washington Products Liability Act. Instead, he jumps right into the analysis. While this strategy would work well with judges who are familiar with the Act, it might not work for judges who are not. Thus. Unless the attorneys know that the judge is familiar with the ACT, he should add a general rule section.

Complaint at ¶ 2.4. They do not allege that they were harmed by the glass in which the orange juice was served, by the garnishes that were placed on the glass, or by any of the other items that were served as part of the Picnic Banquet Breakfast.[21] *Id.* Therefore, under the definition set out in the act, the relevant product is the orange juice because it contained the *Salmonella* "which gave rise to the product liability claim." RCW 7.72.010(3).

B. <u>Sunny Orchard is not a "manufacturer" because all that it did was serve orange juice that it purchased from California Juice.</u>

Although Sunny Orchard is a product seller, it is not a manufacturer. An entity is a manufacturer only if it "designs, produces, makes, fabricates, constructs, or remanufactures the relevant product . . . ." RCW 7.72.010(2).[22]

In the only Washington Products Liability Act case that discusses whether a defendant who serves food falls within the definition of a manufacturer, the defendant altered the food item that caused the injury.[23] *Almquist v. Finley Sch. Dist.*, 114 Wn. App. 395, 57 P.3d 1191 (2002). In *Almquist*, the defendant, the Finley School District (School District), did not just serve the tainted ground beef. *Id.* at 404. Instead, it thawed the beef, cooked the beef, drained it, rinsed it, added seasonings, and then added other ingredients to create tacos. *Id.*[24] In light of these facts, the court concluded that the School District's cooking process fell

Brief in Support of Motion for Summary Judgment - 7

Attorney for Defendant, Sunny Orchard Restaurant, Inc. Address and Phone Number

[21] The defendant's attorney uses detail to emphasize what the plaintiffs have not alleged.

[22] The defendant's attorney starts this subsection by setting out the specific rule in a light favorable to the defendant. Note the attorney's use of the word "only."

[23] The defendant's attorney starts his discussion of the analogous case with a principle-based topic sentence.

[24] Because he wants to distinguish *Almquist*, the defendant's attorney goes into detail in describing the process that the District used in preparing and mixing the tainted beef with other ingredients.

neatly into each of the definitions for "design," "produce," "make," "fabricate," and "construct": the District designed the school lunch and, using the tainted meat, it produced, made, fabricated, and constructed the taco lunch. *Id.* at 405. As the court noted in its opinion, "[t]he reason for excluding nonmanufacturing retailers from strict liability is to distinguish 'between those who have actual control over the product and those who act as mere conduits in the chain of distribution.'"[25] *Id.*

[26]Unlike the School District, which altered the frozen ground beef, Sunny Orchard simply served juice that it purchased from California Juice. It did not do anything to prepare the juice—for example, it did not thaw frozen concentrate, and it did not add anything to the orange juice. All it did was add an orange slice and a sprig of mint to the glass.[27] The orange juice remained in exactly the same form from the time Sunny Orchard purchased it from California Juice until Sunny Orchard served it to its customers. Therefore, Sunny Orchard acted as a mere conduit in the chain of distribution.[28]

C. <u>The orange juice was marketed under California Juice's brand name and not Sunny Orchard's brand name</u>.

Finally, Sunny Orchard did not market the orange juice under its trade name or brand and, therefore, it is not a manufacturer under RCW 7.72.040(2)(e).[29] The key case

Brief in Support of Motion for Summary Judgment - 8

Attorney for Defendant, Sunny Orchard Restaurant, Inc. Address and Phone Number

[25]The defendant's attorney ends this paragraph with a quotation that supports his client's argument.

[26]The defendant's attorney uses this paragraph to distinguish *Almquist*.

[27]To emphasize his points, the attorney uses an example that is based on the facts in *Almquist*.

[28]The attorney concludes this paragraph by repeating language that he quoted in the last sentence of the preceding paragraph.

Although there are other arguments that the defendant's attorney might make, most judges say that they want short, concise briefs. Thus, the attorney makes his key points and then stops. If the plaintiffs make other arguments, he can respond to those arguments in a reply brief or during the oral arguments.

[29]The attorney begins this section of his brief by setting out his assertion and then introducing the key case.

is *Johnson v. Recreational Equip., Inc.*, 159 Wn. App. 939, 247 P.3d 18 (2011), a case in which the plaintiff brought a products liability action against the seller of an allegedly defective carbon fiber fork that fractured and detached from her bicycle. *Id.* at 943. Because both the bicycle and the carbon fiber fork were marketed under REI's brand name, "Novara," the court held REI strictly liable for the injuries caused by the defective product. *Id.*

Unlike REI, which marketed both the bicycle and the carbon fiber fork under its brand name, Sunny Orchard did not market the juice under its brand name.[30] It did not advertise the juice as Sunny Orchard juice and, on its menu it simply states that the juice is "sunny-fresh, orchard-squeezed juice." Pls.' First Am. Compl. ¶ 3.12; Def.'s Resp. to Pls.' Interrog. No. 11. In addition, the Sunny Orchard logo is not on the pitcher or the glasses in which the juice is served. Finally, the orange juice that is sold in the gift shop, which is the same orange juice offered to Sunny Orchard customers, is labeled with the California Juice brand name and not the Sunny Orchard brand name. *Id.* [31]Even if the court were to find that the Picnic Banquet Breakfast is labeled under the Sunny Orchard name, the product that gave rise to the product liability claim is the orange juice containing *Salmonella* and, therefore, it is irrelevant whether the Picnic Banquet Breakfast meets the trade name or brand name exception.

Brief in Support
of Motion for
Summary Judgment - 9

Attorney for Defendant,
Sunny Orchard Restaurant, Inc.
Address and
Phone Number

[30] The attorney uses this paragraph to distinguish REI. In doing so, he sets out the facts that support his position.

[31] In this sentence the attorney counters an argument that he expects that the plaintiffs will make.

Prayer for Relief

For the reasons set out above, Sunny Orchard respectfully requests that the Court grant its motion for partial summary judgment on the plaintiffs' strict liability claims.

Respectfully submitted this 2nd
day of October, 2012.

/s/
Attorney's Name
Attorney for the defendant, Sunny
Orchard Restaurant Group, Inc.
Bar No.

EXAMPLE 4 Plaintiffs' Brief in Opposition to Motion for Partial Summary Judgment

IN THE SUPERIOR COURT OF THE
STATE OF WASHINGTON
IN AND FOR THE COUNTY OF KING

BARBARA DONELY et al., Plaintiffs, v. SUNNY ORCHARD RESTAURANT GROUP, INC. a Delaware Corporation, Defendant.	Case No.: 10-1-02399-2 SEA BRIEF IN OPPOSITION TO DEFENDANT'S MOTION FOR PARTIAL SUMMARY JUDGMENT

Relief Requested[1]

The Plaintiffs[2] request that the Court deny the Defendant's Motion for Partial Summary Judgment on the Plaintiffs' strict liability claims under the Washington Product Liability Act (Act) because there are genuine issues of fact. In addition, even if there are no genuine issues of fact, the Defendant is strictly liable both because it manufactured the relevant product and because it marketed the relevant product under its brand or trade name.

Brief in Opposition to
Defendant's Motion for
Partial Summary Judgment - 1

Attorney for Plaintiffs
Address and
Phone Number

[1] The Washington Rules require a section in which the party submitting the brief sets out the relief that it is requesting. See LCR 7(b)(5)(b).

[2] Although the attorney for the plaintiffs would like to have referred to his clients by name, because the plaintiffs have different last names, she decided to use the more generic label.

Statement of Facts

1. Exposure to *Salmonella* Typhimurium and Resulting Injuries ❸

❹Plaintiffs Barbara and James Donely reside in Omaha, Nebraska. Pls.' First Am. Compl. ¶ 1.1. Plaintiffs Michael and Beverly Steddic reside in Seattle, Washington, and are the parents of Daniel and Charlotte Steddic, the Donelys' grandchildren. Pls.' First Am. Compl. ¶ 1.2. The Defendant, Sunny Orchard Restaurant Group, Inc., is a Delaware public corporation headquartered in California. It operates 132 restaurants in fifteen states. Pls.' First Am. Compl. ¶ 1.3.

On Mother's Day, May 13, 2012,❺ the Plaintiffs visited one of Sunny Orchard's Seattle restaurants where all six members of the family ordered the "Picnic Banquet Breakfast," which the Defendant states in its advertising and menu is like "having a family picnic in a sun-filled orchard!" Def's Responses to Pls' 1st Interr. No. 12. The featured item on the menu is a pitcher of "sunny-fresh, orchard-squeezed juice." Pls.' First Am. Compl. ¶ 3.12; Def.'s Resp. to Pls.' Interrog. No. 11.

2. Barbara Donely's Injuries and Medical Care

❻Two days after eating at the Defendant's restaurant, Ms. Donely became so ill that she had to be hospitalized for seven days. Pls.' First Am. Compl. ¶ 3.14(a). During this time, Ms. Donely underwent a series of tests: a stool

Brief in Opposition to Defendant's Motion for Partial Summary Judgment - 2

Attorney for Plaintiffs
Address and Phone Number

❸Because her statement of facts is long, the plaintiffs' attorney has divided it into subsections and then labeled those subsections.

❹The plaintiffs' attorney begins her statement of facts with a paragraph in which she identifies the parties.

❺While the fact that the plaintiffs ate at the restaurant on Mother's Day is not legally significant, the plaintiffs' attorney has included it because it helps her tell her clients' story.

❻While the defendant's attorney did not devote any space to the plaintiffs' injuries, the plaintiffs' attorney sets out those facts in detail. While these facts are not legally significant, they help the plaintiffs' attorney tell her clients' story.

culture confirmed the presence of *Salmonella* Typhimurium. Pls.' First Am. Compl. ¶ 3.14(c); Def.'s Resp. to Pls.' First Req. for Admis. No. 13.

3. Daniel Steddic's Injuries and Medical Care

While at school on the Monday after he ate at the Defendant's restaurant, nine-year-old Daniel Steddic[7] developed abdominal cramps and diarrhea. Pls.' First Am. Compl. ¶ 3.15. Because his symptoms worsened overnight, the next morning his parents took him to the emergency room, where he was admitted with a temperature of 103 degrees. *Id.* Daniel[8] was in the hospital for three days and was diagnosed with gastroenteritis caused by *Salmonella* Typhimurium, a condition called Salmonellosis. Pls.' First Am. Compl. ¶ 3.22; Def.'s Resp. to Pls.' First Req. for Admis. No. 14.

[7] The plaintiffs' attorney emphasizes that one of the plaintiffs is a young child.

[8] While as a general rule you do not want to refer to a party by just his or her first name, that rule does not apply to children.

4. *Salmonella* Typhimurium Outbreak Investigation

During the week of May 13, 2012, the Washington State Department of Community Health (WSDH) investigated nine *Salmonella* infections that resulted from consumption of "fresh, orchard-squeezed" orange juice at one of the Defendant's Seattle restaurants. Attach. No. 1 to Pls.' Interrogs. 2; Def.'s Resp. to Pls.' First Req. for Admis. No. 1. One of the unopened gallon bottles of orange juice taken from the Defendant's restaurant tested positive for *Salmonella* Typhimurium. Def.'s Resp. to Pls.' First Req. for Admis. No. 15. Pulsed-field gel electrophoresis (PFGE)

Brief in Opposition to Defendant's Motion for Partial Summary Judgment - 3

Attorney for Plaintiffs
Address and
Phone Number

testing concluded that the Salmonella bacteria isolated from this unopened bottle was "a genetically indistinguishable match" to the *Salmonella* bacteria isolated from Ms. Donely's and Daniel's stool cultures. Def.'s Resp. to Pls.' First Req. for Admis. No. 16.

5. Handling of "Sunny-Fresh, Orchard-Squeezed" Orange Juice

[9] The Defendant's Operations Manual sets out detailed instructions for the assembly and service of the "fresh, orchard-squeezed juice" that is served as part of the Picnic Banquet Breakfast. Attach. No. 2 to Pls.' Interrogs. 1. First, servers fill a pitcher with juice from the refrigerated dispenser and tie a gingham kerchief around the handle of the pitcher. Attach. No. 2 to Pls.' Interrogs. 2. Second, servers place the pitcher on a tray and arrange "Sunny Orchard decorative glasses" around the pitcher in a semicircle. Attach. No. 2 to Pls.' Interrogs. 3. Third, servers garnish the glasses by placing a slice of orange on the edge of the glass and tucking the stem of a mint sprig under the fruit slice; at the table, a cherry is added to children's glasses. Attach. No. 2 to Pls.' Interrogs. 4. In emphasizing the importance of these garnishes, the Operations Manual states that "it would just not be Sunny Orchard 'orchard-squeezed juice' without the proper 'picnic' garnishes. Our guests expect and pay for these extra-steps [sic]." Attach. No. 2 to Pls.' Interrogs. 4. Fourth, when they get to the

Brief in Opposition to Defendant's Motion for Partial Summary Judgment - 4

Attorney for Plaintiffs
Address and
Phone Number

[9] Unlike the defendant's attorney, the plaintiffs' attorney goes into detail in describing the process that defendant uses in preparing and serving the juice. The use of "First," "Second," "Third," helps the plaintiffs' attorney emphasize the process involves a number of steps.

table, servers place a napkin with the Defendant's logo on it in front of each guest and then place the glass on the napkin. Attach. No. 2 to Pls.' Interrogs. 5, Def.'s Resp. to Pls.' Interrog. No. 14. Finally, servers pour juice from the pitcher into each glass. As they do so, they say "I hope that you enjoy our fresh, orchard-squeezed juice." Attach. No. 2 to Pls.' Interrogs. 6.[10][11]

Since introducing the Picnic Banquet Breakfast in 2005, the Defendant has served the juice in "decorative glasses." While these glasses now feature seasonal designs, originally the glasses had the Defendant's logo printed on them.[12] Def.'s Resp. to Pls.' Interrog. No. 12. The Defendant advertises the glasses as "seasonal souvenir glasses," and states that many customers collect the glasses by visiting the Defendant's restaurants several times a year. Def.'s Resp. to Pls.' Interrog. No. 12.

Issue Statement

Should the Court deny the Defendant's motion for partial summary judgment when the plaintiffs purchased the Picnic Banquet Breakfast from the Defendant, and the featured product of that breakfast, orange juice served from a pitcher with a kerchief tied around the handle into decorative glasses garnished with an orange slice and a sprig of mint, was contaminated with *Salmonella*?[13]

Brief in Opposition to
Defendant's Motion for
Partial Summary Judgment - 5

Attorney for Plaintiffs
Address and
Phone Number

[10] Although the plaintiffs' attorney could have added a paragraph break, she decided not to. She thought that the long paragraph would highlight the fact that the process was a long one.

[11] Plaintiffs' attorney ends the paragraph with a favorable fact, which she emphasizes by including a quotation.

[12] The plaintiffs' attorney has put the favorable fact in the main clause.

[13] The plaintiffs' attorney frames the question so that it suggests the conclusion that she wants the court to reach.

Although these details make the issue statement longer, they are key facts.

Because she wants to remind the court that some of her clients became seriously ill, she puts the reference to *Salmonella* at the end of the sentence.

Evidence Relied Upon

This Motion is based on Plaintiffs' First Requests for Admission and Defendant's Responses Thereto, Plaintiffs' First Interrogatories and Requests for Production and Defendant's Responses Thereto and their attachments, and the pleadings on file with this Court.

Argument

[14]I. THE COURT SHOULD DENY THE DEFENDANT'S MOTION FOR PARTIAL SUMMARY JUDGMENT BECAUSE THERE ARE GENUINE ISSUES OF MATERIAL FACT AND THE DEFENDANT IS NOT ENTITLED TO JUDGMENT AS A MATTER OF LAW.[15]

[16]A court should deny a motion for summary judgment unless it concludes "that there is no genuine issue as to any material fact and that the moving party is entitled to a judgment as a matter of law." CR 56(c). In deciding the motion, the court considers the evidence and all reasonable inferences drawn therefrom in the light most favorable to the nonmoving party. *Seybold v. Neu*, 105 Wn. App. 666, 675, 19 P.3d 1068 (2001). It is the moving party—in this case, the defendant—that bears the initial burden of showing that there is no genuine issue of fact. *See id.*

A. There is a genuine issue of material fact.[17]

In this case, there is a genuine issue of material fact. Although the defendant argues that the relevant product is the orange juice,[18] the plaintiffs assert that the relevant product is the Picnic Banquet Breakfast and that

Brief in Opposition to Defendant's Motion for Partial Summary Judgment - 6

Attorney for Plaintiffs Address and Phone Number

[14]Because the plaintiffs' attorney has one issue statement, she has one main heading. The issue statement sets out the question, and the heading answers that question.

[15]While the "because" clause makes the heading longer, the plaintiffs' attorney decided to include it because it allows her to emphasize that there are issues of fact, and once she mentions issue of fact, she also needs to mention her alternative argument.

[16]Because judges know the rules governing summary judgment, the plaintiffs' attorney does not go into detail in setting out those rules. She simply sets out the key rules, emphasizing those rules that favor her client.

Compare the way in which plaintiffs' attorney sets out the rules for summary judgment with the way that the defendant's attorney set out the rules in Example 3.

[17]In this instance, the attorney just sets out her assertion. There is no concise way of setting out the facts.

[18]To show that there is an issue of fact, the plaintiffs' attorney sets out each side's assertion. Note that the defendant's assertion is in the dependent clause and the plaintiffs' assertion is in the main clause.

the component part giving rise to the plaintiffs' injuries is the juice that was served, in accordance with detailed instructions, from a pitcher with a kerchief on the handle into decorative glasses garnished with a slice of orange and a sprig of mint.[19]

Almquist v. Finley Sch. Dist., 114 Wn. App. 395, 57 P.3d 1191 (2002), can be distinguished from this case.[20] While in that case the plaintiffs argued that there was an issue of fact, the court noted that the plaintiffs had not raised that issue at the trial court level and that, in arguing the motion for summary judgment, the plaintiffs had referred to the product as the tainted meat and not as the taco lunch.[21] *Id.* at 404. In contrast, in this case the plaintiffs have raised the issue. The jury should be allowed to decide whether the relevant product is the juice or whether it is the product that the Defendant sold and the plaintiffs purchased: the Picnic Banquet Breakfast.[22]

B. <u>The Defendant is a Manufacturer</u>.[23]

The Washington Product Liability Act (WPLA) imposes strict liability on manufacturers of defective products. RCW 7.72.030(2).[24] The WPLA defines both "manufacturer" and "product": the term manufacturer includes a "product seller who designs, produces, makes, fabricates, constructs, or remanufactures the relevant product or component part of a product before its sale," RCW 7.72.010(2), and a product is "any object . . . produced for introduction

Brief in Opposition to
Defendant's Motion for
Partial Summary Judgment - 7

Attorney for Plaintiffs
Address and
Phone Number

[19] The plaintiffs' attorney goes into detail in setting out the facts that support her assertion that the relevant product is the breakfast and that the component part is the juice as it was packaged and served.

[20] Because the defendant cites *Almquist* as authority, plaintiffs' attorney distinguishes it. Note the attorney's use of a strong topic sentence.

[21] The plaintiffs' attorney responds to the defendant's argument without repeating that argument.

[22] Unfortunately, there are no cases that say that the issue is an issue of fact. Thus, the plaintiffs' attorney must rely on assertions.

[23] Once again, plaintiffs' attorney has chosen to set out an assertion without a "because" clause.

[24] Unlike the defendant's attorney, plaintiff's' attorney starts her argument by setting out the applicable sections of the law.

into trade or commerce." RCW 7.72.010(3). In addition, the WPLA defines the term "relevant product." *Id.* The relevant product is "that product or its component part or parts, which gave rise to the product liability claim." *Id.* In discussing these definitions, the *Almquist* court emphasized that the statute applies to all sellers who do "more than merely pass along, unchanged, a previously packaged product." *Id.* at 401.[25]

[25] The plaintiffs' attorney ends this paragraph with a quote that supports her position.

Because WPLA does not define the words "designs," "produces," "makes," "fabricates," "constructs," or "remanufactures," the courts have used the dictionary definitions. *Id.* at 404-05. For example,[26] in *Almquist*, the court stated that the School District had a "design" for cooking the meat: its recipe. In addition, the court held that the District's cooking process fell within the definitions for "produce," "make," "fabricate," and "construct." *Id.* at 405.

[26] Note the attorneys' use of transition.

Like the School District,[27] the Defendant had a design for preparing and serving the juice that was included in the Picnic Banquet Breakfast: the Defendant's Operations Manual sets out in detail the way in which the servers should prepare and serve the juice. The juice is dispensed into a pitcher with a kerchief tied around the handle, the glasses are garnished with a slice of orange and a sprig of mint, and the servers are instructed not only on how to serve the juice but also on what to say as they are

[27] The attorney starts this paragraph with an assertion: that this case is like *Almquist*. She then uses the facts from her case to support her assertion; at the end of the paragraph she compares the facts in *Almquist* to the facts in her client's case. In doing so, the attorney counters the arguments that defense counsel made in his brief, and she tries to create a new rule, that a manufacturer is someone who creates a new product.

Brief in Opposition to Defendant's Motion for Partial Summary Judgment - 8

Attorney for Plaintiffs
Address and
Phone Number

serving it. Thus, just as the School District produced and made a new product when it combined the meat with other ingredients, the Defendant produced and made a new product[28] when it combined juice, fruit slices, mint sprigs, cherries, and various service items and breakfast foods to produce and make its Picnic Banquet Breakfast. Because the Defendant designed, produced, and made the relevant product, it is a manufacturer.

[29]The *Almquist* court also concluded that the School District "was not merely a retailer" because it "did not simply resell frozen ground beef, seasonings, and tortillas as a grocery store would." *Id.* at 405. Instead of simply reselling a product, the District took a product and altered it. *Id.* at 405-06. [30]Similarly, in this case, the Defendant did not act as a retailer, reselling juice, fruit slices, mint, cherries, and the various service items and breakfast foods as separate goods. Instead, it assembled and served these items in an elaborate way, as evidenced by the multi-step procedure outlined in the Operations Manual. The Operations Manual's own words—that restaurant "guests expect and pay for these extra-steps [sic]"—show that the Defendant transformed these items into a unique and valuable product, a product that it manufactured.

Brief in Opposition to
Defendant's Motion for
Partial Summary Judgment - 9

Attorney for Plaintiffs
Address and
Phone Number

[28]Note how the attorney repeats the phrase "produced and made a new product."

[29]In this paragraph, the attorney for the plaintiffs sets out an additional/alternative argument. She uses *Almquist* to argue that the Defendant did more than resell a product.

[30]To emphasize her point, the plaintiffs' attorney goes into detail in describing the facts.

C. In the alternative, the Defendant marketed the Picnic Banquet Breakfast under its brand or trade name.

Even if the Defendant is not deemed a manufacturer, it is still strictly liable.[31] Under the Act, a non-manufacturing product seller is strictly liable for a defective product when it markets that product under its brand or trade name. RCW 7.72.040(2)(e).

In this case, the Defendant falls with the definition of a "product seller" because it sells various food products to the public. *See* RCW 7.72.010(1). In addition, it marketed the Picnic Banquet Breakfast in its advertising and on its menu, stating that the Picnic Banquet Breakfast is [l]ike having a family picnic in a sun-filled orchard!" While the Defendant has not done what REI did and created a special brand name, *Johnson v. Recreational Equip., Inc.*, 159 Wn. App. 939, 247 P.3d 18 (2011), it has done the equivalent.[32] It has used a word from its corporate name, "orchard," and put it in its advertising for the orange juice (the juice is "sunny-fresh" and "orchard-squeezed"). In addition, the Defendant serves the juice in decorative glasses that customers associate with the Defendant's restaurants. Thus, even if deemed a non-manufacturing product seller, the Defendant is strictly liable under Act.

Brief in Opposition to Defendant's Motion for Partial Summary Judgment - 10

Attorney for Plaintiffs
Address and
Phone Number

[31] The plaintiffs' attorney starts this subsection by setting out her assertion. In doing so, she makes it clear that she is arguing in the alternative. She then sets out the specific rule.

[32] In this sentence and the following sentence, plaintiffs' attorney counters the defendant's argument. Note that the attorney does not repeat the defendant's argument. She simply sets out her own argument.

Prayer for Relief

For the reasons set forth above, the Plaintiffs respectfully request that the Court deny the Defendant's motion for partial summary judgment on the Plaintiffs' strict liability claims.

Respectfully submitted this 12th day of October, 2012.

/s/ ______________________
Attorney's name
Attorney for the plaintiffs

Brief in Opposition to
Defendant's Motion for
Partial Summary Judgment - 11

Attorney for Plaintiffs
Address and
Phone Number

CHAPTER 11

Oral Advocacy

Oral argument. For some, it is the part of practice they most enjoy; for others, it is the part they most dread.

Whichever group you fall into, oral argument is probably not what you expect. It is not a speech, a debate, or a performance. Instead, when done right, it is a dialogue between the attorneys and the judges. The attorneys explain the issues, facts, and law, and the judges ask questions, not because they want to badger the attorney or because they want to see how much he or she knows, but because they want to make the right decision.

A. AUDIENCE

In making an oral argument, who is your audience? At the trial court level, the audience is the trial judge who is hearing the motion; at the appellate level, it is the panel of judges hearing the appeal. In both instances, the audience is extremely sophisticated. Although an eloquent oral argument is more persuasive than an oral argument that is not eloquent, form seldom wins out over substance. If you do not have anything to say, it does not matter how well you say it.

At oral argument, the court can be either "hot" or "cold." The court is hot when the judges come prepared to the oral argument. The judges have studied the briefs and, at least in some appellate courts, have met in a preoral argument conference to discuss the case. In contrast, a cold court is not as prepared. The judge or judges are not familiar with the case, and if they have read the briefs, they have done so only quickly.

As a general rule, hot courts are more active than cold courts. Because they have studied the briefs, they often have their own agenda. They want to know more about point A, or they are concerned about how the rule being advocated might be applied in other cases. As a consequence, they often take more control over the argument, directing counsel to discuss certain issues and asking a number of questions. A cold court is usually comparatively passive. Because the judges are not as familiar with the case, most of their questions are informational. They want counsel to clarify the issue, supply a fact, or explain in more detail how the law should be applied.

B. PURPOSE

In making your oral argument, you have two goals: to educate and to persuade. you want to explain the law and the facts in such a way that the court rules in your client's favor.

C. PREPARING FOR ORAL ARGUMENT

The key to a good oral argument is preparation. you must know what you must argue to win; you must know the facts of your case and the applicable constitutional provisions, statutes, regulations, and cases; and you must have practiced both the text of your argument and your responses to the questions the court can reasonably be expected to ask.

1. Deciding What to Argue

In making your argument, you will have only a limited amount of time. depending on the case and the court, you will be granted ten, fifteen, or thirty minutes to make your points; answer the judge or judges' questions; and, if you are the appellant, to make your rebuttal. Because time is so limited, you will not be able to make every argument that you made in your brief. you must be selective.

PRACTICE POINTER

In selecting the issues and arguments that you will make, choose those that are essential to your case. Do not spend your time on the easy argument if, to get the relief you want, you must win on the hard one. Make the arguments that you must make in order to win.

Also anticipate the arguments that the other side is likely to make. Although you do not want to make the other side's arguments, try to integrate your responses into your argument. Similarly, anticipate the court's concerns and decide how they can best be handled.

2. Preparing an Outline

Do not write out your argument. If you do, you will either read it or, perhaps worse yet, memorize and recite it. Neither is appropriate. A dialogue does not have a predetermined text. Instead, prepare either a list of the points you want to cover or create an outline.

Because it is difficult to predict how much of the oral argument time will be spent answering the court's questions, many advocates prepare two lists or outlines: a short version, in which they list only those points that they must make, and a long version, in which they list the points they would like to make if they have time. If the court is hot and asks a number of questions, they argue from the short list or outline; if the court is cold, they use the long one.

3. *Practicing the Argument*

The next step is to practice, both by yourself and with colleagues. Working alone, practice your opening, your closing, your statements of the law, and the arguments themselves. Think carefully about the language you will use and about how you will move from one issue to the next and, within an issue, from argument to argument. Also list every question that you could reasonably expect a judge to ask and decide (1) how you will respond and (2) how you can move from the answer to another point in your argument.

Then, with colleagues, practice delivering the argument. Ask your colleagues to play the role of the judge, sometimes asking almost no questions and at other times asking many. As you deliver the argument, concentrate on "reading" the court, adjusting your argument to meet its concerns. you should also focus on responding to questions and on the transitions between issues and arguments. Before a major argument, you will want to go through your argument five to ten times, practicing in front of as many different people as you can.

4. *Reviewing the Facts and the Law*

You will also want to review the facts of the case, the law, and both your brief and your opponent's brief. When you walk into the courtroom, you should know everything there is to know about your case.

PRACTICE POINTER

In practice, months might pass between the writing of the brief and the oral argument. When this is the case, it is essential that you update your research, and, when appropriate, file a supplemental brief with the court.

5. *Organizing Your Materials*

Part of the preparation is getting your materials organized. you do not want to be flipping through your notes or searching the record during oral argument.

a. Notes or Outline

To avoid the "flipping-pages syndrome," limit yourself to two pages of notes: a one-page short list or outline, and a one-page long list or outline, which you can staple to the inside of a manila folder. Use colored markers to highlight the key portions of the argument.

b. The Briefs

You will want to take a copy of your brief and your opponent's brief with you to the podium, placing them on the inside shelf. Make sure that you know both what is in the briefs and where that information is located.

c. The Record

In arguing an appeal, you will usually want to have the relevant portions of the record in the courtroom, either on the podium shelf or on counsel table. you should also be fully familiar with the record, as with the briefs, knowing both what is in the record and where particular information can be found. Many attorneys tab the record or prepare a quick index so that they can locate information quickly.

d. The Law

Although you do not need to have copies of all of law with you, you should be familiar with the constitutional provisions, statutes, regulations, cases, and court rules you cited in your brief and those on which your opponent's case is based. If you do bring cases with you, have them indexed and highlighted for quick reference.

D. COURTROOM PROCEDURES AND ETIQUETTE

Like much of law, oral argument has its own set of conventions and procedures.

1. Seating

In many jurisdictions, the moving party sits on the left (when facing the court) and the responding party sits on the right.

2. *Before the Case Is Called*

If court is not in session, sit at counsel table, reviewing your notes or quietly conversing with co-counsel. If court is in session, sit in the audience until the prior case is completed. When your case is called, rise and move to counsel table.

3. *Courtroom Etiquette*

Stand each time you are instructed to do so by the bailiff. For example, stand when the bailiff calls court into session and announces the judge or judges, and stand when court is recessed or adjourned. In the first instance, remain standing until the judges are seated, and in the latter instance, remain standing until the judges have left the courtroom.

Also stand each time you address the court, whether it be to tell the court that you are ready to proceed, to make your argument, or to respond to a question.

In addressing the court, you will want to use the phrases "your Honor," "your Honors," "this court," "the court," or, occasionally, the judge's name—for example, "Judge Brown" or "Justice Smith." Never use a judge's or justice's first name.

PRACTICE POINTER

The title judge or justice can vary depending on your jurisdiction and on whether you are in an intermediate court or the jurisdiction's highest court. Make sure that you are using the correct title to address the members of the bench.

Finally, during the argument, do not speak directly to opposing counsel. Instead, address all of your statements to the court. Also remember that you are always "on." While opposing counsel is arguing, sit attentively at counsel table, listening and, if appropriate, taking notes.

4. *Appropriate Dress*

As a sign of respect, both for the court and the client, most attorneys wear suits. Men wear conservative suits and ties, and women wear suit coats and matching pants or skirts. The key is to look professional but not severe. during oral argument, the judge's attention should be focused on your argument, not on your attire.

E. MAKING THE ARGUMENT

Like the brief, the oral argument has a prescribed format. The following example sets out the typical outline for an oral argument.

EXAMPLE 1 **Outline of Oral Argument**

A. *Moving party* (party bringing the motion or, on appeal, the appellant)
   1. Introductions
   2. Opening
   3. Statement of the issue(s)
   4. Brief summary of the significant facts (when appropriate)
   5. Argument
   6. Conclusion and request for relief
B. *Responding party* (party opposing the motion or, on appeal, the respondent or appellee)
   1. Introductions
   2. Opening
   3. Statement of position
   4. Brief summary of significant facts (when appropriate)
   5. Argument
   6. Conclusion and request for relief
C. *Moving party's rebuttal*
D. *Sur-rebuttal* (when allowed)

1. Introductions

Begin your oral argument by introducing yourself and your client. At the trial court level, the language is relatively informal. Most attorneys say, "Good morning, your Honor," and then introduce themselves and the client. At the appellate level, the language is more formal. By convention, most attorneys begin by saying, "May it please the court, my name is ___________, and I represent the [appellant] [respondent], ____________."

PRACTICE POINTER

In many courts, the introduction is also used to reserve rebuttal time. The attorney for the moving party reserves rebuttal either before introducing himself or herself or immediately afterwards: "Your Honor, at this time, I would like to reserve _______minutes for rebuttal." If you do not reserve rebuttal time, the court might not allow you to present a rebuttal.

2. *Opening*

The first minute of your argument should be memorable. The opening sentences should catch the judge's attention, making the case's importance clear, establishing the theme, and creating the appropriate context for the argument that follows.

3. *Statement of the Issues*

a. The Moving Party

If you are the moving party, you need to set out the issues. Sometimes this is best done as part of the opening. From the issue statement alone, the case's importance is clear: "In this case, the appellant asks the court to overrule *Roe v. Wade.*" At other times, such a strategy is not effective. For example, few trial judges would find the following opening memorable: "In this case, the defendant asks the court to suppress identification testimony." In such cases, the opening and the statement of the issues should not be combined.

As a general rule, the statement of the issues should precede the summary of the facts. Before hearing the facts, the court needs a context. There are times, however, when it is more effective to set out the issues after the summary of the facts.

Whenever they are presented, the issue statements must be tailored to oral argument. What is effective in writing might not be effective when spoken. For example, although the under-does-when format works well in a brief, it does not work well orally. In oral argument, the issue needs to be presented more simply: "In this case, the court is asked to decide whether . . . " or "This case presents two issues: first, whether . . . and second, whether. . . . " An issue statement can be even stronger if it is stated as a positive assertion, much like an argumentative heading: "This court should reverse because Mr.Josephy's constitutional rights were violated by the admission of evidence obtained from an unlawful search and by the prosecutor's purposeful discrimination in the use of its peremptory challenges to remove Native Americans from the jury. The search was unlawful because. . . . "

Even though they are streamlined, the issues should be presented in the light most favorable to the client. The questions should be framed as they were in the brief, and the significant and emotionally favorable facts should be included. See sections 10.F and 2.12 [Laurel Currie Oates, Anne Enquist and Connie Krontz, Just Briefs, 3rd Ed.,].

b. The Responding Party

As a general rule, the responding party does not restate the issue or issues. Instead, it states its position, either as part of its opening or as a lead-in to its arguments: "The trial court did not err in denying Mr.Josephy's motion to suppress because the officers had a particularized objective suspicion that the defendant was engaged in criminal activity."

4. *Summary of the Facts*

a. The Moving Party

When arguing to a cold court, you will want to spend one to three minutes on a summary of the facts, telling the court what the case is about. you might also want to include a summary of the facts when arguing to a hot court. If the facts are particularly important, you will want to summarize them, refresh the court's memory, and present the facts in the light most favorable to the client. There will, however, be times when a separate summary of the facts is not the best use of limited time. In those instances, instead of presenting the facts in a separate summary at the beginning, integrate them into the argument.

b. The Responding Party

As the responding party, you do not want to use your time repeating what opposing counsel just said. consequently, for you a summary of the facts is optional even if the court is cold. If opposing counsel has set out the facts accurately, the summary can be omitted. Just integrate the significant facts into the argument. you will, however, want to include a summary if opposing counsel has misstated key facts or has omitted facts that are important to your argument, or if you need to present the facts from your client's point of view.

PRACTICE POINTER

In presenting the facts, you will not, as a matter of course, include references to the record. You must, however, be able to provide such references if asked to do so by the court or if you are correcting a misstatement made by opposing counsel.

5. *The Argument*

Unless the issues and arguments build on each other, start with your strongest issue and, in discussing that issue, start with your strongest argument. This allows you to take advantage of the positions of emphasis and ensures that you will have the opportunity to make your best, or most crucial, arguments. In addition, it usually results in better continuity. Because the moving party's strongest issue is usually the responding party's weakest, the moving party's final issue will often be the responding party's first, providing the responding party with an easy opening for his or her argument.

Moving Party	*Responding Party*
Issue 1 → Issue 2	Issue 2 → Issue 1

In presenting the arguments, do what you did in your brief but in abbreviated form. If you are the moving party, begin by stating the rule, presenting that rule in the light most favorable to your client (see sections 10.J.3 and 2.15.3 [Laurel Currie Oates, Anne Enquist and Connie Krontz, Just Briefs, 3rd Ed.,]). Then argue that rule, explaining why the court should reach the result that you advocate. If you are the responding party, do not repeat the rule unless your opponent has misstated the rule or you are arguing for a different rule. Instead, use your time to make your own affirmative arguments and to counter the arguments that your opponent has made.

In both instances, you must support your assertions. you can do so by making plain language arguments, by arguing legislative intent, by using analogous cases, or by making policy arguments. When appropriate, cite to the relevant portions of a statute or to a common law rule and, when using analogous cases, be specific: explain the rule that the court applied, the significant facts, and the court's reasoning. Although you should have the full case citations available, you do not need to include them in your argument. A reference to the case name is usually sufficient.

Although you want to cite to the relevant authorities, you do not, as a general rule, want to quote them or your own brief. reading more than a line is seldom effective. If it is important that the court have specific language before it, refer the judge or judges to the appropriate page in the brief or, better yet, prepare a visual aid.

There are several other things that you need to keep in mind in making your argument. First, it is usually more difficult to follow an oral argument than a written one. As a result, it is important to include sufficient roadmaps, signposts, and transitions. Make both the structure of your argument and the connections between ideas explicit.

Second, you need to manage your time. do not spend so much time on one issue or argument that you do not have time for the other issues or other arguments. Because it is difficult to predict how many questions the court will ask, practice both a short version and a long version of each argument.

Finally, remember that your goal is to persuade the judge to rule in your client's favor. consequently, do not avoid the "hard" arguments. If you think that the judge already agrees with you on a point, move to your next point.

6. *Answering Questions*

You should welcome the court's questions. They tell you what the court is thinking about your case, what the judges understand, and what they still question. If you are not getting questions, it is usually a bad sign. The judges have either already made up their minds or are not listening.

Questions from the bench fall into several categories. Some are mere requests for information. The judge wants to clarify a fact or your position on an issue, or wants to know more about the rule or how you think it should be applied.

Other questions are designed to elicit a particular response from you. For example, at the appellate level, Judge A might agree with your position and want you to pursue a particular line of argument for the benefit of Judge B, who is not yet persuaded. Still other questions are designed to test the merits of your argument. These questions may have as their focus your case or, at the appellate level, future cases. If the court applies rule A to your case, what does that mean for cases X, y, and Z?

Whatever the type of question, when the judge begins to speak, you must stop. Although judges can interrupt you, you should not interrupt them. As the judge speaks, listen—not only to the question that is being asked, but also for clues about how the judge is perceiving the case.

The hardest part comes next. Before answering the judge, think through your answer. Although the second or two of silence might make you uncomfortable, the penalty for answering too quickly can be severe. Although few cases are won at oral argument, some are lost, usually because in answering a question an attorney concedes or asserts too much. The second or two of silence is by far better than an unfavorable ruling.

When you know what you want to say, answer. In most instances, you will want to begin by giving the judge a one-, two-, or three-word answer. "yes." "No." "yes, but . . . ," "No, but . . . ," or "In some cases, ... " Then explain or support your answer. In doing so, try to integrate key points from your list of bullet points or from your outline. Instead of thinking of questions as interruptions, think of them as another vehicle for making your argument.

There are a number of things that you should not do in responding to a question. First, do not tell the judge that you will answer the question later. It is you, not the judge, who must be flexible.

Second, do not argue with the judge. Answer all questions calmly and thoughtfully. do not raise your voice, and even if you are frustrated, do not let it show. If one line of argument is not working and the point is essential to your case, try another, and if that line does not work, try still another. When the point is not important or you have given all the answers you have, answer, and then, without pausing, move as smoothly as you can into the next part of your argument.

Third, after answering the question, do not stop and wait for the judge's approval or permission to continue. Answer the question, and then, unless asked another question, move to the next part of your argument.

Finally, do not answer by asking the judge a question. In oral argument, it is inappropriate to question a judge.

7. *The Closing*

The closing is as important as the opening. Because it is a position of emphasis, you want to end on a favorable point.

One way of doing this is to end with a summary of your arguments, reminding the court of your strongest points and requesting the appropriate relief. Although this is often effective, it can also be ineffective. Many judges stop listening when they hear the phrase "In conclusion" or "In summary." consequently, when using a summary, avoid stock openers. catch the court's attention by repeating a key phrase, weaving the pieces together, or returning to the points made in your opening.

Another way is to end on a strong point. If you are running out of time, it might be better to stop at the end of an argument or after answering a question than to rush through a prepared closing. like a good comedian, a good advocate knows when to sit down.

8. *Rebuttal*

Perhaps the hardest part of the oral argument is rebuttal. In one or two minutes you must identify the crucial issues and make your strongest argument or response.

If you try to make too many points in rebuttal, you dilute the power of each. Therefore, as a general rule, do not try to make more than one or two points. The points should be selected because of their importance to your case: do not merely repeat what you said in the main portion of your argument or respond to trivial points made by opposing counsel. Instead, make your rebuttal a true rebuttal by responding to significant points made by opposing counsel or questions or concerns raised by the court during opposing counsel's argument.

Because time is so limited, most advocates begin their rebuttal by telling the court how many points they plan to make: "I would like to make two points." This introduction tells the court what to expect. The advocate then makes his or her first point and supports it and, unless interrupted by a question, moves to the second point. Most advocates close by quickly repeating their request for relief.

F. DELIVERING THE ARGUMENT

Every advocate has his or her own style. While some are soft-spoken, others are more theatrical; while some are plain-speaking, others strive for eloquence. As an advocate, you will need to develop your own style, building on your strengths and minimizing your weaknesses. Whatever your style, there are certain "rules" that you should follow.

1. *Breathe*

Before you start speaking, take a deep breath. The breath will allow you to clear your mind, focus, and control your nerves. In addition, if at some point during your argument you lose your place or become flustered, look down at the podium and breathe.

2. *Do Not Read Your Argument*

The first, and perhaps most important, rule is not to read your argument. Similarly, do not try to deliver a memorized speech. Know what you want to say and then talk to the court. you are a teacher, sharing information and answering the court's questions.

3. *Maintain Eye Contact*

If you do not read, you will be able to maintain eye contact with the judge. This is important for several reasons. First, it helps you keep the judge's attention. It is very difficult not to listen to a person who is looking you in the eye. Second, it helps you "read" the court. By studying the judges, you can often determine (1) whether they already agree with you on a point and you can move to the next part of your argument, (2) whether they are confused, or (3) whether you have not yet persuaded them. Finally, eye contact is important because of what it says about you and your argument. An advocate who looks the judge in the eye is perceived as being more confident and more competent than one who does not.

PRACTICE POINTER

When you are arguing to an appellate court, maintain eye contact with all of the judges, even when you are answering a specific judge's question.

4. *Do Not Slouch, Rock, or Put Your Hands in Your Pockets*

In delivering an oral argument to the court, stand erect, but not stiffly, behind the podium. do not rock from foot to foot, and do not put your hands in your pockets.

Although it might be appropriate to move around the courtroom when arguing to a jury, you should not do so when arguing to the court.

5. *Limit Your Gestures and Avoid Distracting Mannerisms*

Gestures are appropriate in an oral argument. They should, however, be natural and relatively constrained. If you talk with your hands, mentally put yourself inside a small telephone booth.

You also want to avoid distracting mannerisms. do not play with a pen, the edge of your notes, or the keys in your pocket. In addition, do not repeatedly move hair out of your eyes or push your glasses back up on your nose.

6. *Speak So That You Can Be Easily Understood*

In delivering your oral argument, speak loudly and clearly enough that you can be easily heard by the judges.

Also try to modulate your voice, varying both the pace and volume of your speech. If you want to emphasize a point, speak more slowly and either more softly or more loudly.

G. MAKING YOUR ARGUMENT PERSUASIVE

In delivering your oral argument, you will want to use many of the same techniques that you used in writing your brief. In stating the issue, frame the question so that it suggests the answer favorable to your client and, in presenting the facts, emphasize the favorable facts by placing them in positions of emphasis and by using detail and sentence structure to your advantage. See sections 10.F.3 and 2.12.5 [Laurel Currie Oates, Anne Enquist and Connie Krontz, Just Briefs, 3rd Ed.,]. Also, present the law in the light most favorable to your client. State favorable rules broadly, use cases to your advantage, and emphasize the policies that support your client's position. See sections 10.J.3 and 2.15.3 [Laurel Currie Oates, Anne Enquist and Connie Krontz, Just Briefs, 3rd Ed.,].

You should also pick your words carefully. Select words both for their denotation and their connotation, and avoid words and phrases that undermine the persuasiveness of your argument. If you represent the defendant, do not say, "It is the defendant's position that the officers violated the defendant's Fourth Amendment rights when they searched his car." Instead, say, "The officers violated the defendant's Fourth Amendment rights when they searched his car." Similarly, do not say, "We feel that the State engaged in purposeful discrimination when it used its peremptory challenges to excuse the only two Native Americans in the jury pool. Instead, say, "The State engaged in purposeful discrimination when it used its peremptory challenges to excuse the only two Native Americans in the jury pool.""

H. HANDLING THE PROBLEMS

Because an oral argument is not scripted, you need to prepare for the unexpected and decide in advance how you will handle the problems that might arise.

1. *Counsel Has Misstated Facts or Law*

If opposing counsel misstates an important fact or the governing law, you will usually want to bring the error to the attention of the court. you should, however, use care in correcting opposing counsel.

First, make sure you are right. If there is time, double-check the record, the statute, or the case. Second, make sure you are correcting a misstatement of fact or law, not the opposing party's interpretation of a fact, statute, or case. Third, correct the mistake, not opposing counsel. Instead of criticizing or attacking opposing counsel, simply provide the court with the correct information and, if possible, the citation to the record or the language of the statute or case.

EXAMPLE **Correcting a Statement made by Opposing Counsel**

> "Ms. Martinez did not see the assailant three times. She testified that she saw him twice: once when he drove by slowly and then when he pulled in front of her."

Finally, correct only those errors that are significant.

2. *You Make a Mistake*

If you make a significant mistake, correct it as soon as you can.

3. *You Do Not Have Enough Time*

Despite the best planning, you will sometimes run out of time. you might have gotten more questions than you expected, leaving you little or no remaining time for your last issue or your final points. When this happens, you have two options. you can either quickly summarize the points that you would have made, or you can tell the court that, because you are out of time, you will rely on your brief for the issues and arguments that you did not cover.

What you do not want to do is exceed the time that you have been allotted. Unless the court gives you permission to continue, you must stop when your time is up.

4. *You Have Too Much Time*

Having too much time is not a problem. you do not need to use all of your allotted time. When you have said what you need to say, thank the court and sit down.

5. *You Do Not Know the Answer to a Question*

Occasionally, you will be asked a question that you cannot answer. If it is a question about the facts of your case or about the law, do not try to bluff. Instead, do one of the following: (1) if you can do so in a few seconds, look up the answer; (2) tell the judge that at this point you cannot answer the question but that you will be glad to provide the information after oral argument; or (3) give the best answer you can.

EXAMPLE **Statements that You can make When You Do Not Know the Answer**

> "So that I can answer correctly, let me quickly check the record."
>
> "I'm not sure what the actual words were. I will check and provide you with that information after oral argument."
>
> "As I recall, the police officer testified that he asked the question twice."

If the question raises an issue that you have not considered, the options are slightly different. you can either trust yourself and, on the spot, give your best answer or you can tell the court that you need to give the question some thought.

6. *You Do Not Understand a Question*

If you do not understand a question, tell the judge and either ask him or her to repeat the question, or repeat the question in your own words, asking the judge whether you understood correctly: "I'm sorry, I'm not sure that I understand your question. could you please rephrase it?" "If I am correct, you are asking whether. . . . "

7. *You Become Flustered or Draw a Blank*

It happens, at some time or another, to almost everyone. you become flustered or draw a blank. When this happens, "buy" a few seconds by either taking a drink of water or taking a deep breath and looking down at your notes. If you still cannot continue with the point you were making, move to another one.

8. *You Are Asked to Concede a Point*

Concessions can work both to your advantage and to your disadvantage. you will win points by conceding points that you cannot win or that are not important to your argument. you can, however, lose your case if you concede too much. Therefore, before you walk into court, decide what you can and cannot concede, concede when appropriate, and otherwise politely but firmly stand your ground. If the court presses for a concession, you can try to move the court past the issue: "Assuming, *arguendo,* that this court decides that the trial court erred, the error was harmless because. . . . "

I. A FINAL NOTE

No matter how much they dread it, initially most individuals end up enjoying oral argument for what it is, a stimulating dialogue among intelligent people.

1. *Checklist for Critiquing the Oral Argument*

I. ***Preparation***

- The advocate has anticipated and prepared rebuttals for the arguments the other side is likely to make.
- The advocate has anticipated and prepared responses to the questions the court is likely to ask.
- The advocate knows the law and the facts of the case.
- The advocate has determined what arguments he or she needs to make to win.
- The advocate has determined what points he or she can, or cannot, concede.

- The advocate has prepared two outlines: a long outline, which can be used if the court asks only a few questions, and a short outline, which can be used in case the court asks more questions.

II. *Content and Organization*

A. Introduction

- The advocate identifies himself or herself and the client.
- When appropriate, the advocate requests rebuttal time.

B. Opening and Statement of Issues or Position

- The advocate begins the argument with a sentence or phrase that catches the attention of the court and establishes the client's theory of the case.
- The advocate then presents the question or states his or her position.
- The question or statement of position is framed so that it supports the advocate's theory of the case and suggests an answer favorable to the client.
- The question or statement of position is presented using language that is easily understood.

C. Summary of Facts

- When appropriate, the advocate includes a short summary of the facts in which he or she explains the case and establishes an appropriate context. When a separate summary of the facts is not appropriate, the advocate weaves the facts into the argument.
- The facts are presented accurately but in the light most favorable to the client. The positions of emphasis and detail are used effectively, and words have been selected for both their denotation and their connotation.

D. Argument

- The advocate discusses the issues and makes the arguments needed to win.
- The argument is structured in such a way that it is easy to follow:
  (1) issues and arguments are discussed in a logical order and
  (2) sufficient roadmaps, signposts, and transitions are used.
- The arguments are supported. The advocate uses the law, analogous cases, policy, and the facts to support each of his or her assertions.
- The law, analogous cases, policies, and facts are presented accurately.
- The law, analogous cases, policies, and facts are presented in the light most favorable to the client.

E. Questions from the Bench

- When a judge asks a question, the advocate immediately stops talking and listens to the question.
- The advocate thinks before answering.
- As a general rule, the advocate begins his or her answer with a short response ("yes," "No," "In this case") and then supports that answer.

- After answering the question, the advocate moves back into his or her argument without pausing or waiting for the judge to give permission to continue.
- The advocate sees questions not as an interruption, but as another opportunity to get his or her argument before the court.
- As he or she listens to the questions, the advocate adjusts the argument to match the concerns and interests of the court.

F. Closing

- The advocate ends the argument by summarizing the main points or on a strong point.
- When appropriate, the advocate includes a request for relief.

G. Rebuttal

- The advocate uses rebuttal to respond to the one or two most important points raised by opposing counsel or the court.

III. *Delivery*

- The advocate treats the argument as a dialogue; he or she does not read or recite the argument.
- The advocate maintains eye contact with all of the judges.
- The advocate has good posture, uses gestures effectively, and speaks so that he or she can be easily understood.
- The advocate does not use phrases like "I think," "We maintain," or "It is our position that. . . . "
- The advocate is composed and treats the court and opposing counsel with respect.

INDEX